The Higher Education Manager's Handbook

The job of the manager in higher education today is not an easy one. Faced with challenges such as increased student numbers and diminishing resources while at the same time having to ensure greater accountability, efficiency and continued excellence in teaching and research, the job can often appear complex and overwhelming.

The Higher Education Manager's Handbook offers practical advice and guidance on all aspects of the manager's role. Drawing on professional best practice and the examples of international university innovators, it tackles all the key areas central to the job of managing in higher education, from understanding the culture of your university and the role it plays, to providing effective leadership and managing change.

This book will be invaluable to anyone involved in a management or leadership role in higher or further education, from heads of departments to vice-chancellors and principals, and is a reliable source of advice that will be referred back to again and again.

Peter McCaffery is Pro-Vice-Chancellor at London South Bank University. He has over twenty years of teaching and management experience, working in a range of institutions from further education colleges to an Ivy League university. As a Winston Churchill Fellow, he has spent considerable time in the US researching effective management in higher education.

To Sean and Kyle so they now know what I do

The Higher Education Manager's Handbook

Effective leadership and management in universities and colleges

Peter McCaffery

 RoutledgeFalmer
Taylor & Francis Group

LONDON AND NEW YORK

First published 2004
by RoutledgeFalmer
2 Park Square, Milton Park, Abingdon, Oxon OX14 4RN

Simultaneously published in the USA and Canada
by Routledge
270 Madison Avenue, New York, NY 10016

Reprinted 2005 (twice), 2008

RoutledgeFalmer is an imprint of the Taylor & Francis Group, an informa business

© 2004 Peter McCaffery

Typeset in Palatino by
Florence Production Ltd, Stoodleigh, Devon
Printed and bound in Great Britain by
TJ International Ltd, Padstow, Cornwall

British Library Cataloguing in Publication Data
A catalogue record for this book is available from
the British Library

Library of Congress Cataloging in Publication Data
A catalog record for this book has been requested

ISBN 10: 0-415-34120-5 (hbk)
ISBN 10: 0-415-33507-8 (pbk)

ISBN 13: 978-0-415-34120-2 (hbk)
ISBN 13: 978-0-415-33507-2 (pbk)

Contents

Illustrations

Figures

Tables

Boxes

Abbreviations

ACAS	Advisory, Conciliation and Arbitration Service
AOB	any other business
ARA	academic-related administration
AUT	Association of University Teachers
CIPD	Chartered Institute of Personnel and Development
CPD	continuous professional development
CRE	Commission for Racial Equality
CVCP	Committee of Vice-Chancellors and Principals
DGB	degree-granting body
DRC	Disability Rights Commission
EQ	emotional quotient
EU	European Union
FE	further education
FTE	full-time equivalent
GMU	George Mason University
HE	higher education
HEFCE	Higher Education Funding Council for England
HEI	higher education institution
HERA	Higher Education Role Analysis
HERDSA	Higher Education Research and Development Society for Australasia
HR	human resources
ICT	information and communication technology
IQ	intelligence quotient
JCPSG	Joint Costing and Pricing Steering Group
MBO	management by objectives
MBO	master of the bleedin' obvious
MBWA	management by walking about
MLE	managed learning environment
NAB	National Advisory Board (no longer current)
NHS	National Health Service

NLE	New Learning Environment – at TVU
OPM	Office for Public Management
OU	Open University
OUP	Open University Press
P4P	Partnerships for Progression
QAA	Quality Assurance Agency
QUT	Queensland University of Technology
RAE	research assessment exercise
RBL	resource-based learning
RRA	Race Relations Amendment Act
SENDA	Special Education Needs Disability Act
SMT	senior management team
SRHE	Society for Research into Higher Education
TA	Teaching Assistant
THES	*Times Higher Education Supplement*
TQA	Teaching Quality Assessment
TVU	Thames Valley University
UCEA	University and Colleges Employers' Association
UGC	University Grants Committee (no longer current)
UUK	Universities UK
UWS	university-wide services

Foreword

Peter McCaffery addresses all the key issues facing those with leadership and management roles today in our higher education institutions. Having recently established the Leadership Foundation for Higher Education in the UK I find it both refreshing and reassuring to see the similarities between his critique and the agenda we have developed at the Foundation.

Absolutely central to this critique is to start not with some idealised model of leadership but with the context of challenges and change issues facing universities and colleges. There probably has not been such a wide-ranging agenda across all our institutions which goes so directly to the heart of how they should be led over the next five to ten years. Many commentators may bemoan the huge emphasis on leadership across this and other sectors at the moment, but none can deny the proposition that the effective management of change can only make for sound leadership.

But, of course, this is not just something that happens from the top. It is, as this book effectively sets out, a 'distributed' process: if it is to succeed, it has to happen both bottom-up and top-down.

Another crucial factor reflected in the book is the need for self-awareness – know your organisation, and know yourself as a leader. Some commentators may still need to be convinced about emotional intelligence, but the basic principle behind it is undeniably true: a good leader needs a high level of self-awareness.

One area where we all have to improve as leaders is in managing performance. In my last role running the Civil Service College, the most sought-after help from senior leaders was in how to manage the performance, both good and poor, of other senior staff.

And, most importantly, the key area of values is considered – integrity, transparency and clarity. The last one in particular means avoiding the jargon of the latest techniques: be straightforward with colleagues and use the language that fits your organisation. Also, set a good role model on work/life balance and be a 'whole person'.

I hope you get much out of reading this very timely handbook.

Ewart Wooldridge CBE, Chief Executive,
The Leadership Foundation for Higher Education

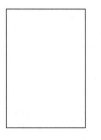

Introduction

The challenge for HE managers

> People are always blaming their circumstances for what they are. I don't
> believe in circumstances. The people who get on in this world are the people
> who get up and look for the circumstances they want, and if they can't find
> them, they make them.
>
> George Bernard Shaw

'Management is a punishment from God!' Pilloried in the media for incompetence, badgered by the incessant demands of government bodies and often vilified within their own academic communities, there can be few managers in higher education who cannot have identified with this popular epithet at some stage in their career. And yet, ironically, this sentiment is strikingly at odds with the vitality of the very institutions which this group purports to manage. For while universities have, like other public sector institutions, experienced unprecedented change over the last quarter century, they have been equally successful, as the 2003 White Paper and the 1997 Dearing Report confirmed, in facing up to the unprecedented demands that successive governments have placed upon them.

In essence, higher education institutions (HEIs), on the one hand, have had to become more accountable for the way they manage their affairs while, on the other hand, they have been obliged to cater to the needs of a mass student clientele, rather than those of a privileged few. While this transition in role and function has been neither smooth nor uncontested HEIs, have, by and large successfully, managed to do 'more' (that is, teach more students) with 'less' (fewer resources) while simultaneously maintaining 'quality'. In the UK, for example, HEIs have accommodated a tripling of student numbers over the past twenty-five years while assimilating a 50 per cent reduction in the unit of public funding per student. More than that, the White Paper, like the Dearing Inquiry, praised HEIs for maintaining their international standing in research while continuing to produce first degree graduates quickly, with low drop-out rates when compared to other countries. Universities, then, can quite rightly be proud of their collective achievement, even if it is a triumph which has too often gone unheralded, and consequently unheeded, beyond the academic world.

Where universities have been much less successful, however, is in managing the internal ramifications of these externally imposed changes. Indeed alienation, cynicism and demoralisation are currently rife within academic communities. Witness one Oxford University Professor of English who, in response to his own question, 'What does the institution of higher education care about?' railed,

> Bleakly observed, the local institution seems to have thrown in the towel. Degree-factory rhetoric is all we hear. New-style university managements are, actually, counter-productive. If you piss off your teachers and researchers you are eating the seed-corn, selling the family silver, sapping the life-blood. You would think our institutions were suicidal, the way they treat us – with the bad pay they collude in, the abolition of tenure they have agreed to, the rash economisings by engineering early retirements of good people, with the weekly questionnaires and the constant abuse of our time and energy and their acceptance of piss-poor TQA-inspired formalisms and abomination of abominations, their utter short-termism (their kow-towing to the silly time-scales of the RAE bods, their iniquitous short-term contracts – you can have your job back at the end of the long vacation if you ask nicely). Managerial cynicism is rampant in higher educa-tion as never before. They (THEY) don't care about the poor bloody infantry. . . . People are fed up, they are glad to give up and retire; they are going into internal exile, clock-watching, minimalising their effort. The government-inspired way, the neo-managerial way, is a mess none of us can survive on.
>
> (Cunningham, 2000)

It is not a surprise then, if no less cause for concern, that an AUT-sponsored (Association of University Teachers) inquiry into the psychological health of university staff in spring 2000 found that 'more than half of those who work in British univer-sities are on the brink of depression or anxiety, while a quarter have suffered a stress-related illness in the past twelve months'. Indeed a broader survey conducted contemporaneously (for the Economic and Social Research Council's 'Future of Work' programme) on the 'professional well-being' of the 140 or so officially recog-nised occupations actually placed university teaching professionals at number one in their 'Job Misery Index'. Nor is this grim picture peculiar to the UK. Researchers at Melbourne Business School and the Australian National University, for instance, have charted how stress levels in Australian universities have risen dramatically over the past decade, generating an epidemic of work-related illnesses across the country's campuses; an outcome which they attribute to, among other things, the role played by university managers (*Times Higher Education Supplement* (*THES*), 2000, 2003). It is also the case that the pressure on universities worldwide to embrace yet still further change is unrelent-ing – and is likely to remain that way for the foreseeable future. Globalisation, informa-tion technology and the emergence of the so-called 'Knowledge Society' all presage a new environment to which universities will have to adapt (Scott, 1998).

The challenge facing universities then, and in particular individual managers, is a formidable one. Nor can they prepare for it with a tabula rasa. On the contrary, as we've seen, 'management' in universities, unlike in other organisations, has long had its legitimacy questioned. Often depicted by academics ('the managed') as an irrelevant business practice which has no place in the (essentially) collegiate environment of the academic world, this view was until recently upheld for the most part by those who occupied such 'management' positions in HEIs. On the other hand, there have been well-publicised instances when 'new managerialism' has allegedly run rampant in its quest to bring the techniques, values and practices of the commercial sector to the university world. Thus where once universities may have been led and managed in an amateurish, complacent or uninformed way in the past, they are now widely perceived to be in the grip of an aggressive managerial cadre determined to run higher education (HE) as a business.

Common to both scenarios is the low status and esteem accorded university management. 'There is no scientific basis to management therefore it does not deserve to be taken seriously' as the intellectual may put it. A view which is too often compounded in university settings by the disregard that some managers themselves have for their positions when it comes to their own training and development. 'Training is for the second eleven' as one pro-vice-chancellor has said (Middlehurst, 1993). Unsurprisingly, the instances of mismanagement and incompetence in universities have exhibited an upward trend. How then, given the prospective changes in the environment, the degree of internal malaise within institutions, and the 'crisis in management', can university managers hope to manage effectively in such a setting? Indeed, how can and should university managers prepare to meet this challenge?

The purpose of this study is to help HE managers – both academic managers and general managers alike – to do just that. It is based on the research on university innovators overseas, which I undertook for the Travelling Fellowship I was awarded by the Winston Churchill Memorial Trust. As dean of school in a 'new' university I had (and naturally still have as a pro-vice-chancellor), like many others with a similar role in the HE sector, both a professional and a practical interest in how our institutional counterparts in other countries were responding to the common dilemma which, as I indicated above, we all face no matter what or where our domicile; namely, how to do 'more' with 'less' while still maintaining 'quality' in an ever-increasing competitive environment. This study, based on a selected number of universities in the US and Australia, not only reports the findings of this inquiry, but also seeks to identify the lessons we can learn from these university innovators and in particular those which we can all apply in practice.

It also draws on my own personal and professional experience of 'crisis management' within the context of 'a failing institution', Thames Valley University (TVU). Indeed the study originated following a visit to TVU by Tony Blair and David Blunkett when – in the week after the former had declared at the annual TUC Conference that his three key priorities in government, if his party were elected to office, would be 'education, education and education' – the then Leader of the Opposition formally opened the new state-of-the-art Paul Hamlyn Learning Resource Centre on the Slough campus with the rejoinder, 'Why, I wonder, can't every university be like TVU?'. At that time, TVU was attempting to establish a self-styled 'New Learning Environment' (NLE); a bold innovation that was to founder, not because the aspiration behind it – to create an education setting which was more learner-centred than teacher-centred – was unsound, but because, as the Quality Assurance Agency (QAA) subsequently pointed out, the scale and speed with which attendant change processes had been introduced (notably, the centralisation of the academic-related administration and the establishment of an internal market) had undermined the University's infrastructure, thereby placing academic standards at risk.

The whole of this process – the conception, and subsequent unravelling of, the NLE; the QAA's investigation into allegations of 'dumbing-down'; the naming and shaming of TVU as Britain's 'first failing university'; and the development of the HEFCE (Higher Education Funding Council for England) recovery plan under the stewardship of Sir William Taylor – conducted, as it was, under intense public scrutiny and in circumstances unprecedented in higher education in the UK, yielded penetrating insights into management practices and processes; both their deficiency and also their efficacy. Not only that, but when contrasted with the examples set by university innovators overseas, it rendered transparent those prerequisites which are essential to effective management and leadership in HE. It is these characteristics which this study seeks to identify. In doing so, it also offers guidance, where appropriate, on tried and tested methods derived from the training programmes and the professional development schemes provided by among others the Cabinet Office, the Work Foundation (the former Industrial Society), the Chartered Management Institute and the Chartered Institute of Personnel and Development. Taken together, this study aims to provide HE managers with a 'best practice' guide to effective management.

Its focus furthermore, unlike the bulk of the literature on university management to date, is on the HE manager per se. That is to say, it is written quite deliberately from the manager's perspective. Much of the research in this area in the past – whether conducted by HE researchers, staff developers or management practitioners themselves – has invariably focused on a particular issue or theme in question (e.g. curriculum, personnel management, staff development, globalisation, and so on). Although an approach which, while quite legitimate given the conception of the subject matter, has very often yielded critical insights into the subject, it is also one which has not always rendered them transparent or explicit from the (subjective) perspective of the reader. Put another way, the received wisdom to date offers HE professionals cogent analysis and advice on *what* one could, or should, do in academic environments, but it is implicit, and not explicit, on *how* one should go about doing it.

Ironically, this same trait is also characteristic of the literature which has been designed by management developers and deliberately targeted at the middle management HE audience. It is almost as if the same affliction which has affected management development in HE in the past – the (false) assumption that any intelligent, educated individual can manage, and there is therefore no need for training – has also influenced many of those who write about HE for a HE audience: namely, they appear to argue that 'since any intelligent and educated individual *can understand* what we say then *ipso facto* they will *automatically* be able to manage it'. Their conception of management within HEIs is also equally if not more damagingly restrictive, in that they invariably exhibit a consensual acceptance of the status quo in universities and a disposition to regard academic staff as an undifferentiated mass, as well as a tendency to view the role of HE managers as confined solely to responding to the needs of the managed.

In this book I have attempted to overcome the deficiencies of the received wisdom by, on the one hand, conceiving of the academic environment from the holistic perspective of the university manager, rather than in terms of a particular theme or issue (i.e. by making the manager the independent variable of the study rather than the dependent variable as has conventionally been the case) and, on the other, by maintaining an open mind about how such environments could or should be organised and managed: namely, by recognising that universities do indeed have distinguishing features – the autonomy of the individual scholar; the precedence of subject over institutional loyalty; the strength of tradition; and the cult of 'the expert' – but that these characteristics are not so *peculiar* in themselves that HEIs *have* to be managed in a particular way. And it is for this reason that I have not drawn any particular distinction between so-called academic managers such as heads of subject departments and general ('support') managers such as 'administrators' of central services; that, and the fact that such distinctions – as the success of the private 'for-profit' University of Phoenix demonstrates – have more to do with the endemic elitist ethos that prevails within many institutions, than they do with the reality of how HEIs will operate in the twenty-first century.

This book, then, seeks to address the needs of all those who manage in HEIs – with a particular emphasis on those who occupy head of department roles – and to make explicit, rather than implicit, the competencies and skills required to be an effective manager. It does not assume that any educated and intelligent individual can be an effective manager *without training*. Nor that universities are unique environments that can only be managed in a special way. And it has been structured and organised accordingly with the manager's 'world-view' in mind: from the examination of HE in the broader context in Chapter 1 and the analysis of HEIs as organisations in Chapter 2; through to the expectations of the role (leading your department, leading by example) and the demands (managing for high performance, developing staff, managing change); and finally to accomplishing mastery of the role (managing up, managing the 'down side', managing oneself). Each of the chapters provides a commentary and analysis of the particular role aspect under review, and offers advice and guidance on good practice, including case study examples and self-assessment tools.

Taken together these chapters argue the case for a professional (or 'managerial') approach to people management in HEIs, and the case *against* amateurist, elitist and reactionary perspectives on university management. They further seek to demonstrate that 'managerialism' is not necessarily incompatible with collegiality, and to show how 'institutions of learning' can indeed become more like 'learning organisations'. More than that, they aspire to inspire. For history teaches us, as George Bernard Shaw implies, that 'nothing has to be as it is' – maybe that even management can be a blessing, as much as a punishment, from God!

Knowing your environment

1

The university is dead; long live the university.
Times Higher Education Supplement (THES),
11 February 2000

'What is the world's largest business corporation in terms of market value?' It is – as management guru Peter Senge suggested in his opening address to the 1998 American Association of Higher Education Conference on Faculty Roles and Rewards – not the one you might readily suppose. Not Microsoft or Coca Cola or IBM or General Motors. It is in fact Visa International. As Senge explained, Visa International is a member-owned, non-stock corporation incorporated in the state of Delaware. Governed by the principle of subsidiarity, it has only 3,000 employees – approximately the same number as that of Selfridge's Department store in London's Oxford Street. Yet it has a stock market value in excess of $500 billion. In other words, Visa International 'is a business but unlike Microsoft which has an Industrial Age model of organisation it doesn't feel like or look like a conventional business'. And while Bill Gates has fallen victim to the same (Sherman) anti-trust legislation which thwarted John D. Rockefeller's Standard Oil monopoly, Visa International is a conspicuous exception. It is indeed a novel phenomenon.

Senge's purpose in posing this simple question was threefold: to draw our attention to the significant changes taking place in the nature and organisation of business corporations; to remind us that the present may not be an accurate guide to the future; and, equally fundamental, to illustrate that the first prerequisite of effective management is an awareness of one's external environment.

His vignette also highlights the difference in perception between the business world and the academic world. In higher education the prevailing consensus is that we do not really face the same changes as those which confront business. After all, the conventional wisdom maintains universities have a history stretching back centuries, and they have proved themselves to be extremely durable institutions, capable of adjusting to different circumstances while still upholding their traditional ideals. They have, moreover, shown that they can accommodate themselves to the new realities of more recent times – principally, the (negative) governmental economic imperative to do 'more' (teach more students) with 'less' (resources) while still maintaining 'quality' and the (positive) pedagogical imperative to cater to employers' expectations of graduate competence, and students' desires for flexible provision. There is, then, no compelling reason, the argument runs, why universities cannot continue in the same vein in the future.

The problem with this argument, however, is that it ignores both the historical and the contemporary reality of the circumstances facing universities. In the case of the latter, for example, it overlooks the fact that the university is no longer the only type of institution capable of fulfilling the role that it has played in the past – namely that of providing access to knowledge, creating knowledge, and fostering learning in students to enable them to use knowledge. And in the case of the former, it overstates the ancient pedigree of universities, for in truth very few of them are old. In Europe, their ancient heartland, four out of five only came into being in the last century and in the UK fully three-quarters have been established in the course of the past four decades; and thirty of them (the former polytechnics) in a single stroke as recently as 1992. In essence, the bulk of universities are very modern institutions and those that can trace an ancient lineage have survived only because they have changed so much. To such an extent, indeed, that today universities seek to present themselves as useful to all comers, from international students to regional development agencies. They have acquired 'multiple callings': to broaden student access, enhance student employability, promote lifelong learning, meet quality benchmarks, diversify income streams, improve research rankings, and so on. In consequence they have become so diverse, so fractured and differentiated that it seems they are no longer bound by any overarching principles or unitary idea. So much so, as some have argued, that the university as a concept or 'idea' has in fact been rendered meaningless (Barnett, 1990; Scott, 1995; Smith and Webster, 1997).

It is perhaps not surprising, then, that many staff in HE have become alienated, and that the prevailing mentality within the sector is survivalist: one of endurance rather than enjoyment. Some even go further and suggest that many universities today are imbued with a 'welfarist' mentality: an outlook of 'whingeing and whining' and ultimately one of dependence upon – and equally subservience to – the public purse (Melody, 1997). Either way, the most common reaction within the sector has been *not* to address the broader issue concerning the *raison d'être* of HE, other than to constantly reiterate the narrowly instrumental defence line stressing the usefulness of universities to government and industry. Rather it has often been to engage in mutual recrimination and penny-pinching within institutions on the one hand, and a common railing against government and the wider community for failing to appreciate the self-evident value of universities on the other.

The difficulty with this approach, however, is that this outpouring is often matched by a deafening silence outside the sector. Crippled by a lack of self-confidence, reluctant to articulate an overriding motivating purpose and contending in a world where hardly anyone is listening, universities, it would seem to appear, are enfeebled institutions facing an uncertain future. Yet the prospect is not nearly so bleak. Higher education is after all a growth industry, and the education-driven economy of the so-called 'Knowledge Society' is likely to keep it this way in the foreseeable future. We also arguably need an 'idea' of the university more than ever, as Barnett (2000) puts it, to make sense of 'the craziness of the world of supercomplexity' in which we now live. The White Paper too (for all the controversy over its recommendations to concentrate research in an elite minority of institutions, to establish 'teaching-only' universities, and so on) does presage a setting in which universities will be encouraged to play to their strengths. If this is indeed the case, then universities will have an opportunity to reassert their importance in the life of the country. Whether or not it is taken or spurned will, of course, be dependent upon their willingness to practise flexibility on the one hand, while simultaneously maintaining their fundamental values on the other.

This first chapter, then, examines the broader context or nature of the external environment in which HEIs and individual managers alike have to operate. It explains, as a means of understanding the pressures on modern universities and the reasons why they respond the way they do, how universities have come to be where they are today, and includes an analysis of the role of HE and of the key influences or drivers of change currently affecting HEIs: globalisation, IT (information technology), the 'Knowledge Society', the contractual state, the postmodern challenge. It also examines the nature of the university identity crisis, the university as an idea and, finally, the case for universities.

The role of universities

Universities are both ancient and modern institutions. Ancient in the sense that today's universities can trace their first beginnings to those universities – Bologna, Paris and Oxford – founded in the late middle ages, and are the heirs to this medieval heritage and the traditions and values that go with it. Modern in the sense that it was only in relatively recent times – in the late nineteenth and early twentieth century – that universities developed into the form recognisable today, and it was not until a generation or so ago that the bulk of Britain's universities were established. Their evolution, moreover, bears witness to a remarkable series of changes in the role that universities have played; one which is reflective of a close association with wider developments in society (and not, as is often held to be the case, a separation or aloofness from them). The ancient institutions of Oxford and Cambridge for instance – the only established universities in England 200 years ago – were founded as Church universities, whose main concern was the training of clergymen and teachers and with it the sustenance of the established Anglican Church. They did not originally seek to encourage progressive science or provide a liberal education – nor to encourage research either for that matter. This former role was undertaken by the dissenting academies such as the 'godless' University College of London which was established in 1826 and provided a practical education with an emphasis on science, medicine and engineering (Scott, 1995; Schuller, 1995; Coaldrake and Stedman, 1998).

It was the Industrial Revolution, and with it the progressive extension of the franchise, and also the rise of professional society, which were to be the three key factors in creating the demand for, as well as shaping the development of, a more elaborate university system in nineteenth-century Britain. And it was the civic universities – Manchester, Leeds, Liverpool, Sheffield, Bristol, and so on – along with the technical colleges and the mechanics' institutes (that were later to develop into the technological universities and the polytechnics) which were established to meet that demand. These three forces – albeit, radically extended to embrace the ever-increasing specialisation of labour, the universal access to mass entitlement, and the ceaseless march of professional 'credentialism' – have continued to mould and shape higher education down to the present day. So much so that the modern university has come to undertake four conventional roles:

- finishing school: the last stage of general education;
- professional school: the training of elite workers;
- knowledge factory: the production of science, technology and ideology;
- cultural institution: the expression of our individual and collective sense of being.

It was the state, though, which was the critical driving force in bringing together the different institutions – Church, voluntary and public sector – into a coherent higher education system. This development drew on two interrelated processes: the subordination of the autonomous universities on the one hand, and the takeover by the state (or nationalisation, if you will) of responsibility for other advanced institutions, on the other. The subsequent abolition of the binary divide between universities and former polytechnics in 1992, along with the quadrupling of student numbers in the last twenty years, set in motion a social and political revolution in British higher education; one which has left the system with far more in common with its counterparts in Europe and North America than it had a generation ago.

This transition from an elite to a mass system – or loss of British exceptionalism depending on your perspective – has been neither smooth nor uncontested and is still also curiously incomplete. For example, in terms of size, there is little doubt that if we apply Martin Trow's (1973) linear model – which defines elite systems as those which enrol up to 15 per cent of the age group, mass systems as those enrolling between 15 and 40 per cent, and universal systems as those which enrol more than 40 per cent – then the UK has acquired the attributes of a mass system. The current age participation index in British higher education, for instance, is in excess of 40 per cent (if we include the UK equivalent of the US community college student population, namely the post-18 HE provision in further education colleges) and the White Paper has reconfirmed the government's target of achieving a participation rate of 50 per cent among under 30-year-olds by 2010.

Much of this growth however has been uneven in that it has taken place primarily in the 'new' universities (the former polytechnics) and moreover has been based not so much on reaching out to new student populations, but rather on exploiting existing student constituencies more fully. Reservations remain as to whether this growth can be sustained, or that government aspirations can be met; doubts compounded by the paucity of evidence of viable student demand for the new foundation degree initiative, and the sharp reality facing prospective students that they will have to bear a far greater proportion of the cost of their studies than their predecessors ever did.

Additionally, this growth has still not yet produced the culture change normally associated with a shift to a mass system. The enduring emphasis on the privileged character of student–teacher exchanges, the fervent belief in pastoral intimacy (and fear concerning its loss, a peculiarly British phenomenon), and the passionate commitment to a research culture (even though as a university activity it is a relatively recent one) all suggest that, in its 'private life' if not its 'public' one, British higher education remains firmly wedded to elite values and practices no matter if it has become a mass system (Scott, 1995).

Nonetheless this expansion, and the universities' and colleges' achievement in accommodating it, has been a remarkable one, particularly since Britain was relatively late in making the shift from elite to mass higher education (the US and much of Western Europe made the transition a generation earlier) and also that it was accompanied by a squeezing of resources, notably a halving in the unit of public funding per student. In the process, the core mission of higher education has been transformed. HEIs have had to redefine their notion of conventional roles such as 'teaching' (where the need to accommodate a more diverse student population has coincided with the emergence of new learning technologies) as well as undertake additional new roles, particularly in the areas of lifelong learning and technology transfer. This transformation, like other developments in the universities' long history, did not emerge in isolation but rather is intimately linked to broader societal and economic trends. Drivers, that is, which are affecting higher education systems in all developed countries in similar ways – the UK, Europe, Australia and the US alike. It is these critical influences in the external environment which are analysed next.

I THE CHANGE DRIVERS

Globalisation

In his last speech as US President on British soil, Bill Clinton chose as his topic 'the intensifying process of economic integration and political interdependence that we know as globalisation'. It is a subject on which few politicians – and UK government ministers in particular – can resist the temptation to say something. And like the latter, with his eye on contemporary circumstance, the President informed his audience that 'in a single hour today, more people and goods move from continent to continent than moved in the entire nineteenth century'. While his assertion may have been ahistorical – in that it understates the contribution of inventions such as the electric telegraph, the telephone and the railway, and overlooks the fact that the world economy was more integrated a century ago than it is today and that the nineteenth century witnessed the greatest period of voluntary mass migration ever known – his motives were entirely laudable. Namely, to draw our attention to the radical impact this extraordinary process has already had on the established institutions and ideas of the modern world – the market, the state and the individual – and the opportunity, as well as threat, it poses to our current social, economic and political order.

That said, we should also recognise there has been considerable confusion concerning the use of the term 'globalisation' – what it is and what it means. This has arisen in part because the term refers both to global processes (from the verb, to globalise) and to certain global outcomes (from the noun, the globe) and in part because it remains a contested concept: namely some commentators view it primarily as an economic and political phenomenon, while others place more emphasis on its cultural and environmental dimensions. Thus the term has been used in a variety of ways to refer to, among others:

- the kinds of *strategies* employed by self-serving transnational corporations;
- an *ideology* promoted by capitalist interests seeking a global marketplace unfettered by (national) government regulation;
- an *image* used in the advertising of products (such as airlines, for example) or in recruitment drives for environmental protest groups (as in the 'fragile earth');
- the *basis for political mobilisation* on a particular issue: for example, famine relief in Ethiopia; the campaign to save the Amazonian rainforest, etc.;
- the *'scapes'* and *'flows'*, or the means (the fibre-optic cable, the microwave channel, the space satellite) and objects (people, information, ideas, messages and images) which now characterise the interconnectedness of the new global environment.

Globalisation, then, is not simply an advanced form of internationalisation writ large. Unlike internationalisation, globalisation is at best indifferent to, and at worst positively hostile to, nation states; it celebrates the 'low' worlds (or *coca-colonisation* and *McDonaldisation*) of mass consumerism, not the 'high' worlds of diplomacy and culture and, as it is not tied to the past, is subversive of, and not supportive of, the established world order.

As an institution that is a creature of the nation state (the university has been reliant on the nation state for the bulk of its revenue, been closely identified with the promulgation of national culture, and its core business, that of teaching, has been standardised through the impact of communication and information technology), it follows that globalisation presents one of the most fundamental challenges, if not *the* most, that the university has ever had to face in its long history (Urry, 1999; Scott, 1998).

The 'Knowledge Society'

Intimately related to globalisation is the growing recognition that national economic success can no longer be guaranteed solely by the mass production of consumer goods, or the physical exploitation of natural assets. Rather, it is becoming increasingly dependent on our ability to create and use new ideas and knowledge. New technologies have radically transformed our capacity to store and transmit information. We can now access a far greater range, diversity and quantity of it with greater speed and greater convenience than ever before. Knowledge though, and this is often misunderstood, is more than simply information, or access to it. It is about how and why we access it, how we make sense of it and how we engage critically with it. In essence, knowledge is about understanding. It is about 'information put to work ... it is what enables people to make judgements, create new products, solve problems and interpret events'. And, of course, it has also been the prime *raison d'être* of the modern university. Indeed, in the past century the university, as a producer of knowledge ('research') and as a developer of knowledgeability ('teaching'), has been a, if not *the*, key knowledge institution in Northern and Western Europe and North America.

This pre-eminence, however, can no longer be taken for granted. There are now, for instance, alternative sources of authority over knowledge readily accessible through the Internet and television. And while it is the case that high-level training and research has always taken place outside the university and public research system in think-tanks, corporate research and development divisions, and so on (indeed half of all spending on HE comes from the private sector), the new 'Knowledge Society' has spawned a proliferation of novel forms of knowledge organisation including the 'for-profit university', the 'mega-university' and especially the 'corporate university' (and perhaps the 'global university' to come?). Their use of the brand name 'university' may be a compliment but it is also a distinct threat for these 'new wave' institutions are earnest competitors for the university's established role. IBM for instance spends over one billion dollars per year on research and boasts eight of its own campuses in which it offers its own university-level education. More than that, there is also the threat that other kinds of knowledge organisation may yet emerge: institutions that might be organised not so much on the university model but on that, say, of management consultancies, market research companies or media organisations. Either way, these newcomers will constitute a formidable challenge which HE will have to rise to meet if it is to maintain its established role (see Box 1.1) (Coaldrake and Stedman, 1998; Daniel, 1996).

Social change

Globalisation and the 'Knowledge Society' have also generated far-reaching implications for higher education through the way in which they have transformed the nature of both our working lives and our daily lives. In today's education-driven economy the message is loud and clear: 'If you don't learn, you won't earn.' And if you want to prosper, then – given that there are no more 'jobs for life' – you will have to commit yourself to 'lifelong learning' in order to maintain 'lifetime earning'. Thus higher education has become (and is almost certain to remain), whether one likes it or not, a growth industry. Indeed at the turn of the millennium there were 1.8 million students in Britain, which was more than double the total a decade earlier. And the participation of young people has increased from fewer than 1 in 10 to more than 1 in 3 in one generation.

More than that, as the participation has risen the 'employment power' of a university degree has, quite naturally, declined, and this outcome has in turn generated a burgeoning demand for still more specialist and stronger academic credentials (as demonstrated, for example, in the 'MBA syndrome'). Hence the surge in growth of ever more postgraduate awards and professional qualifications. Further, the coincidence of this ratcheting (or 'credentialism') with the broadening of professional status, has also placed universities in a strong position to cater to the needs of these new professionals in 'enterprise' (entrepreneurs) and 'welfare' (nurses, social workers, etc.), in the same way they accommodated those of the 'industrial' (engineering) and 'pre-industrial' professions (lawyers, doctors and clergy) (Bargh *et al.*, 2000; Coaldrake and Stedman, 1998).

Whether or not they will be able to take full advantage of this situation, however, or indeed maintain their existing market share, given the threat posed by the 'new wave' competition outlined above, will be contingent on the extent to which they are willing to respond to public expectations of choice, service and quality. Today's discriminating consumer wants, and indeed increasingly demands and gets, personalised service. And there is little reason to suppose that students are any different. Indeed as they are more financially pressed than ever, they are likely to be even more intolerant of standardised ('one size fits all') approaches to services and products, such as the expectations that they should: conform to the rhythms of a narrow conventional learning environment; attend classes at a set time and place; complete assessments that are often 'bolted-on' to courses as an afterthought; and generally learn passively under the overall control of the ('gatekeeper') tutor. In short, an approach which is organised to meet the convenience of the institution and its staff rather than that of the students.

If universities are to meet this challenge then, as a significant minority have attempted, they will have to fundamentally change the way they currently organise their teaching activity. In essence, they will have to turn the existing arrangement on its head, not only putting the student at the centre of the learning process, but also ensuring that provision is tailored to the student's individual needs. In other words, they will need to establish a learning environment which is much broader and more holistic in scope, one in which students are able to tap a wide range of learning resources (for example, their student peers, library, computing and media facilities) free of the constraints of time and space, organise their learning around assessments which are central to their courses, and, above all, one in which they are active participants under the guardianship of the ('facilitator') tutor.

The implications, and rewards, for universities in taking this initiative are both significant and far-reaching. On the one hand, they would have to convince tutors that the transformation in their role – from the traditional one of 'director of learning'

Box 1.1 New wave competitors in higher education

Mega-universities
UK Open University
Academic University Turkey
University of South Africa
Indira Ghandi National Open
   University, India

For-profit universities
Phoenix, Western Governors

Corporate universities
BAE
Disney

Ford
Microsoft
Motorola
Unipart

Private higher education, training organisations
Apollo
Stayer

Sleeping giants
IBM, News International

(or information deliverer) to that of 'facilitator of learning' (or curriculum designer) – was not merely desirable but essential for success. And on the other, they would need to maximise the potential benefits offered by new learning technologies. That is to say, wary of the pitfalls that have already befallen e-banking and e-retailing in seeking a 'technological solution' to provide excellence, universities would also need to ensure that they embrace a 'conversational' (i.e. 'people-to-people') model rather a 'transmission' ('machine-to-people') model of electronic learning. If successful, then they should flourish in today's service-oriented 'new economy'.

'Contractual' government

A further driver – the one which has had the most profound impact to date – is something that universities have had to contend with since their inception, namely, the nature of their relationship with wider society. Up until the second half of the twentieth century, the form and practice of HE was largely a matter of the internal or 'private interest' of the academic community. Since then the state, in the name of the 'public interest', has taken an increasingly active role in HE. Initially to guide, then to steer and direct, and latterly to orchestrate 'the market' in which HEIs operate. This is a shifting pattern of behaviour which reflects the change in the way many governments now relate to their citizens, namely, in a contractual manner as much as the traditional legal and political way.

This 'contractual' view of government in which the state now 'purchases' services on behalf of its 'clients' as opposed to 'providing' them itself (as it had previously done in the case of publicly-owned 'nationalised' industries, for example) has been in the ascendancy since the 1980s. It is most typically associated with the privatisation initiatives of the Thatcher government of that period, and the public sector reforms of similar ilk introduced contemporaneously in Australia and New Zealand. This 'purchaser–provider' separation in the management of public services has also of course had a number of far-reaching implications for – and expectations of – the way in which HEIs are organised, governed and managed (Coaldrake and Stedman, 1998).

'Efficiency gains'

First and most obviously, as we have seen, has been the financial imperative placed on institutions to do 'more' with 'less' (resources): to generate that is, in policy-speak, 'efficiency gains'. And they have in this regard been very successful, managing to accommodate a tripling of student numbers over the past twenty-five years while assimilating as the Taylor Report (2001) repeatedly pointed out 'a 38 per cent reduction in real terms since 1989 following a decrease of 20 per cent between 1976 and 1989'. Or, put another way, achieved an efficiency gain of more than 30 per cent in the 1990s alone, measured in terms of expenditure per student. Not only that, but they also managed to sustain, in spite of the unprecedented introduction of means-tested tuition fees and the abolition of student maintenance grants in 1998, a higher student completion (or lower drop-out) rate than anywhere else in the world (with the single exception of Japan).

By the start of the millennium, however, the consensus within the sector was that this momentum was no longer sustainable, at least not without damaging 'the continued reputation for quality of our higher education system'. And particularly because half of Britain's universities were collectively in debt to the tune of £200 million and staff–student ratios had deteriorated from an average of 9 to 1 in 1980 to 17 to 1 in 1998 (or 23 to 1 if funding for research which is included in the average unit of funding is excluded). This view finally prevailed when the government, recognising the need to 'reverse years of under-investment', committed itself in January 2003 to increasing public spending on HE by 6 per cent a year in real terms from £7.6 billion in 2003–4 to £9.9 billion in 2005–6. A cash injection that will be buttressed by a further £1.5 billion a year from 2006 when, in another volte-face on student finance, up-front tuition fees will be replaced by a top-up fee of up to £3,000 a year and maintenance grants will be restored for students from low-income families: namely the government will finally introduce in 2006 the measures which the Dearing Inquiry originally recommended back in 1997. That said, the absence of political consensus on these proposals means that this income stream cannot be taken for granted. And the debate on where and how alternative sources of funding may be raised – to meet the estimated £8 billion investment shortfall – goes on (see Table 1.1).

'Initiativitis'

A second implication has been the apparent retreat from central planning, or, more accurately, the shift in emphasis from overt to covert planning. The higher education funding councils for the home nations (e.g. HEFCE, the funding council for England, from 1992 to date) are nothing other than agents of government – unlike their predecessor the University Grants Committee (1918–89), which acted as a buffer body between universities and Whitehall, and which generated a strategic overview for the sector consistent with universities' core values. Their role, and there is confusion about this within the sector, is not to lobby or act as a mediator, but rather to implement the government's predetermined objectives through second order policies. As their name implies, they are not intended to be planning bodies. Since strategic development is the responsibility of individual HEIs they confine themselves, supposedly, to funding institutions against their own strategic plans rather than seeking to impose any particular system-wide pattern of development (Scott, 1995). Well, that is in theory, at least.

Such is the spate of special initiatives, however, emanating from the funding councils – on access and widening participation; institutional collaboration and restructuring; the development of learning and teaching strategies; the improvement of poor estates; the facilitation of links with business and the community; and so on: projects amounting to £627 million or 13 per cent of the total funding for HE in England alone in 2001–2 – that one could be forgiven for thinking that HEFCE was indeed HEPCE. The biggest and most controversial of the funding councils' initiatives, accounting for a further £888 million or 18 per cent of total funding in England in 2001–2, is of course the Research Assessment Exercise; the four- or five-yearly peer review (or exercise in 'informed prejudice' by 'elitist amateurs' as its detractors put it) of university research output (HEFCE 01/14, 2001; Cohen, 2000).

Table 1.1 Funding options for higher education

Option	Strength	Weakness
Increased public funding	• Readily identifiable • Government commitment to acknowledged priority	• No guarantee of government commitment • Electorally unpalatable (allegedly)
Market fees	• Differential ('top-up') fees would accurately reflect the costs of providing teaching • Would encourage diversity among HEIs and offer greater choice • The government's chosen option: January 2003	• Would increase graduate indebtedness and threaten student participation • Potentially damaging to access-oriented HEIs • The absence of political consensus
Institutional endow-ments (or 'perpetual loans') – proposed by the Conservative Party, 2001	• £1.6 billion scheme which offers HEIs increased autonomy and independence of action • Could facilitate further development of world-class universities and niche institutions and also the culture of 'giving' (as in the US)	• Contingent on scale and scope of deregulation permitted by government • May have negative impact on widening participation • Could not be applied universally in the short term. Would create new binary division
Income contingent on graduate contributions (or 'graduate tax') – similar to Cubie and Australian systems	• Abolishes up-front (fee) contributions in favour of fixed repayments shortly after graduation • Endowment fund would meet shortfalls in learning and teaching (unlike Cubie)	• Would increase dependency on public funds and reduce equity in the short term • May still deter prospective students without incentivising those who do enrol to pressurise HEIs to provide improved 'value for money'
The Cubie – Scottish Parliament scheme *(same as one immediately above except . . .)*	• Endowment fund provides additional support for students	• Raises no extra money for HEIs
Increased maximum fee contribution with income contingent loans	• Doubling the current fee level (to £12,000) would yield English HEIs an additional income of £800 millon	• Government likely to seek claw-back of some additional funding • Increases disincentive to study. Unlikely to lead to an improvement in quality
Full-cost fees and scholarships administered by independent trust – advocated by social market foundation	• Would increase institutional autonomy and give students greater influence	• The burden of funding for students would be likely to remain unchanged
Individual learning accounts	• Would provide greater transparency for individuals and give real meaning to lifelong learning • More a method of building up and distributing many different types of funding to and from individuals	• No ready means of controlling in advance the demand without complex rationing systems • Not a true funding option

Source: adapted from the Taylor Report, 2001

Each of these initiatives are accompanied by the usual bureaucratic paraphernalia and form-filling – the information circular, the consultation document, the invitation to tender, etc. – so much so that for those in the thick of it, it can feel like an endless treadmill of bidding rounds and game playing amid a snow blizzard of information.

Niche institutions

Even more painful is the realisation that these initiatives are likely to remain unrelenting. For despite the rhetoric of free enterprise they are, in essence, national planning interventions thinly disguised as quasi-market competition, the chief purpose of which is to establish a more highly differentiated HE system. A modus operandi, reflected in the funding councils' separation of funding for teaching and for research, which, if logically extended (and there is every sign that it will be), would produce a 'super-league' of (elite) research universities co-existing alongside, though largely segregated from. the bulk of HEIs, whose role would be confined primarily to a social one, that of providing (mass) teaching (HEFCE 22, 2003).

The rationale behind this drive for greater institutional segregation has been the desire to protect elite research universities from the pressures of massification on the one hand, and access-oriented HEIs from the temptations of so-called 'academic drift' on the other. Or, put another way, to preserve and enhance 'excellence' in HE while simultaneously satisfying political and public pressures for mass participation. This aspiration is, of course, most clearly articulated in the 2003 White Paper which anticipates the creation of just such a setting: namely a research elite, centres of teaching excellence, fair access for all and a network of 'Knowledge Exchanges' to promote links between 'non-research-intensive universities' and the business community. The White Paper notwithstanding, this drive has to date not been as successful in practice as national policy makers would have wished.

On the contrary, it could be argued that, formally at least, the HE system has become less stratified, not more. The elite universities, for example, have shown a marked reluctance to forego their broader social responsibilities. An inclination borne out in the celebrated case of Laura Spence, the Tyneside state school applicant, whose rejection by Oxford, and subsequent acceptance at Harvard, was deemed by the Chancellor of the Exchequer to be an 'absolute scandal'. Irrespective of whether or not this individual student should have been turned down, the furore it generated – 'I have never seen Oxford in such a lather of indignation' as one don put it – showed that, although the university may be acutely sensitive to allegations of elitist bias, it also had a keen appreciation of the need for broader student access. Likewise the former polytechnics have shown a similar reluctance to foresake research in favour of an existence based solely around teaching. Indeed they have, by and large, sought to expand their research base, in the belief (if not one shared by the authors of the White Paper) that without such activity they would not be taken seriously as 'a university'.

The government has been more successful, however, in its expectation of universities to take on brand new roles, reaching out to new student constituencies and to the business community in particular. For example, the establishment of science parks as incubators for private enterprise, the commercialisation of intellectual property, the provision of consultancy (both to generate income and to assist global economic competitiveness), the development of electronic and distance learning, the extension of continuous professional development provision, and the accommodation of lifelong learning and of work-based learning are all radically new activities which go well beyond the traditional notions of 'research' and 'teaching'. A myriad of callings have in fact opened up for universities providing opportunities which institutions have exploited to a greater or lesser extent. Thus differentiation is emerging not so much at the system level – where fuzziness, which was the norm even before the binary division between universities and polytechnics was abolished in 1992, has increased still further – but at the institutional level. Put another way, it would appear that we have all become niche institutions or, at least, are expected to be one; that 'instead of trying to do everything' we should, as HEFCE advises, 'focus on what we do best', even though, ironically, the 'Knowledge Society' is evolving in the exact opposite direction to an environment in which easy categorisation and ready-made demarcation are conspicuous by their absence (Bargh, 2000; Scott, 1995).

Accountability

'Paper, paper, everywhere', 'Trial by paper' and 'Academics swamped by bureaucracy' are familiar press headlines which bear testament to a further, and also bitterly contested, implication of the government's contractual relationship with HE. Namely, the former's insistence that the latter should adhere to new forms of accountability. This expectation, which has drived from the expansion of provision in HE, has a number of drivers. One is the financial imperative that, given HEIs receive over £6 billion of public money a year, they should do their utmost to deliver 'value for money'; a performance indicator which is monitored by the national funding councils. Another is quality assurance: the view that academic quality cannot be guaranteed if it is exclusively reliant on academic self-regulation and that quality ought to be managed, rather than assumed, in order to demonstrate that provision is 'fit for purpose', the monitoring of which is undertaken by the QAA.

Still another is the desire for greater transparency – that stakeholders have a 'right to know' and should therefore have access to accurate, consistent and comprehensive information on HEIs enabling them to make informed choices; a process which is invariably aided and abetted by the publication of university league tables in the national media. In consequence HEIs have found themselves required to respond to external requests for information, inspections, audits, submissions and bids for funding from an increasing variety of stakeholders: the QAA, the HEFCE, the Higher Education Statistics Agency, the Teacher Training Agency, the National Health Service, the European Commission, Research Councils, and so on (see Figure 1.1). Though this requirement is no different from that expected of other public sector institutions, and is in fact symptomatic of the emerging audit society which has developed as a corollary of the nascent 'Knowledge Society', it has had a more profound impact on HEIs for a number of reasons.

First, universities, and in particular the traditional ones, have had a longer and deeper attachment to institutional autonomy and professional collegiality than other comparable public sector organisations; an ethos reinforced in the past by the emphasis placed on planning resources (inputs), but undermined nowadays by the current vogue for auditing policies (outcomes). Second, the strength of this tradition has meant that these new requirements have, rightly or wrongly, been widely perceived as having replaced a self-governing system based on trust among competent professionals with one based on a presumption of mistrust and incompetence. A perception which, accurate or otherwise, has not surprisingly had a predictably depressing effect on morale within the universities. Third, the other reservations prevalent within universities concerning audit, that the processes are overly bureaucratic, time consuming and expensive, and needlessly stressful, do in fact appear to be borne out in practice, as the funding council's review indicates. This review inquiry found that the cost of accountability was approximately £250 million (or 4 per cent of the £6 billion of public funds which HEIs receive each year) but, since 'the overall regime [was] a patchwork of legacy requirements from different stakeholders, responding to different concerns, at different times, with little overarching design, coordination or rationale', concluded that this investment 'represents poor value for money both for stakeholders and for institutions'. Further the review team found that, among other things, the regime: encouraged 'inappropriate behaviour' (such as game playing, positional planning and short-term opportunism); contributed to 'planning blight' (by exacerbating uncertainty); placed academics' professional reputations (and even their careers) at risk; and fostered a 'something for something' culture which incurred further costs in administering extra funding which were, ironically, often disproportionate to the extra money awarded (HEFCE 00/36, 2000; Smith and Webster, 1997).

The reviewers recommended, therefore, that a new paradigm be established, namely an investor/partner model, for the relationship between HE funding agencies and institutions: one which would be less burdensome and less interventionist, and which, by channelling demands on HEIs through a single body (the funding council),

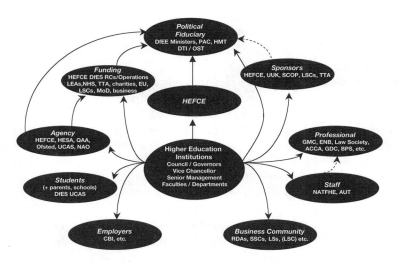

Figure 1.1 Stakeholders in the English higher education sector

Source: HEFCE Report 00/36, 2000

would eliminate 'the duplication, confusion and conflicting demands of overlapping systems' symptomatic of the current accountability regime. While this proposal has, along with the QAA's much trumpeted 'lighter touch' for institutional and subject review, been broadly welcomed, a significant number in HE believe that these reforms do not go far enough. On the contrary, they argue that given the propensity of bureaucratisation to stifle rather than enhance creativity and innovation, and the fact that half of all academics spend more than 15 per cent of their time on administration, the external government assessment process should be eliminated altogether, in favour of an unregulated market system in which freedom, competition and choice can flourish.

There are sharp divisions then concerning the best means of ensuring effective accountability. But either way, the goal remains constant: how do we achieve the optimal balance between the needs of public assurance (that funds are spent properly and to good effect) and those of private governance (of the health and interest of institutions).

Active management

A final implication, and one which has been equally divisive in consequence, has been that universities have been compelled to be far more proactive in the way they manage their affairs. Two generations ago, universities were self-governing collegial communities of scholars presided over by vice-chancellors, whose *raison d'être* was essentially that of a ceremonial figurehead. Their autonomy went unchallenged and their affairs were 'administered' by a bursar and a registrar, whose combined complement of staff rarely exceeded 10 per cent of the total payroll for a typical 1950s 'redbrick' university. Today, universities operate as professional bureaucracies with vice-chancellors whose authority rests more on managerial competence than it does on collegial charisma and who wield power akin to their role, and to that of their counterparts in the private sector, as the institution's chief executive officer. External intrusion has become a daily fact of life, university departments have become 'basic units' and 'cost centres', and 'central services' administration now consumes well over one-third of the average university budget. More than that, universities have acquired the typical organisational panoply – the mission statement, the guiding principles and strategic plan, the corporate brand, etc. – characteristically associated with that of contemporary private sector enterprise. And in many instances, have sought to apply techniques, values and practices derived from the commercial sector. Simply stated, the 'donnish dominion' has been supplanted by managerial sovereignty (Halsey, 1992).

Government expectations that new universities (the former polytechnics) would take on additional responsibilities (for industrial relations, estates management and strategic planning) subsequent to incorporation, and that all universities would both generate efficiency savings and adhere to new forms of accountability, have, as we have noted, played a significant role in precipitating this volte-face in institutional management. It would be wrong, however, to assume that government pressure was the sole driver. On the contrary, the growth of managerialism is as much attributable to the internal dynamics of institutional development, as any other external pressure. Institutional expansion alone on the scale that we have witnessed (the size of the average British university today, *c.*17,000, is more than double that of forty years ago) would have required that universities be far more actively managed than had previously been considered necessary. As it is, it is more than simply a matter of size: universities have also become increasingly complex institutions. The relentless specialisation and sub-specialisation of scholarship, the acquisition of new roles (such as technology transfer and lifelong learning), and the formation of collaborative partnerships with FE (further education) institutions and private enterprise, have all contributed to making universities far more heterogeneous than in the past. In addition the redesignation of the former polytechnics as universities in 1992 also diluted the organisational exceptionalism still further. For all these reasons, then universities would, government pressure notwithstanding, have been obliged to manage their affairs in a much more self-conscious way than hitherto (Bargh, 2000; Scott, 1995).

Either way, the very fact that universities do need to be managed in a more proactive way has meant that issues concerning the internal operation of universities – principally, how should universities be optimally organised and how should they be managed (in an entrepreneurial or collegial way, for example) – have assumed far greater importance and significance in contemporary HEI (higher education institution), a theme which we will return to later.

Academic specialisation and the postmodern challenge

The two final change drivers have, unlike the previous ones, arisen from *within* rather than outside HE. One, the ever-increasing specialisation of scholarship, as a consequence of the growth of knowledge; and the other, postmodernism, as an intellectual challenge to the prevailing (modernist) epistemology of knowledge. The former trend is one which has in turn given rise to the professionalisation of knowledge: to the practice, that is, of scholars writing primarily for a specialist audience, invariably their academic peers rather than a general one. It has become a common and generally accepted practice.

Postmodernism, on the other hand, is a more contentious and less well understood phenomenon. A significant minority view it as so much 'academic globaloney'; as a change in form and style, rather than one of any real substance. And indeed its very nature – its lack of coherence, and of opposition to 'Big Ideas' of the past and present – does not make it easy to define. The origins of postmodernism are obscure, though it appears the movement sprang from a seemingly disparate range of sources: the apparent demise of grand ideologies; the idea of post-industrial society; the theories of the post-structuralists (Derrida and Foucault); and the aesthetic reaction against the 'international style' of modern architecture. Roots, that is, united more by what they reject, modernist discourse, than in what they have in common to one another. Put another way, according to the postmodernists, the relationship between the researcher (the subject) and the object of study is a lot more delicate and complex than modernists have assumed to be the case. Indeed, in the postmodern view, modernist research is fatally flawed because of the way in which language is used, *unproblematically*, within any discourse to picture the essentials (atoms, neurons, economies, etc.) of 'reality'. So much so, in fact, as to call into question the very notion of objectivity which has underpinned traditional methods of scientific inquiry to date (Reed and Hughes, 1991).

The impact of postmodernism in practice, then, has been profound. In subverting the conventional belief in the possibility of objective knowledge and scientific truth, it has not only undermined the epistemological basis on which the modern HE system developed, but has also spawned an academic environment characterised by *difference*; i.e. one in which – in the absence of any particular hierarchy of subjects or notion of authoritative knowledge – a plurality of mutually contestable knowledges (or 'multi-vocalism') prevails. Or, put another way, it has precipitated a transformation in the organisation of knowledge in universities away from what has been termed Mode I knowledge (traditional, homogeneous, hierarchical subject disciplines rooted in an apprentice–master relationship) towards Mode II knowledges (which are non-hierarchical, pluralistic, transdisciplinary, fast changing and socially responsive to a diversity of needs). A trend which has itself been compounded by the relentless drive towards ever-increasing subject specialisation (Smith and Webster, 1997).

In practice, these two drivers have had a largely unsettling effect on academic communities. On the one hand, postmodernism has, not surprisingly, reduced, if not in all cases, the confidence and self-esteem of many intellectuals in their work – in both what they produce and the value of it. And on the other, specialisation has brought about a decline in the number of intellectuals who write for the wider public. For the simple reason that it fosters scholarship, which places a premium on writing for the sake of professional advancement at the expense of contributing to public affairs. Indeed, the scale of fragmentation in many disciplines is such that sometimes academics, even within the same faculty, cannot discuss their areas of expertise without misunderstanding. And this is particularly manifest in areas such as the post-structuralist school of thought where self-styled 'radicals' (usually securely tenured at renowned universities) proffer opinion in language which is excessively and unnecessarily convoluted, self-referential and socially exclusive. In rebarbative jargon, in short. And it these same 'radicals', ironically, who have repeatedly railed at the language used by proponents of 'new managerialism' (Jacoby, 1997).

In consequence, then, the university community has become ensnared by its own peculiar notions of intellectual expertise. Many intellectuals have retreated to this private world, apparently incapable of or unwilling to engage with a wider public and public issues. And this is at a time when, as we have seen, universities have come under greater public scrutiny than ever before. It is as if the university then has 'lost the plot' just when it can least afford to. More than that, in challenging the ethical base as well as the epistemological one on which the university rests, post-modernism has shorn the university of any particular value structure. Thus we cannot assume any longer that the contribution of a university is necessarily a given 'cultural good'.

II THE UNIVERSITY IDENTITY CRISIS

When we place these outcomes alongside the consequences of the other change drivers we have examined – notably, the loss of organisational exceptionalism, the acquisition of novel roles and the emergence of 'new wave' competitors – it is readily apparent why some commentators such as Ronald Barnett have concluded that the university faces a crisis of identity and even the prospect of terminal decline. Today, these commentators may argue, the university can mean all kinds of things in a mass system, yet it does not stand for anything in particular; nor does it have any essential qualities. As such, the university in their view is redundant both as a concept and as an institution.

The challenge this bleak prognosis presents is self-evident. It goes to the heart of the *raison d'être* of higher education. Yet the response from the academic community has for the most part been defensive or, as Smith and Webster (1997) put it, 'passive'. Reluctant to articulate an overriding purpose, or unifying theme, for HE for the reasons given earlier, universities have tended to justify themselves primarily, and indeed with some justification, on practical grounds: on the contribution they, and their graduates, make to the wealth creating resources of the nation. Frustratingly, however, this message is not always recognised outside the sector. Others, by contrast, maintain we need the 'idea' of a university more than ever before and that a broader and more profound case can be made for the institution. In their view the prospect is not nearly so bleak: on the contrary, the university is more likely to prosper than it is to wither in their future scenario.

What then is, or should be, the 'idea' of the university? What case can we make in defence of it?

The university as an 'idea'

The irony of today's condition – the absence of a commanding model or expressive vision of the university – is that it is an entirely novel experience in the university's long history. For in the past HE has always been supported by a number of just such ideas, that is, visions which are invariably invoked by those seeking to defend the university ideal.

The first, and also the most famous, was of course the one embodied in Cardinal Newman's *The Idea of a University* published in 1852. A former Oxford tutor and Anglican convert to Catholicism, Newman's vision was of an institution that was not a tool of business, the state, nor indeed, to the surprise of his sponsors, the Church. Universities needed 'elbow room', Newman argued, in which to pursue 'a knowledge which is its own end . . . liberal knowledge'. Not to train up imperial rulers, as has sometimes been argued, but rather to cultivate in its students the values of civilised reflection. In Newman's view, then, knowledge is valuable for its own sake, not for the uses to which it can be put. And his university ideal, in keeping with the scholastic tradition of the mediaeval university, was that of a setting in which knowledge and culture, with a special emphasis on classical Greek culture, were conserved and passed on. His university, then, was strictly non-utilitarian; one in which there was no place for either professional training or indeed organised research. Rather it was teaching that was the activity at the heart of what Newman called 'the business of a university' (Pelikan, 1992).

A second model, and one in marked contrast to Newman's ideal, was the research university. Initially conceived by the Prussian education minister Wilhelm von Humboldt as an instrument for national rebuilding in the wake of the Napoleonic Wars, the university in this model drew on science as well as philosophy, and prioritised graduate research rather than undergraduate teaching. Centred on the all-powerful departmental professor, this model, in which graduate students served their apprenticeship for a Ph.D. in much the same way as journeymen had done in the medieval guild, also embraced academic freedom and student freedom of choice. It was soon adopted elsewhere, notably the United States where the Humboldtian university was most clearly epitomised in the establishment of Johns Hopkins University (1876), Clark University (1887), Stanford University (1891) and the University of Chicago (1892).

The German notion of the university as an instrument of national culture fell into disrepute with the rise of fascism in the 1920s and 1930s, and it was left to the existentialist philosopher Karl Jaspers to reassert the independence of the institution. 'The University,' he wrote famously in *The Idea of the University*, 'is a community of scholars engaged in the task of seeking truth.' In Jaspers' scheme, then, the transmission of culture was based strictly on critical enquiry but, interestingly, unlike Newman he did not believe that the university should be preoccupied solely with the pursuit of 'pure learning'. There was also room in Jaspers' university for professional education too.

A third model was that of the 'modern' university; a concept developed by the American educationalist, and former Johns Hopkins graduate, Abraham Flexner in his *Idea of a Modern University*, published in 1930. Reacting against the dominance of what he termed the 'service station' role of universities – the expectation that universities should provide vocational education and demonstrate their practical usefulness to the country – as well as his perception that much university research output was of poor quality, Flexner argued for the establishment of a 'modern' institution, which combined the ideas of Newman and von Humboldt within a 'unity of purpose' to pursue excellence. Flexner's 'modern university' ideal exerted, as one might expect, a very powerful attraction at the time of its publication, one indeed which has persisted in many quarters undiminished to the present day. This was in spite of (or maybe because of) the ideal's antipathy to mass participation, and the fact that, as Clark Kerr pointed out as long ago as 1960, Flexner, like Newman, was describing an institution that had already ceased to exist (Coaldrake and Stedman, 1998).

A fourth model was the 'multiversity' developed by Clark Kerr, President of the University of California and celebrated in his *Uses of a University* published in 1963. Kerr's model, symptomatic of the idealistic aspirations of post-war American society, conceived the university as having not one single community but multiple ones: namely different communities of students, of academics, and different external communities of alumni, government, business, and so on. His 'multiversity' is a city, a 'City of Intellect', in which staff and students identify with particular subcultures rather than with the whole. A concept which Kerr sought to make reality, first through the building of a multi-campus public research university system, unique in not having an official flagship campus, and second as the architect of the 1960 California Master Plan for Higher Education. The latter, called a 'treaty' by Kerr, outlined a vision for the entire state – to spread opportunity to all its young citizens; to raise the skill levels of human resources; and so on – and established a three-tier system each with its own function and specialisation. Thus the elite campuses of the University of California offer world-class research and teaching facilities; the California State University concentrates primarily on undergraduate teaching; and the state's many community colleges provide low cost and locally focused access to higher education. The Plan attracted admirers and critics in equal measure but remains the classic example of a stratified system of HE provision, and potentially the source of renewal, as recognised in the White Paper, for a vision of HE in the twenty-first century (Kerr, 2001).

The home-grown British response to the same forces which produced a mass system in the US saw the establishment of the 'Polytechnic Experiment' (1965–92), on the one hand, and the creation of the greenfield campus sites of the county (or Shakespearian) universities – York, Lancaster, Warwick, Sussex, Essex and Kent – on the other. Twin initiatives, that is, which combined a visionary aspiration (largely unmet) to redraw the map of learning with the more pragmatic, and eventually successful, goal of providing vocational and technical education (Scott, 1995).

The case for universities

Contemporary HE is heir to all these earlier visions – but, as we noted earlier, a dispossessed one. For there is nothing today to match these past visions which have, to varying degrees, been either undermined or discredited. It is, however, possible to identify some elements which testify to the uniqueness and special value of the institution – and to why, ultimately, universities matter.

In the first instance we need to remember, as Daniel Bell (1966) began reminding us forty years ago, that what gives our universities their defining purpose is that *they retain the monopoly for granting of credentials*. And while this purpose may be fraught with risk, in that potentially it could reduce the university to being a servant of the professions, employers and industry, the very fact that universities have maintained a virtual monopoly in the awarding of legitimate credentials testifies to the vitality of academia.

Second, universities, the virtual campus notwithstanding, are *particular* sorts of gathering places. And even in the postmodern era, when knowledge is uncertain and contested, they remain *the primary site of cultural engagement; a physical locale* where people come together to engage in intellectual endeavour.

Third, and more problematically, is the unashamedly and unapologetic modernist contention that, in spite of postmodern claims to the contrary, the university remains *the locus of disinterested research, scholarship and teaching*; a guiding principle which should underpin all institutions bearing the name. This is not inconsistent with the White Paper's view of universities having different priorities and in some instances maybe even a 'teaching only' brief. Such a conception indeed would mark the reassertion of what Newman always maintained was the (single) core activity of universities.

Fourth, the uncertainties of the new postmodern age, a 'world of supercomplexity', have bestowed as Barnett (2000) points out a new set of responsibilities on universities. There is a need to: reorganise research to engender daring new frames of understanding; utilise pedagogy that enables us to understand the character of this world; and empower individuals both within itself and in the wider society to live purposefully amidst supercomplexity. Put another way, the university should complement critical thinking, as it always has done, with critical self-reflection and critical action, and in that way establish itself as *a site of the continuing formation of critical being*. That is, as *an emancipatory institution* which empowers students on the one hand, and acts as *a key instrument in maintaining an open society* on the other (Smith and Webster, 1997).

Taken together, these distinctive features offer a basis for revivifying the university both as a concept and as an institution, to enable it, potentially, to fulfil a uniquely significant role that no other type of institution can properly provide in a free and responsible society. And when we combine these features with the significance which the institution holds, as an object of aspiration and as a crucial *rite de passage*, for an increasing proportion of the population, as well as the practical contribution which universities make (summarised in Box 1.2), then the future prospect is indeed a bountiful one.

It remains the case however, as we have seen, that universities will have to re-define themselves to operate successfully at the forefront of change: to ensure flexibility, that is, while still maintaining loyalty to traditional values. If they do not, then they run the risk of being overwhelmed and will have no one but themselves to blame for the outcome. Institutional management and the professoriate alike, then, have a shared responsibility in ensuring that universities take the former path. If successful there is no reason why universities cannot be more important than ever in the future.

Box 1.2 The aims and functions of universities

Functions

- Pursuit of research and scholarship
- High-level specialised education and training
- Fulfilling the manpower needs of the 'expert society'
- Performance of leadership roles in intellectual activities
- Provision of services to the region and immediate community
- Acting as a screening mechanism for entry to the professions
- Operating as an avenue for social mobility

Aims

- To generate a highly educated and trained population
- To generate a population able to work and live together. The British universities' concept of collegiality, and their strong pastoral systems, help to promulgate the ideal of a civilised society, able to settle dissent through democratic and rational means
- To generate a society that reflects certain inherent moral values
- To transmit a shared culture – one which is not in any way inconsistent with an ideal of cultural diversity
- To preserve and transmit knowledge
- To assist in spreading the benefits of informational and technological advances
- To enable its graduates to play an active part in wealth creation of the nation
- To generate a population skilled in the wide range of specialised activities necessary to sustain a complex society

Source: adapted from National Conference of University Professors, 1996

2 Knowing your institution

The University is a community of scholars engaged in the task of seeking truth.
Karl Jaspers, 1923

I find the three major administrative problems on campus are sex for the students, athletics for the alumni and parking for the faculty.
Clark Kerr, President, University of California, 1958

'This proposal, you know, might have to go to a Congregation.' This constantly reiterated mantra came to haunt John Kay soon after his appointment as the founding Director of Oxford University's Said Business School in 1996. His brief – to introduce a new subject into an ancient institution – was a difficult one, but given that the project was being underwritten by an external sponsor, in the form of a £20 million gift, and since Kay himself was a long-standing Fellow of St John's College and therefore familiar with 'the Oxford way', his task should have been, as Kay anticipated, rendered more straightforward. And indeed it was initially, for Kay's immediate priority, to establish a developmental strategy, was enthusiastically endorsed by colleagues (Kay, 2000a).

When he sought to advance the initiative further, however, through the implementation of an agreed action plan, Kay found that the university had no mechanism for proceeding with such discussions. Instead he was advised to turn his strategy document into specific proposals which could then be considered by relevant committees; a disastrous consequence, from Kay's perspective, for none of these committees had an overarching brief, and his initiative would be tackled in a piecemeal fashion. Worse still, they were all averse to reaching a definitive conclusion anyway. Indeed Kay discovered that the Oxford committee system had elevated the avoidance of decision-making into an art form. The 'eight oars of indecision', as Kay dubbed them (deferral and referral; procedural objection; the wider picture; evasion; ambiguity; precedent; and denial), were all techniques which were invariably deployed by committee members to thwart his proposals (Kay, 2000b).

In exasperation Kay turned to those university officials who held executive titles only to find they did not have executive functions or authority. Even his suggestion that they hire a project manager to oversee the construction of the building, a normal business practice, was overlooked in favour of appointing yet another committee of academics solely for this purpose. As a last resort Kay could have appealed to the Congregation (the 'parliament' of all the Oxford faculty, some 3,000 in number and the source of ultimate authority in the university) but he knew this would be fruitless as this course of action had been repeatedly recommended to him by opponents, in the knowledge and spirit that 'you haven't got a hope in hell of getting this through so you might as well give up now'. Kay opted to resign in frustration in 1999 and become a fellow once more of St John's College. The university restructured its operations the following year (devolving decision-making and resource allocation to the local level) and it was left to Anthony Hopwood, Kay's successor, to establish the Said Business School as a major intellectual and physical centre of the institution (Kay, 2000a).

Kay's experience highlights how Oxford's greatest strength – academic freedom and innovation flourishing within a federalist, organic and diverse structure ('the collegiate academy') – is also potentially its greatest weakness: an inability to grasp change as opportunity. From our perspective, it also underlines the importance, as a manager, of understanding the nature of one's organisation *even when you believe you know it well enough already*! Kay's detractors argued that he did not do enough either to work with the grain of a complex academic institution, or to convince others of the efficacy of his vision for a US-style business school operating on the banks of the Isis. To be an effective manager, then, you must have a keen appreciation of the distinctive features and nuances of your institution, notably its climate, structure, politics and culture.

We should also recognise that, despite the tendency to treat HEIs as if they are all organised along similar lines, no two institutions are alike. The participative democracy that characterised Oxford's deliberations over Kay's proposals, for example, contrasts markedly with the way in which decisions were reached under a former vice-chancellor at Bradford University. Here there was no ambiguity, nor was there much else. The vice-chancellor simply exercised his executive authority without any reference to others, on the basis that the deadline for response set by the HEFCE 'means that there is no time for democracy'. This sharp divergence in practice also illustrates how the management of HEIs has become increasingly differentiated. More than that, several HEIs have pioneered new paths of development: some have sought to establish themselves as 'entrepreneurial universities' or 'business excellence universities' while others have attempted to become 'virtual universities'.

This second chapter considers the institutional context or nature of the internal environment in which individual managers have to operate. It explains, in general, how HEIs have come to be managed as they are today and, in particular, the nature of organisational culture peculiar to HEIs. In doing so it offers analytical tools which managers can use as a means of understanding their own individual circumstances and context. It also examines exemplars of the new models of institutional organisation (the 'entrepreneurial university', the 'virtual university', and so on) and speculates on the alternative ways in which HEIs might develop and organise in the future: the university 2025?

The management of HEIs

A 'community of scholars' or a 'degree factory'? These two epithets, and the contrast in the connotations associated with them, have come to characterise the increasingly bitter debate in academia on how universities are, or should be, organised. The 'community of scholars', and its depiction of autonomous professionals pursuing knowledge for its own sake within a collegial academy, where authority is derived from academic expertise, has always been, and still is, a powerful and evocative ideal for most academics. The 'degree factory', by contrast, conjures up an image of the university as a large corporate identity where functions and resources are consciously 'managed', and where the concepts of relevance and service have primacy.

The reality however, both historical and contemporary, is more complex than this simple dichotomy suggests. While it is true, for instance, that the term 'management' is relatively novel in higher education (it was first used with reference to institutional planning in the late 1960s), it is also the case that, Oxford and Cambridge apart, there was significant lay involvement in the government of 'old' universities from the outset. Put another way, contrary to popular belief, most 'old' universities, although autonomous in the sense that they are not state institutions, have not always been run by academics. The ancient Scottish universities of Edinburgh and Glasgow, for instance, were controlled by their respective town councils until well into the nineteenth century. And the governing councils of most civic universities established in Victorian England were dominated by networks orchestrated by founding patrons and their heirs, Chamberlain in Birmingham, Wills in Bristol and Palmers in Reading (Warner and Palfreyman, 1996; Scott, 1995).

It is possible to discern, as Scott has demonstrated, four main phases in the internal government of 'old' universities: civic (late nineteenth to early twentieth century); donnish (1920s to early 1960s); democratic (late 1960s to 1970s); and managerial (1980s to date) (see Table 2.1). A pattern of development which is indeed more evolutionary than revolutionary: each phase reflecting the, quite logical, response which universities made to the changing environmental circumstances they encountered. The donnish phase, for instance, emerged as a consequence of the state's growing stake in HE and the subsequent change in source of university income – from town council and industrial subsidy, and student fees (symptomatic of the civic era) to direct state 'block' grants meted out by the UGC (University Grants Committee) set up for this very purpose in 1919 (to 1989). Under the new funding arrangements the influence of founding patrons waned and power passed from lay councils to academic senates. The elite collegiality characteristic of this donnish phase was, in turn, challenged by the student protests of the 1960s, and the increasing heterogeneity of staff and student populations of the 1970s. The democratic phase proved to be short-lived, however, and the managerial university emerged in the 1980s as a response to a newer harsher environment, characterised by fewer resources, greater accountability and increased complexity. Viewed historically, then, this current managerial phase is not a radical departure from the past, nor should we assume it is an eternal one. It has, as we noted earlier, been as much a positive response to institutional growth and development, as it has been a defensive one, to manage successive cuts in public funding.

'New' universities have arrived at a similar point, though by an entirely different route. Originally local authority institutions, by and large, they only acquired independent status in 1989. Consequently they do not have the same deep-rooted attachment to institutional autonomy and collegiality which prevails in 'old' universities. Their academic boards for instance are, despite their formal power, lightweight compared to the academic senates, their equivalent in the traditional sector, and are often overshadowed by powerful senior management teams. Their governing bodies too – given that the independent member majority appoint their successors (in a similar vein to a closed corporation) – are arguably not sufficiently accountable either. Nor do 'new' universities enjoy the financial security which underpins many of their 'older' counterparts. Cambridge, for example in 2001, was worth 170 London Guildhalls in financial terms (Sanders and Goddard, 2001).

Significant though these differences are, management systems and practices in 'new' and 'old' universities alike are no longer so dissimilar. Line management has become the norm in both types of institution. They each invariably have a 'vice squad', a senior management team of pro-vice-chancellors and deputy vice-chancellors with specific portfolios of responsibility, and are headed by a vice-chancellor whose role, in most cases, is now firmly a chief executive one. It is also the case that the majority working in higher education understand and accept that institutions have had to be more actively 'managed'. Where there has been criticism (and often rightly so), and why managerialism has attracted such opprobrium, is because of the *way* in which institutions have handled this process. The style of management in these instances has almost always clashed with the prevailing institutional culture. *Effective* management, on the other hand (management that harnesses the commitment and skills of all staff), is contingent upon getting the 'fit' between management style and organisational culture right. That is, ensuring that the management style, whether it be formal, rational, consensual, hard-driving, or political, etc., harmonises with, rather than rubs against, the distinctive character of the institution. Without it, institutions will never realise their full potential. Sensitivity towards and understanding of institutional culture then is an essential prerequisite of effective management. But what is organisational culture – and how can we manage it?

The culture of HEIs

What is culture?

A notoriously slippery concept to define, 'culture' has been invoked by 'all persons to mean all things'. Traditionally, it has been used as a reference guide to, as well as judgement on, patterns of societal development; though nowadays, it is employed more usually as a (non-judgemental) means of differentiating between societies as well as organisations. Common to both approaches is the notion that 'culture' is a distinct (static and fixed) entity; a unitary phenomenon, that is, which has clearly defined attributes (derived from beliefs, stories, norms, rituals, and so on) and which all nation states and organisations 'possess'.

More recent perspectives in organisational science, however, such as those in anthropology, sociology and new social history, view this interpretation of 'culture'

Table 2.1 The government and management of UK universities

'Old' universities

Phase period	Civic *late nineteenth to early twentieth centuries*	Donnish *1920s to early 1960s*	Democratic *late 1960s to 1970s*	Managerial *1980 to date*
Characteristics	• Dominance of lay patrons and governing council	• Elite collegiality; vice-chancellor and senior professors • Pre-eminence of academic senate; supervisory lay council	• Democratic collegiality • Extension of democracy to staff and student 'rank and file'	• Reordering of internal authority • Senior management influence increases; effective (if not formal) power of organs of academic self-government decreases
Management	• Non-issue	• Minimal; 'lightest of light touch'	• Consensus	• Heads of department as line managers; formation of senior management teams (SMTs)
Administration	• Skeletal	• Subordinate	• Professionalised: Conference of University Administrators (CUA)	• Managerial cadre (including planning, strategy)
Role of vice-chancellor	Chancellor substitute Ceremonial figurehead	Charismatic leader Institution builder	Chief executive – crisis manager; political lobbyist; returns officer; efficiency champion; fund-raiser	

'New' universities

Phase period	Municipal *pre-1989*	Transitional *1970s to 1989*	Corporate *1989 to date*
Characteristics	• Local authority institution • No form of institutional democracy • Underdeveloped	(i) Establishment of academic boards in HEIs	• Polytechnics established as free-standing institutions (1989); creation of unified university system (1992); establishment of new, smaller governing bodies with majority of independent members (a closed corporation)
Management	Bureaucratic hierarchy, regulatory	(ii) Gradual devolution of local authority responsibilities	• Fully-fledged; pre-eminence of SMT (senior management team) 'overshadows' academic board
Administration	• Key functions the responsibility of local authorities	(iii) Creation of national policy environment, via National Advisory Board (NAB)	• Professionalised and formalised; takeover of local authority residual responsibilities (industrial relations, estates management, strategic planning)

Source: adapted from Scott, 1995; Bargh *et al.*, 2000

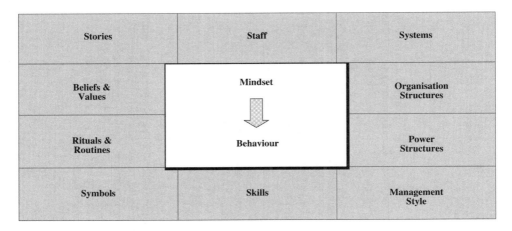

Stories	Staff	Systems
Beliefs & Values	Mindset	Organisation Structures
Rituals & Routines	Behaviour	Power Structures
Symbols	Skills	Management Style

Figure 2.1 The cultural web of an organisation

Source: adapted from Alexander, 2001

as being unduly mechanistic; that is, one which fails to convey either any sense of dynamism with regard to workplace activity, or any 'real' understanding of it from the 'insider's' viewpoint. Advocates of this revisionist school argue that 'culture' should in fact be conceived not as a distinct static entity, but as a dynamic social process; i.e. an ongoing and proactive 'process of reality construction that allows people to see and understand particular events, actions, objects, utterances, or situations in distinctive ways'. In other words, such revisionists consider organisations to *be* cultures as opposed to *having* cultures: that culture is, in essence, a process rather than an entity (Morgan, 1997; Frost *et al.*, 1991; Allaire and Firsirotu, 1984).

Either way, it is a lot more complex (as Figure 2.1) illustrates, than the popular understanding of the term which prevails within organisations – that culture is simply 'the way we do things round here'. Organisational culture is indeed reflective of, and embedded in, the 'working out' of a variety of powerful influences: the distribution of power within the organisation; the way in which work is structured and controlled; the attachment to history and tradition; the 'ownership' of the organisation; the rituals, routines, stories, symbols and gossip which shape everyday working life; and so on. All of which profoundly affect, and are affected by, the 'mindset' and behaviour of staff and management. Culture is thus a combination of values, structure and power which has implications for every aspect of an organisation's operations, its external relationships and, ultimately, the realisation of its institutional mission.

Academic cultures

Drawing on Karl Weick's (1976) characterisation of the classic collegial academy as a 'loosely coupled system' and Charles Handy's (1993) categorisation of organisation cultural types, Ian McNay (1995, 1996) has developed a model which helps us to not only interpret the nature of organisational culture peculiar to HE, but also explore how HEI cultures have changed over time. McNay's model – based on the degree of 'tightness' or 'looseness' on two dimensions: policy definition and control over

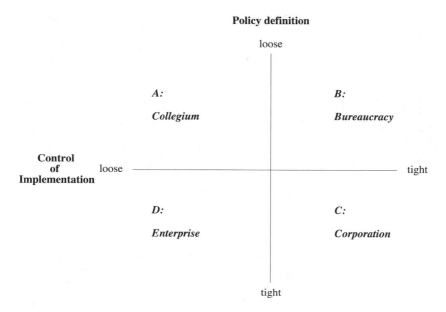

Figure 2.2 Models of universities as organisations

Source: McNay and Dopson, 1996

implementation (see Figure 2.2) – generates four organisational types of HEI, each with their own distinguishing features (see Table 2.2).

Type A, with loose policy definition and loose control over implementation, is *the classic collegial academy*. Here the focus is on freedom to pursue professional and personal goals uninhibited by external constraints. Discipline-based departments headed by senior professors are the dominant organisational units, and the management style is permissive and consensual. Evaluation is by peer review and students are regarded as apprentice academics.

Type B, the *bureaucratic university*, has a loose policy frame but exercises tight control over implementation. Its focus, as one would expect, is on rules, regulations and procedures. The management style is formal–rational and decision-making is formalised in committees. Evaluation is based on external audit and students are perceived as statistics.

Type C, the *corporate university*, exercises tight control over both policy and implementation. Here the focus is on loyalty to the organisation and in particular to the senior management team and chief executive who make up the dominant institutional unit. The management style is political–tactical and decision-making is centred in senior management working groups. Evaluation is monitored through performance indicators and students are seen as units of resource.

Type D, the *enterprise university*, combines a tight policy frame with loose control over activity. Its focus is in competence and its orientation is as much external as it is internal. The management style is supportive of devolved leadership and decision-making and is centred on project teams. Evaluation is based on attracting repeat business and students are treated as valued customers.

Table 2.2 Summary characteristics of four university models

Factor	Collegium	Bureaucracy	Corporation	Enterprise
Dominant value (Clark, 1983)	Freedom	Equity	Loyalty	Competence
Role of central authorities	Permissive	Regulatory	Directive	Supportive
Handy's organisation culture	Person	Role	Power	Task
Dominant unit	Department/individual	Faculty/committees	Institution/senior management team	Subunit/project teams
Decision arenas	Informal groups/networks	Committees and administrative briefings	Working parties and senior management teams	Project teams
Management style	Consensual	Formal/'rational'	Political/tactical	Developed leadership
Time-frame	Long	Cyclic	Short/mid-term	Instant
Environmental 'fit'	Evolution	Stability	Crisis	Turbulence
Nature of change	Organic innovation	Reactive adaptation	Proactive transformation	Tactical flexibility
External referents	Invisible college	Regulatory bodies	Policy makers as opinion leaders	Clients/sponsors
Internal referents	The discipline	The rules	The plans	Market strength/students
Basis for evaluation	Peer assessment	Audit of procedures, e.g. IS9001	Performance indicators	Repeat business
Student status	Apprentice academic	Statistic	Unit of resource	Customer
Administrator roles: servant of . . .	The community	The committee	The chief executive	The client, internal and external

Source: McNay, 1995

Research in the UK and Australia suggests that in broad terms HEIs have, as a consequence of the changes in the environment they have faced over the last two decades, moved in a clockwise direction from A to B to C to D. A pattern of development which is consistent with the environmental 'fit' (evolution, stability, crisis, turbulence) associated with each of the four cultures. It would be wrong to assume, however, that this pattern is either a universal or a consistent one. Cambridge and Imperial College, London, for example, have arguably moved from A to D without passing through B or C. It is also the case that none of these different cultures are mutually exclusive and it is likely that all four co-exist in most HEIs (Coaldrake and Stedman, 1998; McNay, 1995).

What is your university or college culture?

The point is: what is the nature of the organisational culture which you work in? There are no easy answers. We need to recognise that there are difficulties in examining culture whatever one's perspective. Insiders, as well as outsiders, find it difficult to analyse simply because so much of culture is 'taken for granted'. Or as Edgar Schein (1997) memorably put it: 'Culture at its deepest level is the assumptions we do not see'. And for all that it is *your* perspective which may, or may not, tally with that of your colleagues. For this reason you may wish to share the activities which follow with the other members of your department.

I   One simple yet very effective way of realising 'hidden' staff perceptions, as the UK Open University has demonstrated (Russell and Parsons, 1996), is to ask them to draw their own individual picture of the institution as they perceive it. You should then share these with your department and discuss the outcomes (see Figure 2.3).

II   Another more structured approach – given that organisational cultures, as Tony Becher (1996) reminds us, operate in three arenas: front-of-stage (the public arena); backstage (where deals are done) and under-the-stage (where gossip is purveyed) – is to attempt to articulate these 'official' and 'unofficial' cultures (see Table 2.3). The questionnaire outlined below is designed to help you do this: to develop, that is, your own 'fine-grained' understanding and analysis of your own institution still further (see Table 2.4).

Again, you can complete this questionnaire either on your own or share it with colleagues. If the latter, examine the differences between their responses and your own. More importantly, try and establish the reasons for these differences and identify what you can do about them.

III   Once, you have completed the questionnaire, use the scoring mechanism in Table 2.5 to quantify your perception of the current 'cultural balance' of your institution.

- Think of your institution as it was five years ago and repeat the scoring exercise.
- Anticipate how your institution will develop over the next five years and repeat the exercise again.
- Plot the outcomes to determine the shift in your organisational culture.

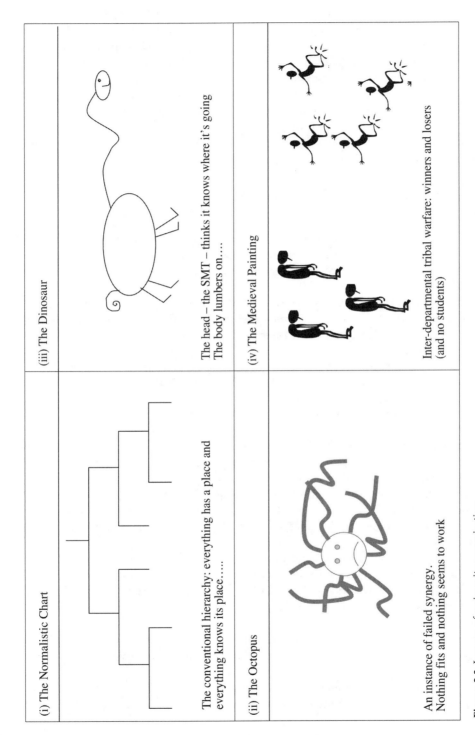

(i) The Normalistic Chart

The conventional hierarchy: everything has a place and everything knows its place......

(ii) The Octopus

An instance of failed synergy.
Nothing fits and nothing seems to work

(iii) The Dinosaur

The head – the SMT – thinks it knows where it's going
The body lumbers on.....

(iv) The Medieval Painting

Inter-departmental tribal warfare: winners and losers
(and no students)

Figure 2.3 Images of university organisation

Table 2.3 Understanding the culture of your HEI: I Illustration

Gossip and the informal stories that provide everyday conversation yield a penetrating insight into organisational culture – in themselves and in the messages they convey

HEI	Conversation theme	'Message'
'New' university, southeast England	Q What's the difference between the vice-chancellor and the rest of the staff? A He's chauffeur-driven and we are all student-driven!	There is one law for some of us and another for the rest of us.
	The removal of the staff pigeonholes from X campus.	Irrefutable proof of the management conspiracy against dedicated staff.
Regional research university, Eastern USA	The 'meat-axe administrator' and his refrain: 'We already did that yesterday!'	It's a Darwinian jungle in this state and we're ahead of the game.
	'They slough it off here, slough it off there, slough it off everywhere.'	Outsourcing is all the rage here and we could be next.
Regional research university, Northeastern USA	'He (the President) used to come out of the 'puzzle palace' with a guard of honour.'	Who knows what the executive does or thinks – you can't get near them.
	'It was like Moses coming off the mountain with the tablets (The Strategic Plan).'	Collegiality? You gotta be kidding.
University of technology, Eastern Australia	'A lot of the staff here have greater credit card bills than the debt of the university.'	Whatever else this university can be accused of – financial laxity isn't one of them.
Research university, Eastern Australia	'You need the personality of a Sherman tank to survive as head of department here.'	It's rough, it's tough and there is no end in sight. The industrial model is just not suited to an HE environment.
Research university, Western Australia	'X has just been R . . . d.'	Given a severance offer he couldn't refuse. We don't carry any 'deadwood' here, no matter what you might think.
Regional university, South Australia	'I've been parking my car under that tree for 28 years or more.'	The latest change initiative can just go hang. 'Wake me when it's over.'

Table 2.4 Understanding the culture of your HEI: II Questionnaire

The culture of your institution is embedded in the images, metaphors, beliefs, values, norms, rituals, language, stories, legends, myths, and other symbolic artefacts that decorate and give form to the experience of everyday working life.

Think about your institution.
How would you describe its culture?

Try to be systematic in your analysis by identifying specific examples of the symbolism in use:

– What are the principal images or metaphors that people use to describe your institution?
_____
_____
_____

– What *physical impressions* do the organisation and its artefacts create? Do these vary from one place to another?
_____
_____
_____

– What are the dominant *stories or legends* that people tell? What messages are they trying to convey?
_____
_____
_____

– What *reward systems* are in place? What 'messages' do they send in terms of activities or accomplishments that are valued, and those that are not?
_____
_____
_____

– What are the favourite topics of *informal conversation?*
_____
_____
_____
_____

– What kind of *beliefs and values* dominate your organisation? (officially / unofficially)
_____
_____
_____
_____

– What are the main *norms* (i.e. the dos and don'ts)?
_____
_____
_____
_____

– What are the main *ceremonies and rituals* and what purposes do they serve?
_____
_____
_____

– What *language* dominates everyday conversation (e.g. buzzwords, clichés, catchphrases)?
_____
_____
_____

– Think of three *influential people*: in what ways do they symbolise the character of your institution?
_____
_____
_____

– What are the *identifiable subcultures* in the organisation? How are they differentiated? Are they in conflict or in harmony?
_____
_____

– What *impacts* do these subcultures have on the organisation? What functions do these groupings serve for their members? Is the overall effect on the organisation positive or negative?
_____
_____

Compare your analysis with:

a) The sequential pattern of development (A, B, C, D) implied in McNay's model. Has your institution followed the same path? If not, how do you account for the differences?

b) Those of your colleagues. Where do you agree? Disagree? Are the differences significant. Is the management style consistent with the organisational culture?

IV   Repeat the first three activities and on this occasion focus solely on your own department or unit rather than the whole institution. Compare the outcomes.

a) In what ways is the culture of your department or unit similar to and different from that of your institution. Account for the differences.

b) What are the strengths and weaknesses of your institutional culture? Departmental culture?

c) Is your perception consistent with those of your colleagues? What are the key differences? Do they relate to your management style? Do you need to change it?

The management of culture?

A systematic examination of our own organisational culture then yields a number of significant benefits. It enhances our own self-realisation, gives insight into the hidden perception of others, and ultimately develops our understanding of the 'social reality' of the institutional context in which we have to operate.

Understanding organisational culture, however, begs the question whether it should be changed in some way, and, if so, what can we do to change it. Certainly many people in the private sector reason that, since the creation and maintenance of a 'strong' organisational culture is a critical determinant of company success, 'managing culture' must be an effective way of generating competitive advantage. Not all such efforts are successful however. Too often such initiatives have floundered because they have been based on the, arrogant, assumption that, as an entity, culture (like dough) can somehow be consciously moulded by senior managers sitting above the fray. More successful have been those instances which recognise culture (as a process which) embraces all players within the organisation (Trowler, 1998; Frost *et al.*, 1991).

In either case, the lesson learned is to remember that 'our actions speak so much more louder than our words'. Thus, it would make little sense, and serve to foster deep antipathy, for an HEI to have, say, a mission statement extolling how much the institution valued excellence in teaching if the criteria it used for staff recruitment and promotion were based solely on performance in research. Put another way, we can all contribute to sustaining, or shaping, our organisational culture by the way in which we act. Our actions demonstrate to others what we really value. And in the context of HEIs the criteria we use for recruitment, promotion and redundancy, the way in which we respond to critical incidents and institutional crisis, celebrate achievement, operate budgets, and so on, all send important signals which reinforce or alter the perception of others. These may, in turn, affect their outward behaviour and indeed

Table 2.5 Understanding the culture of your HEI: III Scoring mechanism

Each of these items contains four descriptions of organisational features. Distribute 100 points between the four descriptions based on how similar the description is to your own institution. None of the descriptions is any better than the others: they are just different. For each question, please use 100 points.

In question 1, for example, if A seems very similar to mine, B seems somewhat similar, and C and D do not seem similar at all, I might give 70 points to A and the remaining 30 points to B.

1 Dominant characteristics (divide 100 points)

My institution is ....

(a) A very personal place. It is like an extended family. People seem to share a lot of themselves.
(b) A very formalised and structured place. Bureaucratic procedures generally govern what people do.
(c) Very competitive in orientation. A major concern is with getting the job done. People are very production- and achievement-oriented.
(d) A very dynamic and entrepreneurial place. People are willing to stick their necks out and take risks.

2 Organisational leader (divide 100 points)

The university vice-chancellor/principal/president is generally considered to be
....

(a) A mentor, a facilitator, or a parent figure.
(b) A coordinator, an organiser, or an efficiency expert.
(c) A hard driver, a producer, or a competitor.
(d) An entrepreneur, an innovator, or a risk-taker.

3 Organisational glue (divide 100 points)

The glue that holds my institution together is ....

(a) Loyalty and commitment. Cohesion and teamwork are characteristic of this organisation.
(b) Formal procedures, rules, or policies. Maintaining a smooth-running organisation is important.
(c) An emphasis on production and goal accomplishment. Marketplace aggressiveness is a common theme.
(d) A focus on innovation and development. The emphasis is on being at the cutting edge.

4 Organisational climate (divide 100 points)

The climate inside my institution ....

(a) Is participative and comfortable. High trust and openness exist.
(b) Emphasises permanence and stability. Expectations regarding procedures are clear and enforced.
(c) Is competitive and confrontational. Emphasis is placed on beating the competition.
(d) Emphasises dynamism and readiness to meet new challenges. Trying new things and trial-and-error learning are common.

5 **Criteria of success** (divide 100 points)

My institution defines success on the basis of ....

(a) Its development of human resources, teamwork and concern for people.
(b) Its having unique or the latest 'products' (in teaching, research and consultancy). It is a product leader and innovator with a keen interest in stakeholder satisfaction.
(c) Efficiency and equity. Dependable delivery, smooth scheduling, low cost production and the maintenance of standards are critical.
(d) Its position in the external league tables. Being number one relative to the competition in the marketplace is a key objective.

6 **Management style** (divide 100 points)

The management style in my institution is characterised by ....

(a) Teamwork, consensus and participation.
(b) Security of employment, longevity in position and predictability.
(c) Hard-driving competitiveness, production and achievement.
(d) Individual initiative, innovation, freedom and uniqueness.

[(a) collegium (b) enterprise (c) bureaucracy (d) corporation]

Source: adapted from Cameron and Quinn, 1998

inner consciousness. This is an issue we will return to in Chapters 3 and 7 when we discuss leadership and the management of change respectively. Some HEIs, however, have deliberately and purposefully sought to adopt a particular organisational model. And it is to these types of institution we turn next.

The entrepreneurial university

The notion that a university could, and should, be run along the same lines as a private business company is a prospect many academics view with horror. Such a proposal is invariably dismissed for at least one, if not all three, of the following reasons. First, it is maintained that if universities were to embrace a commercial ethos then the consequences for the concept or *idea* of the university would be dire. For in such a setting universities would have no core business and no responsibilities, and ultimately would be reduced to the totality of market opportunities on offer. Thus the 'soul of the university' would simply wither and die in this environment (Pratt, 2000). Second, it is argued that even if universities wanted to adopt this approach, then the *practical* differences between them and commercial enterprises – the tradition of consensual management; the primacy of quality over profit; the greater degree and range of accountability; the tension between academic freedom and commercial confidentiality; the political interference in policy making; the difficulties in measuring value and outputs; and so on – would render this aspiration nigh-on unworkable. And third, it is recalled that the *legal* status of universities – typically that of a registered charity – would preclude such a possibility ever gaining credence.

These barriers, however, have not dissuaded all universities from taking this path. Far from it. 'Caught in a crossfire of expectations' at 'a time of disquieting turmoil with no end in sight', universities, as Charles Vest, the President of MIT put it, are 'overextended, under-focused, overstressed and under-funded' (Clark, 1998). The pressure on them to innovate then is considerable, if not overwhelming. Indeed such is the overload of demands on universities – to accommodate more students and different types of students; to satisfy the lifelong training needs of an increasingly specialised labour market; to assimilate the careening growth of knowledge; to do 'more' with 'less'; and so on – that, as Burton Clark (1998) argues, universities have little option but to take an entrepreneurial path if they wish to secure their future. To do nothing at all would be to run the risk of institutional breakdown; a far more daunting prospect, surely, than the inherent dangers associated with entrepreneurialism.

As it is, some universities have taken the lead in this regard and there are five European ones in particular – Warwick (England), Strathclyde (Scotland), Twente (Netherlands), Chalmers (Sweden) and Joensuu (Finland) – which Clark has identified as role models worthy of emulation. Innovators, that is, who all sensed the need to transform their traditional character by becoming 'more enterprising, even aggressively entrepreneurial'. In the case of Warwick, for example – one of seven new 'greenfield' research universities founded in the 1960s – the university's 'tough-minded recognition' that the Thatcher government of the 1980s 'had become an undependable university patron and often a hostile one' led it 'to work hard to place the institution in an independent posture – to stand on its own feet by earning its way'. An institutional idea whose enthusiastic adoption has enabled the university to generate almost half of its income from non-governmental (or third-stream) sources, and establish Warwick as 'the success story of the [English] university world'.

Strathclyde, too, has reaped a similar reward for its endeavours. Different in pedigree to Warwick, this Glasgow institution, a former mechanics institute turned technical college and eventually technological university, chose to adopt its traditional ideal of '200 years of useful learning' in confronting the contemporary prospect of 'death by a 1000 cuts'. So successful was this initiative that the ideas of useful learning, strategic research and technology transfer have 'come together as a belief system that has become an all-university culture'. And the university, no longer Scotland's poor relation, has taken on a semi-comprehensive form in which three of its five faculties (business, education and the arts) are now concentrated on research, teaching and service outside science and technology.

Joensuu, a modest regional university in rural Finland, was, in sharp contrast to Warwick and Strathclyde, positively encouraged by the government to experiment with innovations in university management, notably the radical idea (for the highly centralised Finnish national system) of doubly decentralising budget-based control all the way down to the departmental level. The university's early acceptance of a second novel innovation, that of flexible staff workloads, has secured Joensuu's burgeoning reputation as a 'piloting' institution: one which operates in a significantly different manner from those in still following the traditional Finnish style. Of humble origin, Joensuu has successfully 'strengthened its sense of self and its place in the world'.

Likewise, Chalmers University of Technology also established a distinctive identity for itself when, in 1994, it chose to become a 'foundation university'. An institutional definition which virtually all other Swedish universities were unable or unwilling to consider. This 'opt-out' from a national system characterised by 'central government controlled standardisation' caused a sensation, but one which the university desired in order to gain 'simultaneous right of disposition over all resources', 'a more flexible organisation', and to have 'greater opportunity for our own organisational and financial initiatives'. Grounded in the idea that the university should have 'a plurality of special places for innovative behaviour', Chalmers has flourished as a 'one-of-a-kind' institution.

Twente, the last of the five, is also arguably the most ardent subscriber to this particular model of development. A provincial Dutch university founded in the 1960s, Twente, responding to growing marginality and fuelled by a desire to evolve from an 'education university' to a 'research university', defiantly declared itself in the early 1980s to be '*the* entrepreneurial university', though Twente initially barely knew what this term might mean in practice. It turned out to mean two things: adopting an 'attitude' and a sense of 'doing business on one's own account and at one's own risk'. The result was that Twente achieved its goal, and in 1996 hosted the inaugural meeting of the new European Consortium of Innovative Universities.

The similarities between these innovators are not confined solely to the nature of their response. They also extend to the manner in which they sought to transform themselves: namely, even though these innovators may have differed markedly from one another – in terms of their institutional origins and character, the nature of their national settings and the stimulus which prompted them to action – they all chose to adopt common 'organisational pathways of transformation'. Five elements, that is, which Clark argues are not only characteristic of these particular innovators but 'constitute an irreducible minimum' for any university which seeks to follow in their path.

The strengthened steering core

The first element involves recognising that universities can no longer continue to be managed in the conventional way they have in the past. Not, that is, if they wish to respond effectively to the 'overload' of demands placed upon them. In order to do so universities must develop a capacity which they have conspicuously lacked in the past, namely, the ability to steer themselves. Elite universities, of course, can afford to ignore this imperative (though possibly not indefinitely) and continue to rely on their outstanding reputations and political clout for maintaining resources and status. All other HEIs however, the wannabes, the marginal and the desperate, do not have this luxury. A strengthened steering core then, which enables the institution to respond more quickly, flexibly, and consistently to expanding and changing demands, is thus a necessity. And in the case of the five innovators, the key to their achievement in this respect lies, as Clark demonstrates, in the nature of the cores they established: ones which not only embraced *both* central managerial groups *and* academic departments, but also reconciled new managerial values with traditional academic ones.

At Warwick, for example, the university has, and indeed prides itself on, a 'flat structure' of (a strong) centre and (strong) departments linked together by a web of central committees, notably the Vice-Chancellor's Steering Committee, the Earned Income Group and the Senate Budget and Resources Committee. Faculties and deans are conspicuous by their absence. At Strathclyde a 'soft' centre characterised by 'a lassitude of purpose' and with responsibility diffused 'in a rabbit warren of over fifty committees' was replaced in 1987 by a University Management Group (UMG) or 'private sector model of management'. The UMG was the institution's considered response to the 1985 Jarrett Report on the (in)efficiency of British universities and it 'became the action group that could get-up-and-go'. It reports to the court and senate, but is a creature of neither.

This process of strengthening institutional steering capacity was, of course, not unproblematic. At Warwick, for example, there was bitter student and staff protest against what some regarded as the establishment of 'Warwick University Ltd.' while at Strathclyde faculty 'warriors routinely stalled' reform initiatives by vetoing 'disagreeable issues'. Why these changes were ultimately accepted at Warwick and Strathclyde is because each took pains to ensure that faculty were directly represented – by departmental chairs or elected pro-vice-chancellors and deans – on these central cores. In this way, 'management points of view, including the notion of entrepreneurship, were carried from centre to academic heartland, while faculty values infiltrated the managerial space'. And, in consequence, all members of these cores 'worked to find resources for the institution *as a whole*'.

The expanded developmental periphery

The second element derives from the belief that academic departments by themselves can no longer do all the things that a contemporary university has to do. And that the latter therefore must make up the difference. Namely, by reaching across old university boundaries and seizing the initiative to develop links between itself and the wider world. This activity has, as in the case of the five innovators, typically focused on the establishment of professionalised outreach units – on knowledge transfer, industrial contact, intellectual property development, continuing education, and the like – and the creation of externally-oriented (Mode II knowledge-based) research centres.

At Warwick for example the University's 'developmental periphery' embraces:

- the Warwick Manufacturing Group which has sales of £80 million a year and 500 companies and governments worldwide as customers;
- a conference business which generates £12 million a year from 2,000 en suite bedrooms;
- a science park 'hothouse' which accommodates 65 high-tech companies employing more than 1,500 staff;
- a fully-fledged business school of international repute; and
- an arts complex that attracts 250,000 visitors a year.

Similarly at Strathclyde 'peripheral' activity has centred on:

- a research and consultancy service which has facilitated the creation of twenty-two spin-off companies (more than any other Scottish university) and the collection of £7 million a year from intellectual property rights;
- an Institute for drug research which generates £2.5 million a year in royalties and twenty research centres, including cutting edge ones in the social sciences and European regional development.

While the focus is similar in each of the five cases, the same cannot be said of the way in which these activities are organised. New outreach administrative units and research centres are sometimes closely linked to the steering core and academic departments and sometimes not. There is no one way, no one model. What these development peripheries have done, though, in all five instances is bequeath a common legacy: namely, they have moved each of the five innovators towards a dual structure of basic units in which (specialist-based) traditional departments are supplemented by (project-based) centres linked to the outside world. They have, in effect, spawned a matrix-like structure which fulfils the institutional need to acknowledge the continued importance of discipline-based academic departments, on the one hand, while simultaneously enabling it to cater for the growth of the service role of the university, on the other.

If developed further, an enhanced periphery could indeed, in organisational terms, move a university toward the character of a shopping mall. And while it might add to the organisational complexity of an institution, this is arguably a minor inconvenience compared to the benefits an enhanced periphery brings. Not simply in economic terms, as an income generator, but also in academic ones too – in its contribution to new modes of thinking and problem-solving, to interdisciplinarity, and to the production of useful knowledge, and so on.

The diversified funding base

The third element arises from the broad acceptance that the traditional and staple source of funding for HEIs (i.e. government) is no longer reliable nor munificent. On the contrary, mainline institutional support from government as a share of total budget has declined virtually everywhere. Not only that, the emergence of 'contractual' government has robbed universities of the ability to plan for the long term with any degree of confidence. Enterprising universities recognise this trend and turn it to their advantage. That is, rather than passively fall in line with a government-determined agenda (experiencing parallel financial increases and decreases as government stimuli wax and wane), they actively intervene by deciding to pursue additional sources of income. In other words, they accept and promote as their maxim a general truth offered by two percipient American observers (H.D. Babbidge and R. Rosenzweig, 1962) over forty years ago: 'a workable twentieth-century definition of institutional autonomy [is] the absence of dependence upon a single or narrow base of support.'

Our five innovators are no exception. They each set out, with remarkable success, to build a diversified funding base: initially by competing more vigorously for research grants and contracts from second-stream sources (research councils), and latterly by systematically constructing an ever widening and deepening portfolio of third-stream sources, that stretch from industrial firms, local governments and philanthropic foundations to royalty income from intellectual property, earned income from campus services, student fees, and alumni fund-raising. By the mid-1990s each of the innovators had reduced their dependence on government as a funding source to the extent that third-stream activities accounted for a significant proportion of their overall income – Strathclyde 51 per cent, Warwick 47 per cent, Joenssu 27 per cent, Twente 21 per cent and Chalmers 20 per cent. This achievement is an invaluable one as it offers the innovative university far greater freedom for manoeuvre than that enjoyed by its less enterprising counterpart. It not only increases total resources but also allows a university to 'roll with the punches' (a loss here is made up by a gain there), to build up reserves, to borrow additional monies, and ultimately to take innovative steps (as Warwick did when it used accumulated surpluses from its earned income to fund fifty new research fellowships aimed at 'further enhancing and strengthening the university's research reputation').

Diversified funding, however, does not come without a price. The perennial debate within universities, for example, concerning the internal disposition of funds raised through diverse sources – over the range and amount of central top-slicing, the degree of institutional cross-subsidisation, and so on – are invariably, and legitimately, contentious. It is though a price worth paying, for without diversity in financing universities would lose the ability to be adaptable, to make choices, and with these, in effect, the opportunity to be better-focused institutions.

The stimulated academic heartland

The fourth element recognises that, while traditional academic departments may no longer be able to do all the things that a contemporary university has to do, they are still nevertheless vitally important in the shaping of an institution's future. For it is in the heartland, after all, where traditional academic values are most firmly rooted and, therefore, it is the arena in which entrepreneurial innovation is most likely to fail. This is not to say that the traditional heartland is characterised by the absence of enterprising action. On the contrary, virtually all science and technology departments have become entrepreneurial to some degree, as have some social science departments and even humanities departments. The point is that such enterprising action has typically been unevenly spread within institutions. The entrepreneurial university, by contrast, is one in which enterprising activity is widely diffused across the academic heartland.

The key to the latter's achievement lies as ever, as shown in the case of the five innovators, in the way that entrepreneurial activity is fostered: not by hard managerialism but rather by maintaining and even increasing collegial integration; by bringing faculty, that is, into the central steering groups, and by insisting on faculty–management collaboration throughout the process. At Warwick, for example, such collegial entrepreneurialism manifested itself in a number of ways: through the establishment of a pioneering university-wide graduate school; the creation of the institutional research fellowship scheme; the building of numerous research centres under departments; and the melding of the periphery (e.g. the Warwick Manufacturing Group) with traditional academic departments (such as engineering). In each case – characterised as 'the Warwick Way' – an initiative was identified, a framework developed and a leading academic (or 'product champion') was 'given their head' to realise the opportunity (Warner and Palfreyman, 2001).

Likewise, at Chalmers, it was a science professor who pioneered the Chalmers Innovation Centre and inspired 'the transfer of new product ideas and new technology from university to industry'. And at Strathclyde, the university has been able to file over a dozen patents from the work undertaken by the department of electronic and electrical engineering, its leading academic department. At Joensuu, the university relied on 'dialogue' and 'information systems' to monitor departmental 'inputs' (sources of support, unit costs) and 'outputs' (degree completion, course coverage, research productivity, etc.) as a means of asserting the broader institutional interest and its successful piloting of budget-based departmental self-regulation.

In all of these instances, the innovators were more than simply inclusive. They empowered individuals and departments to take responsibility for their actions and to establish their priorities. In this way, they successfully managed to 'install a spirit of collegial entrepreneurialism' by 'unhooking collegiality from defence of the *status quo* and the love of the *status quo ante*' and orienting it in favour of adaptiveness and change. In return, the innovators were rewarded with, and entrepreneurial universities are characterised by, *selective* substantial growth in their basic units.

The integrated entrepreneurial culture

The fifth and final element recognises that entrepreneurial universities are not only differentiated in operational terms from their less enterprising counterparts, but also in a cultural sense – in the ideas, values and beliefs they espouse. Put simply, entrepreneurial universities accept the notion that change and adaptation is a continuous and never-ending process and typically develop, as in the case of the five innovators, a work culture which reflects this proposition: one, that is, which successfully reconciles (not jettisons) traditional academic values with newer managerial ones.

Cultural transformation of this order does not, of course, occur overnight. In the case of the five innovators this process developed in all instances over a period of at least ten to fifteen years. Indeed they each have 'a story' (or *saga*) to tell – of institutional perseverance in the face of adversity – which has itself become part of their cultures. And they all, in turn, have shared a common pattern of cultural transformation: namely, all five innovators moved along the same 'ideational road'; from the initial teasing out of a working *idea*, to the cultivation of institutional *beliefs*, the dissemination of a new *culture*, and the formation of a new unifying *identity*; or as in the case of Warwick, for example, from the tentative notion promulgated in the early 1980s that the institution should 'earn its way', to the growing belief in the efficacy of the earned income approach; its unprecedented success in this regard and the collective acceptance of this modus operandi – 'the Warwick way' – celebrated, literally and symbolically, on the twenty-fifth anniversary of the university's founding.

At Strathclyde, the leading idea was not nearly so well defined, but in time the initial managerial idea expressed in a distinctive central steering group, a productive periphery, and an entrepreneurial 'spirit' in some heartland departments, became folded into a generalised belief system of 'useful learning'. A doctrine which, like that of Warwick's, was at the centre of the university's bicentennial celebration in 1996.

These new belief systems did not emerge in isolation from other institutional structures and processes. On the contrary, they were sustained by the practical development of the other elements. In other words, the first four elements provided the *means* by which these transforming ideas became operative. And herein lies the key to the innovators success – and the lesson to be drawn by those seeking to emulate them. Namely, successful transformation is contingent on the interaction of *all* of the elements: not one or two, but all five of them. It cannot be achieved, for example, by simply relying, as advocates of top-down approaches might have it, on a strengthened steering core. In other words, each of the elements by themselves can make little difference: the capacity for transformation lies in their collective interaction (Clark, 1998).

Such has been the success of the five innovators in this regard that they have not only managed to transform their organisations internally, but have also been able to carve out a distinctive identity for themselves in the marketplace. In short they have all achieved what they set out to do: to have more control over their destiny. And they have done it by harnessing collegiality, not spurning it. They have shown that entrepreneurialism need not compromise traditional academic values; that it may actually present universities with the best alternative in the difficult circumstances now facing them.

The virtual university

Attractive as the above proposition may be it is not the only option universities are considering. An equally compelling vision to many in higher education is the notion of the 'virtual university'. Unlike the entrepreneurial university which emerged as a reaction to a negative economic imperative (the universal squeeze on funding) the 'virtual university' is usually perceived as a positive response to a technological driver and pedagogical need. That is to say, faced with rising demand and rising expectations (students' desire for flexible provision, employer requirements of graduate competence, and so on) – with, in effect, the challenge of turning 'mass time' into 'quality time' for students – universities tend to view the enabling potential of new technologies as a godsent opportunity. They see it as able to provide them, that is, with the practical means, and arguably the only realistic one, of increasing scale at a sensible cost yet without sacrificing quality. Not only that. Such technologies, if intelligently adopted, would enable them to meet the newly emergent challenge posed by corporate universities – currently six in the UK (Body Shop, British Aerospace, Ford, Motorola, PricewaterhouseCoopers and Unipart) and a host of others in the US including McDonald's Hamburger University, the Disney Institute, Microsoft and Sears.

Not surprisingly, HEIs have mobilised to capitalise on this incentive and a conspicuous minority have broken new ground in establishing themselves at the forefront of 'borderless education'. Some such as the University of Melbourne, Deakin University and New York University, for example, have established their own private subsidiaries – Melbourne University Private Ltd, Deakin Global and NYU Online – in order to enable them to operate more flexibly and to extend their international reach (CVCP (Committee of Vice-Chancellors and Principals), 2000; Robins and Webster, 2002).

Others have joined with like-minded HEIs in developing new international consortia, often in collaboration with commercial organisations. *Universitas 21*, for example, initially established in 1997 as an informal network of elite research-intensive universities from the UK, the US, Canada, Australia, New Zealand, Hong Kong, Singapore and China, is now an incorporated British company seeking to position its eighteen university members worldwide as a 'global brand'. One in which, as Alan Gilbert, Vice-Chancellor of Melbourne University and founder of the original network put it, in classic marketing-speak – 'the centuries old brand value of the individual partners is invested in an international cross-jurisdictional brand signifying and symbolising a singular level of quality and quality assurance' (Cohen, 1998). It has also established a joint venture company with Thomson Learning, a subsidiary of the Thomson Corporation, and launched its own on-line university: U21 Global. EUROPACE 2000 is another consortium that has likewise sought to establish a virtual campus and distance education network. In this instance, to support 'learning on demand' by bringing together forty-five European universities, and a host of private enterprises (including Alcatel, IBM and Philips) and international agencies, to facilitate the delivery of lifelong learning.

Still other HEIs have sought to broaden their use of new technologies beyond that of course delivery to include their own internal operations. To become, that is, not simply Web-based but also *Web-enabled*. Such initiatives, however, have not always produced the outcome that was anticipated. Visionaries at three northeast England universities, for instance, found that when they attempted to harness new technologies – in developing a new finance and human resources management information system (Newcastle University), extending the work of the Learning Development Services unit (Sunderland University) and promoting excellence in the use of C&IT (Northumbria University) – electronic processes 'did not displace traditional ways of doing things but simply co-existed in a tense symbiotic relationship'. They adjudged that far from leading to a break-up of the traditional university, new technologies actually require 'a re-institutionalisation of the university as a more corporate kind of organisation where goals, roles, identities, rules and operating procedures are made more explicit'; that is, a far more 'concrete' organisation, ironically, than the one currently existing in many universities. As such, they concluded that the quest for the 'virtual university' is a fruitless one, for the premise on which it is based – 'a university without walls' – is flawed (Goddard, 1999).

While it may well be that the idea of the virtual university underestimates how universities as institutions (currently) work, and perhaps overstates what communications technologies can do, it would be premature to discard the notion altogether (van Ginkel, 1995). Particularly since we already have successful exemplars of this model in operation: institutions, that is, characterised by the fact that they have all differed from the traditional university since their inception. One such 'virtual university' we should acknowledge and which is very well-known is, of course, the UK Open University (OU). Established in 1969 to provide higher education opportunities to individuals whose circumstances did not permit conventional full-time residential study, the Open University fused the technologies of correspondence education with those of broadcasting and a unique student support network. An open (no formal entry requirements at undergraduate level) and distance learning institution whose courses cost 40 to 60 per cent less than conventional face-to-face provision in the UK, the OU today boasts 'an academic community on which the sun never sets'. It currently has more than 164,000 students in forty-one countries – including Hong Kong, Malaysia, a number of Eastern European countries, and Russia – and 80,000 of its students are networked to the OU as well as to each other from home computers (Daniel, 1998).

One of a dozen or so mega-universities, the OU is still very much an industrial model of higher education delivering a mass product to a mass audience. While it may be a 'virtual university', in that it functions independently of any physical location, it does not operate as a 'virtual corporation' (one which is flexible, tailored to individual or corporate needs, and fluid in structure). It is precisely this attribute which is the hallmark of our second 'virtual university' exemplar: the University of Phoenix, the most famous private for-profit higher education provider in the United States. A subsidiary of the Apollo Group first accredited in 1978, Phoenix deliberately positioned itself to respond to what it saw as the failure of most traditional institutions: to consider the adult population. And it has sought to differentiate itself from the traditional university ever since. It has done this not simply in its provision of an on-line library to complement its on-line campus but also through:

- Its 'cornerstone philosophy': to focus on providing professional education for working adults who have established personal and professional goals (rather than the younger college student still deciding on a career).
- Its organisation of curriculum and pedagogy: programmes are offered on a year-round basis with students studying courses sequentially (rather than concurrently) over a five- to eight-week period in an atmosphere of 'concentrated immersion'. Classes mirror business practice and students are grouped into problem-solving teams and self-help study groups.
- Its modus operandi: a small administrative centre and an army of 6,000 non-tenured part-time teachers ('working practitioners' hired on the basis of what students will learn rather than their academic credentials) provide specialist training 'anytime, anywhere' to individual and corporate clients alike, via a network of 170 campuses and 300 corporate sites (in 37 states) situated, for convenience sake, on the edge of freeways and in shopping malls.

Initially derided as the founder of 'McEducation', Phoenix currently has a national enrolment of 140,000 students, including 40,000 registered (in class sizes of 9) with Phoenix Online, making it the largest accredited private institution in the United States, and the leading provider in its field (de Alva, 2002).

Phoenix's success, like that of the OU, is attributable then not so much to new technologies per se, but to the way in which they have been harnessed and *integrated* – as a *means* to an end, rather than an *end* in itself. While operationally differentiated from one another, neither has forgotten (unlike some enthusiasts of e-learning) that learning is, in essence, a social activity, and that the key ingredient is not computers but rather the *interaction* between student and tutor and students with their peers. They have thus sought to organise themselves around a genuine (dialogue-based) *conversational* model of learning rather than the traditional (tutor-centred) *transmission* model or (environment-simulated) *constructivist* model so characteristic of the many initial, and ultimately disappointing, institutional attempts at Internet delivery (Laurillard, 2001). They also recognise that learning in the future will be as much network-based (university, home, place of employment, local community) – something which the Dearing Inquiry failed to grasp – as it is campus-based. And their market performance bears testament to the fact that a virtual university, based on such principles, can indeed deliver 'more' for 'less' without sacrificing quality.

All this is not to say that the apocalyptic predictions proffered by futurists and management gurus such as Alvin Toffler (1991) and Peter Drucker (1993) – that 'the big university campuses will become relics' and 'the college won't survive as a residential institution' – will come to fruition. Far from it. More probable, as we noted in Chapter 1, is the likelihood that the university will still retain a physical manifestation: a particular sort of gathering place. Indeed, the greatest threat to the hegemony of the residential university ideal has not, ironically, been the prospect of a 'virtual takeover' based on innovations in new technologies, but rather the increasing tendency of universities to recruit students from their home region. Or, more accurately, the growing propensity of students (well over a half of all undergraduates in the UK) to apply solely to those universities based in their locality (largely for reasons of financial constraint). Either way, the 'virtual university', like the entrepreneurial model, offers universities yet another alternative with which to respond to the unprecedented circumstances now confronting them. What though of the university of the future? What might the reformed post-millennial university that has adapted to this new environment look like – the university of 2025?

The university of 2025?

Projecting forward is, of course, a hazardous business. It would be very easy, for example, to get carried away, as some futurists have done, by the prospect of a techno-fantasy in which modems take over from people, databases from discourse, and computers from culture. More sober reflection anticipates three alternative paths of development: one, the 'post-Fordist' university, grounded in changes in the way the university is internally managed; and the other two, the 'core university' model and the 'distributed university' system, based on the break-up of the traditional university as we know it. These three institutional variants offer competing visions of the future university. Let us consider each in turn.

The 'post-Fordist' university

The first anticipates the emergence of a 'post-managerialist' culture within universities: a transition that is similar in scope to that of the last two decades, during which managerialism replaced collegialism as the dominant cultural form within most UK universities. Managerialism, then, it is foreseen, will in turn suffer a similar fate as that which befell collegialism, and be replaced by what Peter Scott and David Watson (1994) have dubbed a 'strategic' (or 'reflexive') culture.

This presumption, they argue, is a logical corollary to the massification of HE in that it recognises that institutions have to be managed differently according to their size and complexity. Thus, where once it may have been appropriate, say, for small elite HEIs (*c*.7,000 students), with uncomplicated missions, to be managed along collegial lines, this was no longer possible with the emergence of a mass system characterised by heterogeneity and diversity and large-scale institutions (10,000 to 20,000 students). Equally, the managerialist characteristic of this transition will no longer be suitable, Scott maintains, as HEIs evolve beyond 20,000 FTEs (full-time equivalents). Indeed, increasing size, complexity and differentiation within institutions will 'compromise the need for strong centralised direction' and senior management once the locus of most decision-making will 'shrink to a slimmed-down strategic core'. That is, its role would be limited to safeguarding the financial, and legal, integrity and academic mission of the university while providing management services to its basic units, which would enjoy far greater operational freedom beyond that of responsibility for devolved budgets. Consequently institutional hierarchies would become much flatter and may even be replaced by loosely coupled networks.

In essence, Scott and Watson anticipate universities evolving in much the same way as many successful private corporations have done (and particularly those knowledge-intensive enterprises which employ highly skilled workers) by developing an institutional setting which facilitates flexibility and synergy while accommodating volatility: one, that is, which bears the hallmarks of an organisation commonly typified as 'postmodern' or 'post-Fordist'. This new transition to a strategic culture they stress, however, would neither represent a return to old-style collegiality, nor a retreat from managerialism, but rather 'a reinterpretation and recombination of both to meet the radically different challenge of managing mass institutions'.

The 'core university' model

Our second institutional variant anticipates, by contrast, a very different HE environment. Principally, the establishment of a framework in which universities, reconfigured to have as their primary role the commissioning of courses and programmes, would invite bids from newly self-employed academic staff to teach within them. Such a setting, the brainchild of the Office for Public Management (OPM), could and should be created, the OPM argues, by restructuring higher education along the lines of the NHS (National Health Service): that is, by accepting the academic community for what it is – a world in which tutors cling resolutely to their autonomy and to their subject loyalties – and seeking to change it from without, not within: namely by 'reformulating the staff "contract", both legally and psychologically to reflect this underlying reality' (Albury, 1997).

In this new environment academic staff – perhaps in partnerships, consortia, trusts or other organisational forms based on particular subjects, disciplines or approaches: for example, the Progressive Particle Physics Partnership or the Renaissance in the History of Art Trust – would be free to tender for the delivery of courses and programmes in any number of universities and colleges. They would also have the freedom to choose (the exigencies of making a living notwithstanding) *not* to teach subjects in which they had no interest, as well as to pursue other activities (e.g. research and consultancy) which they personally valued. Equally, universities, now reduced essentially to their senior managers and administrative support, would be able to create real choice for students by offering courses which the students demand rather those which the staff want to teach. And the key, and by no means trivial, task for senior managers would be to act as champions of the 'stakeholders' of their university or college, by developing strong forms of engagement with potential students, targeted communities, employers and relevant agencies to ensure the needs of these various parties are met.

The establishment of such an environment would in effect turn the HE 'business' on its head, making it market-driven rather than producer- or supply-driven. In this sense the proposal is a logical extension of the 'contractual' view of government which, as we noted earlier, has emerged as the dominant orthodoxy in the management of public services over the last two decades. For staff in HE it would herald the 'end of tenure' and the 'start of tender'. Implementation, however, may be another matter for this very reason. Tenure enjoys iconic esteem in academia, particularly so in the US, and any proposal which seeks to drastically reshape the contract between academic staff and institutions, as this one does, could only be successful if there was sufficient strength of political character and will to carry it through.

The 'distributed university' system

Our third alternative also anticipates the emergence of a new configuration within HE and again, like the second variant, envisages a radical change in the contractual status of academic staff. The latter however, in this instance, is a second order outcome rather than the prime motivating factor. The distributed university system takes as its cue, not the legal and psychological reality of the staff contract, but rather the needs of all learners, electronic as well as face-to-face, for access to communities of scholars on the one hand and the acquisition of credentials from universities on the other. It recognises that the digital age will change the relationship between these two and that as such the days of the traditional (and inflexible) monolithic university are numbered.

Indeed the model, as propagated by two Californian cybernetic researchers (Brown and Duguid, 1996), envisages the university system broken up into its four main constituent parts: a degree-granting function, academic staff, campus facilities and students. Elements, that is, which may have hitherto been considered all part of a single institution but which in reality there is no inherent reason (historical precedent notwithstanding) for them to be so or remain so. Take them apart, and the system of HE would become much more *flexible*, particularly so for the learner. In such a setting, for example, the university's role would be confined primarily to that of one granting credentials, and as a degree-granting body (DGB) per se the 'new' university (or DGB) would own little beyond its own administrative competency and a building in which to house its staff. Thus liberated of the need to make the massive capital investment that a university requires now, these DGBs would be able to evolve to meet the needs of students, faculty and employers far easier than their predecessors.

Faculty, likewise, would be free to become independent contractors. Like doctors who contract to NHS Trusts, they would have to find DGBs to sanction their teaching and, like doctors, they might find more than one to do this. They could also contract either individually, or in teams, but would not, unlike now, all have to assemble in one place. As for payment, remuneration could be linked to the type of teaching (lecture, tutorial, research seminar, etc.) or the teacher's ability to attract high-quality students to the DGB. Or alternatively, as in the case of eighteenth-century academics such as Adam Smith, scholars could simply collect a fee directly from the students they personally attract. Equally flexible arrangements could be put in place for research.

Facilities would probably look very much like the campus of today, the significant difference being that they would be quite independent of either the DGB or the faculty. As such, the physical campus, if it is to survive and prosper, would have to ensure that the standard of its facilities was of sufficient quality to attract the students, staff and DGBs within its region. Conversely, faculty and students would not have to travel to their DGB, but might travel to be close to superior facilities. Nor would they be locked into one set of facilities. In well-endowed areas, for instance, some faculty and many students may well indeed use more than one facility.

For students *choice* grows dramatically if the university is divided up in this way. Their central choice would involve finding a DGB appropriate to their needs. Such a decision would, like now, draw on a whole array of factors: the DGB's insistence (or not) on conventional campus life; its willingness to accredit prior experiential learning; the exchange value of the degree in question; the presence and commitment of quality staff; and so on. Once that decision had been made students would then have to choose how they would like to study: on-line or off-line; home-based campus-based, or work-based; in class, with mentors, or on their own; or simply a mix of all the permutations on offer. They would not, however, have to commit to working with the faculty of a single campus or a single region. In essence, a student's university career would not be through a particular place, time or pre-selected body of academics, but rather, in the same way as their current explorations of the Internet, through a network of their own making, yet endorsed by the DGB and its faculty.

This model then does not anticipate the wholesale destruction of the university system. On the contrary, it seeks to combine the strengths of the old conventional system with the resources of the new digital age: the local and the distant, the real and the virtual. And it does so in such a way as to enhance flexibility and freedom, competition and choice.

Whether or not the university of the future will look anything like this picture, or like that of the post-Fordist or 'core university' model, we cannot tell. But what is clear is that these models, along with the virtual and entrepreneurial ones, do offer universities a genuine way forward. That is, they all offer a model of the university that does not seek to preserve the 'glories of the past' but, rather, to use what is appropriate and relevant for the future. And for that they warrant our undivided attention if not our agreement. For what is certain is that the traditional university will not remain as it is today.

<table>
<tr><td>3</td><td>

Leading your department
</td></tr>
</table>

As I went to bed at about 3 a.m., I was conscious of a profound sense of relief. At last I had the authority to give directions over the whole scene. I felt as if I were walking with destiny, and that all my past life had been but a preparation for this hour and for this trial.

Winston Churchill on becoming Prime Minister, 10 May 1940

[Seven weeks later and France had fallen to Hitler's armies. A shattering blow that left Britain to fight on alone.] Clementine Churchill wrote to her husband on 27 June 1940: 'My Darling Winston, I hope you will forgive me if I tell you something that I feel you ought to know. One of the men in your entourage (a devoted friend) has been to me and told me there is a danger of your being generally disliked by your colleagues and subordinates because of your rough sarcastic and overbearing manner . . . I was told "No doubt it's the strain" – I cannot bear that those who serve the Country and yourself should not love you as well as admire and respect you. It is for you to give the Orders and if they are bungled – except for the King, the Archbishop of Canterbury and the Speaker you can sack anyone and everyone. Therefore with this terrific power you must combine urbanity, kindness and if possible Olympic calm. . . . Besides you won't get the best results by irascibility and rudeness. They will breed either dislike or a slave mentality. Please forgive your loving devoted and watchful Clemmie.'

'Winston Churchill', Ed Morrow the American broadcaster based in London in 1940 observed, 'mobilised the English language in defence of the free world against the tyranny of Nazism – and much else besides'. In Clemmie, Churchill was fortunate to have a devoted partner unafraid to remind him that the qualities of sound leadership were needed more than ever in a time of crisis. And, great leader that he was, Churchill had the good sense to heed such wise counsel. 'God knows where we should have been without him', commented Field Marshall Lord Alanbrooke of Brookeborough, Chief of the Imperial General Staff in his memoirs, in 'deep-rooted admiration' of the way in which Churchill's leadership averted defeat in 1941, as the nation's darkest hour turned into its finest (Alanbrooke, 2001; Churchill, 1996; Soames, 1998).

It is of little wonder then why Churchill – and leaders of similar ilk such as Franklin D. Roosevelt, Mahatama Gandhi and Martin Luther King Jr – should have been the subject of so many research inquiries into leadership. If we can identify the distinguishing characteristics which sets leaders of this stature apart, it was reasoned, then we can look for these factors when selecting future leaders. These endeavours have not been nearly so straightforward in practice, however. On the contrary, the quest to reach an understanding of leadership – on its nature and essence, its style and meaning, its exercise and practice – has come to resemble the pursuit of the Holy Grail. The source of the difficulty, as Warren Bennis (cited in Syrett and Hogg, 1992) puts it, lies in the fact that 'leadership is an endless subject and endlessly interesting because you can never get your conceptual arms fully around it . . . I always feel like a lepidopterist chasing a butterfly'. And as is often the case in such pursuits, opinion on the subject has moved full circle. Thus where leadership was once perceived as the preserve of the few who were born to the role, it is now widely regarded as an attribute that can be acquired, or learned, and therefore open to all.

Leadership has itself, in the process, become a growth business, not least for HEIs themselves. University business schools have become veritable 'cash cows' for their institutions as literally hundreds of courses on the subject have been established worldwide, usually in response to overwhelming demand from private organisations who themselves have, in turn, often set up their own in-house leadership develop-ment programmes. All these programmes, to a greater or lesser extent, have been created in the belief, quite rightly, that leadership and management capacity is a crit-ical determinant of organisational success. This is a view which many argue, and most agree, holds equally true for the public sector as for the private one. As the late Tory Education Minister Sir Keith Joseph used to say, the nearest thing we have in educa-tion to a magic wand is an outstanding head teacher. And this is even more the case given the new tough environment in which public services now operate: one in which consumer demands for tailor-made service, employee expectations of empowerment and governmental insistence on 'value-for-money' all vie for attention, under the critical gaze of a voracious media.

Either way, it is a principle that the government has taken to heart and rendered it a lynchpin of their public sector 'modernisation' agenda. And prima facie there appears to be good reason for them doing so. For we now live in a time when the National Health Service sends patients abroad for treatment as a means of easing congested waiting lists, rail safety is at an all-time low and passenger complaints an all-time high, and so on. We should be wary, however, of a knee-jerk reaction in which a 'private sector knows best' approach, or copycat management style, is adopted. After all much the same pejorative discourse on the management and provision of public services dominated the politics and newspapers of all major cities in nineteenth-century Britain and America. And yet today their legacy is widely regarded as the 'unheralded triumph' of the Victorian age (Teaford, 1984).

We should also remember it is now broadly accepted that effective leadership is as much contingent on *context* as it is on personal attributes and qualities. That is, leadership is not simply a matter of who one is, or what one does, but also involves doing the right thing at the right time in the work environment. This applies equally to HE as it does to every other working situation, public and private. The point is, how can one lead in a university setting? What is the nature of leadership in such an environment? In what ways do leadership and management differ in HE? Can one be a leader as well as a manager? How should you lead?

These questions have too often been ducked within HE in the past: HE is not immune from the forces sweeping across other parts of the public sector. Nor do we do ourselves any favours pretending otherwise. Too much academic leadership, as we noted earlier, has been characterised by unprofessionalism; excessively lax and responsive at one extreme, or dumbly aggressive and assertive on the other. Both kinds have had devastating consequences in practice. This chapter, and those that follow, seek to confront these issues and address this deficiency.

This third chapter explores the concepts of leadership and management, outlines the similarities and differences between them and articulates the nature of leadership in theory. It also demonstrates how leadership can be applied in practice within the HE context by focusing, in this instance, on leadership in the formulation of departmental strategy.

Leadership versus management

> Leaders do the right thing, managers do things right.
>
> Peter Drucker

Some commentators use the terms 'leadership' and 'management' interchangeably as if they are synonymous with one another, while others use them in a very deliberate sense to convey that they are, in fact, quite different. Still others regard one (leadership) as a subset of the other (management). In academia we tend to shy away from using the terms altogether! It is not surprising then that the lay person's understanding of these terms, like that of academia too, is very often an unclear one, if not downright muddled. It is a misconception we need to straighten out.

Organisational effectiveness, it is broadly accepted, is dependent upon both capable leadership and sound management. It does not follow from one or the other, only from the successful combination of the two. Their very complementarity, however, as the sine qua non of organisational success, has often prevented us from recognising that there is indeed a very real difference between the two. One, that is, exemplified not only in the characteristics and activities of managers and leaders, but also in the perceptions of them in the workplace, as well as, indeed, in the origins of the words themselves (Turner, 1998).

'Manager', for example, is derived from the Latin *manus* (or 'hand') which is the root of the sixteenth-century Italian word, *maneggiare*, a reference to the handling, training and control of horses. British soldiers subsequently brought the word back from Italy and applied it to the handling of armies and the control of ships: vital duties performed by people who became known as 'managers'. The word gradually came to be applied to anyone who had a responsibility for organising activities and controlling their administration. And the activities or functions associated with it, planning, staffing, budgeting, coordinating, decision-making, and so on, came to be the guiding principles (and organisational theory) on which the classic business corporation was later formed. This association of management with 'gaining one's ends' through control and organisation, and perhaps too by implication manipulation, also helps explain why in some HE cultures the term is often perceived as a pejorative one – indeed as a 'dirty word'.

While management is unfairly, and wrongly, viewed as a simplistic, unnecessary and bureaucratic process, leadership by contrast is invariably portrayed as a difficult and noble art. The word 'leader' is derived from *laed*, a word common to all the Old North European languages, meaning 'path', 'road', 'course of a ship at sea' or 'journey'. A leader is therefore someone who accompanies people on a journey guiding them to their destination, and by implication who holds them together as a group while steering them in the right direction. Present-day dictionaries typically define a leader as *one who rules, guides or inspires others*.

This linguistic dichotomy is also mirrored in the workplace perceptions of these activities and analyses of these roles as shown in two national surveys (see Box 3.1). The key difference between the two, exemplified best perhaps in Drucker's (1974) phrase, 'leaders do the right thing and managers do things right', also highlights the symbiotic nature of their relationship. That is, there is limited value in doing things right if you don't know where you are going. And equally, it is of little use knowing where you're going if you haven't got the wherewithal to get there. The roles, however, are not wholly mutually exclusive and we should be wary of exaggerating the differences between them; and likewise of concluding that an effective manager cannot also be an effective leader or, conversely, a charismatic leader will necessarily be a poor manager. Each role after all poses challenges which draw on complementary sets of competences (see Box 3.2). It also may not be simply a question of being one or the other: the everyday expectation in the workplace is that individual post-holders will be capable and proficient in both. And this is particularly the case for those holding departmental (or 'middle management') positions, where leadership and management functions are more closely integrated, than at the broader institutional level.

The situation in HE is no different, even if we would like to think otherwise. The traditions of academia, like those of other professional groups, have long upheld a separation between leadership and policy making on the one hand, and policy implementation and administration on the other. This distinction was manifested clearly in the traditionally separate roles of academics (whose domain included academic leadership and policy formation) and administrators (whose domain included advice on policy and the responsibility for policy execution), and is one which lives on in the nomenclature which is still often used, even today, to differentiate between the two. Thus, whether the post is head of a service department of a physical support character (such as residential accommodation or estates), or one essentially academic in nature (such as registry or the library), or indeed an academic department outright, all three post-holders are invariably lumped together (sometimes by the post-holders themselves) under the catch-all heading 'administration' (Warner and Palfreyman, 1996). It is only relatively recently that the title of 'manager' has been conferred in some of these areas (and not always readily accepted); and the national representative body is still entitled the Association of University Administrators rather than what would be the more accurate epithet: 'Association of University Managers'. It is also

Box 3.1 Workplace perceptions of leaders and managers in the UK

MANAGERS

– were viewed as:

- Planners
- Controllers
- Implementers of policy
- Resourcers
- Administrators
- People who are results-oriented

LEADERS

– were viewed as:

- Motivators
- Enablers
- Mentors
- Communicators
- Innovators
- People who are energetic

A MANAGER

- ☐ Is a copy
- ☐ Administers
- ☐ Maintains
- ☐ Focuses on systems and structure
- ☐ Relies on control
- ☐ Has short-range view
- ☐ Asks how and when
- ☐ Has his/her eye on the bottom line
- ☐ Accepts the status quo
- ☐ Is the classic good soldier
- ☐ Does things right

MANAGERS

- Plan and budget
- Organise and staff
- Control and solve problems
- Establish order

A LEADER

- ☐ Is an original
- ☐ Innovates
- ☐ Develops
- ☐ Focuses on people
- ☐ Inspires trust
- ☐ Has long range perspective
- ☐ Asks what and why
- ☐ Has his/her eye on the horizon
- ☐ Challenges the status quo
- ☐ Is his/her own person
- ☐ Does the right thing

LEADERS

- Set direction
- Align people and groups
- Motivate and inspire
- Produce change

Source: adapted from Turner, 1998

Box 3.2 The leadership and management challenge

LEADERSHIP

Style	Strategic vision	Team building	Influencing	Environmental building
e.g. making a personal impact, leading by example	e.g. creating a vision of the future and deciding how best to meet objectives by focusing on outcomes	e.g. inspiring people to work together and give of their best	e.g. using negotiation and persuasion to achieve desired outcomes	e.g. creating the conditions to foster creativity, innovation and risk-taking

MANAGEMENT

Change	Complexity	Networks	Ambiguity	Creativity
e.g. assessing drivers, communicating, envisioning and delivering	e.g. processing information and ideas	e.g. using others to leverage results, share best practice and learn	e.g. handling difficult situations with limited information	e.g. drawing on experience and new ideas to improve results

even more unusual for a 'dean' or 'head (chair) of department' to be styled 'academic staff manager' or something similar. Even so, the world beyond academia would readily recognise, if the organisation of HE was more transparent, that the functions being carried out by these post-holders are analogous to those carried out elsewhere in the public and private sectors by leaders and managers. But what is it that makes for effective leadership and management?

Being an effective leader and manager

> Go to the people
> Live amongst them
> Start with what they have
> Build on what they know
> And when the deed is done,
> The mission accomplished
> Of the best leaders
> The people will say,
> 'We have done it
> ourselves.'
>
> Sun Tzu, Chinese philosopher, *c*.500 BC

> [The general should be] ingenious, energetic, careful, full of stamina and presence of mind . . . loving and tough, straightforward and crafty, ready to gamble everything and wishing to have everything, generous and greedy, trusting and suspicious.
>
> Xenophon, Greek historian, 504 BC

Leadership is one of those rare topics – like war and peace, with which it has been particularly associated – which has enthralled and fascinated scholars and the public alike, ever since records began: an attraction which remains as powerful today as it has ever been. Popular debate on the subject dates back as far as Homer and his peers, while the first scholarly output can be traced to Plutarch and the biographies of great persons he penned in the first century AD.

Proper scientific research on leadership, however, only really began at the start of the twentieth century. Since then, literally thousands of formal research studies have been carried out, which have, in turn, spawned a whole host of theories. Nevertheless the mystique of leadership has remained intact, for none of these theories have fully explained the phenomenon. Rather the inquiries that generated them were as much a reflection of the way in which our assessment of leadership roles has changed over time, as they were an impartial examination of the intrinsic nature of the subject itself (see Table 3.1) (Sashkin, 1995).

Either way, the quest to determine just what makes a leader effective – and the reason the subject is still so compelling (especially in the light of the corporate and societal needs of the new millennium) – is because it remains as elusive today as it has ever been. This is not to say our understanding of leadership has not advanced. On the contrary, the substantive research to date has yielded an array of illuminating insights into the subject. And it is to an initial consideration of this work we turn first. What can the received theoretical wisdom tell us about leadership and management in practice?

Table 3.1 Overview of twentieth-century theories of leadership

Period	Theory/approach	Theme	Advocates
Up to late 1940s	Trait theories	Leadership ability is innate and linked to personal qualities	Hunt (1992)
Late 1940s to late 1960s	Behavioural theories	Leadership is associated with behaviour and style	Adair (1983); Blake and Mouton (see Blake and McCanse, 1991); Likert (1967); Mintzberg (1973)
Late 1960s to present	Contingency theories	Leadership is affected by the context and situation	Fiedler (1978); Hersey and Blanchard (1992); House (1988); Vroom and Yetton (1973)
Late 1960s to present	Power and influence theories	Leadership is associated with the use of power	Bass (1985); Bennis and Nanus (1985); Burns (1978); Kouzes and Posner (1985)
1970s to present	Cultural and symbolic theories	Leadership is the 'management of meaning'	Deal and Kennedy (1982); Smith and Peterson (1988)
1980s to present	Cognitive theories	Leadership is a social attribution	Cohen and March (1986); Hunt (1992)
1990s to present	New leadership theories	Leadership is linked to organisation building and transformation	Kakabadse and Kakabadse (1998); Senge (1995); Turner (1998)

Sources: adapted from Middlehurst, 1993; Kakabadse and Kakabadse, 1998

The 'great person' approach

The first serious researchers into leadership (in the 1920s) assumed, as alluded to earlier, that effective leaders were born and not made, and as such set out to identify their distinguishing traits. This so-called 'great person' approach (the individuals were usually male, but not exclusively so) dominated research inquiries for the next two decades and gave birth to what critics later dubbed the 'myth of the heroic leader'. Based on the concept of the military hero, this cult was buttressed by the reading public's penchant for biographies – and has been bolstered still further in recent times, by the contemporary practice of headhunters, who, in seeking to 'fit' literally 'the right person to the right job', have lent even greater credibility, however unwittingly, to the mystique of searching for the 'great person'. Such inquiries have generated all kinds of epiphenomena: the greatest American presidents were stubborn and grumpy; the British boardroom executive today is more than likely 'a mummy's boy', and so on (Brodie, 2001; Frean, 2001). They also indicated that leaders were generally a bit smarter, a bit more outgoing, slightly more inventive, and even a little taller than the average. None of these traits however, nor any others, stood out sufficiently to be clearly or strongly associated with leadership.

Behavioural theories

The focus of leadership research therefore changed. By the late 1940s researchers became less concerned with identifying individual traits of leadership, *who leaders are*, and more interested in leadership behaviour: *what leaders do* and how they do it; their actions and the style in which they perform these actions. These inquiries identified two essential aspects of effective *managerial* leadership: *task-oriented* behaviour (the importance of leaders providing clear instructions and directions) and *relationship-oriented* behaviour (the need for leaders to provide personal support and encouragement). Initially it appeared that the puzzle of leadership was finally resolved. For if everyone simply learned how to engage in these two types of leadership behaviour, and did so with sufficient acumen, then there would be no shortage of successful leaders. In practice, however, the benefits of such behaviour proved to be quite limited and did not ensure outstanding performance on the part of either followers or leaders.

Situational leadership

The emphasis within research therefore shifted again, and the 1960s witnessed the emergence of a new perspective stressing the importance of situational factors (or 'contingencies'); the nature of the task, the type of external environment, the abilities of followers, and so on. If effective leadership is not *who they are* nor *what they do*, it was reasoned, then perhaps it arises from the interaction between leaders, followers and situations and involves leaders *doing the right thing at the right time*. The most influential of these contingency theories has been the situational leadership model developed by Hersey and Blanchard (1992) which also forms the basis of, and lends its name to, one of the most widely used management improvement approaches in the world today.

In essence, Hersey and Blanchard argue that a leader's style, whether 'participating', 'delegating', 'selling' or 'telling', varies according to the degree of a subordinate's ability and willingness to undertake the task at hand. And their model reflects this proposition. That is, it incorporates the two dimensions on leadership behaviour we identified above and also includes a third; an environmental variable denoting follower 'maturity' or 'readiness'. Managers can then use the model, not only to assess the willingness and capability of followers to do a job, but also to determine what combination of task and relationship behaviour will be most effective in a particular situation. Indeed, in emphasising the importance of flexibility in leadership behaviour (in contrast to earlier searches for an all-purpose leadership style) and by demonstrating the potential for facilitating follower 'maturity', this model gave managers their first real *practical* insight into enhancing their effectiveness as leaders. A model which is readily understood and which managers find as relevant and useful today as their predecessors did when it was originally conceived (see Figure 3.1).

Transformational and transactional leadership

Further insight came from an unlikely quarter, the American historian James MacGregor Burns (1978), not an unfamiliar source and his examination of distinguished national, social and moral leaders. In Burns's view, such leaders were so successful because they were able to transcend the customary (Hobbesian) norms of traditional leadership, i.e. the self-interested *transaction* of rewards and benefits in exchange for compliance and loyalty, by engaging with their supporters on a 'higher' plane. By appealing that is to their altruistic motivations (to their notions of liberty, justice, equality and the like) rather than their self-interested ones of money, status, praise, and so on. In doing so, a cycle of mutual reinforcement was set in train, in which both leaders and followers raised each other's motivations and sense of purpose. To such an extent, indeed, that their behaviour and aspirations were *transformed* well beyond their original expectations. This notion of leadership – as transformation – was, of course, not a new one. The emotional appeal and power of leadership based on charisma (or 'god-like gift'), for instance, is an idea of ancient pedigree. Particularly germane at moments of crisis, it is also one which we have witnessed ourselves in recent times, for example, in the aftermath of the atrocities of September 11, 2001.

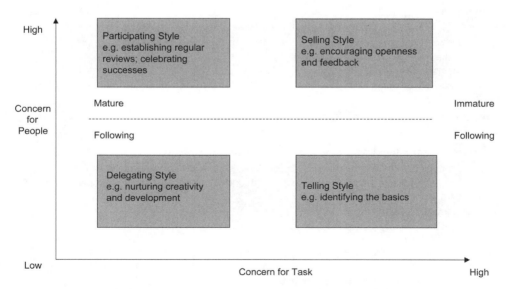

Figure 3.1 Situational leadership: leadership style and follower 'maturity'
Source: Adapted from Middlehurst 1993; Hersey and Blanchard, 1992

Burns's critique, however, provided us with the first clear delineation between leadership as a moral process – or *transformational* one – as distinct from that which is essentially *transactional* or exchange-based in nature. A distinction which some argued mirrored the essential difference between leadership and management (they were, in Burns's view, the opposite ends of his transactional–transformational continuum). A view disputed by others, notably Bass (1985) and Kotter (1990), who persuasively argued that transactional strategies, such as rewards for good performance, are not only compatible with transformational leadership but indeed, as we noted earlier, are an essential corollary to it, if organisational effectiveness is to be realised. Where the substantive difference between leadership and management really lies, these commentators implied, and this is significant, is the way in which these individuals are *perceived by their staff*. For while a management relationship can be conducted in a cool, job-oriented and perfectly satisfactory (transactional) manner to both parties, a leadership relationship cannot. The latter, if it is to succeed – that is, if followers are going to give their consent to be led (or transformed) – has to involve the emotions. Thus, for effective managers to become equally effective leaders, there must be warmth, inspiration and a stirring of the blood in their relationship with their staff.

For this reason still others have used Burns's typology as the basis for developing new approaches to leadership in practice: models of 'new leadership' that is – the visionary leader, the 'learning organisation' leader, the liberating leader and the

Box 3.3 The visionary leader

The behaviours, personal characteristics and culture-building activities common to all effective transformational leaders

Behaviours

1 Focus – providing a clear focus on key issues and concerns, i.e. on the right things
2 Communication – getting everyone to understand this focus through effective organisational communication practices
3 Consistency – acting consistently, over time, so as to develop trust
4 Respect – demonstrating through actions that they care for and respect the organisation's members
5 Empowerment – creating empowering opportunities that involve the organisation's members in making the right things their own priorities

Personal characteristics

1 Self-confidence – a grounded belief in one's ability to make a positive difference
2 Being comfortable with empowerment – a grounded belief in the ability of others to make a positive difference
3 A long-term vision span (*c.*10 years)

Culture building

A propensity for building strong cultures by instilling assumptions, values and beliefs that support four key organisational functions: managing change, achieving goals, coordinating teamwork and maintaining a vibrant organisational culture.

Source: adapted from Sashkin, 1995

discretionary leader – which have come to dominate contemporary thinking on the subject. All these approaches are grounded, to varying degrees, in transformational theory and as such this literature is often suffused with a quasi-religious, moralistic fervour. What practical insights though do they offer us on effective leadership?

Models of 'new leadership'

The visionary leader

Based on the work of Warren Bennis (1985), James Kouzes and Barry Posner (1995), Marshall Sashkin and W.E. Rosenbach (1993), visionary leadership theory is the most comprehensive attempt to focus Burns's initial ideas on organisations. Its exponents argue that if leadership is to be effective then it has to be based on not just one but three major aspects of transformational leadership: behaviours, personal characteristics and organisational culture-building activities. The implication is a clear one: to be an effective leader you must have the requisite qualities listed in Box 3.3. Daunting as this may initially appear, however, the model's advocates do insist that these qualities are all competences we can learn to develop. That the goal of the self-actualising visionary leader is indeed one within all our reach.

The 'learning organisation' leader

The role and nature of leadership as well as the expectations of it are, as one would expect, different in the context of the learning organisation. Popularised in the 1990s by Peter Senge (1990b) among others, the 'learning organisation' was grounded in the widespread belief that 'the rate at which organisations learn may become the only sustainable source of competitive advantage in the future'; that in a context of rapid change only organisations capable of flexibility, adaptivity and productivity could expect to flourish. As such, many enterprises sought to establish themselves as 'learning organisations where people continually expand their capacity to create the results they truly desire, where new and expansive patterns of thinking are nurtured, where collective aspiration is set free, and where people are continually learning to see the whole together'.

The implications for leadership in such settings are quite profound. In the first instance Senge (1990a) argues would-be learning organisations need to abandon the traditional conception of leadership (one that is 'based on assumptions of people's powerlessness, their lack of personal vision and inability to master the forces of change, deficits which can be remedied only by a few great leaders') and embrace a new view that centres on 'subtler and more important tasks'. In Senge's model, leadership is focused on three critical roles – those of *designer*, *teacher* and *steward* (or servant). These functions in themselves are not new, in the sense that they each have antecedents in the ways leaders have contributed to building organisations in the past, but, in the context of the learning organisation, they take on new meanings since they demand new skills – to 'build shared vision', 'surface and test mental models' and develop 'systems thinking' (see Box 3.4).

Box 3.4 The leader's new work: building learning organisations

The learning organisation

Based on five disciplines (or component technologies)

Each 'discipline' is a series of principles and guiding practices to master

1   Personal mastery
2   Mental models
3   Building shared vision
4   Team learning
5   Systems thinking – the conceptual cornerstone that integrates the first four

New roles of leader

Leader as designer – teacher – steward

New skills of leadership

Building shared vision

- Encouraging personal vision
- Communicating and asking for support
- Visioning as an ongoing process
- Blending extrinsic and intrinsic visions
- Distinguishing positive from negative visions

Surfacing and testing mental models

- Seeing leaps of abstraction
- Balancing inquiry and advocacy
- Distinguishing espoused theory from theory-in-use
- Recognising and defusing defensive routines

Systems thinking

- Seeing interrelationships, not things and processes, not snapshots
- Moving beyond blame
- Distinguishing details complexity from dynamic complexity
- Focusing on areas of high leverage
- Avoiding symptomatic solutions

Source: adapted from Senge, 1990a

Leadership is also a distributive phenomenon in Senge's model. That is, if organisations really wish 'to tap people's commitment and capacity to learn at *all* levels', then leadership must be devolved throughout the organisation via a web of executive leaders, local line leaders and internal networkers. Only then, when these leadership criteria are met, Senge maintains will enterprises have the opportunity to establish a 'learning organisation'. To become that is masters of 'generative' learning and not simply of 'adaptive' or survival learning (Senge, 1990b).

The liberating leader

The concept of the leader as liberator developed, like that of the 'learning organisation' leader, as a response to the sweeping changes in the external environment

Box 3.5 Characteristics of the liberating organisation

Feature	Purpose
A flat organisational structure	To cut out functionalism, bureaucracy and the worship of status
Inversion of the pyramid	Leaders and managers support employees who interface directly with customers, i.e. 'leadership from behind'
Organisational democracy	To value the contribution of all alike and to promote their self-esteem: colleagues not subordinates
A liberating climate	To encourage healthy development and growth
Genuine empowerment	The unequivocal transfer of authority, responsibility and resources to those closest to each group of tasks
A 'blame-free' culture	To use mistakes as learning opportunities, not to levy punishment
Self-managed teams	Independent workgroups with the authority and responsibility to achieve their agreed targets
Mutual trust	The rock upon which all effective working relationships are built
Ownership	Established through shared information, the provision of user-friendly procedures and the celebration of successes
Vision	An inspirational view of the future, communicated to all, that acts as an organisational headlamp, lighting the path ahead
Values	The principles, beliefs and standards to which the organisation holds
Communication	To be open, comprehensive and without hidden agendas; clarifying rather than clouding and natural without affectation
Development	An integral part of working, managing and leading: coaching and encouragement to learn are second nature
Innovation	Sensible risk-taking is encouraged and fear is banished
Attitude	Proposed changes are seen as challenges to be met and managed rather than opposed

Source: adapted from Turner, 1998

(in working patterns, access to information, the nature of competition, global economics, and so on) which has affected all organisations since the 1990s. In this instance, however, the source of competitive advantage was perceived to be, not so much the rate of organisational learning, as the degree to which organisations 'unlock the potential and creative energies of all their employees'. Or, put another way, the extent to which they establish a 'liberating organisation', one which 'creates a climate of trust, empowerment and stability by devolving authority and responsibility and harnesses the latent energy within its walls' (see Box 3.5) (Turner, 1998).

In this environment, leadership, as in Senge's model, is not confined to the top. Indeed, in its outright rejection of position, status and hierarchy and its commitment to 'democracy at work', the 'liberating organisation' takes Senge's notion of devolved leadership a stage further, by fostering liberating leadership at all levels. Such leadership, as the name implies and as the ideal behavioural profile outlines, is modelled on the assumption that effective practice is about *what leaders do and the way they do it which, in turn, reflects what they believe* – self-belief, belief in and beliefs about others, and belief in fairness (see Box 3.6). Liberating leaders then jettison old-style command-and-control ways of working. They 'create situations where continuous improvement can occur; demonstrate, by their own behaviour, how people can be liberated to maximise their skills; recognise the need for continuing change and urge everyone to meet the challenges that this brings; and, finally, act as facilitators, coaches and supporters, encouraging those closest to the tasks to take their own decisions'.

Dismissed by some as a fanciful new Utopia, the supporters of the model view it as 'a managerial blueprint for the new millennium'; one that can be customised to meet the needs of all organisations. And given the substantial number of organisations that have successfully adopted it there is every reason to believe they may well be right.

The discretionary leader

The 'liberating organisation' and the 'learning organisation' concepts both share a common belief in the ability of individuals to shift perspectives and make themselves and their organisations more effective. The same is equally true of the concept of the discretionary leader. Though in this case the focus is not so much on the 'one size fits all' approach to leadership, characteristic of the two grand schemes above, but rather on the scope for, and use of, discretion on the part of individual leaders per se.

Taking its cue from Socrates, that no one remains 'within a box' unless they are bounded by their own perspective, the discretionary concept recognises that, while the scope for discretion is more limited at the lower levels of an organisation where roles are more prescribed, individual leaders in all cases can, and indeed should, draw on the wide range of approaches open to them in fulfilling their roles. And the key to effective leadership in fact lies in *the flexibility as well as ability of leaders to utilise the most appropriate approach according to the context in which they operate*. In other words, it recognises that not only do different organisations require different types of leadership, but since present-day organisations are invariably characterised by diversity, dissension and difference, then leaders also need to be able to reconcile contradictions *within* the same organisation. In addition, since no one individual, no matter how gifted, is likely to be able to fully appreciate the different requirements of different contexts, this model also emphasises the need for leadership based on and around teamwork (Kakabadse and Kakabadse, 1998; Kakabadse, 2001).

These emphases on the individual and collective contextualisation of leadership constitute, the model's advocates maintain, the best way forward for organisations seeking to master the internal and external repercussions of the 'new economy'. And, by implication, those individual leaders who choose not to exercise their discretionary roles will, like their organisations, suffer the consequences.

Box 3.6 Profile of the liberating leader

LIBERATES

- Does not blame people for mistakes
- Encourages the people closest to the job to take their own decisions
- Listens to their staff
- Encourages full and open communication
- Operates systems based on trust, rather than suspicion
- Encourages staff to develop new ideas

ENCOURAGES
AND SUPPORTS

- Accepts responsibility for the actions of their staff
- Gives praise where it is due
- Recognises, and acts to minimise, other people's stress
- Supports staff when they need support
- Regularly meets with individuals to clarify direction
- Makes people feel important and shows that they have faith in them

ACHIEVES
PURPOSE

- Achieves results
- Agrees demanding targets with individuals or teams
- Consults those affected before making decisions
- Is willing to take unpopular decisions in order to move forward
- Seeks out future challenges/opportunities
- Regularly communicates an inspirational view of the future
- Constantly seeks to improve the way things are done

DEVELOPS
PEOPLE AND
TEAMS

- Encourages other people to learn
- Encourages people to work together as a team
- Regularly meets with the team, as a whole, to review progress
- Takes time to develop and guide their staff
- Deals effectively with breaches in standards of behaviour
- Treats other people's mistakes as learning opportunities

EXAMPLE TO
OTHERS

- Actively encourages feedback on their own performance
- Communicates an air of enthusiasm
- Works on their own learning
- Practises what they preach
- Openly admits mistakes
- Sets a good example to others by their own behaviour

RELATIONSHIPS
BUILT ON TRUST

- Does not put self-interest before the interests of their staff
- Keeps promises and does what they say they will do
- Is in touch with, and sensitive to, people's feelings
- Is calm in a crisis, and when under pressure
- Is honest and truthful
- Does not take personal credit for other people's work
- Is always fair

Source: Turner, 1998

Guiding principles of leadership and management

A definitive understanding of leadership continues, as we have seen, to elude analysts. And indeed some analysts maintain that the subject will remain an unexplained phenomenon in perpetuity. Even so, these four models of 'new leadership' along with the received wisdom to date, do provide us with a series of pointers to the nature and exercise of leadership in practice – a set of guiding propositions, if you will, which can aid us in seeking to be effective leaders and managers in practice. These can be summarised as follows:

I   Leadership and management are not mutually exclusive: there is no reason why an effective manager cannot also be an effective leader and vice versa. And the work-place expectation, particularly at departmental level, is that individual post-holders will be proficient in both capacities. Whether an effective manager does indeed become an effective leader is determined, in the final analysis, by the way they are perceived by their staff ('followers'). It is your colleagues who determine if you are a leader.

II   Leadership is not confined to, nor vested in, a single great figure. Nor is it the preserve of, or related to, formal positions in an organisation's hierarchy. Rather, it is a distributive phenomenon. The skills of leadership, and the exercise of leadership, can exist at all levels in an organisation. *Ipso facto*, it is incumbent on those who wish to be genuinely effective to foster these qualities within their department. Effective leaders grow people, bad leaders stunt them.

III   The stereotypical young, dynamic whizz-kid is no more representative of effective leadership than is the traditional 'captain-of-the-ship' concept of leadership. Both notions are as unfounded as they are outdated. Leadership is as much to do with groupings and group behaviour – the formation and operation of top teams, departmental teams, project teams, and so on – as it is to do with individuals and individual behaviour.

IV   Leaders are, by and large, made, not born. They are learners and as such can be helped to develop themselves, in particular to master the key competences associated with transformational leadership, all of which can be learnt, namely:

- visioning skills, including creative thinking;
- critical evaluation and problem-detection skills;
- communication and linguistic skills;
- expectation-management skills;
- empowering skills; and
- the confidence to challenge traditional ways of working.

V   The mastery of competences and the development of self-confidence, however, are not in themselves sufficient to guarantee effective leadership. Not unless individuals are also motivated to that end: that is, to use power and influence (publicly) to benefit the organisation and its members, rather than simply (privately) to satisfy their own personal desire for power, status and achievement.

VI   The essential attributes of an effective leader are much the same whatever the environment. It is the context (the organisation's particular needs) and the leadership approach taken which are the key variables. As such, effective leaders seek to utilise their discretionary role to the fullest extent. In doing so, they recognise:

–   what works in one context may not do so in another (and equally, what makes you successful in one job may not necessarily do so in another);
–   the need to develop and maintain both a flexible and a broad mindset sufficient to cope with multiple different contexts;
–   the importance of harnessing this (rational) mindset with an equally well-developed sense of emotional intelligence: that is, of tackling both the 'hard' stuff and the 'soft' stuff together with a similar degree of insight and maturity. (Too often in the past, leaders have been imbalanced one way or the other. Maximum strategic insight is of little use if combined with limited (emotional) sensitivity. Equally, emotional maturity will only get you so far and no further if you lack strategic organisational insight. One needs to complement the other if leadership is to be effective.)

VII   Effective leadership is a dynamic process and, at best, a transformative one. It is about, as the industrialist John Harvey-Jones put it, 'lifting peoples' vision to a higher plane, raising achievement beyond what might normally be expected and getting extraordinary results from ordinary people', and, in the process, also transforming oneself as a leader through continued reflection, self-development and personal change (Turner, 1998).

VIII   Finally, effective leaders, and aspiring ones, accept they will be judged on the results or outcomes they produce, not simply the leadership competences they possess.

Leading and managing in HE

> To rephrase the corny words of the song, you have to do it your way.
> John Monks, TUC General Secretary

In applying these principles, it follows that if individuals are to be effective leaders then they must, in the first instance, understand both themselves and the particular context in which they operate. And this is as true for prospective leaders and managers in HE as it is for aspirants in other environments. As such then, our examination of leadership in HE begins with those who occupy, or aspire to, such roles: that is: you and your particular HE environment. The questions set out in Boxes 3.7 and 3.8 are designed to help you 'reach within yourself', to probe your modus operandi, to increase your self-awareness and reflect on your state of being. Their purpose is to provide you with an initial self-assessment, an on-the-spot 'health check' of how you are doing in your role.

There are more formal and systematic ways of conducting a self-assessment which you should also consider. Indeed there are literally scores of such instruments on the market. The most popular and widely used include:

Box 3.7 Conversations with yourself

Take each question in turn, take time to reflect on it and write down your answers on a sheet of paper. Discuss the accuracy of your judgements with someone whose opinion you value and trust.

- **What is expected of me in my role?**
- **How am I doing in my role?**
- **How do I know?**

[These are the basic questions which every employee in any organisation should be able to answer – including those who work for you. If you have difficulty answering them fully, you should consult the individual you report to immediately]

What do I stand for, what are my values, do they match those of my HEI?

- What or where is the level of fit?

Do I have the right level of dissatisfaction with the status quo and the way things are?

- Do I challenge the way things are?
- Do I encourage others to do so too?

What are my comfort zones and how, if I choose, do I move out of them?

Do I aim big and just fall short, or aim smaller and hit the target?

- How do I set goals and are they the right ones?
- Do I really stretch myself?
- How much do I push boundaries?
- Is my mindset 'better safe than sorry' or 'nothing ventured, nothing gained'?
- Do I aim for the upper reaches of the possible or the lower level of the impossible?

How much am I engaged in Activity and how much in Action?

- Do I mistake being busy with making things happen?
- How much of what I do is tangential to actually achieving things?
- Do I do things because I am interested in them or because they need to be done?

What motivates me to act?

How much of the day do I spend thinking about the past – the present – the future?

- Do I have to feel right about the past before taking action in the present to create the future?
- Do I live out of my imagination or memory?

Do I know how to hit my pause button?

- Do I suspend assumptions and preconceptions?
- Do I know what winds me up and how to stop that from happening?
- In what ways do I add/destroy value?
- What mindsets usually drive me?
- Do I have a mind which is usually open to new possibilities?

- Do I have a positive inner voice?
- Do I know when not to interrupt others but to listen to their ideas?
- Do I hear what people are actually saying?

How do I get that 'fresh feeling', how do I declare myself satisfied, how do I close the loop?

- Am I satisfied at the end of each day that I have done all I can . . . and draw a line under it?
- I got a 'fresh feeling' when I moved house, changed jobs, moved offices, completed that project, etc. . . . how could I have that feeling at the end of each day?

How could I redefine the issues and problems that face me?

How do I feel each evening when I walk through the door at home?

- How long does it take me to unwind?
- How do I recharge my batteries?
- If someone asks me how the day has gone what do I usually say?

What do I put my energy into?

How do I dance on a shifting carpet?

- Do I move ahead with change or feel like the rug is (sometimes) being pulled from under me
- Do I strive for step change or incremental change

Where will I be in five years time?

What do I want to achieve with the rest of my life?

- **Now look in the mirror, literally . . .**

- **What image and what example do I convey to others day-to-day about the quality of life I lead?**

- **Are they the right ones? How should I change them?**

- Visionary leader behaviour questionnaire (Sashkin, 1995): a survey which enables you to compare your own perceptions of your approach to leadership with those who work for you (subordinates), alongside you (peers) as well as who you report to (your line manager): namely, it provides '360 degree contextual feedback' on your leadership behaviour, your leadership characteristics and your effect on the organisation as a leader.
- Myers-Briggs (personality) type indicator (Myers and Myers, 1977): an instrument which enables you to assess the deeply-held ways – extrovert or introvert; senser or intuitive; thinker or feeler; judger or perceiver – in which you prefer to work. And hence is an indicator of how you are likely to behave in practice in solving problems, reacting to change, communicating, and so on.
- Thomas-Kilmann conflict mode instrument (Kilmann and Kilmann, 1974): a mechanism which enables you to assess the styles you have learned to develop (competing, accommodating, avoiding, collaborating and compromising) in handling workplace conflict.

Box 3.8 The top ten 'stoppers and stallers' to effective leadership

Consider each of the following 'stoppers and stallers' which have been identified as the most common obstacles to effective leadership. To what extent, if any, do these factors apply to you. How do you propose to overcome them?

- Failure to build a team

  The most common shortcoming; failure to give credit to staff, to say thank you or to encourage them

- Arrogance

  An asset on occasion at some levels, otherwise a drawback

- Lack of composure

  Failure to handle pressure or stress well; tendency to become sarcastic; hostile or abrasive when things get tough

- Lack of ethics

  Failure to recognise where the limits of proper behaviour lie; to lose the confidence of others in the organisation

- Betrayal of trust

  Saying different things to different people, not keeping promises

- Poor administration

  Being bad at the detail

- No strategic thinking

  The converse of the previous fault; tendency to concentrate exclusively on tactics and detail

- Over-managing

  Checking up on subordinates all the time and demanding constant information on how things are going

- Failure of networking

  Failure to maintain external links or to keep up with what others are doing

- Inflexibility

  Failure to adapt; an expectation that increases with seniority yet can become more difficult with age

Source: adapted from Industrial Society training course, 1996

These three instruments, while useful in their own right, are especially incisive, given the critical insights they yield on quite different aspects of behaviour, when used in conjunction with one another. And this has become common practice across the private sector and parts of the civil service and public sector as well. They can be just as illuminating for teams as well as for individuals and you may wish to consider using them with your own team or a team of your peers, say the senior management team.

Either way, a 'health warning' is in order. Such instruments can generate feedback and outcomes which some people, and maybe even you, might find hurtful or offensive. The key, of course, is not to take offence nor to deny the validity of the feedback, but rather to act on it propitiously. However, not everyone will be sufficiently able to do this, so you should enlist the support and help of your management and staff development adviser, or alternatively a reputable career management consultant, before undertaking this initiative. You should not be deterred, however, for the received wisdom to date indicates that the benefits of this activity, both collectively and individually, have far outweighed any particular drawback.

This theme of self-assessment and the implications for learning and development for ourselves, as well as for others, is one which we will return to in Chapters 4 and 9. For the moment we turn to perhaps the most critical aspect of your role, or indeed of any leader's role. One that both contributes to, and is shaped by, your own environmental context, that is the articulation of a strategic vision for your department.

Establishing a vision: developing a strategy for your department

Vision without action is a daydream, action without vision is a nightmare'.
Japanese proverb

We live in an age when even a humble sandwich bar cannot open without the fanfare of an accompanying statement of mission or vision: the strength of this trend is matched only by the degree of scepticism which such gestures can often engender in their intended audience. Why they have been received in this way is not difficult to discern. Invariably such statements reflect the design of a single individual or group, are often prone to grandiose new-age rhetoric, if not outright slogans, and have quite rightly been regarded as presenting an unmerited claim or unwanted imposition, or both, by staff and customers alike.

It is also a pattern from which HEIs have not been immune. Their initial attempts to articulate their institutional missions in the early 1990s, for instance, generated statements which, as one reviewer put it, were either 'unashamedly publicity instruments' or declarations 'of a five year plan' or worse still 'definitions of the management's role within the institution, not the institution's role within HE'. This proved to be an initiative which, above all, bred 'confusion and fudge' while spawning apathy and dissent in equal measure (Earwaker, 1991). As relative latecomers to this activity, HEIs have also been surprisingly slow, compared with organisations in the private sector, to learn and adapt from this initial experience. Which may in turn be symptomatic of the resistance to the idea of diversity which persists in UK higher education.

Either way, the prevailing scepticism over notions of 'mission' and 'vision' both within and outside HE, and their collective debasement in the literature on management, cannot and should not detract from the fact they are vitally important issues, if not desperately so for HE, given, as we noted earlier, the overwhelming pressure on HEIs to change and to diversify. Indeed vision, as we have seen, is at the heart of leadership. A vision is a 'dream', not a pipe-dream, but a realistic long-term ambition; a picture of the future that you want to produce. As in – Where do you see your department headed? What could it achieve? How could it be special? Distinctive? Cutting edge? Envisioning necessarily calls for creativity, imagination and optimism. More than that, it also requires animation, inspiration and passion on your part if it is to enlist others in 'building a shared vision' and agreeing to a strategy which realises this vision. How, though, should you set about this task? That is, how do you develop a strategic vision? And how do you engender collective ownership of it?

In the first instance, we need to recognise there is no single right way. Some commentators, for example, argue that vision springs from the 'collective mind' of the staff group and it is the role of the leader to tease out and articulate these latent ideas. Others maintain the exact opposite: that such visions emanate from the ideas developed by the head of department who then encourages staff to develop a commitment to them. Nearly all agree, however, that shared visions are unlikely to emerge from a series of formal departmental meetings called 'To develop a strategic plan' (Ramsden, 1998). In reality, their emergence varies according to the nature (the culture, needs and organisation) of the particular institutional context. Thus a method which works in one environment may not do so in another, and vice versa.

The common variable in all cases is the ability and willingness of the leader to take the initiative – and this applies equally to developing the content of a strategic vision, in the first instance, as much as it does to the building of a consensus around it. In the case of the former, if not the latter, there is indeed a set of guiding principles or common framework which you can, and maybe expected to, follow given that HEIs are now invariably held externally accountable for producing their own particular institutional plans, as in the UK since 1992, for example. Put another way, HEIs in common with other organisations all adhere (at least the great majority does), nuances of style and approach notwithstanding, to a framework which is broadly similar: a three-stage cycle of planning, documentation, and implementation and monitoring, each with its own particular sub-elements which together provide a comprehensive guide to the process of strategy formulation (see Figure 3.2).

What is strategy?

All of which begs the questions – What is strategy? Why do we need it? What is its purpose? How should you formulate it in your department? 'Strategy' is another of those terms in management which has come to mean many different things. In essence, the origins of the word relate to 'generalship' and political leadership and the process involves standing back from day-to-day activities and taking an overview from the perspective you hold: e.g. organisation-wide, departmental, personal, and so on. In the case of work, it is 'about defining and agreeing the nature of your organisation or department'. Or as Alexander (2001) suggests, it is 'the framework which guides those choices that determines the nature and direction of the organisation. It is what an organisation wants to be'. The role of strategy then essentially is to:

- facilitate strategic decisions by providing a framework for choosing;
- arrest strategic drift, by acting as a prompt to assess progress and to identify, build and maintain a leading edge;
- foster coordination, by providing a mechanism for reducing wasted and conflicting efforts;
- enhance motivation, by generating a sense of being in control, on a winning path;

Or, put another way, strategy at its simplest – and this is important as it is often overlooked when participants are embroiled in the process – involves, at whatever level, the alignment of three basic elements: aims, capabilities and opportunities (see Figure 3.3). Historically, each element has in turn being regarded as the critical focus of strategy. 'Aims' in the 1960s by those who believed that once a mission was established and people were 'on board' everything else would follow; 'opportunities' in

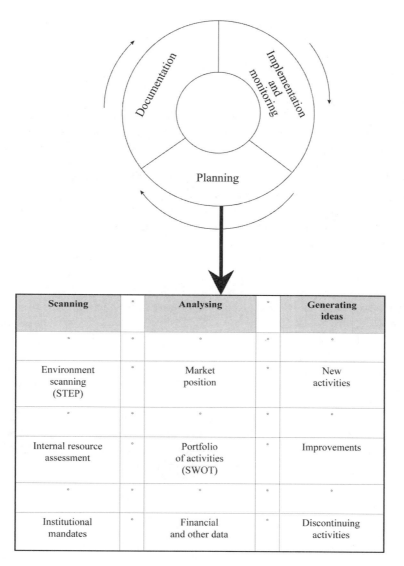

Figure 3.2 The strategic planning process

Source: HEFCE 00/24, 2000

the 1970s and early 1980s by Michael Porter and the Boston Consulting Group who maintained that salvation lay in mastering the forces of competition in the external environment and latterly 'capabilities' by those who argue that organisational success is contingent first and foremost on the effective mobilisation and integration of all internal competences and resources. Nowadays all three are regarded as significant: none more so than the other, the critical aspect now being their mutual integration rather than their sovereign singularity (Porter, 1998; Mintzberg, 2002).

The strategic planning process

Step I: *Identify the 4–5 key aims, capabilities and opportunities of your department – as you see them*

This simple overview provides us with the ideal starting point for a preliminary analysis of your department. As head of department it is incumbent on you to take the initiative in this regard, in part because your colleagues and those at the head of your institution will expect you to, and in part because you should be at least better informed than either group on the particular capabilities and opportunities in your area. But most of all because as a putative leader the articulation of a departmental strategic vision should, in the first instance, begin with you – your own *personal* perspective. This is not to say that you should foist your view on that of your colleagues but rather that, if you want them to engage in an informed and meaningful way in this process, then you need to put yourself through the same searching self-examination that you expect of them. The alternative of simply asking staff 'blind' to express their views will – in the same way as an ill-informed student seminar in the hands of a poorly prepared tutor – generate little heat, even less light, excite no one and fail to do justice to the full range of opportunities and issues in the broader environment.

Furthermore, if you are going to be transformative, this self-examination also provides you with the opportunity to kindle your own passion and beliefs in what your department can achieve beyond the mundane. A genuine conviction, that is, which is visible to others and one they can share. In Senge's (1990a) terminology, you need to 'surface and test' your own 'mental models' first, as a means of 'building a vision' you can believe in as well as potentially share with others.

Using the overview, then, reflect on and write down the four to five key aims, capabilities and opportunities for your department as you perceive them. What assumptions do your perceptions rest on? Are they accurate ones? Are you satisfied

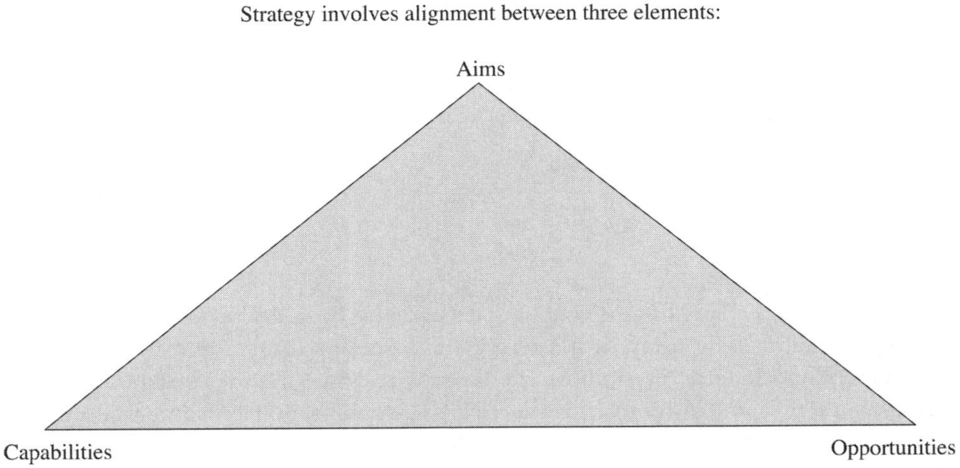

Strategy involves alignment between three elements:

Figure 3.3 Strategy as alignment

- Market size
- Market competition

- Market prospects
- Cost effectiveness
- Optimal staff resource
- Demographic patterns
- National significance
- Government policy

- Stakeholder attitudes
- STEP: Social, Technological and Political trends
- Employment prospects
- Image and Perception
- Etc.

SUBJECT AREA STRENGTHS

Size of department
Market size and share
Market image and reputation
Number of applications
Nature and Diversity of student body
Graduate employment
Cost effectiveness
Staff Profile
Teaching Assessment
RAE Publications
Research and Enterprise income
Research and Enterprise potential
Range of Partnerships
Other Resources: human, financial, material

UNIVERSITY STRENGTHS IN THE SUBJECT AREA

	High	Medium	Low
High	'A Star' Overall Expansion	Selective Growth/ Niche specialisation	'A Cash Cow' Consolidation
Medium	Selective Growth/ Niche Specialisation	Consolidation	Contraction and planned withdrawal
Low	'A Problem Child' Consolidation or planned withdrawal?	Contraction and planned withdrawal	'A Dog' Plan withdrawal and redeploy

Figure 3.4 The strategic directional policy matrix

Source: Sizer, 1982; Porter, 1998

all your responses reflect (genuine) reality and not simply wishful thinking or in-house rhetoric? Is there a match between your aims, capabilities and opportunities? If not, how will you achieve alignment?

Step II: *Examine your department systematically and comprehensively from each of the different perspectives – 'scanning', 'analysing' and 'generating ideas' – of the strategic planning model (Figure 3.2). Test, develop and refine your initial self-assessment accordingly*

You are now in a position to probe, develop, test and refine your ideas further – and just as likely add to them. To do so you need to undertake a more systematic full-blown examination of your department. One that encompasses, not simply what is often referred to colloquially as SWOT (strengths, weaknesses, opportunities and threats) and STEP (social, technological, economic and political factors) analyses, but all of the elements and sub-elements of the strategic planning process identified in Figure 3.2. Thus you need to both research and analyse your department from each of these different perspectives as outlined and exemplified in Table 3.2 (Luffman *et al.*, 1996). An alternative way of conceiving this process, and an extremely useful one for conventional subject departments, is the directional policy matrix developed by Sizer (1982). You can use this matrix to assess the strengths of your own subject area in relation to that of other subjects within your institution, as well as with your counterparts in other HEIs (see Figure 3.4).

Table 3.2 The strategic planning process illustrated

Purpose	Research and analysis	Example of outcome
I Scanning		
(i) Environmental (STEP) scan		
• To discern changes in the business environment which are either planned or emergent and which will affect the department	• Social developments	The level of mature student participation in HE remains high but has, again, not risen for the third consecutive year, indicating the local market has indeed reached saturation point. Emergent growth in number of young, whitecollar professionals – a new potential market for CPD provision.
	• Technological developments	Impending launch of new 'managed learning environment' (MLE) using WebCT platform is likely to transform programme delivery and prevailing teaching orthodoxy. Strong potential for improvements in both quality and resource efficiency. (Immediate need for staff training and development.)
	• Economic change	Funding council decisions – to claw back money on basis of unmoderated student target numbers (rather than the revised figure) and to withdraw financial support for units of assessment graded 3b in the RAE – will impact disproportionately on the department. Threat of course closure and job losses. Buoyant currency exchange rates in Asia may yield even greater international student numbers. Specific skills demand in key business sectors in local and regional economy still unmet. A shortfall we could make good.
	• Political change	Government commitment to 50% participation rate for 18–30-year-olds by 2010 provides opportunity to develop 'partnerships for progression' (P4P) with our local FE providers and the elaboration of our own sub-degree provision.
(ii) Internal resource assessment		
• To ensure that the resources needs of plans are identified and can be met (i.e., the strategy is deliverable)	• Staffing resource	Staffing establishment currently fully utilised. Reliant on cadre of part-time staff to deliver 20% of core teaching activity.
	• Staff skills	Majority wedded to conventional pedagogy. Use of ICT (information and communication technology) a minority interest. Almost all are dedicated researchers though expertise is limited in commercial and outreach activity.
	• Learning resources	Existing stock more aged and incomplete than ever. Uniform configuration of physical facilities

(iii) *Institutional mandate*
- To ensure there is a 'fit' between the departmental strategy and your institution's overall strategic operation

- Core value/'mission' — reinforces conventional pedagogical style. Potential for resource-based learning, and for MLE, untapped.

- Strategic orientation — 'To excel as a dynamic learning community'; 'access and opportunity'; 'the pursuit of excellence'; 'to be No 1'; 'entrepreneurialism'; indeterminate, unknown, 'no sense of mission'? Business planning sequence: Plan – Act – Evaluate (defender); Act – Evaluate – Plan (prospector); Evaluate – Plan – Act (analyser); Act – Plan – Evaluate (reactor).

II Analysing

(iv) *Market position*
- To locate the department in comparison with other HEIs as well as to other departments within our university

- Teaching and research performance — Outstanding reputation for teaching reflected in 'excellent' TQA (teaching quality assessment) (23/24) though performance rating in RAE (3b) below what we had anticipated (3a/4). Overall a 'consolidated' market position compared with our rivals elsewhere and relative to the other departments across our university.

(v) *Portfolio analysis*
- To identify the most, as well as the least, successful areas of our provision

- Academic programme portfolio — Applying the university's new costing and pricing model to our departmental courses indicates that: 80% – are consistently successful in academic and financial terms; 10% – are successful academically but not financially (our 'loss leader' access programme to attract local mature entrants; our singular Master's programme); 10% – are successful financially but not academically (our unacceptable drop-out rate, 30%, on the postgraduate diploma); 0% – consistently unsuccessful in academic and financial terms (not applicable).

III Generating ideas

(vi) *Action plan*
- To identify areas for action based on analysis

- New activities — Articulate and develop new short course portfolio aimed at young, whitecollar professionals keen on CPD.

- Improvements to existing activities — Re-appraise postgraduate diploma and develop local action plan to improve student retention. Develop closer links to, and establish joint projects with, local commerce and industry. Deploy designated staff – to develop RBL (resource-based learning) and to utilise WebCT – to help propel change and to promote greater teaching efficiency.

- Discontinuance of selected activities — Replace our singular Master's programme with a series of Master's pathways based on a common foundation year programme.

Step III: *Critically review the mission statement and strategic plan of your HEI*

Either way, there is a recurring theme or constant variable to which you need to give the most careful consideration, as it is often the greatest single source of difficulty (we have alluded to this earlier), and that is the degree of 'fit' between your departmental perspective on strategic orientation and that of your institution in the broader sense. We noted in the last chapter how an analysis of organisational culture can generate critical insights into the context in which you operate. In this instance you need to examine in fine detail the more formal aspects of your institution. That is, you need to put aside any scepticism or prejudice you have and critically review the mission and strategy of your HEI.

Such matters, as we noted earlier, have often courted publicity and controversy in equal measure – and with it, to be frank, a good deal of nonsense too. The penchant for mission statements, for example, parallels the trend towards 'flatter', less hierarchical organisations. And their publication has invariably been designed to exert a centrifugal 'pull' within this new type of institutional environment. If a mission statement is to be useful or effective however, it has, as Colin Marshall (former chairman of BA) put it: 'to be much more than an outline of good intentions and fine ideas. It should offer a framework for the entire organisation. The values which drive the organisation and the belief that the organisation has in itself and what it can achieve' (Luffman *et al.*, 1996). Indeed conventional wisdom suggests that any mission worth its salt must have four discrete qualities, namely an expression of:

*   purpose – *why the organisation exists*: an inspiring purpose which avoids playing to the selfish interests of one or another set of stakeholders;
*   strategy – *the organisation's competitive position*: the identification and specification of the organisation's strategic position;
*   values – *what the organisation believes in*: the moral and cultural values of the organisation identified and expressed in such a way as to engender pride in all employees.
*   standards and behaviours – an indication of *the standards and behaviours expected of staff* in pursuing the organisation's strategic goals.

So now ask yourself the following questions:

1   To what extent does your HEI's mission statement measure up against these four criteria. Where is it deficient – and why? When was it last reviewed and revised?
2   Turning to your institution's strategic plan you need to consider the degree of synchronisation between the latter and the former. Is the strategic plan a logical corollary to your HEI's mission statement? What and where are the gaps? Are they significant?
3   How does your HEI define its market position according to its strategic plan? As a 'star' (high growth; high market share), a 'cash cow' (low growth, high market share); a 'problem child' (high growth, low market share) or as a 'dog' (low growth, low market share)? (Porter, 1998)

4　How does your HEI view its environment according to the plan? As a defender (of its market position), a prospector (for market growth) or as an analyser (of its market position)? Or is it a reactor (out of step altogether)? What are the implications of this market position and strategic orientation? (Miles and Snow, 2003)

5　To what extent does the plan exhibit symmetry and consistency between the 'first order' (or 'upstream') strategies which identify your HEI's long term objectives; 'second order' ones which affect the institution's operation; and, finally, 'third order' (or 'downstream') strategies which determine the most appropriate use of human resources? What are the implications of any inconsistencies? (Boxall and Purcell, 2002)

6　What does your HEI strategic plan imply about the stage of the organisational life-cycle of your institution: entrepreneurial, collectivist, formalised and controlled, or adaptive? (Cameron and Quinn, 1998)

7　What else does your institutional plan tell you about the assumptions and forecasts on which it was based (the integration, or otherwise, of supporting strategies), the capacity for genuine self-critical scrutiny and stretch (i.e. the scope of institutional ambition), and so on.

Putting together these answers should provide you with significant insight into the self-perception of your HEI. It should demonstrate that there is an informed and meaningful stratagem to underpin your HEI's claim to be a 'research-led' institution, a 'community university' or an 'opportunity university', etc. If not, though this is unlikely, you should seek immediate clarification from your institutional planning director or your line manager. If still not satisfied, then you may want to consider mounting a challenge to the rationale. If so you are likely to make more headway if you remember that, despite appearances to the contrary, planning documents are meant to be 'living documents' and not unchanging formal monoliths set in stone for the duration of their span.

Step IV: *Examine the degree of 'fit' between your departmental perspective on strategic orientation and that of your HEI*

Assuming there is indeed consistency in your HEI's claim, you now need to determine where and how your perspective on your department's strategic orientation measures up against that of your institutional one. There should be an alignment, if not perhaps in the fine detail, between the broad aims, opportunities and capabilities of your department as you see them, and those of your HEI. Put another way, there should be sufficient scope within your HEI's strategic plan to enable you to develop a departmental perspective which, while customised to your particular circumstances, fits comfortably within this overall institutional framework. Again if not, you need to consider why. Are the differences matters of style or substance? If the latter, you should go back and review your own perceptions once more. If these remain unchanged then you need to consider the implications, political as well as practical, of these differing perspectives and be prepared to spell them out when it comes to articulating your view of the options facing the department.

In practice, substantive differences in the rationale underpinning departmental or institutional strategies are relatively infrequent. More often than not the relationship between the two is characterised by symmetry and consistency. Where significant – and critical – differences do arise, however and not surprisingly, is over the extent to which the rationale is perceived to match the everyday reality of institutional life.

Put another way, you may have a mission statement and strategic plan and it may even be pinned to the wall, but, far more importantly, do the staff in your department and across your HEI have *a sense of mission*. Are they driven by a sense of purpose? Are they aware of how to realise it? In management-speak, is the 'espoused theory' consistent with the 'theory-in-use'?

Step V: *Measure the 'espoused theory' (the rhetoric) against the 'theory-in-use' (the reality); the knowledge of mission against a 'sense of mission'.*
Design and formulate your strategic options accordingly, from the perspective of your colleagues

The perceived differences between institutional rhetoric and everyday reality go to the very heart of why mission statements have attracted so much opprobrium – and you need to be especially sensitive to such concerns, if you wish to avoid a similar fate in the case of your department. As we all view the world through a different lens, so you need to give careful consideration to the style as well as the substance of the options you see facing the department. You will get short shrift from your colleagues, for example, and rightly so, if you propose objectives which while consistent with your institutional plan seem hopelessly out-of-kilter from their perspective, and doubly so if you couch them in language and vocabulary which, while echoing your HEI's mission, do not resonate with them.

This is not to say you should bow to the status quo or qualify your ideals either. Far from it. Visions and strategic plans, if they are to succeed, are necessarily positive. They anticipate the realisation of an idealised and desirable future state. Equally, they are not concerned with the negative: the problems of the here-and-now, the raking over of past mistakes or the outlining of reasons why aspirations cannot be realised. Nonetheless, you must remember that if your departmental vision is to be realised then your colleagues will need to believe in it as much as yourself. As such you should articulate your vision in the first instance from their 'world-view', not one derived from the 'infallibility' of your institutional mission plan, or in anticipation of a leap of faith in or wholesale conversion to it.

Yet we should also be wary of being overly sceptical, and certainly not cynical, in this regard. HEIs have tended to make heavy weather of their institutional mission plan. Universities are too large and too complex, it is often argued, not to say peculiarly distinctive, *sui generis*, and as such are not always environments conducive to a sense of mission among staff. Evidence from the private sector, however, indicates that this does not always have to be the case; that such reasoning is indeed seriously, if not fatally, flawed. BP Amoco, to take one example, has an organisational infrastructure of global proportions, as one would expect of a world leader in the supply and distribution of oil. It has also set itself an ambitious global mission – to be performance-driven, progressive, innovative and green. What is equally impressive, however, is the way in which these core values have been disseminated both within and across the organisation. To such an extent indeed that first-hand investigation confirms that whether a BP respondent is a Norwegian fitter on a North Sea oil rig, a Belgian engineer in a Dutch oil refinery or a Spanish operative in a Madrid filling station, each is similarly imbued with an acute understanding and genuine commitment to the company's mission and its values. If BP Amoco is able to generate a sense of mission, despite its size and complexity, and the breadth of its global operation, there is no reason, in theory, why HEIs cannot do likewise.

In the case of your department, then, it is important you strike a balance between the need to engage your colleagues on the one hand, and your impulse to embrace your institutional mission on the other. This is something only you can judge, based on your understanding of your colleagues and the extent of their knowledge and commitment to the institutional mission. You should then articulate your departmental perspective accordingly. Whatever the style or substance of your deliberations you should aim to develop a paragraph or 5–6 bullet points for each of the sequential elements of the strategic process which follow, namely:

(i)   Where are we now? (Analysis, not navel-gazing.)
(ii)   Where could we go? (Option formulation, not generating confusion.)
(iii) Where do we want to go? (Option selection, not post-rationalising.)
(iv)   What will help us get there? (Engineering coherent support, not changing the rules.)
(v)   What do we do today? (Implementation, not fire-fighting.)

It is important that you go through each of these stages step by step. You should resist the temptation to skip any of them. That way you will avoid the danger of making assumptions about the status quo on the one hand, and underestimating the potential for, as well as the implications of, future developments on the other. In doing so you should also, as we noted earlier, accentuate the positive. The alternative is to run the risk of lapsing into navel-gazing, generating confusion and becoming mired in fire-fighting (Luffman *et al.*, 1996; Mintzberg, 2002).

Step VI: *Ensure your departmental perspective includes an assessment of risk as well as a number of key targets: i.e. your 'critical success factors' or SMART (not DUMB) objectives*

Finally, you should remember to build in to your perspective two aspects which have not always been given due consideration in the past but which are nowadays increasingly an expectation, if not a requirement, of statutory authorities, an assessment of risk, and a list of your key targets.

In the case of the former you should outline the risk implications for embarking on your proposed course of action and equally important the consequences of *not* undertaking it. The rationale for such risk assessment is to help avoid excessive risk-taking on the one hand, and facilitate the seizure of new opportunities on the other, while simultaneously reassuring stakeholders you are unlikely to be blown off course by unforeseen circumstances. The irony, of course, is that in the case of many HEIs the greatest single risk facing them is their *fear* of taking a risk in the first place.

As for target-setting, the idea, quite correctly, is to provide you with an indicator of progress towards your goal (how we will know when we've got there), an incentive towards achieving it, and a means of monitoring your collective activity. Such targets, it is commonly accepted, are most effective if they are SMART ones: i.e. specific, measurable, achievable, realistic and time-bound. And you may well have had experience of developing objectives of this nature in the past. If so, you will know that in practice many targets which claim to be SMART are anything but; that is, they are often written to satisfy 'the system' rather than address the real task at hand, are invariably inflexible, and frequently set goals that are either too high or too low (Rose, 2000). You should take extra care then to ensure you do not fall into the same trap: that is, you should develop your indicative targets in such a way as they are *not* DUMB – defective, unrealistic, misdirected and, perhaps worst of all, simply, bureaucratic.

Step VII: *Share and test your 'mental model' of the department's strategic orientation with those of your colleagues. Revise and agree, collectively, a 'shared vision' for your department*

With your personal perspective on the department completed, you are now in an position to undertake the most difficult task of this whole process: that of securing the agreement of your colleagues on the best way forward for your department.

Your research and analysis of what the department could and should do will count for nought if you are unable to engage your colleagues in establishing a 'shared vision' on your collective future. There is, as noted earlier, no single right way. However, our understanding of leadership, together with the examples of good practice extant in some HEIs, do provide us with a way forward. You have anyway already taken steps to help you in this regard: through your own self-assessment ('paving the way' – the 'first leadership act' in Senge's view (1990b)); and in your willingness to 'encourage the heart' by articulating your vision from your colleagues' perspective. You now need to go further and test your 'mental model' with them.

More than that, in order to 'enable others to act', you need to encourage your colleagues to put themselves in your shoes and develop their own indicative 'mental model' of the department. This need not be a grand design, simply a one-page summary of their visions and strategies for the department. Either way, their critique of your perspective along with their own conceptualisation should enable you to revise, enhance and maybe even dramatically reshape your own initial ideas. This interchange between an individual leader's ideas and the collaborative thought of colleagues is at the heart of vision formation, and it is contingent on your willingness, as a putative transformational leader, to invite your colleagues to share in the process of leadership.

Strategic planning in practice

Northeastern University, Boston

We can see these elements and processes at work in the institutional examples of good practice offered by Northeastern University, Boston and George Mason University, Virginia. The former, a large, private 'national research university' that is 'student-centred, practice-oriented and urban' with 'a strong community service mission', set itself the goal of 'creating a New Home for Faculty' as part of its 'self-study for re-accreditation'. A 'home' which envisages faculty working in new ways; where 'mentoring, advising, collaboration and curriculum development are recognised, assessed and rewarded along with teaching, research and scholarship as integral elements of professional performance' (Baer *et al.*, 1998). The experience of departments in attempting to make this vision a reality provides us with an illuminating insight into the variation in approaches to departmental planning. Two model ones in particular, the Departments of Mathematics and Cardiopulminary Sciences, highlight the difference.

In the case of Mathematics, a large department with an international research reputation and a heavy service load, the chair found it virtually impossible, in the first instance, to generate any interest on the part of his colleagues in the process. Indeed they felt threatened by the prospect of defining departmental goals consistent with the university's mission, as if they were 'losing control over one's life' as one faculty member put it. To overcome this difficulty the chair did two things. First, he sought to make the process more meaningful by focusing preliminary discussions on an issue (or 'hook') of particular interest to the whole department – in this instance the hiring of junior faculty. And, second, he attempted to give 'ownership' to the department by asking one of his colleagues to write a first draft based on the debate. The tactics worked. Staff estrangement was arrested and turned around. The process of draft writing and circulation, feedback and revision soon developed its own momentum and a collective agreement was finally reached. From the chair's viewpoint the key to this successful outcome was 'to listen and feel the emotions of people in your group, to find an appropriate activity that stimulated the interests of the group and to move ownership of the process in ever widening circles'.

In Cardiopulminary Sciences (a smaller department oriented towards applied research and professional development), by contrast, the attraction of a new and different setting, and with it the prospect of greater professional fulfilment, exerted such a 'pull' on staff that the chair had no difficulty in arousing staff interest. On the contrary, her main concern was how best to harness this enthusiasm. After consulting colleagues she arranged for staff to work through their initial ideas in groups of two or three. She then organised a series of departmental retreats (or 'away-days') at which these ideas were presented, discussed and ultimately voted upon formally (all votes having equal weight) by every department member. While, in theory, a high-risk strategy in itself, in that there was no guarantee that staff would necessarily vote for goals consistent with the university's mission, the chair found that, in practice, this was not the case. Not only that, but the goals which the department finally adopted were those on which there was near unanimity. Indeed she concluded that the process had made her department 'feel more like a team than ever before'.

George Mason University, Virginia

George Mason University (GMU) likewise has sought to improve staff participation and commitment in a similar way; in this instance, in developing a strategic plan for the institution as a whole. A 'commuter school' catering for minority populations in the Washington DC metropolitan area, yet, ironically, based in America's wealthiest county (Fairfax, north Virginia), GMU is relatively under-funded compared to its more illustrious state neighbours: the University of Virginia, William and Mary, and Virginia Tech. What it lacks in tradition and continuity it has sought to make up for, with commendable drive and ambition, by aiming to be 'if not the biggest, then the best-managed university in the world'. In this spirit, and in a conscious attempt to foster community-building, the university's executive charged a faculty group task force with the job of identifying the objectives, or alternative scenarios if you will, which the university could and indeed should set itself.

Working to the brief set by the Provost's office – to establish attainable goals; to focus on audit, dialogue and 'friend-raising'; and to include alumni, the local Round Table and legislators in the consultation – the group produced a visionary guide, *Engaging the Future* (Wood *et al.*, 1997), which outlined a range of viable alternative options open to the university. Put another way, they posed the questions, anticipated future scenarios, and, above all, established a framework for institutional discussion and decision-making. They also, in addition, included concrete recommendations which were subsequently adopted, notably: the creation of three-year faculty second-ments for senior scholars to the Provost's office; the launch of a video-based 'constituency conversation' on university citizenship; the establishment of a credit-based staff development account for individual faculty members; and the formation of a 'New Century College' aimed at providing 'the finest small college education in the context of a large state university'.

Such has been the success of this initiative, indeed, that the Commonwealth of Virginia has adopted it as a mandatory practice for all universities in the state, including William and Mary, etc. An instance of one-upmanship that we should certainly not begrudge, given we can all learn and benefit from it. Indeed, it is a model of best practice we could, and would, all do well to follow.

4 Leading by example

I know that I can save the country and that I alone can.

William Pitt

...Is that right?

When George W. Bush entered the White House in January 2001 few believed his administration would not have to struggle to assert itself. Indeed as the 'minority' victor in the most controversial presidential election since the Hayes/Tilden contest of 1876 many – including much of the Washington media – believed his presidency would be crippled from the outset. And yet, within the space of just one month, the same sceptics were openly baffled at the smooth way the new president had moved into the old office; of how the White House had become more akin to 'Bush Corp'; an organisation defined by a business culture with the president as chairman of the board.

Much of the explanation for this remarkable turnaround can in fact be traced to the sole, but significant, characteristic which differentiates Bush Jr from all forty-two of his predecessors in the office. Sons may have followed fathers (as in the case of the Adams) into the White House before, as have twenty-six lawyers and seven soldiers for that matter, but George W. Bush is the first president ever to hold an MBA. And while his business career may not have been an untrammelled success, he has managed to apply the lessons he learnt at Harvard Business School to the business of running a government to telling effect.

His management style bears all the hallmarks of the MBA handbook. From the appointment of cabinet members (chosen on the basis of complementary expertise combined with an element of rivalry, alongside imperfectly defined portfolios to foster 'creative tension' among advisers), to the approach to strategy (one theme per week, one speech per day), to the insistence on a strict code of dress and behaviour. Bad language, poor timekeeping and 'dress down' Fridays have been made taboo. On the other hand, staff are encouraged to follow the president's lead and not overdo the overtime – to maintain in effect the balance in their lives between commitment to work and responsibility to family and community.

It is a management style which perceives politics as being a matter of perform-ance goals more than motive, and of results more than process. For Bush the business of government is just that – less a matter of ideology than a theory of management. His job, as he sees it, is to sell 'the plan', get the right people to put it in motion and then stand back. A modus operandi we see most clearly in the 'corporate' relation-ship that exists between president and vice-president; between Bush the chief executive officer who deals with the broad-brush strategy and Dick Cheney the chief operating officer who puts it into practice.

Now while it is the case that the new president may well have been motivated to differentiate his administration from the informality characteristic of his immediate predecessor, and that his adoption of MBWA ('management by walking about') and the use of joshing nicknames could be interpreted (as indeed it was) as a deliberate 'charm offensive' to wrong-foot his opponents, it is equally the case that his actions demonstrate an astute business-based manoeuvre. One that has reaped a handsome dividend and one from which we can all learn. That is, irrespective of whether one shares the president's conception of politics or the beliefs espoused by his adminis-tration, the style, tone and manner in which he reorganised the White House provides us with an exemplary model of leadership by example: of how to undertake a new role, shape it to your design and make it your own. In Bush's case to live up to his own maxim that: 'a good executive is one that understands how to recruit people and how to delegate. How to align authority and responsibility, how to hold people accountable and how to build a team' (Macintyre, 2001).

This practise of reflecting on leadership, of how one should embrace a new role or tackle an existing one, is a trait not often found in HE, unfortunately. Indeed to judge from a leadership study of UK university vice-chancellors it is a characteristic conspicuous by its absence. As exemplified in the typical response which researchers met when they probed individual vice-chancellors on their preferred or adopted leadership styles: 'I don't really think about these things frankly. I just try and get on with the job. Basically I don't read books about it. I just get on with it' (Bargh *et al.*, 2000). It may be, and one would like to think it is, that the vice-chancellors in this case study do not simply rely on 'playing it by ear'. That they do in fact consciously deliberate on their modus operandi but did not feel inclined to admit to doing so for reasons of culture or personal modesty. Either way, the point is, it is an activity we ignore at our peril. Private sector organisations indeed set such store by it that they invariably hire coaches to ease new post-holders through this process; an investment they willingly and regularly incur in the knowledge that the benefits which accrue will far outweigh the initial expense. In HE the hiring of coaches is beyond the reach of most HEIs, yet, even if it wasn't, it is doubtful many would regard it as a priority for funding. For, as we noted earlier, leadership and management within HE is bedevilled by the low status and esteem in which it is almost universally held. A parlous situation exacerbated still further by the tendency of some managers to treat their role as if it were a temporary distraction from their 'real' work of teaching and research (see Box 4.1).

We all have a collective responsibility to address this malaise and as individual managers can do so, in the first instance, through the personal example which we set: the way in which we conduct ourselves; the style, tone and manner we set in managing day-to-day affairs; the ways in which we support colleagues, handle meetings, make decisions, resolve conflict, establish standards; and so on. To be an effective manager requires you to give serious consideration to these issues. Put another way, if you are to make a real difference to your colleagues and make a distinctive contribution to your institution – and also, critically, one that meets with your own satisfaction – you need to consider these matters in a deliberative, reflective and self-conscious way. This fourth chapter seeks to help you do that by systematically examining these particular 'public' aspects of your role: namely, the establishment of a modus operandi, the chairing of meetings, the making and taking of decisions, the handling of conflict and the building of teams.

Paving the way

> I wish some power the gift would gi'e us, to see ourselves
> as others see us.
>
> Robbie Burns

One of the most difficult things to learn – and one of the last things we ever learn about ourselves – is the personal impact we have on those around us. Yet without such self-knowledge we cannot begin to determine how effective we are in our roles. Our path to self-realisation, however, has been made still more difficult in recent times. For, like it or loathe it, we cannot ignore the fact we operate in a radically different political and social world from our forebears: one which seemingly celebrates fame over originality, 'image' over 'reality', style over substance, soundbite over reason and 'spin' over news story.

Plotting a course of action in such a setting is no easy task. It requires that you are genuinely attuned to the needs and feelings of others as well as those of your own. Indeed leadership development programmes nowadays are less about testing the leadership capacity of individuals through various outdoor pursuit challenges and the like, and more concerned with getting participants 'to reach inside themselves' to find the leadership style of their own that would most successfully mesh with their organisation. We began to explore this issue in the last chapter and identified a variety of ways you could gain more self-knowledge through formal feedback instruments (such as the visionary leader behaviour questionnaire, the Myers-Briggs (personality) type indicator and the Thomas-Kilmann conflict mode instrument) as well as in conversation with the person who knows you best – yourself.

We can – and you should – extend this journey of self-exploration further in order to prepare you for the role you have undertaken.

I   First, examine that aspect of your personality which will have a critical bearing on whether, or not, you will be successful: that is not so much your IQ – a common mistake made in gauging individual's leadership potential, not least in universities, as in 'X is highly intelligent and must therefore be able to lead' – but rather your 'EQ' (emotional quotient). Popularised by American psychologist Daniel Goleman (1996), 'emotional intelligence' is defined as the ability to perceive one's own feelings

Box 4.1 'New manager assimilation': San Diego State University

Not all universities are hesitant or sceptical of hiring external consultants to facilitate the assimilation of new managers. San Diego State University is a case in point.

The context

The desire of the newly appointed university president 'to take charge', 'to begin building strong, positive and productive working relationships' with his eight-strong cabinet of top administrators. His predecessor had served twenty years in office.

The approach

The external facilitator, hired to help in the leadership transition, meets with each of the cabinet members for forty-five minutes on a one-to-one basis.

The one-to-one meetings are organised around a common set of questions (see below) which the new president has agreed in advance with the facilitator. Ground rules provide for anonymity.

The facilitator concludes the process by convening the entire cabinet group including the new president and summarising the outcomes.

The findings

1 *What do we want to know about the new president?*
   - He came from a state college: Does he understand research, graduate education and Division I athletics?
   - He seems to have a consultative management style: How does that really work?
   - How will he utilise the cabinet?
   - What does he need from us?
   - How will the campus relate to the system administration now?
   - Is it Dr Weber? Stephen? Steve?

2 *What should he know about us?*
   - We have a terrific faculty and staff
   - We have an entrepreneurial culture, which, as such, maybe resistant to change
   - Our mission and identity need clarification

3 *What does he need to know to be successful here?*
   - Use your transition process to convey messages about the future of the campus.
   - Become highly visible in the community.
   - Bond with the faculty and the staff as soon as you can.
   - Consultation is important, but don't forget that the President must make the executive decisions.
   - You will be given an extended honeymoon – don't squander it!

4 *What significant issues need to be addressed quickly?*
   - Establish and define your presidency, as soon as possible.
   - Get 'up to speed' on athletics!
   - Don't be afraid to delegate.
   - Make any planned personnel changes as soon as possible.
   - Improve our planning and budgeting processes.

5 *What specific suggestions do we have for addressing the issues we have identified?*

- Develop a shared vision and value system for us to use in decision-making.
- Don't get 'used up' in your first year – save a little for the ' third act'.
- Get to know us, use us to help advance your agenda, work with us as a team.

The feedback

- Participants agreed the transition dialogues did facilitate an extremely valuable exchange of information in a way that was far less protracted than would be the norm. More than that, however, they also enabled:
- The president to signal he was 'eager for the views of senior officers and valued their feelings as professional colleagues'.
- Cabinet members to be more 'self-confident and comfortable in delivering bad news or identifying problems and issues that needed resolution'.
- Cabinet meetings to proceed 'with less game playing and more honest conversation'.
- The 'top team' to approach an immediate crisis incident (a campus triple homicide) with 'a higher degree of readiness and effectiveness' than would otherwise have been possible.

Source: Krinsky and Weber, 1997

and those of others. Thus the more emotionally intelligent person is characterised by a high sense of self-worth, an ability to express and understand their emotions and to understand their personal values. They tend to be more aware of their own strengths and limitations and also able to recognise these things in people working around them and accommodate them. Such individuals invariably outperform their less sensitive counterparts and not surprisingly EQ has come to be regarded as equally important as IQ, if not more important, in determining professional effectiveness and progression.

So, how do you fare? Box 4.2 enables you to assess your own level of emotional intelligence; a task you need not approach with undue reticence for, if you do not score as well as you anticipate, you can always take remedial action, since it is still possible to significantly increase your EQ in later life (unlike your IQ).

II   A more conventional way of assessing your preparedness is to examine your degree of competence for the role. The management competence framework, outlined in Box 4.3, is a generic template which one 'new' university in the UK has developed to clarify to managers the (benchmark) standards of performance expected of them, to help them assess their performance and to guide them in determining their development needs. You should take each of the nine core competencies in turn:

- Grade yourself strong, average or weak against the skills and qualities in each subcategory.
- Determine your overall average for each of the nine core competencies.
- Discuss your profile with a 'critical friend', someone whose opinion you value and trust: in what aspects are you strong, less strong, underdeveloped or undeveloped? Focus on the gaps and the weaknesses in your profile. What can you, ought you, do about them?
- Commit to an action plan to address them.

Box 4.2 Emotional intelligence questionnaire

Test your emotional intelligence. Tick a single response to each question then add up your score.

	Never	Rarely	Sometimes	Routinely	Always

Awareness of feelings

Recognising one's emotions and their effects

	Never	Rarely	Sometimes	Routinely	Always
1 Do you know which emotions you are feeling, can you say why and accurately label them individually?	☐	☐	☐	☐	☐
2 Do you recognise the chain from experiencing an emotion to taking action based on it (i.e. the links between your feelings and what you think, do and say)?	☐	☐	☐	☐	☐
3 Do you recognise how your feelings affect your performance, the quality of experience at work and your relationships?	☐	☐	☐	☐	☐

Personal insight

Knowing one's key strengths and frailties

	Never	Rarely	Sometimes	Routinely	Always
1 Are you aware of your strengths, weaknesses and emotional boundaries in relationships?	☐	☐	☐	☐	☐
2 Are you, or do you consciously make time to be reflective?	☐	☐	☐	☐	☐
3 Are you open to candid feedback, new perspectives, continuous learning, and self-development?	☐	☐	☐	☐	☐

Self-assurance

Sureness about one's self-worth and capabilities

	Never	Rarely	Sometimes	Routinely	Always
1 Do you present yourself with self-possession; have poise but with warmth?	☐	☐	☐	☐	☐
2 Can you celebrate diversity in teams, voice views that are unpopular?	☐	☐	☐	☐	☐
3 Are you decisive, able to make sound judgements using emotional and analytical information, despite uncertainties and pressures?	☐	☐	☐	☐	☐

Scoring

Always: Add 4 points for every tick. **Routinely:** Add 3 points for every tick. **Sometimes**: Add 2 points for every tick. **Rarely**: Add 1 point for every tick. **Never**: No points.

Score 36–27

Congratulations. You have a high to exceptional awareness of your own emotions, thought and resulting behaviour. You would have the ability to reflect on incidents that did not go well or as expected and analyse your part in that sequence of events.

Score 26–18

Well done, but reflect on the reasons that you put a 'sometimes' response. Think about questions you could ask others in future to check out what their motive is for their behaviour or their responses to you. Try to stop yourself from repeating mistakes.

Score 17–9

You may be puzzled by the way you act or the responses you get from others. You may feel misunderstood a significant amount of the time. Enlist the help of a friend to develop a plan for taking steps to improve yourself.

Score 8–1

You are very honest. Showing integrity is a great EQ strength. You would benefit from a course to help you to increase your self-awareness. Your score shows you are not particularly aware of how or why you behave the way you do.

Source: Chartered Institute of Personnel and Development (Dann, 2001)

III   A further, and by no means trite, consideration as to your 'roadworthiness' is image – your own image and that of your immediate surroundings. We cannot overlook the fact that one of the consequences of living in an increasingly image-conscious age is that first impressions really do count – particularly at work, and especially when dealing with external clients. Conventional wisdom, for instance, tells us that when we walk into a meeting, people form an impression which is based 70 per cent on our personal image, 23 per cent on the sound, pitch and modulation of our voice, and just 7 per cent on the content of what we're actually saying (Hanscombe, 1998).

If you are to make the right impression then attention to your image is as critical as with any other aspect of your role. Put another way, it is as important to 'look the part' and 'feel the part' as it is to 'fit the part'. This is not a question of acquiring an expensive wardrobe or of becoming 'the packaged executive'. Such techniques, like the penchant for 'power-dressing' in the 1980s, are rarely sustainable or desirable for they are, in reality, transparently manipulative. Rather it is a matter of reflecting on the example you convey to others about the quality of life you lead. It is about projecting a positive image – thinking positively and being positive. This is not always easy for everyone. Indeed we're all familiar with the individual who has the unfortunate tendency to enter a room as a kind of walking apology – 'Sorry, it's only me'. Again however, as with emotional intelligence, there are ways in which we can cultivate such positive habits and we will be exploring them later in Chapter 9, 'Managing Yourself'. And while it might mean you do indeed need to refresh your

Box 4.3 Performance expectations of senior managers at one UK 'new' (post-1992) university

Strategic ability

- Balances immediate needs against longer term objectives
- Ensures day-to-day tasks and activities are clearly linked to the longer-term aims of the business
- Develops a coherent picture of the school's/ UWS's (university-wide services) contribution to overall university goals and communicates this
- Influences and contributes to wider university issues

Leadership

- Creates and secures commitment to a clear vision
- Initiates and manages change in pursuit of strategic objectives
- Is visible, approachable and earns respect
- Inspires and shows loyalty
- Builds and supports a high performing team
- Acts decisively having assessed the risks
- Accepts responsibility for the actions of the team

Communication

- Negotiates effectively and can handle hostility
- Is concise and persuasive orally and in writing
- Listens to what is said and is sensitive to other's reactions
- Chooses the methods of communication most likely to secure effective results
- Is comfortable and effective in a representational role
- Builds, maintains and uses an effective network of contacts

Judgement and decision-making

- Ensures necessary information or evidence is collected and weighs the value of advice against its source
- Assesses the degree of the risk in major plans and decisions, and balances against potential disadvantages
- Takes timely decisions in uncertain situations or based on limited inform-ation, where necessary
- Evaluates the potential impact of a decision on school/UWS priorities or on broader university objectives
- Remains objective in assessing information when under great pressure

Management of people

- Develops staff to meet challenging organisational needs
- Establishes and communicates clear standards and expectations
- Delegates effectively, knowing when to step in and when not to
- Makes best use of skills and resources within the team
- Gives regular face-to-face feedback and recognition
- Addresses poor perform-ance, builds trust, good morale and teamwork
- Responds to feedback from staff
- Secures commitment to change through appro-priate involvement of staff

Management of financial and other resources

- Secures value for money
- Challenges existing practices and leads initiatives of new and more efficient use of resources
- Negotiates for the resources to do the job, in the light of wider priorities
- Commits and realigns resources to meet key priorities
- Uses management information to monitor/ control resources
- Demonstrates commitment to using IT as a resource

Delivery of results competence	Personal effectiveness	Expertise and professional
• Defines results, taking account of customer or other stakeholder needs • Manages relationships with customers/other stakeholders effectively • Organises work processes to deliver on time, on budget, and to agreed quality standards • Strives for continuous performance improvement and encourages others to do the same • Assesses and manages risk • Monitors performance and incorporates feedback in future plans	• Adapts quickly and flexibly to new demands and change • Manages own time well to meet competing priorities • Shows resilience, stamina and reliability under heavy pressure • Takes a firm stance when circumstances warrant it • Is aware of personal strengths and weaknesses and impact on others • Shows commitment to own personal and professional development • Offers objective advice without fear or favour • Pursues adopted strategies with energy and commitment	• Earns credibility and influence through depth and breadth of expertise • Ensures that decisions are informed by relevant technical/specialist expertise • Understands and operates effectively within the university framework • Accepts personal responsibility for quality of professional work • Gives professional direction to others • Seeks and applies best practice from other organisations

wardrobe, the important point is that your credibility with colleagues and clients is intimately related to the image you project. You will get back, be it positive or negative, what you give out.

Equally, the impression others have of you is often informed by your surroundings as much as yourself. As such you also need to cast a critical eye on your immediate working environment, notably your office. If you have one – and we tend to assume it is essential we do, even though it may not really be so – what does your office say about you? Is it a stimulating or stale environment? Organised or disorganised? Tidy or cluttered? Bright or dull? Green or barren? As Churchill once said, 'we shape our buildings and afterwards our buildings shape us'. The same can equally be applied to offices if we allow them to. You therefore need to consciously reflect on the 'messages' your office gives to colleagues and to visitors about you. Does the way in which you have utilised the space, decorated the walls, furnished the surroundings and personalised it convey what you really want. For example, if you have a desk – and again we tend to automatically assume we should have one even if it may not be necessary – how is it positioned? In the centre with you behind it? It may convey to your visitors, made to sit in front (of it), the sense that you like to be the 'controlling adult' in your environment; alternatively, they might feel you are an insecure manager with something to hide; or simply both. Placed alongside one of the walls, the position of your desk conveys a quite different impression: one of a person who is willing to share their space on an equal footing with others, although you may simultaneously run the risk of being thought a soft touch. Either way, the point is you need to ensure that, whichever way you choose to organise your office, and again we will pick this issue up later, it reflects your personal style.

IV In developing your own way forward you also, as we noted earlier, need to consider aspects of not only yourself but of your institution: its distinguishing characteristics; its climate, structure, politics, culture; and so on. You then need to determine which leadership approach is likely to have the most successful effect in your working environment. Some such as Senge (1990b) argue that 'taking a stand' is the first leadership act. And in his case, he argues that the 'learning organisation' is a 'good idea' but will remain only a good idea unless, and until, individuals make a conscious and deliberate choice to build such organisations.

There are, too, other models from which you can draw, the visionary leader, the liberating leader, the transformational leader, the transactional leader, and so on.

Box 4.4 The seven habits of highly effective people

In *The Seven Habits of Highly Effective People*, Stephen Covey identifies seven key steps that will lead to truly effective behaviour, whether at work or at home.

The first three habits are 'private' steps the individual must take personally before being able to achieve significant results in the outside world. The next three habits are 'public' activities for the public realm where interaction and, crucially, interdependence is called for. The final habit is to stay fresh.

- **Be proactive.** Covey does not use the term proactive in the more recent sense (where· it is synonymous with 'active'). He genuinely means taking responsibility for your life and your actions. A key principle for Covey here is that 'between stimulus and response people have the freedom to choose'.

- **Begin with the end in mind.** This means having clear goals and knowing what it is you want to achieve. Covey even suggests drawing up a personal mission statement that is based on your most valued principles.

- **Put first things first.** Effective management of time, tasks and responsibilities. This includes developing trusting working relationships, delegating effectively.

- **Think win/win.** Creative problem-solving, not aggressive negotiating or feeble passivity. The approach transcends current difficulties and finds alternatives.

- **Seek first to understand . . . then to be understood.** Covey talks about 'empathic listening'; allowing others to express themselves, letting them know they are being listened to and understood.

- **Synergise.** This for Covey is the 'miraculous' part – catalysing, unifying and unleashing the greatest powers within people. The whole is greater than the sum of its parts.

- **Sharpen the saw.** This is about renewal and staying fresh. The man struggling to cut down a tree is too busy to sharpen his saw, so it takes him far longer.

If you observe these seven habits, Covey believes you can constantly renew yourself.

Source: adapted from Covey, 1989

The general management literature is also awash with sage advice on everything from *Thriving on Chaos* (Peters, 1987) to the *One Minute Manager* (Blanchard and Johnson, 2000). Of this, two further generic perspectives are worth considering. One, Stephen Covey's *The Seven Habits of Highly Effective People* (1989) because it is one of the few successful codes of behaviour to have stood the test of time, and because it also provides you with a sound reference point to question your actions (see Box 4.4). And the other – a transformational leadership model for the public sector – because it offers an approach more closely suited to universities than probably any other. One that is which not only recognises the critical differences (in governance and management and accountability) between the public and the private sector (principally, the lack of clarity and greater complexity of the former compared to the latter), but also reflects the variation in the perception of leadership of those who work in the two areas (see Box 4.5). In the private sector the greatest expectation of the leader is to be a role model while in the public sector the most important

Box 4.5 Characteristics of the transformational leader in the public sector

Leading and developing others

- Has genuine interest in staff as individuals; values their contributions; develops their strengths; mentors; has positive expectations of staff abilities.
- Trusts staff to take decisions and initiative on important matters; delegates effectively; develops potential; supportive of mistakes.
- Approachable and not status conscious; prefers face-to-face communication; accessible and keeps in touch.
- Encourages staff to question traditional approaches to the job; encourages new approaches/solutions to problems; encourages strategic thinking.

Personal qualities

- Transparency; honest and consistent in behaviour; more concerned with the good of the organisation than personal ambition.
- Integrity; open to advice, criticism and disagreement; consults and involves others in decision-making; regards values as integral to the organisation.
- Decisiveness: decisive when required; prepared to take difficult decisions and risks when appropriate.
- Charisma: in touch; exceptional communicator; inspires others to join them.
- Analytical and creative thinking: capacity to deal with a wide range of complex issues; creative in problem-solving.

Leading the department/organisation

- Inspiring communicator of the vision of the organisation to a network of internal and external stakeholders; gains the confidence and support of various groups through sensitivity to needs and by achieving organisational goals.
- Clarifies objectives and boundaries; team-oriented approach to problem-solving, decision-making and identifying values.
- Has a clear vision and strategic direction, engages various internal and external stakeholders in developing; helps others to achieve the vision.

Source: Alimo-Metcalfe and Alban-Metcalfe, 2002

prerequisite for a leader appears to be what they can do for their staff. An inclination that closely resembles the model of leader as servant (Alimo-Metcalfe and Alban-Metcalfe, 2002).

This is not to say, however, that leadership is simply about meeting staff needs. On the contrary it suggests that while individuals may ascribe characteristics to (distant) leaders such as charisma, vision, courage, passion, and so on, these are not necessarily the same qualities they value in their own immediate boss. Here it would seem public employees set greater store on line managers who have attributes such as: being sociable, open and considerate of others; having a sense of humour; being credible in their field of expertise; being intelligent; and setting high performance standards for themselves and for others. In other words, leaders who set an example by 'practising what they preach' (see Box 4.6). In this context then leadership is about engaging others as partners in developing and achieving a shared vision and enabling staff to lead. It is about creating a fertile supportive environment for creative thinking and for challenging assumptions about the status quo, as well as having genuine sensitivity to the needs of a broad range of internal and external stakeholders. It is in short the transformational model of leadership, that of the *democratic* leader who seeks to take an organisation through change while transforming people's beliefs in themselves and encouraging leadership in others. This approach has clear implications for management too and the role managers are expected to play: i.e. principally, not so much a case of 'hands-on' as 'hands-off' (see Box 4.7).

Either way, the options are for you to consider and the choice of approach yours to make. Ultimately it is about finding out what works for you. There is, as we noted

---

Box 4.6 Leadership by example

To lead by example you must ensure you:
- Work hard to high standards.
- Actively encourage feedback on your own performance.
- Communicate an air of enthusiasm.
- Help out/walk the job.
- Work on your own learning.
- Practise what you preach.
- Openly admit your mistakes.
- Set a good example to others by your own behaviour.
- Are *corporate*.
- Don't compromise yourself.
- Don't panic.
- Don't let it get you down.

You should **never** say (and should try to resolve):
- No one tells me . . .
  - what's going on;
  - what my exact job is;
  - what my responsibilities are.
- The university should do . . .
- It is not down to me.

Box 4.7 The new public sector manager

As public bureaucracies evolve . . .

from mechanistic organisations
which build on:

- rules
- procedures
- job descriptions
- structures
- rationality
- planning
- management by objectives
- control

to more human organisations
which build on:

- values
- meanings
- commitments
- shared understanding
- rituals
- communication
- learning
- collaboration

. . . then the role of the *new manager* moves

from close control – 'hands-on'
with the manager as:

- supervisor
- expert
- director
- controller
- constraint

to remote control – 'hands-off'
with the manager as:

- resource
- coach
- catalyst
- explorer
- orchestrator
- boundary manager
- networker
- champion
- politician
- negotiator
- conflict raiser/resolver

earlier, no magic formula to leadership and management. In developing a personal style, however, which is consistent with your beliefs and values and with your working environment you will be well on the way to becoming an effective leader and manager. How, though, does this (theoretical) effectiveness translate into your (practical) day-to-day activities. It is to these seemingly mundane – yet in terms of your ultimate success, critically important – aspects of your role we turn next.

Meetings, meetings, meetings

> I chair from the front.
> Margaret Thatcher

> Wilt stared out of the window at the new Electronics building and wondered for the umpteenth time what it was about committees that turned educated and relatively intelligent men and women, all of them graduates of universities, into bitter and boring and argumentative people whose sole purpose seemed to be to hear themselves speak and prove everyone else wrong. And committees had come to dominate the Tech.
>
> Tom Sharpe, *Wilt on High*

Meetings are one of, if not *the* most distinguishing characteristics of university life. Whereas in business such commonplace gatherings are rightly regarded as an important part of work, academic caricature has elevated them into a celebrated art form. This satirical tradition, stretching from F.M. Cornforth at the start of the last century to Laurie Taylor in this, tells us 'what everyone knows' about HE: that it is beset by committees in which people spend hours of their time while someone takes minutes (Lucas, 1995; McNay, 1996). An activity whose prodigious consumption of time many staff believe, with good reason, is an unwelcome distraction from their 'real and proper work'.

Unlike business, academia is, of course, characterised by a far greater range of forms of authority. Indeed Burton Clark (1983) has identified no fewer than nine such forms of authority in academic settings: four based on disciplines (personal rulership (professorial), collegial rulership (professorial), guild authority and professional authority); two characteristic of institutions (trustee authority and bureaucratic authority); and three operating at the level of the system (bureaucratic authority, political authority, and what he calls 'system-wide academic oligarchy'). These various forms of authority, and the stakeholders they represent, help explain why HEIs have developed an elaborate network of committees to accommodate them. But this development in itself is not the root cause of staff disaffection. After all there is, too, an equally long-standing commitment to collegiality within academic cultures, and with it an express (and to outsiders, probably excessive) desire that consultation and decision-making are both extensive and mutually deliberative processes.

The real source of staff grievance appears to lie in the fact that this 'system theory' is rarely adhered to in practice. Critics, for instance, invariably complain that committees often have an unclear remit or are poorly controlled, or both; that they are sometimes used as devices to, at one extreme, deliberately stall or avoid reaching a decision, or, at the other, disguise the fact that decisions have already been made elsewhere. Collegiality, as the last criticism implies, is breached as much as it is honoured in practice and, as such, can alienate a significant minority of staff. More than that, collegiality also allows negative, as well as positive, attitudes and behaviours to flourish unchecked, which the determined and the unscrupulous may well exploit without being held to account. When other new forms of authority are introduced into such a setting, and in particular, ones such as those exercised by managers which many insiders regard as illegitimate, it should not surprise us that staff perceive it as yet another unwarranted and unwanted intrusion on their autonomy, their time and their energies (McNay, 1996; Ramsden, 1998).

The challenge for managers then is a considerable one. Indeed credibility in your authority will stem from:

- the way in which you determine to schedule meetings (or not);
- the types of meetings you hold;
- the way in which they are organised; and
- the manner in which you chair them.

Your mastery of these critical key skills, moreover, will not only enable you to enhance your effectiveness as a leader *within* your department or service but also, given that performance targets nowadays are invariably dependent on a far greater degree of internal collaboration than hitherto, your contribution as a member representing your area in different forums *across* the institution.

How to do it, though?

To meet or not to meet, that is the question

It is widely accepted that the committee culture symptomatic of academic institutions is, as we noted earlier, simply a reflection of the plurality of forms of authority and of the collegiate tradition that persists within them. The harsh reality, however, is that this culture is also fuelled by those who enjoy, or have most to benefit from, such gatherings: i.e. managers and others in authority. Indeed it is not uncommon to come across managers who pride themselves on having diaries that are 'wall-to-wall' with meetings. It is as if they have adapted Parkinson's Law and expanded their number of meetings to fill the amount of time they have available. It is also a mistake you will find yourself making unless you exercise the most stringent self-discipline.

After all, we need to recognise that *meetings can be seductive* in the sense that they are social occasions in which you meet with other colleagues: they get you 'out of the office'; they can fill you with a sense of importance; are often relatively undemanding; and, usually, free from interruption. They can also have a fatal attraction too, for they can delude you into thinking that 'I am busy therefore I must be being effective'. Nothing, however, could be further from the truth. Being occupied is not the same as making things happen. Activity is not the same as taking action. Indeed, as a 'rule of thumb', Senge (1998) maintains that, as a manager, you should divide your time in roughly equal proportion between that spent in meetings and that devoted to action outside of them.

Is a meeting really necessary?

This is the first question you should ask yourself when either planning to hold a meeting yourself or when you have been asked to attend one organised by others. What is the purpose of the meeting? What do you want to get out of the meeting? What do you want others to get out of the meeting? What would be the consequences of *not* meeting? Are you meeting for meeting's sake? Could you not instead send an e-mail, a voice-mail, a memo, make a telephone call, or write a report?

You should not proceed with a meeting unless you are able to respond positively to these questions. And if a meeting has been arranged by someone else you should seek clarification of its purpose from the chair prior to the meeting. If not satisfied you should lobby other attendees and challenge the purpose at the meeting itself or, so long as your interests are not threatened, opt not to attend giving your reasons why.

That said, we need to recognise, of course, that meetings can have very different *purposes* and that there are indeed many different *types* of meeting.

Purposes of meetings

All meetings serve one or more of four main purposes:

1	information-giving	–	'have I got news for you!'
2	information-gathering	–	'what do you think of this?'
3	decision-making	–	'what are we going to do?'
4	problem-solving	–	'how should we resolve this?'

They are also invariably used to satisfy one or more of the following objectives:

- to test colleagues reaction to information given (inviting opinion);
- to gain their acceptance of the given information;
- to identify the need for further information;
- to pool ideas and experience on a particular subject (to learn from one another);
- to gain understanding of each other's point of view (to gain cooperation);
- to give individuals the opportunity to test their ideas and attitudes with those of others (and possibly change them);
- to build group morale.

Types of meetings

Meetings too can vary in many different ways according to their:

- size: large, small, mass or one-to-one;
- status: formal, informal; official, unofficial; open, closed; academic or management;
- scope: team-, group-, unit-, department-, faculty- or institution-wide;
- function: steering group or working party; exam board or user group; think-tank or project team; mitigation panel or public forum; course committee or staff seminar; etc.;
- nature: brainstorming or briefing; presenting or discussing; monitoring or evaluating; negotiating or consulting; lobbying or assessing; etc.

You need, therefore, to give careful consideration, then, as to how you want to organise meetings in your own area. You should not fall into the trap, as so many others do, of assuming that the 'all-purpose meeting for all staff' is the most appropriate, nay, only viable, way to manage the work of your department. Such gatherings can indeed improve team spirit and resolve difficulties. Too often, though, they invariably waste time and money, increase hostility, treat 'acorns and oak trees as if they are alike', and skim over deep divisions among staff. You can take much of the heat out of such meetings, and simultaneously make them more meaningful and effective, by preparing your audience sufficiently beforehand. By arranging that is to hold, or have others hold, separate meetings to satisfy different purposes (as suggested above). Small advisory meetings, say, to gather and exchange information, others to test new ideas, still others to develop policy papers, and so on.

You also need to consider the types of meetings you intend to have with staff on a regular basis: team briefings, team meetings, all-staff meetings, one-to-ones, and so on (see Boxes 4.8 and 4.9). Their nature and frequency will depend on the size and complexity of your department or service.

- If for instance your department is a relatively small (under fifteen), stable, single-site operation you should anticipate holding all-staff meetings either once a term or twice a semester, and one-to-ones with one or two individuals who have a particular and significant responsibility every other week, e.g. subject coordinator, course leader, team leader.
- If you have responsibility for a university service, your meetings with staff should be of greater frequency, typically every other week, and you may like to consider alternating them with team briefings.
- Likewise, if your department is a large academic one with multiple programmes on different campuses and a diverse range of interests, you should anticipate holding additional staff meetings and alternating them between sites. You will also need to build in additional one-to-ones to ensure you embrace the full range of your department's interests and responsibilities, e.g. with your research director, enterprise activity coordinator, community liaison officer, and so on.

Box 4.8 One-to-one meetings: key features

Why have them?

- One-to-one meetings offer you one of the most effective and efficient ways to manage your department while also indeed developing your own management team at the same time.
- You should aim to hold them with the two to three individuals in your department who have a particular and significant responsibility either for an activity (e.g. admissions, research, community links) or the management of staff (e.g. team leader, programme leader, subject coordinator).

Key features

You need to ensure, if you are to achieve your goals, that your one-to-ones:

- Are scheduled on a regular basis, typically one hour, every other week (a great time saver and not a time waster for regularity ensures that you and your colleagues do not feel obliged to interrupt the other, every time a development arises).
- Are literally (rather than virtually) a face-to-face discussion in private.
- Caters for a discussion which reviews the whole of the role, not just a single aspect of it.
- Are structured meetings and not just a casual chat.
- Include a discussion of the past, present and future (up to three months in either direction).
- Are a genuine two-way dialogue aimed at assessing and reviewing the effectiveness of both parties as a partnership.
- Have outcomes (revised or amended targets, agreed deadlines, etc.) that you record briefly in writing on a file note; specific action points that are to be picked up and form the basis of your next regular meeting.

Source: adapted from Moores, 1994

Box 4.9 Team briefings: key features

Why have them?

Team briefings, as the term implies, are more like a systematic flexible drill than a conventional meeting. A well-established practice, which has its origins in the commercial sector, it has been increasingly adapted to good effect in public sector organisations, including HEIs. Briefings, of course, have an obvious practical application if you are responsible for a university-wide service but they can and have been used equally well by academic leaders who tend to place more emphasis on the format of the briefing (the 5Ps, see below) and play down the enforced formality of these occasions (often substituting half-hour informal meetings over lunch in their stead).

Either way, team briefings can be particularly useful in helping you to:

- Correct misunderstandings within your group.
- Reduce the effect of damaging rumour, of the grapevine, etc.
- Seek cooperation from your colleagues in preparing for change.
- Improve the commitment and morale of group members.
- Reinforce your role as leader and manager of the department.

How do they work?

- Face-to-face; to facilitate a free range of Q and A.
- Small teams (four to fifteen people).
- Regular: thirty minutes every other week or once a month depending on circumstance.
- Relevant: the focus and information must be on the 'here-and-now' if the briefing is to command sufficient interest and commitment.

Format: the 5Ps

- ► • Progress – How we are doing in relation to our targets? Budgetary, planning, admissions, etc.
- ▷ • Policy – New initiatives; changes in policy, systems and routines.
- ▷ • People – Who is coming, who is going and why; promotions, scholarship, publications, professional development opportunities.
- ► • Points for action – What do we have to do before we meet again. Agree on who will do it.
- ▷ • Praise – For the group and for individuals as appropriate.

    [► at every briefing   ▷ not necessarily every briefing]

Source: adapted from Moores, 1994

Now you have decided the combination of meetings, both regular and occasional, which best suits your and your department's needs, you face a more difficult task still, that of conducting them.

Effective chairing

Academics are fond of remarking that management is little more than common sense. If that were so then the poor reputation of meetings, chaired by academics as well as managers, suggests common sense is a commodity in relatively short supply in universities. Staff complaints, as we noted earlier, are manifold. The most common being:

- an unclear remit; a lack of clear purpose or objective;
- the absence of an agenda, or a poorly prepared agenda, or an overambitious agenda;
- held at the wrong time, with the wrong people there, or in the wrong environment;
- behavioural problems: getting sidetracked, going round in circles, individual soapboxing and gamesmanship, time-wasting and waffling;
- interruptions from outside the meeting: messages, phone calls, etc.;
- too lengthy; no time-frame;
- no agreed actions; poor minutes.

These complaints, however, are all attributable to a common source: poor organisation and control on the part of the chair. You will be well on your way to being an effective chair if you do not fall foul of any of the above. To that end, you should treat these serial complaints as a checklist of don'ts.

Put another way, the effective chair pays due regard to the planning and organisation of all aspects of the process, not just parts of it. They recognise that a successful outcome is as much dependent on what is done *before* the meeting, as it is on what happens *during* it, and equally what action is taken *after* it. As such they place equal value and importance on each stage.

Before the meeting

You should:

I   Plan

- Be clear about your precise objectives and why you need the meeting.

Meetings, as we've noted, often lack such objectives. Indeed they are invariably no more than a list of activities: e.g. a discussion of the latest government initiative on widening participation, and so on. The real objective would be the desired outcome from this activity, for example, 'to elicit people's points of view', 'to agree a course of action', 'to plan a course of action', 'to decide a response', etc. That is, the objective should be clear, explicit and challenging (and not implied, vague or non-existent). Objective setting is critical, for without it, it is unlikely the meeting will have an appropriate structure – and the structure of the meeting should flow logically from your objectives.

- List the subjects for:

  - information-giving (this may entail clarification: either way, this aspect should be kept to a minimum; circulate information via e-mail, voice-mail or internal post instead);

- information-gathering;
- decision-making;
- problem-solving.

II Inform

- Anticipate which people and what information may be needed.

In identifying participants you need to take into account that:

- the ideal meeting size is probably around seven to ten and certainly no more than fifteen (formal rules governing the membership of academic boards and senates, notwithstanding);
- meetings are not just time-consuming, but very expensive too: do your participants need to be there the whole time, or simply for a single item?

- If you need information, ask individuals to prepare a 'position statement' in advance of the meeting: one to two sides of A4 (maximum) in bullet point format.

- Ensure everyone knows what is being discussed and why.

There is nothing so irritating, nor so unnecessary, as for individuals to be asked to assemble in ignorance of the matter at hand. It not only guarantees a 'cold start' to any meeting but also limits the potential contribution of participants from the outset.

III Prepare

- Draw up a logical agenda and circulate, with papers, in good time; i.e. at least forty-eight hours in advance.

  - Schedule the most important, difficult or contentious items first to catch people when they are fresh.
  - Try to save a 'high note' item for the end to send people away in an upbeat mood. (Or, in the event that the meeting does not go well, you should at least be prepared to thank participants for their honesty.)
  - Do not permit 'any other business' (AOB), other than important announcements, unless it is cleared with you before the meeting. Otherwise you run the risk your meeting will be hijacked. It also encourages sloppy practice and time-wasting. To give of their best, participants need to be forewarned of an issue not confronted with it 'on the spot'.

Anticipate the length of the meeting, up to one hour preferably, certainly no more than two, and allocate time for each item on the basis of its importance. Some chairs also advertise this time limit for *each* item though it is a practice that can backfire, as it leaves you open to challenge for being presumptive, manipulative, etc., which itself precipitates yet more time-wasting. A more prudent course of action is to set a time limit for the meeting as a whole and to start the meeting at an unorthodox time, at a quarter to or quarter past the hour rather than on the hour. That way you convey the message to participants that time is important to you and also to them.

Determine and establish the most suitable physical setting for the meeting. It may seem self-evident that the actual layout and configuration of the meeting rooms can make a critical difference, yet it is surprising how often in practice this is left simply to chance, typically an inheritance from the room's former occupants. You should be proactive in this matter. Ideally you should hold your meetings in a convenient place, in surroundings that are reasonably comfortable (but not too comfortable), and arrange the seating in such a way that you have a clear view of everyone and they in turn have one of you and of everyone else. In other words, you should avoid the political gamesmanship inherent in the meeting configurations of some universities (the raised platform, the 'top table', the 'over-long' rectangle, the elongated tuning fork, the linear ranking, and so on). Depending on the circumstances, there may be occasions when you need, or want, to alter the group dynamic (for example, to facilitate group consultation or formal negotiation or team building, etc.). In which case you should consider assigning places to named individuals or alternatively breaking up the collective group into smaller sub-groups organised around different tables (for example, laid out in a circular fashion or in management parlance, 'cafeteria style'). Either way, the point is you should consciously reflect on the optimal physical configuration that will help you to realise your meeting's objectives.

During the meeting

You should aim:

- to keep control of the subject under discussion;
- to keep control of the people at the meeting.

This is far easier said than done. All your planning and preparation, however, will have been in vain if you fail to do so. As such you need to recognise that one of the main reasons why chairs fail in their duty is due to the inherent contradiction within their role: namely the expectation they should, as chair, remain uninvolved, disinterested and impartial, and suppress the impulse to intervene, even though they invariably have a direct and personal stake in the discussion in hand. In reality few can resist the temptation to participate. Getting involved in the subject matter of a meeting, however, while simultaneously chairing it, are two quite different things that simply do not mix.

And it is, of course, the case that some chairs deliberately choose to ignore this contradiction (often those intent on outright manipulation) while others bask in it (usually those eager to parade their knowledge, the so-called 'sage-on-the-stage'); and still others flounder on regardless (perhaps through misunderstanding, lack of self-esteem or other personal shortcomings). All these examples of poor practice, of role models *not* to follow, are familiar to many in higher education (see Box 4.10). To avoid joining them you must 'manage this contradiction' in a positive and constructive way. How? By conceiving of your role as that of 'facilitator' rather than 'chair'. These terms

Box 4.10 Chairing meetings: chairs we have endured . . . role models *not* to follow

- **The pedant** Sticks to the script and nothing but the script. A stickler for protocols and is obsessive about procedures rather than the process. Can't see the wood for the trees and doesn't let others in who can

- **The 'populist pretender'** A dedicated follower of fashion: unstintingly politically correct. Poses as 'man of the people' yet support for social inclusion and mass participation does not extend to those around the table. Speaks 'left of centre', acts well to the right.

- **The philosophiser** Takes (academic) 'heart on sleeve' very seriously. Boldly goes where few have gone before. An interesting and diversionary journey yet never arrives at a destination.

- **The 'fat controller'** Often well-meaning but has not graduated beyond traditional pedagogic style. Applies a didactic approach which yields predictable outcomes: apathy, boredom and non-engagement on the part of the majority.

- **The benevolent dictator** A charming and engaging character who leaves nothing to chance. Has it all 'done and dusted' beforehand, presents the group with a fait accompli and lines up the troops accordingly.

- **The dictator** As above, though without the style, wit, grace or charm. An unadorned bully.

- **The functioning cypher** Suffers from a distorted perception of corporate responsibility. Acts as a cypher for a higher authority. Abrogates responsibility for any decision or action. A 'yes man' who adds nothing, contributes nothing and alienates everyone.

- **The 'collegio-phile'** Wants to please all the people all the time. So wedded to, and self-conscious of, the collegiate tradition, is paralysed by indecision for fear of upsetting any colleague. More led by the gang than a leader of the gang.

are invariably used interchangeably to describe the conduct of meetings, yet they are in practice very different types of modus operandi (see Box 4.11).

As facilitator you are more a 'guide-by-the-side' and less the 'sage-on-the-stage'. This is not to say, however, that you have to deny any interest in the issues at stake, or have to adopt a laissez-faire approach to proceedings. On the contrary, you are there as 'custodian of the process' to guide the meeting in an informed and transparent manner. Thus, for example, you don't go into the meeting and say 'What shall we do?'. You go in and give a sense of direction: you present the case, outline the alternatives and say 'We can do a, or b, or c – what do you think?' To do otherwise is to abrogate your responsibility (see Box 4.12).

Put another way, it is your duty to:

- First of all, enforce time discipline. So start the meeting on time: 'on the dot'. Make no allowances for latecomers: i.e. start as you mean to go on.
- Clarify the objectives at the outset and check that all participants have a shared understanding.

Box 4.11 The differences between chairing and facilitating a meeting

The chair system	The facilitator system
Chair often has a direct and personal stake	Is impartial, looking only for a successful outcome
Relies on rules and procedures	Is rooted in common sense and courtesy
Identifies each idea with its owner	Uses teams and group dynamics
Calls for immediate valuation of input	Requires deferred judgement
Controls the flow of ideas and inputs	Ensures a free market for contributions
Is commonly rooted in mistrust	Is transparent, with no hidden agendas
Frequently is 'win–lose'	Aims for 'win–win' and consensus
Is open to manipulation	Ensures good behaviour, protects individuals
Underpins the 'sage-on-the-stage'	Offers a 'guide-by-the-side'

- Introduce each topic (the 'what') succinctly by putting it into context, explaining the purpose or objective (the 'how'), and outlining the alternatives (the 'means').
- Use your 'internal clock' to control the pace of the meeting so that the time allotted is proportionate to the gravity of the issues at hand.
- Keep the discussion to the point; ask questions of clarification and summarise at frequent intervals.
- Conclude each topic with a summary of what has been agreed or decided.
- Conclude the meeting by recapping the actions that have been placed on individuals and checking that all participants have a shared understanding.

These responsibilities are well known but, as we've said earlier, are not necessarily well done. The way in which you have physically configured the meeting should help you in this regard. And while there may be no substitute for experience, there are some practical guidelines you can follow which will make your task that much easier and your performance as chair more effective:

Seek to establish ground rules for your meetings, for example: to start and finish on time; no food or drink; no interruptions, and no side-bars when an individual is talking; a three-minute time limit for each speaker; etc.

Just as teachers face the difficult task of individuating learning in a mass system of HE, so you, as chair, must respect, value and foster contributions from all meeting participants. Ideally, all colleagues should feel able to, and be encouraged to, contribute in an open, honest and enthusiastic way. As not all colleagues will be so inclined, you will also need strategies to hand to deal with the many varied and idiosyncratic characters who populate university gatherings (see Box 4.13).

Do stick to a systematic approach to discussion: specify the issue or proposition; produce or hear the evidence; hear the arguments for and against; summarise the arguments; come to a conclusion or verdict; decide and record what action to take.

Box 4.12 The five stages of decision-taking: the five Cs

As guardian of the decision-making process, you should:

- Rehearse by yourself the five different stages involved in the solving of problems and the taking of decisions.*
- Be prepared to lead your colleagues through the same process – the five Cs.

(i) *Consider the issue and clarify the facts*
- Don't immediately react to the problem or issue. Take time to think about it.
- What is the problem or decision? Have you got all the facts? What additional information do you need?
- Who is involved in the problem or decision?
- How urgent is it? Must it be done now? What would happen if it were delayed?
- Are you dealing with the actual problem or just the symptom?
- What is the effect of the problem? What is the real cause?
- Why has this situation arisen?

(ii) *Consult with your colleagues*
- Use the meeting to draw on the existing experience and skills of your colleagues.
- Generate ideas, options, scenarios, alternatives.
- Identify the outcome you would like.

(iii) *Commit to a decision*
- Summarise the options available to you.
- Elaborate the pros and cons of each option.
- Make the decision.

(iv) *Communicate the decision*
- Take the action you have decided on.
- Communicate with all the individuals involved who will be affected by the action, using e-mail, voice-mail, memo, briefing, 'walk the job'.
- Explain the rationale for your decision and the process by which it was reached.
- Be assertive in helping to 'sell' the decision.

(v) *Check and evaluate the implementation*
- Monitor that the agreed actions are in fact being carried out.
- Has the problem or issue been solved?
- How can you avoid it reoccurring?
- What have you learned from the process?
- How can you pass that knowledge on to others?

By practising the five Cs you will avoid the most common causes of *bad* decision-making:

- **Complacency**   • **Taking the easy way out**   • **Prejudice**

* Decisions that is which require reflection and consultation – not the predictable operational ones which form part of the everyday norm or the ones you need to take in an emergency.

Source: adapted from The Industrial Society, 1996

Box 4.13 Chairing meetings: contributors you will recognise . . . and must handle

- **The rustler**   Always has papers ready and prepared for the meeting they've just come from and the meeting they're going to next but never the one they're actually in now! As such, constantly rifles through their material. Pin down quickly and identify papers for them lest distraction persists.
- **The chatterer**   Already thinks they're at the next meeting. Always wants to hold a separate meeting to the one they're actually attending. Shame them into silence by asking their opinion on the item they were not listening to. Remind them of the no side-bars rule.
- **The 'late arrival'**   Usually a recidivist. Do not make any allowances unless justified. Put them 'on the spot' soon after they arrive. They may reform their habit sooner rather than later.
- **The doomsday merchant**   'The department is doomed, the university is doomed. We're all doomed'. Don't necessarily take the interjection seriously. Test out the views of others. Carefully dissect the nature of the issues at hand. Stick strictly to the facts, not opinion.
- **The cynic**   'Who gives a stuff anyway?' Appeal to others to respond. If not forthcoming then respond yourself but keep it brief. A prolonged dialogue may do more harm than good. Make a mental note to have a one-to-one with the individual within the next three days.
- **The oppressed**   'We've had enough. We can't do anymore'. Has full-blown victim complex. Time and energy wholly consumed in worrying. Review workload and agree a customised professional development programme including counselling, if necessary.
- **The 'Trot'**   Wears several hats. Is often engaging in private if menacing in public. Espouses the most radical of political ideologies yet typically practises the most conservative of teaching pedagogies. A revolutionary keen on upholding academic tradition (and preserving their own privileges). Don't let the irony get the better of you. A 'straight bat' is the safest bet.
- **The comedian**   In moderation – a terrific aid in facilitating the work of the group; one to cherish. In excess – one to muzzle outside the meeting.
- **The 'old sea dog'**   'Been there, seen that, done it and got the T-shirt to prove it.' Often has much to offer, and is willing to, if you can get beneath the world-weariness. Cajole and encourage to give more and do it yet again!
- **The maverick**   A loose cannon in every sense. Nobody's fool, proud and independent and not without influence. Often has much to offer yet too unpredictable. Prime them in advance. Seek out their views beforehand and respect and value their contribution.
- **The barrack-room lawyer**   A pedant of the rule book and champion of 'points of order'. Engage with first time round. Use group members to assert the primacy of the (agreed) process over that of formality and procedure. Don't let them sulk. Bring them back into the fold.
- **The unsung hero**   A hidden gem. For whatever reason too self-effacing by half. Often a font of wisdom and an invaluable source of new ideas. Sees things others don't including you. Nurture and encourage at every opportunity.
- **The MBO**   'Master of the bleedin' obvious'. Invariably means well but has the irritating habit of reiterating what everyone knows already. Can be an asset when you and others have 'lost the plot'; otherwise interject without giving offence – summarise – and move on.
- **The 'tribune of the people'**   A class warrior with mono-mania tendencies. Is only too willing to let you know they've got 'your number'. Don't rise to the bait but do show you're not 'just another suit'. Make a genuine effort to get them to make the valuable contribution of which they're capable.
- **The oracle**   A loyal pillar of the institution, touchstone of the department and a fount of stories, gossip and myths about the past. Knows where you've been and how you got there. Respect and value their contribution and they will more often than not be a godsend in times of change.

Unite *the group*

• Be open, honest and enthusiastic yourself. Genuinely aspire to a win–win outcome.

• Be open about acceptable forms of dissent and negativity.

• Do not, however, resort to gimmicks, unless you and your group jointly agree them. And even then, think again about the consequences. The decision by the BBC for example, like that of an American HEI, to import football's yellow card system into meetings (encouraging participants to wave a yellow card bearing the words 'Cut the crap, make it happen' at anyone perceived to be blocking a good idea) is more symptomatic of a public corporation desperate to change its bureaucratic culture, than it is a considered or viable means of achieving change (Snoddy, 2002). Which is not to say such devices are not effective. On the contrary, they can be a very powerful tool in influencing behaviour. However, the risks associated with them are much greater because the device is particularly open to abuse and the likely consequences can be as often negative as positive.

• If there is a disproportionate number of procrastinators in your group, schedule your meetings either prior to lunch or towards the end of the day. The desire to get away will often focus people's attention and curb their natural propensity to verbosity.

• Don't be afraid of 'healthy' aggression. Allow others to let off steam; to 'get things off their chest'.

• Do be wary, however, of 'unhealthy' aggression which invariably leads to 'a stand-off dialogue between the deaf'. In such instances, do not take sides. Remain impartial. Be aware of those who 'withdraw from the group' and seek to bring in others. Ask value-free questions. Stick to facts, not opinions. Never ask an individual for their opinion if they're aggressive.
If the aggression is aimed at you – do not feel obliged to respond to every remonstrance. Keep an even temper, even if provoked (if you lose your temper in public, your credibility will suffer too). Stick to the same approach. Remember not everyone will agree or feel comfortable with the aggrieved parties even if it might seem that way. Agree to meet with the aggrieved parties – but not later that same day. Move on to the next business.

Focus *the group*

• Stay alert. Keep 'a hand on the wheel'. Steer clear of rogue issues and red herrings.

• Be proactive. Keep asking questions. Test the group's understanding.

• Paraphrase the debate and seek approbation. Modify as appropriate.

Mobilise *the group*

- Protect and draw out the quieter members of the group.

- Do not jump to 'quick fix' instant solutions. Take time to consider the pros and cons of alternatives.

- Check round the group if two or three individuals are dominating the discussion.

- Record suggestions as they're stated.

- Be open to, and build up, ideas, including those you may initially feel are 'whacky'.

Take 'a leaf out of the book' of others. Just as there are some chairs who set a poor example there are others who offer an exemplary one. Like the referee of a football match who has a 'good game', these are conspicuous by their apparent absence. Yet they will invariably have done their homework beforehand: by eliciting support for a particular proposal, having others introduce it rather than themselves, and by gaining the confidence of those might oppose them. During the meeting they always manage to strike the right balance between direction and consultation, have a catlike sensitivity for those who may feel excluded, and maintain a brisk pace, sound order and good humour throughout, even in the most difficult circumstances. Most important-antly they 'get the job done' by moving beyond the inevitable divisions of opinion towards an agreed plan of action. It is these role models, those who chair seamlessly with such apparent ease, you should seek out in your own institution. Observe them, learn from them. Emulate them.

After the meeting

You should:

- Reflect and review whether or not the meeting was successful in achieving the set objectives; what went well? What could have gone better? Test your perceptions against the views of others whose opinion you value.

- Double-check and proof-read the 'minutes' and circulate them to all participants as soon as practicable after the meeting and no later than three days afterwards.

- Minutes in the literal sense, i.e. a detailed summation of arguments and actions, are not always necessary or indeed desirable. They are usually required nowadays only (and not always even then) in the case of formal academic committees. For the purpose of 'business meetings', however, you should focus on producing a brief set of notes with transparent action points. As this is not always so straightforward – and there is indeed a general tendency within universities to underestimate and under-value minute-taking as a skill – be prepared to take advantage of the professional guidance your minute-taker can offer. Fortunately there is now just such a pro-fessional cadre of minute-takers in most universities; a legacy for the most part of the demands made on HEIs by external agencies such as the QAA. If your assistant is not one of them you should ensure they are trained in like manner. This small investment will reap you a great dividend.

- Most importantly, check that:
  - those who are responsible for taking actions actually receive the notes of the meeting;
  - they do indeed carry out the actions as agreed: that is, you should not let the process simply slide into abeyance but rather monitor their progress (without 'over-managing' them) in implementing the action(s) in accordance with the agreed timescale.

Team building

The ability to schedule, organise and handle meetings in constructive ways which lead to meaningful action, is a critical leadership skill, albeit an underrated one. Your success in this regard will make a significant contribution to the way in which your department operates. You will need to develop this momentum, however, if your department is to build and realise its collective 'shared vision'. In particular, you need to examine ways in which you can actively and deliberately promote dialogue, collaboration and teamworking.

Put another way, you must avoid making the same mistake that has ensnared so many other leaders: i.e. assuming (falsely) that you can achieve everything by yourself. Attractive though this proposition may be, and particularly so to those of a very self-confident disposition, its adherents invariably share the same tragic fate: total burn-out to no good effect. The simple reality is that much of what we can achieve as leaders can be done only with the help and consent of others. Hence the necessity for collaboration.

This need is more difficult to meet, however, in an academic setting than in the conventional business one. We are all familiar, for example, with the celebrated practices of the lone researcher and the teacher who proclaims: 'I am God in the universe as soon as I close the classroom door', as well as the contention that universities are characterised by a tribal culture rather than a team one – a condition famously reflected in the observation, now a tired cliché, that managing university academics is akin to 'herding cats'. And yet it is equally the case that the nature of teaching and research is evolving in ways which will necessitate collaborative effort if they are to be fruitful: the shift towards the facilitating rather than the directing of learning; the external assessment of research on the basis of unit rather than individual contribution; etc.

Nor is it nearly so alien as traditionalists would have us believe. At Miami University, Ohio, for instance, teamwork is explicitly acknowledged as one of six core values which make up the university's 'academic quality model', a conceptual framework that is applied to all the institution's units (department, division, college and office) (see Figure 4.1). Three values drive unit relationships: leadership, mutual trust and teamwork. Leadership entails 'creating a shared vision of a quality culture and

ACADEMIC QUALITY MODEL

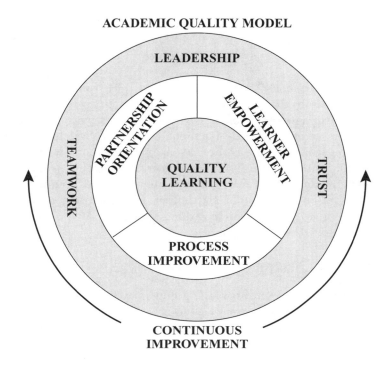

Figure 4.1 Academic quality model: Miami University, Ohio
Source: Shulman, 1998

modelling behaviours consistent with that philosophy' while trust refers 'to the positive expectations (openness, reliability, caring and competence) between chair and department members'. And teamwork 'enhances collaboration to create synergistic outcomes that surpass the wisdom of individuals'.

An additional three values are recognised as guiding individual actions: learner (faculty/staff) empowerment, the acquisition of process improvement skills and a partnership orientation. Learner empowerment involves 'giving faculty and staff the permission, power and protection to make decisions so that they become involved, self-sufficient, responsible, committed and intrinsically motivated'. Process improvement uses 'objective and subjective data for analysis of the work system and decision-making'. And finally, a partnership orientation anticipates 'focusing on satisfying the validated needs of people engaged in professional relationships (i.e. internal and external department constituents)' (Shulman, 1998).

How then can you develop teamwork as a means of enhancing the effectiveness of your department?

I   First, cognisant of the above *you should be wary of the language you use*. Talking about 'teamwork' in an abstract sense is more than likely to have the opposite effect you wish, a collective mental 'switching-off'. Rather you should regard your role as that of fostering and nurturing a dialogue with colleagues on the concrete matters that collectively face you. Indeed for Senge (1990b) 'the discipline of team learning starts with *dialogue*, the capacity of members of a team to suspend assumptions and enter into a genuine "thinking together"'.

You need to help establish an environment in which colleagues feel confident enough to do just that: to discuss their ideas openly; to articulate their assumptions without ridicule; to disagree in a constructive sense; to discover insights not attainable individually – in other words, a setting in which collegiality can genuinely flourish. Again you will need to lead, by personal example, in the way in which you seek to lay the foundations of such an environment: principally, as indicated in the Miami University model, that of trust and, one might also add, mutual respect. The irony of course, and one you should use, is that, far from being an alien business concept, teamwork in its essence is nothing other than the positive aspect of the collegial spirit writ large.

II That said, you need to recognise that:

• *Teams are not the same as groups*. While groups may be little more than a collection of individuals who believe themselves to be a group, teams are special in that they manage to accomplish more than the sum total of its individual members. They evolve from groups who have learned to work together skilfully and achieve, in management jargon 'synergy' or as it is sometimes expressed '1+1=3' (because you count the 'plus', which represents the interaction between different people, the 'ones'). In fact, 'a real team' as Jon Katzenbach (1997) puts it is characterised by a 'discipline of team basics': that is, it is 'a *small number* of people with *complementary skills* who are committed to a *common purpose, performance goals* and an *approach* for which they hold themselves *mutually accountable*'. In other words they can, in practice, differ from groups in almost every conceivable way (see Box 4.14).

Box 4.14 Characteristic differences between teams and groups

Activity	Members of groups tend to be ...	Members of teams tend to be ...
Dependence	Independent	Interdependent
Ownership	'Hired hands'	Owners of the process
Contribution	Directed	Encouraged
Climate	Divisive	Trusting
Communication	Cautious 'game players'	Open and honest
Training	Constrained by dominant supervisors	Mutually supportive of development
Involvement	Individually uninvolved	Collectively engaged

Source: based on Maddix, 1998; Fraser and Neville, 1993

- *It is the differences rather than the similarities between members that is the critical factor in determining team success*: the interplay of different individuals with different ways of behaving and their willingness to undertake a specific role. Meredith Belbin (1990) has, as is well known, demonstrated that effective teams tend to be comprised of eight such role types (see Box 4.15). Put another way, and this is significant in terms of the HE environment, team success is not simply a function of talent and intelligence. Indeed, Belbin discovered that the teams that managers were predisposed to select (invariably the cleverest and most talented people they could find) were, in fact, the ones most likely to fail in practice!

- *Teams are not static but have their own internal dynamic*. They typically evolve through four different stages of development, forming, storming, norming and performing, each of which has its own distinctive characteristics requiring you to adapt your leadership style accordingly (see Box 4.16).

- *Team performance is often hampered by the persistence of a number of enduring myths*:
  - *That a team should function as a team whenever it meets*. This myth suggests that every task to be tackled, no matter how routine, should automatically qualify as a team opportunity. In practice, routine matters are better handled by meeting as a working group and teamwork reserved for the tougher more challenging activities.
  - *That teams need to spend more time together building consensus*. This myth assumes that building consensus is synonymous with reducing conflict and that less conflict will somehow lead to more team-like behaviour. In practice, real teams do not avoid (constructive) conflict – they thrive on it. Nor is it always the case that decisions built on consensus are necessarily better than those handed down by individuals.
  - *That teamwork will automatically lead to improved team performance*. This myth assumes that, by focusing solely on the four Cs of effective teamwork (communication, cooperation, collaboration and compromise), an improvement in team performance is guaranteed to follow. In reality teamwork and team performance are two different things and the latter will only be achieved if team members are equally rigorous in applying the 'discipline of team basics'.
  - *That teams composed of the 'brightest and the best' will inevitably outperform any other*. Or, put another way, assuming that those immediately around you have the necessary requisite skills to be an effective top-performing team. This is simply not always the case, not even for senior management teams and so-called 'top teams'. See Belbin (1990).

III   Whether starting from scratch or having inherited an existing group of individuals *you should consider your options carefully*. Teams go by a variety of different names according to their various purposes and goals.

One common way forward is to collectively bring together as a departmental management team those you intend holding one-to-ones with on a regular basis, i.e. those individuals with significant responsibilities.

Box 4.15 Belbin's eight individual types that contribute to effective team performance

Type	Team role	Positive qualities	Allowable weaknesses
Chair/ coordinator	• Coordinates the way the team moves towards group objectives • Makes the best use of team resources • Recognises team strengths and weaknesses • Maximises the potential of each team member	• Welcomes all contributions on their merit • Strong sense of objectives	• Is unlikely to be the most creative member of the team
Shaper	• Shapes the way in which team effort is channelled • Directs attention to the setting of objectives and priorities • Seeks to impose a shape or pattern on group discussions and outcomes	• Drive and a readiness to challenge inertia, ineffectiveness, complacency and self-deception	• Prone to provocation, irritation and impatience
Plant	• Advances new ideas and strategies • Pays special attention to major issues • Creative approach to problem-solving	• Imagination, intellect, knowledge	• Inclined to disregard practical details or protocol
Resource investigator	• Explores and reports on ideas and developments outside the team • Creates external contacts	• Capacity for contacting people and exploring anything new • Ability to respond to challenge	• Loses interest once the initial fascination has passed
Monitor/ evaluator	• Analyses problems, evaluates ideas and suggestions • Enables team to take balanced decisions	• Judgement, discretion, hard-headedness	• May lack inspiration and ability to motivate others
Implementer	• Turns concepts and plans into practical working procedures • Carries out agreed plans systematically and efficiently	• Organising ability, practical common sense • Self-discipline, hard-working	• Lack of flexibility, unresponsive to new or unproven ideas
Teamworker	• Supports team members in their strengths • Builds on suggestions • Compensates for team members' shortcomings • Improves communication between members	• Ability to respond to people and situations • Promotes team spirit	• May be indecisive at moments of crisis
Finisher	• Ensures nothing has been overlooked • Checks details • Maintains a sense of urgency	• Capacity for follow-through • Perfectionism	• Tendency to worry about small things • Reluctant to let go

Source: adapted from Belbin, 1990

Another, the optimum size of teams as 6–10 members notwithstanding, is to conceive of your whole department as a team.

And still another is to identify and establish a variety of single purpose groups organised around the main challenges facing the department – e.g. a strategic issues group, a departmental policy forum, a learner experience set, a commercial development group, a research and innovation body, a quality circle, etc. – and then staff them on the basis of the range of skills individuals will bring to their respective teams, rather than on the basis of their formal title or position.

Each of these ways is equally valid and you should not feel obliged to stick rigidly to any particular one. Indeed you should above all aim to be open-minded and flexible in your approach irrespective of the size of your department.

IV   *You should indeed attend to the basics of effective teamwork by actively seeking to nurture the four Cs.*

• Agree a team code of conduct such as:

    – to respect each member;
    – to criticise ideas, never people;
    – to listen actively;
    – to seek to understand before being understood;
    – to contribute thoughts, feelings and questions;
    – to keep an open mind;
    – to share responsibility;
    – to attend all meetings.

• Undertake formal team building activities through away-days, retreats and the like: away-days, that is, in the genuine sense of the term, organised sessions held off-site to 'step back' and explore issues over and above the everyday run-of-the-mill and not, that is, as they are too frequently (mis-)used nowadays, as a vehicle for an elongated meeting, held on-site more often than not, and devoted to matters of immediate concern. See the CIPD's (Chartered Institute of Personnel and Development) portfolio for an extensive range of authenticated activities that you can use in promoting effective teamwork within your own group.

• Establish peer support networks in:

    – research – fortnightly or monthly seminars; grant application syndicates; publications workshops; 'brown bag' luncheons to discuss 'work in progress'; outside speakers forum;
    – learning and teaching – a peer review of teaching scheme; a pedagogical innovation workshop; a learning and teaching research seminar; an employers' liaison forum.

V   *You should seek to encourage and increase individual team member's awareness of their team role by analysing the composition of your new or existing or inherited team.*

One way of doing this is by asking all your team members to complete the questionnaire Belbin himself devised to identify self–team role preferences (see Fraser

Box 4.16 Moving through the four stages of team development

Characteristic behaviours

Stage 1: Forming

- Attempts to define the task and decide how it will be accomplished
- Attempts to determine acceptable group behaviour
- Attempts to determine how to deal with problems
- Decisions on information to be gathered to solve a problem
- Abstract discussions of concepts and issues, and for some, impatience with such discussions and a desire to get on with the task in hand
- Discussions of symptoms or problems not relevant to the task in hand
- Difficulty in identifying relevant problems
- Complaints about the organisation and barriers to the task in hand

Stage 2: Storming

- Arguing amongst members even when actually agreeing on the real issues
- Defensiveness and competition between team members
- The emergence of factions and 'taking sides'
- Questioning everything: 'why should we do it this way?'
- Establishing unrealistic goals
- Concerns about excessive work
- A perceived 'pecking order', leading to disunity, tension and jealousy

Stage 3: Norming

- An attempt to achieve harmony by avoiding conflict
- More friendliness, confiding and a sharing of personal problems
- Better discussions and the development of effective team dynamics
- A sense of team cohesion, with a common spirit and goals
- The establishment and maintenance of team ground rules and boundaries
- Clearly defined roles
- The establishment of a framework of formal and informal communication

Stage 4: Reforming

- Humour used in a constructive way to progress the task
- Constructive self-change
- The ability to prevent team problems or work through them
- A close attachment to the team
- Accepting responsibility for themselves and for the achievement

Sources: adapted from Fraser and Neville, 1993; Turner, 1998

Development actions

Leader's style: *Tell*

- Get to know and access one another
- Examine the function and purpose of the team
- Look at the skills, knowledge, cohesiveness and balance already present
- Identify the blocks, frustrations and culture
- Don't jump to conclusions too quickly and impose 'instant' changes

Leader's style: *Sell*

- Debate risky issues
- Consider wider options
- Encourage openness and feedback
- Handle conflict positively
- Remember it takes time to build trust
- Bring in external help if necessary

Leader's style: *Participate*

- Maintain openness
- Regular team review
- Encourage challenges to established ways of doing things
- Celebrate success
- Focus on individual as well as team developments

Leader's style: *Delegate*

- Be wary that established methods do not become an end in themselves
- Remember to look outwards
- Nurture creativity

and Neville, 1993). This activity is a relatively low-risk one for both individual members and the team in that it is confined to highlighting strengths and 'allowable weaknesses'. There are thus no winners or losers in the analysis.

More than that, it not only satisfies the inherent curiosity of individual members who want to 'see how I come out and how others score in my team', but also yields a most valuable insight on others' self-perception, which in turn typically generates an animated and usually good-natured discussion on the outcomes. It, furthermore, enables the team to modify its behaviour to compensate for any obvious omissions in its role make-up highlighted by the questionnaire. Thus the team, for example, which struggled to meet deadlines in the past for want of an obvious 'finisher' could formally assign an individual to undertake this responsibility for each task or project as it arises.

That said, there can, of course, be drawbacks to team role indicators: they are based on subjective perceptions that can lead to stereotyping (as in, 'What do you expect? Colin is a shaper!') and having all the roles filled does not automatically guarantee success. Overall, however, team role awareness should enable you to heighten both the sense of expectation and responsibility on the part of your individual members while simultaneously enhancing the degree of your collective group consciousness for the better.

VI *You should seek to identify your team's development needs, and to raise your collective group consciousness still further, by reviewing your team's progress along the 'forming, storming, norming, performing' development continuum.*

Again, this activity, like the previous one, is based on self-perception and self-assessment. Unlike the previous one, however, which your team should find relatively straightforward to handle itself, this activity has a greater likelihood of generating a more authentic and reliable outcome if facilitated by an outside party. As such, you should enlist the services of your management development adviser, or an experienced colleague respected by all your team's members, or perhaps an external consultant. Whichever you choose, their role would be to tease out your members' perceptions, both individually and collectively, of the functioning and effectiveness of the team.

One simple, yet very illuminating, way of doing this is to conceive of the team development process as a 'clock face', with the undeveloped (forming) team starting at midnight, and evolving through the experimenting (storming) and consolidating (norming) stages to reach maturity (the performing team) within twenty-four hours.

In essence you and your team members should be aiming:

- to identify which stage of development, or 'time on the clock face', the team is currently at; and to share your views freely with one another;
- to identify and explore any issues of concern around the team's development and the *internal* and *external* perceptions of your team;
- to explore and identify strategies which can take your team forward to the next stage;
- to identify team development needs and how they can be met.

Put another way, this 'team development clock' activity will help bring out perceptions which are often striking in contrast, but which would otherwise remain hidden;

Box 4.17 School management team development at one UK 'new' (post-1992) university: characteristic perceptions and behaviours

Undeveloped team →→→ **Experimenting team**

Undeveloped team

- Unclear objectives, values and guiding principles
- Bureaucracy and lack of informal communication
- Weaknesses covered up
- Poor listening skills
- Workplace is only for work
- Feelings and stress not dealt with
- Role conflict and lack of recognition of individual's areas of expertise and accountabilities
- No 'rocking the boat'
- Lack of equality in team
- One or more team members seen as outsiders or scapegoats
- Head of school takes most decisions and seen as a strong leader without vulnerabilities

Experimenting team

- Greater openness
- Experimentation and risk-taking
- Increased listening
- Challenging and confronting each other
- Issues of concern debated and grievances aired
- Failure regarded as learning opportunity
- Questioning of problem-solving and decision-making methods
- Review of team performances begins
- Head of school offers high level of facilitation and begins to share her/his own needs

Mature team ←←← **Consolidating team**

Mature team

- Experimentation *plus* consolidation *plus* flexibility
- Bridges built with other teams inside and outside the school
- Willingness to learn from other teams
- Team leadership changes with the needs of the task
- Experiments with different forms of leadership
- Insularity and a sense of being better or different is resisted
- Team provides enhanced input into meeting wider needs of university
- Team functioning open to external evaluation
- Maximum use of individual and team energy
- Team and individuals are role models and change agents for other school teams
- High levels of support given to each other
- All members contribute equally to the facilitation of continuing team development

Consolidating team

- Agreed procedures and established ground rules by which the team and individual members operate
- Balance of experimentation and methodical working
- Team problem-solving and decision-making skills develop
- Team develops capacity to compensate for individual weaknesses
- Individuals' skills are developed
- Strengths are shared and successes are celebrated
- Team performance and objectives regularly reviewed and improvements implemented
- Increased levels of support given to each other
- Head of school gives moderate level of facilitation and enables other team members to develop facilitative skills

differences of view, that is, which are invariably stimulating in themselves and which you can use to enhance the working of your team.

One UK 'new' university used this development tool to good effect when it established a new academic structure based on schools of study. In doing so, it identified the characteristics that typified school management teams as they evolved through different stages (see Box 4.17). Can you identify where your team is in this cycle?

VII   *Finally, you should develop the habit of reviewing your team on a regular basis.* This practice is as important for teams as it is for individuals. Use the signifiers listed below as a checklist to guide the review of your team's performance every three months. Regular reviews, when combined with your understanding of team development and your support in helping your team to move through the different stages, can have a significant impact on your team's effectiveness (Moores, 1994).

Checklist for reviewing your team's performance:

- clarity and understanding of roles;
- achievement of the team's objectives;
- openness and confrontation;
- support and trust;
- cooperation and conflict;
- procedures;
- appropriate leadership;
- development of individuals;
- good relationship with other groups;
- good communications (Woodcock, 1989).

Handling conflict

Team building is neither a smooth nor uncontested process. Not everyone is prepared to help or to give their consent. On the contrary, since people, psychologists tell us, do not really 'change their spots' between home and work, that is they bring their 'unseen baggage' with them to work even if they believe they don't, you should not be surprised if emotions run high. Put another way, you need to recognise that conflict is an inevitable corollary of the team building process. And you must anticipate and prepare to handle it (Fraser and Neville, 1993).

We have already noted that conflict is not without merit; that it can be constructive as much as destructive and that good teams thrive on it. This is because conflict is used in such a way, as a source of energy and creativity, to allow new ideas to surface and to create positive forces for innovation and change. Handled constructively then, conflict enables individuals to examine their ideas and beliefs and to stretch their imagination, thereby providing the team with a wider range of options and the prospect of a more favourable outcome. Conflict is unhealthy, however, when it is either avoided or approached solely on a win–lose basis. Handled destructively in this way, conflict will manifest itself, at best, in a breakdown in communication and a deterioration in mutual trust and support, and, at worst, in open hostility and revolt. Either outcome would have a deleterious effect on your department, your institution and your own credibility. How then can you avoid such a scenario? How do you handle conflict constructively?

I   *By not being taken off guard.* Conflict does not come out of the blue and you should be alert to the early warning signs: silence and withdrawal, anger, dissent and intransigence escalating to open dispute and meeting walkouts.

Put another way, understanding your departmental environment and knowing that conflict arises from individuals' 'unseen' (but, often, not unknown emotional) 'baggage' (i.e. their differing needs, objectives, values and beliefs; perceptions and motives; expectations and levels of commitment), you should be able to anticipate the degree to which prospective changes or issues are likely to be contentious, and to monitor them. Thus knowing how the conflict is developing you will be better equipped to deal with it.

Conversely, if you have a group in which everyone gets on well together and there are no public disagreements you should not delude yourself into thinking you have an effective team. Very often such teams are inhibited by *group think*, the reluctance to discuss individual members' ideas openly for fear of upsetting the group consensus. A condition which not only perpetuates poor decision-making and low performance, but also may conceal the cumulative build-up of individual frustrations and resentments too.

II   *By recognising there is no single best way of handling conflict; or that the alternatives are limited solely to fight or flight.* There are in fact five different ways in which we can approach conflict:

non-confrontational strategies
* avoiding: 'leave well enough alone';
* accommodating: 'kill your enemies with kindness';

control strategies
* competing: 'might makes right';

solution-oriented strategies
* collaborating: 'two heads are better than one';
* compromising: 'split the difference'.

Each of us is capable of all five conflict-handling modes (Thomas and Kilmann, 1974). Their effectiveness, however, is of course dependent both on the circumstances and the skill with which they are applied. You need to ensure therefore that, since all five are useful in some situations, *you select the 'right' mode to fit the particular requirements of the conflict situation* (see Box 4.18).

Knowing *when* and *where* to apply it is one thing. *Doing* it, however, is quite another. Each of us, for example, has our own set of social skills, our different predispositions and our preferred ways of handling discord. You need to recognise, however, that these may lead you to rely upon some approaches more, or less, than you should. To use them, that is, in situations which do not warrant it while neglecting other approaches which would be better suited. Taken too far your predisposition could well have adverse consequences. Box 4.19 helps you to identify the potential dangers and the associated risks which you must counter. Again you should take heart, these warning signs and risks are not insurmountable, for they are a legacy of the styles you've learned or failed to learn in the past. There is no reason why you cannot develop anew.

III *Through the adoption of an assertive rather than an aggressive or non-confrontational approach in those instances in which your goal is conflict resolution (i.e. the great majority with which you will have to contend).*

You should recognise that while there may be occasions when it is best to let things go (why risk losing the war for the sake of a minor battle?) and others where prudence is the most appropriate course of action (is the benefit really worth the amount of hassle?), the option that offers the greatest potential is that of facing the conflict rather than avoiding it or diffusing it. How you face it though makes all the difference. Tackling it aggressively for example, by: exaggerating your case; belittling and interrupting the other party; dogmatically refusing to make concessions, and so on – may well reap you dividends but the effect will not be lasting, and you are more than likely to alienate your colleagues. Handling it assertively, on the other hand, offers you not only the best prospect of resolving the conflict but also in a way that may benefit all.

Managing conflict assertively means you should seek to do the following:

–   Examine the cause:

  • work with the other parties;
  • attack the problem, not the people;
  • allow others to 'let off steam';
  • listen actively, show you understand their views;
  • value openness.

–   Clarify expectations:

  • focus on interests and compatible areas;
  • list interests;
  • ask questions, don't make statements;
  • encourage questions;
  • be hard on the problem, not the people.

–   Develop options for mutual gain:

  • divide the problem into smaller and more manageable units;
  • agree on common areas of interest;
  • clarify remaining areas of disagreement;
  • look for new ways or thoughts; brainstorm; generate new ideas;
  • ask for their preferences;
  • involve other parties (if helpful).

Box 4.18 The five ways to handle conflict and when to apply them

Style	Conflict management approach	Characteristic context: the circumstances in which you should apply it	Assessment
Competing 'I win, you lose'	• Assertive and uncooperative • Must win at all costs • Entails 'standing up for your rights' • Defending a position which you believe is correct	• When quick, decisive action is vital, e.g. emergencies • On important issues where unpopular courses of action need implementing; e.g. discipline, cost cutting, enforcing unpopular rules • On issues vital to the organisation's welfare, and when you know you are right • To protect yourself against people who take advantage of non-competitive behaviour	• A power-oriented mode you should be careful in using • Are the benefits worth the cost, possibly in lost goodwill?
Accommodating 'I lose you win'	• Unassertive and cooperative (the opposite of competing) • Agreeable to others at the expense of oneself • Entails selfless generosity • Yielding to another's point of view when you would prefer not to	• When you realise that you are wrong – to allow a better position to be heard, to learn from others and to show that you are reasonable • When issues are more important to others than to you – to satisfy others and maintain cooperation • To build up social credits for later issues • To minimise loss when you are outmatched and losing • When preserving harmony and avoiding disruption are especially important • To help other develop by learning from mistakes	• Not good strategy if done out of fear or reluctance • Good if the issue is more important to the other person and you want to show goodwill
Avoiding 'I lose, you lose'	• Unassertive and uncooperative • Does not address the conflict • Entails sidestepping or postponing an issue	• When an issue is trivial, or more important issues are pressing • When you perceive no chance of satisfying your concerns	• Fine when the issue is unimportant but wrong if burying it stores up long-term trouble

- Or simply withdrawing

- When potential disruption outweighs the benefits of resolution
- To let people cool down and regain perspective
- When gathering more information outweighs the advantages of an immediate decision
- When others can resolve the conflict more effectively
- When the issues seem tangential or symptomatic of another more basic issue

Collaborating
'I win, you win'

- Assertive and cooperative (the opposite of avoiding)
- Working with others for mutual gain
- Entails digging into an issue, exploring disagreements, learning from one another and searching for creative solutions

- To find an integrative solution when both sets of concerns are too important to be compromised
- When your objective is to learn – e.g. to test your assumptions; understand the views of others
- To merge insights from people with different perspectives
- To gain commitment by incorporating other's concerns into a consensual decision
- To work through hard feelings which have interfered with an interpersonal relationship

- Overcoming hard feelings and assimilating different concerns and perspectives could lead to a superior solution when commitment to that is important
- It is not a good approach, however, when time is pressing

Compromising
'I win and maybe let you win more'

- Intermediate in both assertive-ness and cooperativeness; a middle ground between competing and accommodating
- Entails seeking an expedient, mutually acceptable solution which partially satisfies both parties

- When goals are moderately important, but not worth the effort or potential disruption of more assertive modes
- When two opponents with equal power are strongly committed to mutually exclusive goals, for example in management–trade union bargaining
- To achieve temporary settlements to complex issues
- To arrive at expedient solutions under time pressure
- As a back-up mode when collaboration or competition fails to be successful

- Not as good as many would have us believe
- Both parties can be unhappy at giving up something
- Decisions are fuzzy

Source: adapted from Thomas and Kilmann, 1974

Box 4.19 Potential risks of your own preferred style of handling conflict

Questions you should ask yourself if you rely on this approach more or less than you should   *Risk*

Competing

If more: – Are you surrounded by 'yes men'? – You close yourself off from vital information

– Do colleagues find it difficult to confess ignorance and uncertainties to you? – You fail to help those around you to learn

If less: – Do you often feel impotent in situations? – You restrict your influence unnecessarily

– Do you find it hard to take a firm stand, even when you see the need? – You exacerbate the suffering and resentment of others

Accommodating

If more: – Do you feel your ideas and concerns do not receive the attention they deserve? – You lose influence, respect and recognition within the department

– Do staff have a casual approach to fulfilling obligations? – You lose the respect of other stakeholders

If less: – Do you find it difficult to build up goodwill with colleagues? – You miss opportunities which are important to others, if not yourself

– Do colleagues consider you to be unreasonable? – You will not be able to garner support when you need it most

Avoiding

If more: – Do others complain about getting your inputs on issues? Is your coordination impaired as a consequence? – You become a 'lame duck'

– Does it often seem that others are 'walking on eggshells'? – You ignore issues that urgently need addressing

– Are decisions on important issues made by accident rather than design? – You end up with a poor decision and maybe the wrong one

If less: – Do you often find yourself stirring up hostility in others? – You stoke up unnecessary conflict through your lack of discretion

– Do you often feel swamped by a number of competing issues? – You fail to prioritise what is really important

Collaborating

If more: – Do you devote a disproportionate amount of time and effort on issues that do not warrant it? – You waste your most precious resources – time and energy

– Is your collaborative behaviour failing to elicit a collaborative response from others? – You may be overlooking some cues – defensiveness, impatience, conflict, competition

If less:	– Do you find it difficult to see differences as opportunities for mutual gain?	– You are being unduly pessimistic
	– Are your colleagues uncommitted to departmental decisions and policies?	– You will not establish 'ownership' if their concerns are not addressed

Compromising

If more:	– Do you focus so much upon the practicalities and tactics of compromise that you sometimes lose sight of the 'bigger picture': principles, values, objectives, institutional welfare?	– You compromise your own position
	– Is the emphasis on bargaining and negotiating creating a cynical climate of gamesmanship?	– You sacrifice the merits of the issues being discussed
If less:	– Are you embarrassed or too sensitive in bargaining situations to be effective?	– You lose an opportunity you can ill afford
	– Do you find it difficult to make concessions?	– You make a 'rod for your own back'

Source: adapted from Thomas and Kilmann, 1974

–   Agree a course of action:

   • relate the problem to your work objectives;
   • ask for their solutions;
   • present your preferred solution;
   • agree mutual actions;
   • explore ways of avoiding repetition of conflict.

All this, of course, sounds fine in theory, but will be harder to achieve in practice. And particularly so since our reasoning is strongly affected by our emotions, and most of us find it difficult to be completely rational when dealing with conflict. Nevertheless, provided you have, or are prepared to develop, the necessary advanced interpersonal skills (self-awareness, strong listening and observational skills, empathy, and a fundamental belief that the other person's point of view may be right, as well as the ability to 'read situations'), you are, or will be, well equipped to achieve control in conflict situations. Acquiring and maintaining such skills and applying the most appropriate conflict-handling mode will not be easy. And you may well need professional training to help you. Either way, there is no reason why, with practise and growing confidence, you should not succeed, or be denied the satisfaction that conflict resolution can bring: a job well done.

5 Managing for high performance

It is immoral to misuse people, under-use them and abuse them but it is highly moral to call forth and make use of the talents that are in people. It is also certain that people will not use their gifts to the benefit of the organisation unless they are treated as people with all the needs that people have.

St Thomas Aquinas, 13th century

While Marx wrote of the horrifying intensification of the working day, most university managers are, unfortunately, pre-Marxist – they only know how to flog the horse.

UK regional union official, December 2000

'The University recognises that its staff are its most valuable resource and the key to the achievement of the Strategic Plan and all its objectives.' 'But for the contribution of our staff the University would not have established the reputation it enjoys today.' 'The staff of the University are our greatest asset . . .' We have all read or heard these familiar refrains many times over. In many staff though they raise a hollow laugh, not simply because such claims have become virtual clichés, but rather because of the glaring mismatch these staff perceive in their daily lives between what their institution says and what it does in practice. To them, and they do appear to be in the majority, universities have an enormous credibility gap to fill, for, as employers, they do not seem to act or behave in a way that suggests they actually believe in what they claim. And for that, staff, quite rightly, hold management directly accountable. Indeed the degree of staff dissatisfaction and alienation is such that one national survey of UK post-1992 universities found that, just a decade later, more than half of employees considered the management of their institutions to be either 'poor' or 'mostly unreasonable' (Natfhe, 2002).

Only the foolhardy and the unreflective would dismiss this scale of criticism as just so much whingeing. The shame, as well as the irony, of course, as the private sector readily acknowledges, is that it is indeed people who make all the difference. In management parlance, the quality of a company's people is the only significant strategic variable for any enterprise. It is their contribution that most affects 'bottom line' performance. The surprise is that it has taken the university sector so long, not just to acknowledge it but rather to recognise and act on it. The UK Bett Report (1999) on pay and conditions in HE still felt it necessary, as late as 1999, to recommend that 'the management of people should be given greater priority at all levels of the HE system'. Not before time, UK universities have begun to put in place a strategic framework for enhancing and developing leadership and management in higher education and the 2003 White Paper anticipates the creation of a leadership foundation.

This initiative notwithstanding, you should be under no illusion that managing the staff in your department – motivating them, developing their competence, improving their performance, realising their potential and maximising their contribution – constitutes your biggest challenge. It is at the heart of your responsibilities as head. The challenge is particularly tough not simply because of the degree of internal malaise we noted, which you may well have to overcome, but also because of the peculiar character of the academic world in which you have to operate: the penchant for peer review and collaborative decision-making; the autonomy of the individual scholar; the precedence of subject over institutional loyalty; the strength of tradition; the cult of the 'expert'; and so on.

More than that, you will also be expected, quite rightly, to 'value diversity'. You will need to establish, that is, an environment based on trust and mutual respect; one in which everyone can, and is encouraged to, play their full part irrespective of their gender, age, background, race, disability or sexual orientation. This is a matter that universities, at least in the UK, have not, to date, grasped with the conviction that their stakeholders are entitled to expect, as the enduring pay inequalities and under-representation within the professoriate testify.

Finally, as well as the 'equality challenge', you will also have to contend with working in a setting in which management is at best regarded as inessential or intrusive and at worst discredited, or simply predictable and unimaginative. How then are you to rise to these challenges? The purpose of this chapter and the one that follows is to help you do just that. It seeks to demonstrate how you can establish and sustain high performance within your department. In doing so, it explains how you can and should manage staff performance; motivate staff; develop staff; manage diversity as well as recruit and select staff.

Managing staff performance

Managing staff performance is demanding even in the best of circumstances. You could be forgiven for thinking it doubly so in the unfavourable climate which prevails in so many academic institutions. And it remains one of the most enduring and contentious issues for those working both inside and outside the HE sector. For many academic staff their experience to date of institutional attempts to guide and support academic work, principally through staff appraisal, has made many of them dismissive, if not contemptuous, of such initiatives. Indeed, staff frequently perceive them (and not always unreasonably) as an unwelcome intrusion on their academic freedom, a barrier to their creativity and freedom, a 'dumbing-down' of their expertise or simply (and maddeningly) as yet another example of bureaucracy at its worst – just so much time consuming form-filling.

To many outsiders, however, academia seems content to remain an unreformed and unaccountable bastion of privilege, out of tune with other public sector professional groups; one in which the penchant for form-filling takes precedence over the quest for genuine performance improvement, and in which underperformance is too frequently tolerated by managers who themselves end up underperforming in the process (Murlis and Hartle, 1996). As far as governments are concerned there is a common consensus that this issue is a priority that must be addressed. In the UK, for instance, the HEFCE (01/16, 2001), as part of the government's public sector modernisation programme, made additional resources available to universities for the first time in summer 2001 specifically to enable them to reward and develop staff. Such funding was contingent on universities developing their own particular human resources strategy. And these strategies in turn were expected to make provision for 'regular reviews of all staff, based on open and objective criteria with rewards connected to the performance of individuals including where appropriate their contribution to teams'. They were further expected to explain how the university intended to tackle instances of poor performance.

It is likely then that you will find yourself in a setting where you will be required both to contribute to, as well as implement, your university's HR (human resources) strategy and, more specifically, the performance management dimension of it. To meet this challenge, you will, as has been suggested, need to prepare yourself for a long and difficult haul ahead. More than that, self-evidently, you will also need to fully understand the principles of performance management and how to apply them. This, however, is not nearly so straightforward, for the concept in practice has itself been the source of much confusion, misunderstanding and indeed rancour in academic environments. Let us begin by clarifying and specifying what exactly is meant when you're asked to undertake 'performance management'.

What is performance management?

A commonplace practice outside the public sector, performance management is a relatively novel phenomenon within higher education. Simply put, it is basically a method of connecting organisational objectives to the people who are there to carry them out. Or as Michael Armstrong (2001) defines it: 'performance management is a strategic and integrated approach to developing the capabilities of individuals and teams in order to increase organisational effectiveness.' It is, in fact, the latest in a long line of attempts (people approaches, work process approaches, management by objectives (MBO), staff appraisal, etc.) to devise the perfect management technique. Where it differs from its predecessors is in its:

- focus – prospective rather than retrospective;
- scope – holistic rather than limited;
- application – tailored rather than packaged;
- emphasis – support rather than control.

Indeed performance management has itself evolved over the last decade. Where once it was regarded as a top-down monolithic appraisal system driven by HR departments, it is more likely nowadays to be a flexible supportive process owned by line managers (Armstrong, 2000; Armstrong and Baron, 1998). Such has been the shift then, it is not surprising that the term has generated so much misunderstanding. In essence, performance management has evolved:

From	*To*
emphasis on:	emphasis on:
systems	processes
appraisal	joint review
outputs	outputs and inputs
PRP	development
ratings	less ratings
the top-down	360 degree feedback
direction	support
the monolithic	flexibility
ownership by HR	ownership by line managers

Either way, the concept is perhaps more accurately termed 'performance and development management' (Armstrong, 2001), for it is essentially about:

- personal development;
- continuous improvement;
- dialogue, support and agreement;
- teams as well as individuals;
- managing performance *throughout the year*;
- managing the organisation.

Performance management then is most definitely *not* just about:

- pay;
- direction and control;
- poor performance;
- individuals;
- form-filling;
- going through the motions.

Principles of performance management

Putting the above together we can identify a number of key principles which characterise effective performance management.

- **Effective organisations need effective performance management**

Or, put the other way, organisational effectiveness is not possible without performance management. That is why we have it. Among other things, to:

- facilitate the integration of individual and organisational objectives and values;
- develop a performance-orientated culture;
- to identify and meet individual development needs;
- to identify those with potential;
- to identify poor performers;
- to provide a basis for valuing people;
- to improve the quality of management.

- **Performance management is concerned with performance across the entire range from A (poor) to Z (excellent)**

It is not, as is often perceived, simply a device to deal with difficult people at point A of the scale. Nor is it something to hit people with when they are down. Rather it is about identifying standards of performance and understanding where your staff are located across the range.

- **Effective performance management is critically dependent on the manager's ability to deliver**

Managers who not only have an open and honest management style but who also provide support and direction through:

- having a thorough understanding of their institutional strategy and the 'big picture' and being wary of any assumptions they may hold about their staff's interest in such matters before engaging with them on such issues.
- recognising that appraisal is not about supervision but is more concerned with helping individuals set strategic goals for themselves that are consistent with those of the organisation.

- **Performance management is a cyclical process centred on learning and development – not a fixed one-off event**

Performance management does not just happen, as is often (wrongly) assumed, at an annual event set up for the purpose. Formal appraisal is but a single aspect of the process. At heart, performance management is about learning and development, i.e. a continuous and ongoing activity. And as such it is one which, like all the best learning experiences, is more effective if it is planned in advance, experienced, reviewed and evaluated on a regular basis; thus emulating and reinforcing the 'learning cycle' (Honey and Mumford, 1995). A critical aspect of the learning cycle of course is that of feedback on progress and achievement. And in this respect staff are no different to students. We all need high-quality regular feedback if we are to develop. Indeed conventional wisdom tells us that any feedback, even if it is negative, is better than none at all. Managers, then, need to be not only particularly skilled in this regard they must also (stop making excuses and) seek every opportunity to provide feedback to staff, to make it in fact an everyday feature of working life.

- **Performance management is about how we manage people; it is a natural process of management – it's not 'a system'**

Performance management goes to the heart of how an organisation views its employees. This may not necessarily entail following 'best practice' per se but rather 'doing what we deem is best for us'. Either way, the focus will, or should, invariably be on changing behaviour, not paperwork, and on the process rather than 'the system'; to help the organisation get to where it wants to be in its performance culture. Performance management works best and succeeds most when it is aligned with the climate, culture, values and aspirations of the organisation, that is, when it complements 'the way we do things round here'. It invariably fails however, and quite rightly, if it is perceived to be (as has so often been the case in many organisations including universities) an artificial implant grafted on to the existing order of things.

- **Good processes alone cannot deliver good performance management – only you can**

It may seem perverse but it is not unknown for organisations to have excellent paper systems yet exhibit no demonstrable improvement in performance, and for those without such systems to demonstrate appreciable achievement in performance management. On the contrary it is very often the case in practice, and herein lies the danger inherent in funding council requirements: the prospect that accountability may not only bureaucratise the process but also yield no appreciable gain either. You ought not, however, let the 'dead hand' of compliance distract you from your goal. You should aim to exceed, and not be confined by, HEFCE guidelines. And your university will, in view of the far greater competitive environment in which we now all operate, certainly want you to do so.

Implementing performance management

Viewed in this way then there is no compelling reason why performance management cannot operate in a university environment. Indeed, far from being an alien practice, the principles on which it is based are central to the values that underpin universities as learning communities. How though should you proceed in implementing performance management?

Assess and reflect on your own approach

Performance management, as we've noted, is about consistency and about how we manage people. It should not make you behave any differently, therefore, from the way you normally function day to day. That said, it is important in the first instance that you take time to reflect on your own leadership style and on the assumptions you make about people and human nature. For understanding your own personal perceptions is of critical significance to the way you will approach performance management. On the one hand it raises your consciousness of them (and of the need perhaps to modify or adapt them) and on the other it will alert you, as Douglas

Box 5.1 Are you a traditional or contemporary leader?

Directions: This questionnaire is designed to help you better understand the assumptions you make about people and human nature There are ten pairs of statements. Assign a weight from 0 to 10 to each statement to show the relative strength of your belief in the statements in each pair. Higher points indicate greater belief in the statement. The points assigned for each item pair must total 10. Answer all items.

1   It's only human nature for people to do as little as they can get away with.   ___ (a)

When people avoid work, it's usually because their work has been deprived of its meaning.   ___ (b)   10

2   If faculty/staff have access to any information they want, they tend to have better attitudes and behave more responsibly.   ___ (c)

If faculty/staff have access to more information than they need to do their immediate tasks, they will usually misuse it.   ___ (d)   10

3   One problem in asking for the ideas of faculty/staff is that their perspective is too limited for their suggestions to be of much practical use.   ___ (e)

Asking faculty/staff for their ideas broadens their perspective and results in the development of useful suggestions.   ___ (f)   10

4   If people don't use much imagination and ingenuity on-the-job, it's probably because relatively few people have much of either.   ___ (g)

Most people are imaginative and creative but may not show it because of limitations imposed by supervision and the job.   ___ (h)   10

5   People tend to raise their standards if they are accountable for their own behaviour and for correcting their own mistakes.   ___ (i)

People tend to lower their standards if they are not punished for their misbehaviour and mistakes.   ___ (j)   10

6   It's better to give people both good and bad news because most want the whole story, no matter how painful.   ___ (k)

It's better to withhold unfavourable news about the university because most faculty/staff really want to hear only the good news.   ___ (l)   10

7   Because a leader is entitled to more respect than those below in the organisation, it weakens prestige to admit that a subordinate was right and the leader was wrong.   ___ (m)

Because people at all levels are entitled to equal respect, a leader's prestige is increased by admitting that a subordinate was right and the leader was wrong.   ___ (n)   10

8   If you give people enough money, they are less likely to be concerned with such intangibles as responsibility and recognition.   ___ (o)

If you give people interesting and challenging work, they are less likely to complain about such things as pay and supplemental benefits.   ___ (p)   10

9   If people are allowed to set their own goals and standards of performance, they tend to set them higher than the chair would.   ___ (q)

If people are allowed to set their own goals and standards of performance, they tend to set them lower than the chair would.   ___ (r)   10

10 The more knowledge and freedom a person has regarding his or her job, the more controls are needed to keep him or her in line.   ___ (s)

The more knowledge and freedom a person has regarding his or her job, the fewer controls are needed to ensure satisfactory job performance.   ___ (t)   10

Scoring: To get your scores, add up the points you assigned to the following:

Theory X score = sum of:		*Theory Y score = sum of:*	
(a)	___	(b)	___
(d)	___	(c)	___
(e)	___	(f)	___
(g)	___	(h)	___
(j)	___	(i)	___
(l)	___	(k)	___
(m)	___	(n)	___
(o)	___	(p)	___
(r)	___	(q)	___
(s)	___	(t)	___
X Total ___		**Y Total** ___	

So which are you? To what extent do you have traditional assumptions about people and human nature and to what degree contemporary? Are you surprised? What are the implications? What changes do you need to make?

Source: Shulman, 1998; adapted from Myers, 1991

McGregor (1960) has convincingly shown, to the danger that exists for creating self-fulfilling prophecies. Thus, for example, if you believe people are lazy, uninterested in work or responsibility and thus must be pushed and cajoled in order to get anything done (assumptions which McGregor dubs Theory X), you will manage them in a way that is consistent with these assumptions: look over their shoulders all the time, and the like. This behaviour in turn could cause staff to feel that they essentially have little responsibility in their job and lead them to work hard only when you are watching them closely. A self-fulfilling prophecy has thus begun and will be continually reinforced.

The questionnaires in Boxes 5.1 and 5.2 are designed to help you probe and better understand your current predisposition. Box 5.1 enables you, in a formal way, to measure your assumptions about human behaviour against McGregor's Theory X–Theory Y dichotomy wherein Theory Y (McGregor's principle of 'management by integration and self-control') assumes the exact opposite of Theory X: that people want to work, that they enjoy achievement, gain satisfaction from responsibility and are naturally inclined to seek ways of making work a positive experience. Box 5.2 enables you in an informal but no less penetrating way to reflect on the way you actually behave in relation to others at work. Taken together you will not only be able to determine whether you favour a traditional or contemporary style of leadership, but also the extent to which you are guilty of what is an allegedly common practice in universities, if the education press is to be believed, that of 'mushroom farming'. Hopefully you will not fall foul of the latter but, if you do, you should take immediate steps to remedy it. You should also reflect on the relative merits of Theories X and Y and how Theory Y (surely the more attractive of the two) has provided the framework on

Box 5.2 Are you a mushroom farmer?

The old joke about 'mushroom management' (keeping people in the dark and showering them with manure) isn't really funny when you're the mushroom.

Here is a short list aimed at sorting out the leaders from the mushroom farmers.
So which are you? There are no scores, but it's easy, if you're honest with yourself, to draw your conclusions.

- Do you ensure colleagues are given an adequate induction to the university and your department very shortly after they join?
- Can you honestly say you're doing all you can to develop your colleagues 'on-the-job'?
- Do you give your colleagues credit for good work with
  - face-to-face congratulations?
  - written notes after exceptionally good results?
  - telling your own line manager about it?
- Do you know how many children your colleagues have, their ages and personal things about them?
- Could you list the current domestic concerns or causes of celebration amongst your colleagues?
- Do you show favouritism? Do the same people in your department tend to get the mundane tasks?
- When did you last get your team together to discuss progress? Was the session a monologue?
- After reproaching someone, do you appear to forget it and start again, or keep the grudge alive?
- Can you say you give someone a fair hearing before turning them down on an idea or request?
- Are you considered a good listener?
- When did you last send a birthday, seasonal or get well card to a colleague?
- When were you last approached for advice on a strictly personal (non-working) matter?
- When did you last send flowers or anything else to say thank you?
- Are the words 'please' and 'thank you' a regular part of your working vocabulary?
- Finally, can you look yourself in the eye and say that in the past year, you have never taken credit for someone else's work or good idea?

which contemporary notions of continuous quality improvement and individual empowerment have been built. More than that, the process of completing the questionnaires should not only reveal how McGregor's conceptualisation highlights the inherent complexity of human behaviour, but also confirm how essential it is for you as a department head to be similarly flexible and adaptable in your own leadership behaviour.

Foster staff 'ownership' of their own development; encourage a questioning culture

Performance management has something of a 'dirty word' in universities over the past decade and not without good reason, Often narrowly conceived as a retrospective 'appraisal scheme', such devices have not surprisingly been regarded by staff as an externally imposed mechanism aimed at controlling them, rather than developing them. At best such initiatives have tended to breed staff compliance and defensiveness and at worst open hostility and defiance. Either way, staff invariably bemoan the waste of time taken up by such schemes, to so little effect. A complaint often borne out by managers themselves who, in routinely struggling to complete the necessary paperwork on schedule, tacitly acknowledge by their behaviour that the process is of little or no real value.

It is against this kind of backdrop, then, that you are likely to be expected to operate, and are likely to be given a 'performance management system' by your university to implement in your department. In doing so, you will need to take positive steps if you are to avoid repeating the mistakes of the past. For example, you need to ensure that:

- You do not get bogged down in the trivia and ritual of your particular institutional scheme. If it is a good scheme, i.e. one based on broad consultation with staff, then you shouldn't.
- You should not 'allow the tail to wag the dog'. It is the *process* not the form that is important.

More importantly still, and equally more difficult:

- You need to foster an environment in which performance and development is recognised by staff as *something they do and not something which is done to them by management*. Ideally you should be seeking to establish a setting in which a staff member can say: 'Here's my personal strategic plan for the year. What do you think of it?'

While it is the case, as we noted before, you may not be able to 'manage culture' per se your role is a critical one in influencing it through your leadership and management behaviour. In this instance, as before, you should be seeking to establish an 'open' departmental culture; one which, as Gerard Egan (1995) advises, encourages staff to ask questions about themselves, their role, their needs, their work objectives and their career plans (see Box 5.3).

Box 5.3 Performance improvement: questions you and your departmental culture should encourage staff to ask

Objectives	What are the key or strategic things I need to accomplish this year?
Delegation	What authority do I have? How far can I go?
Work plans	What are the best routes to my destination?
Initial training	Do I have the skills to implement these plans and achieve these targets?
Facilitation	What can I expect from my head of department in helping me to achieve them?
Feedback	What kind of feedback can I expect from my head of department? What kind of feedback am I expected to give him/her?
Tracking	What is the best way of monitoring my progress?
Recognition	What kind of recognition can I expect for my accomplishments?
Development	How can I prepare myself to do even bigger and better things in the future?

Source: adapted from Egan, 1995

Conversely you can, and should, also assess the degree to which you are being effective in this regard by putting yourself in the place of each of your colleagues, and completing the survey outlined in Box 5.4. You should then test out the accuracy of your perceptions and assumptions against those of your colleagues directly by (burying any embarrassment you may have, which in itself may be an indicator of avoidance or lack of openness on your part) inviting a representative sample of them to go through the survey with you.

As this is, or should be, an exercise grounded in ignorance, the disparity between your perceptions and the reality of your colleagues' experience should not be that great. (If it is you should address your 'out-of-touchness' urgently by instigating regular 'surgeries' with your colleagues.) More tellingly is the extent to which you and, each of them, were able to respond positively to each of the questions. Ideally, all, or not far short (10–12) of them. If anything less, there may be a common difference between you and your colleagues which you need to address, or perhaps there is a variety of different perceptions particular to each individual. Either way, you should respond with urgency.

Identify and specify standards of performance for staff; communicate and disseminate these standards

The controversy over performance management in universities and the difficulties in implementing it has not just arisen from differences of a theoretical nature (the legitimacy and appropriateness of performance management in such a setting). It also

Box 5.4 Measuring your effectiveness in performance management

Put yourself in the place of your colleagues or better still invite them to answer the following questions:

What do I get?

1 Do I know what is expected to me?

2 Do I have the materials and equipment I need to do my work right?

What do I give?

3 Do I have the opportunity at work to do what I do best every day?

4 Have I received recognition or praise for my work in the last month?

5 Does my head of department seem to care about me as a person?

6 Does my head of department encourage my development?

Do I belong here?

7 Are my opinions valued?

8 Does the university mission make me feel my role is important?

9 Are the colleagues in my department committed to doing quality work?

10 Do I have a best friend at work?

How can we all grow?

11 In the last six months, has my head of department talked with me about my progress?

12 This year, have I had the opportunities at work to learn and grow?

Scoring: Award one point for every positive response: 12, outstanding; 10–11, very good; 9, good; 8, fair; 7 and below, poor.

Source: based on Buckingham and Coffman, 2001

stems from concerns that are innately practical: principally the difficulty in unravelling the 'mystery' of academic work and, in particular, the very 'private' activity of teaching. Put another way, received wisdom had it that, even if the theoretical difficulties concerning performance management were overcome, such is the complexity of academic work it couldn't be effectively applied in universities anyway.

The reality is more prosaic. HEIs have traditionally not been very good at clarifying or explaining to staff their expectations of them. In truth, they have not, until recent times, needed to be. But it does not follow from this (the contentious and voluminous debate on what constitutes 'good teaching', as we will see later, notwithstanding) that it cannot or should not be done. Indeed it is essential that this is done, for, without it, how can we expect individuals to perform to their full potential. In this respect, academics are no different from other professional groups, and, like them, they need help in determining their targets, charting their progress towards them and developing their careers. It is a fallacy, as well as irresponsible, to assume that it could otherwise be the case. Academics may be autonomous professionals, but they are not going to realise their full potential independent of others, particularly if they do not know what is required of them in the first place. It is incumbent on you, then, to address this deficiency. Good practice tells us that in order to maximise their potential, individuals need to know the following, and it is your responsibility as manager to ensure:

Staff need to know:	*As a manager you must:*
• What is my role? Why do I exist?	Develop the job role
• Who is my immediate line manager?	Establish accountability
• What is expected of me?	Specify standards of performance
• What are the priorities?	Establish SMART targets
• How am I doing?	Measure and give feedback on performance
• Where can I go from here?	Identify and resource staff
• How can I get there?	development needs

In the first instance, you should aim to determine and clarify for staff the standard of performance expected of them, and the key to developing that is through an analysis of their particular job role(s).

Your predecessor or your HR representative may already have undertaken a preliminary analysis of this nature, but you should not be surprised if you have to start from scratch. In all likelihood you will inherit a situation in which academics are on 'general contracts' which have relatively loosely worded terms and conditions of employment (the norm for 'old' universities in the UK where the emphasis is on 'research, teaching and administration', typically in that order, or 'teaching, scholarship and service', as is often preferred in state universities in the US), or on a national professional contract (as is the case in the 'new' universities in the UK) where staff can be expected to undertake up to a maximum of 550 hours formal scheduled teaching, as well as participate in 'research and other forms of scholarly activity, examining, curriculum development, administration and related activities'.

Whatever your context, you are also likely to find (including those who work exclusively in academic administration) some staff will have job descriptions and others will not, and, of those that have them, many will be outdated. Either way, you too need to be clear about what you have to do. You need to focus on 'job roles', rather than on 'job descriptions' per se, which so often tend to be little more than a shopping list of different tasks and duties that are neither exhaustive nor eternal. Unlike job descriptions, job roles are competence-based rather than task-based. They articulate the responsibilities of the role, the competencies which the post-holder will need to fulfil them, and the standard of performance, or measure of success, the appointee is expected to achieve, i.e. an objective yardstick for determining whether performance is at an acceptable level (Erban, 2001).

Job roles are also invaluable in that they provide an objective, or at least a much less subjective, basis on which to offer feedback, assess development needs or determine rewards. Indeed, when applied in academic settings, they offer an additional

Box 5.5 Code of professional conduct for academic staff in one UK 'new' (post-1992) university

Academic staff are expected to commit to:

1   Doing things on time
2   Being punctual, courteous, caring
3   Being available
4   Taking responsibility for supporting and guiding students' learning
5   Being properly prepared, including knowing how to use teaching and learning facilities
6   Preparing materials to time and quality
7   Continuing own learning
8   Engaging in intellectual work; scholarly activity; research
9   Evaluating learning as a means of evaluating teaching
10 The vision and values of the university

particular benefit in that they open up the possibility, by relying on an evidential base to measure success, for universities, *if they so wish*, to recognise and reward effective teaching on an equal footing with research. The role analysis outlined in Appendix 1 shows how one UK 'new' university has attempted to define the expectations it has of staff, in this instance principal lecturers (the equivalent of senior lecturers in the 'old' university sector, and of associate professors in the US system). The 'role map' sets out the core competences or key responsibilities pertaining to the role, as well as identifying the skills, styles and qualities (or competencies) needed to fulfil the role and the criteria of success by which individual performance is measured. (On an explanatory note: competence = the 'what', e.g. typing a letter; and competency = the 'how', i.e. the skills and behaviour needed to type a letter well.) The same university also sought to establish a common professional standard which it expected all academic staff to adhere to, irrespective of status; a basic minimum standard of performance that is by which to gauge academic conduct and practice (see Box 5.5).

It is this competence-based approach you need to adopt for the staff roles in your department, and, while this may seem a daunting task, breaking it down into stages will make it seem far less so. Better still, you are likely to find it much easier if you attempt this undertaking jointly with your peers in similar roles across the university, aided by your HR expert. That way, you should not only achieve a more informed and accurate outcome, but, equally important, one that should also guarantee institutional consistency. Either way, you should first identify the number and variety of roles in your department – demonstrator, technician, lecturer, professor, research fellow, administrative assistant, section head, etc. For each role ask yourself: What is my purpose? Why do I exist? Summarise your answer in a succinct statement or short number of bullet points. For instance, if you think of your own role as, say, head of an academic department or dean of faculty then it might be defined as follows.

Role of dean of faculty

- To develop and implement a strategy for the work of the faculty, provide academic leadership and to manage the faculty's human and other resources.
- To contribute to the overall academic development of the university.
- To represent the faculty and the university to the wider community.

Role of head of subject

- To provide subject leadership and with the dean take responsibility for securing the effective deployment and development of academic staff.
- To take line management responsibility for staff in the subject area.

Next you need to identify the five to six key competences or areas of responsibility for each role. Again, if we use your own as an example these may well include: strategy and policy formulation; academic leadership (in teaching and/or research); budget and resource management; managing staff performance; teamwork; career and professional development. You then need to specify, as illustrated in the principal lecturer example shown in Appendix 1, the requisite competencies and success criteria for each of these areas of responsibility. Once specified you need to communicate them accurately, clearly, creatively and assertively, in meetings and briefings, as part of induction and appraisal, as well as through MBWA and documentation; the university's mission; the departmental strategic plan; job roles; and so on.

Negotiate and agree SMART (not DUMB) goals and targets with individual staff

More than that, you now have an established framework within which to agree specific goals with your staff. Goals are different to standards in that they are negotiable, minimum performance standards are *not*. Goals are concerned with priorities; immediate concerns 'over and above the job'. As such, their emphasis is on individual progress and growth in the role rather than simply routine maintenance matters. In practice, therefore, they tend to accommodate both work and developmental objectives and are as likely to be apportioned to teams as they are to individuals (Moores, 1994). In either case, as we noted earlier in discussing your departmental strategy, goals should always be SMART – specific, measurable, achievable, realistic and time-related – and not DUMB – defective, unrealistic, misdirected or bureaucratic.

Put another way, you should aim to:

- identify, negotiate and agree a small number of specific goals (typically no more than six) with each individual or team;
- focus on goals that make a difference; *that will improve performance* and not just a list of routine or ongoing events;
- make them consistent with your department and your university's strategic aims;
- quantify the goals and specify the actions (targets) needed to achieve them;
- ensure that they are set in areas within the control of the individual or team;

- ensure they challenge and stretch the team or individual concerned, i.e. they are not set either too low lest they encourage underachievement relative to potential, or, just as damaging, too high lest they lead to underachievement relative to others' expectations;
- establish, by staggering deadlines, a realistic timescale for completion while recognising the need for flexibility should circumstances change;
- ensure that the SMART quest for rigid performance objectives does not hinder you from recognising ongoing accomplishments by staff in realising your department and your university's aspirations (see Box 5.6 for examples of good and bad SMART targets).

Box 5.6 SMART – and not so *smart* targets

SMART	Not so *smart* targets
• Develop, negotiate and agree an admissions compact with three local providers by the end of year	Establish closer liaison with local schools and colleges
• Establish regular meetings of the course team on the first Wednesday of each month beginning in September	Improve communications with course team
• Conduct a SWOT analysis of personal development planning schemes for students and present three alternative models to the course committee for their adoption by the end of semester	Improve student support
• Identify a dozen local employers and arrange a programme of breakfast seminars on work-related learning and employer involvement in curriculum design and validation. Establish employer register and enrol six by the end of year	Improve links with local businesses and employers
• Select one module as a pilot and using WebCT develop and establish an e-learning infrastructure centred on information (bulletin board), learning (discussion forum) and (formative) assessment for next academic year	Explore the potential for e-learning
• Organise a focus group of ethnic minority students to evaluate their experience; to report to the course committee with findings and recommendations by Christmas	Improve the minority student experience
• Submit a finished article to one refereed journal of international repute and negotiate and agree a monograph contract with an international publisher by the end of year	Publish my research findings

While you may know what SMART goals are, you still have the tricky business of negotiating them – no easy task given the degree of scepticism which prevails over such matters in so many HEIs. As such, it is vital that you prepare for your one-to-ones with staff by anticipating and rehearsing your responses to the arguments which they might raise against this process including the perennial ones:

- My role doesn't lend itself to target-setting.
- You are wasting my time requiring me to do irrelevant things.
- Why should I work hard for no extra reward?
- I have had responsibilities passed on to me which are rightly management's, and carried the can too. Why should I do more?
- I have enough on my plate as it is.
- Why is management always changing the goalposts?
- What's the point!

In each case you must be prepared to discuss the objections openly and honestly with the individual concerned. You should not dismiss such claims out of hand or ride roughshod over them. On the contrary, take the trouble to examine them thoroughly. You may not convince every unbeliever, but probing these assertions invariably unearths more substantive deep-seated concerns; issues which very often prompt a more meaningful dialogue. You must also not forget that the great majority of people prefer to do a good job and want to do so. And while it is the case that you need to remind them that goals and targets are simply a way of setting sights on the future (and yes, we do live in a world of changing goalposts), it is incumbent on you to be positive – to encourage reflection. One proven method that works well is to ask individuals:

- What do you see as your main accomplishments over the last six months or year?
- How do you see them supporting the strategic aims of the department and the university?

Or alternatively,

- What are the four or five points by which you would recognise whether you've had a good semester or a bad semester?

Either way, the responses are almost invariably couched in relation to the aspirations and modus operandi of the department or university – and as such provide both you and them with the raw material on which to build, shape and agree an appropriate set of SMART targets.

Measure performance and give feedback to staff on their performance

Performance improvement is, or should be, a matter of everyday concern. Whether it is or not, of course, is dependent to a large extent on the prevailing mindset within your department. If it is a positive one, then, provided that staff do indeed have targets that are authentically SMART, measuring performance should present no real difficulty. Unfortunately this is rarely the case in practice, and not simply because the everyday expectations and standards of professionalism are not as high as perhaps they should be, but rather because of the tardiness with which managers very often approach performance monitoring and staff feedback. A condition which, historically at least, has been a characteristic feature of so many academic environments. That is to say, university managers have, on the one hand, too often sought to rely on appraisal as the sole means of measuring staff performance (thereby psychologically allowing 'the tail to wag the dog') and, on the other, have been far too grudging in the manner they have given feedback to staff on their performance. In this respect, ironically, managers are guilty of doing unto staff what staff themselves are ritually accused of doing unto students – namely, failing to offer students feedback on their learning which is clear, accurate and consistent as well as comprehensive. These are errors of omission you should aim *not* to repeat.

Thus you need to recognise, and should utilise, the multiple ways in which you are able to monitor staff performance. For example:

- by collecting specific, concrete data;
- through 'number crunching';
- management by walking about;
- by engaging in a collaborative endeavour with staff;
- team monitoring;
- through one-to-one supervision;
- through one-to-one appraisal.

If you do so you will ensure that the dynamics of performance management are prospective rather than retrospective; that performance improvement does indeed become an integral aspect of everyday life and that appraisal becomes the creative (rather than the reactive) process it should be; one in which staff take the lead.

Measuring teaching effectiveness

A critical weakness of performance management in universities in the past has, as we noted earlier, been the perennial difficulty of assessing staff effectiveness in teaching. This deficiency has meant that a large part of an academic's work has not only been unevaluated, but also unrecognised and consequently unrewarded. More than that, it has institutionalised the position of teaching as the poor relation of research. Put another way, even if a university was minded to reward teaching and research in a equal fashion, it is argued, the difficulties in demonstrating achievement in teaching compared to that in research (where performance indicators such as research grants, published works in academic journals or books, and citations by other authors are relatively easy to document) are such as to thwart all but the most determined of institutions. Some universities have shown, however, that this need not be the case – that the issue can in fact be tackled afresh in innovative ways.

The University of Ballarat (Australia), for example, has sought to 'overcome the old staff tension between teaching and research' by adopting a vision of scholarly life derived from the work of Ernest Boyer. A new, small, regional university, Ballarat has even more unusually sought to apply Boyer's theoretical conception of the four inter-related scholarships, those of teaching, integration, application and discovery, to all aspects of its operation (see Boyer, 1990). Thus the university's budget, the activities of university-wide services and schools, and the allocation of job titles and roles are all conceived and measured on the contribution they make towards the integration of the four scholarships.

The same is equally the case for academic staff: that is, they are all obliged to demonstrate they are competent in all four of Boyer's categories, and not simply one or two as is usually the case. This they do through the 'personal development port-folio' they are required to maintain. Essentially, a record of professional practice and achievements, the portfolio is comprised of evidence collected by the individual staff member, including that obtained by 360 degree feedback; self, peer, student and super-visor (Kemmis and Maconachie, 1998).

Arizona State University has likewise adopted an integrative approach to this issue (Krahenbuhl *et al.*, 1998). In this instance, by constructing a conceptual model that articulates the full range of faculty activities. One that:

- breaks down the arbitrary boundaries that surround teaching, scholarship and service;
- displays the multiple effects of the specific activities that constitute faculty work;
- provides a visual management tool for allocating different workloads across and within academic units.

Thus it not only recognises and caters for the fact that faculty interests, skills and motivations may change from year to year and over the course of a faculty member's career; it also provides department heads with a framework with which to assess their department's (collective staff) contribution to the university's mission on the one hand and that of the individual staff member's role in this process on the other (see Appendix 2).

The teaching portfolio

A key driver in the initiatives developed by Arizona State University and Ballarat was the respective institutional desire in each case to broaden the traditional concept of scholarship to reflect more fully and accurately the true range of tutors' work. Not all universities have gone this far, but many nevertheless have sought to promote, principally through the 'teaching portfolio', the documentation of individual staff performance in teaching. It is a trend you would do well to emulate: not simply because such portfolios will indeed provide you with the evidential base by which 'to assess how far individual staff members make sense of, engage with and learn from the professional practice of helping students to learn', but also because of the addi-tional equally important benefits such systematic documentation, observation and critical reflection would bring in facilitating still further improvements in both the learning of students and the learning of staff.

Nor does the compilation of such teaching portfolios have to be as difficult as others would have us believe. For unlike academics, students have no such doubts as to what constitutes 'good teaching'. While it is the case we certainly need to recognise that teaching is a dynamic, not a static activity, and encompasses a much broader range of tasks beyond classroom performance (assessment, course design, the production of learning materials, the stimulation and supervision of independent learning, and so on), we also should remember that students repeatedly emphasise the same qualities (Martin, 1999), i.e.:

- *enthusiasm* for and *knowledge* of the subject matter;
- regular and timely *feedback* for students;
- a capacity to engage students with the *mystery and importance* of key ideas;
- ability to give a *clear explanation* of these ideas.

That said, the portfolios that work best, and deliver most, are those which are premised on this basis: in other words, those that use criteria to tap into and bring out evidence of these qualities (see Box 5.7 for an exemplar model).

Giving feedback to staff

The teaching portfolio will enable you to assess aspects of academic work that hitherto may have been undocumented. Your obligation does not end there, however, for there is still the matter of giving staff adequate and proper feedback on their performance; a duty which managers have often been either reluctant, or downright negligent, in undertaking in the past. Why this has been so is largely rooted in the erroneous assumptions which managers may make about their staff, for example:

- staff don't need it, don't want it and wouldn't appreciate it;
- as self-motivated and self-evaluating professionals, academics are best left alone to get on with it;
- positive feedback will only encourage staff to rest on their laurels;
- the annual appraisal interview is sufficient in itself to keep staff on track;
- staff know managers have competing demands and do not expect them to waste time giving unnecessary feedback.

The reality of course, as we noted earlier, is the exact opposite. We all need quality feedback on a routine basis if we are to develop, let alone excel, and any feedback, even negative, is better than none at all. It helps us learn from our mistakes, encourages reflection, develops persistence and gives us a sense of making progress. Thus you should regard giving feedback as a critical and not marginal aspect of your role. Nor should you underestimate the impact it will have on the recipient. As such it is a key skill you must master. In the first instance by recognising that:

- feedback can be given in a variety of ways, formally as well as informally, orally as well as in writing;
- feedback is more effective and constructive if given promptly in the most appropriate way, in public or more likely in private;

Box 5.7 The teaching portfolio: bespoke criteria for evaluating teaching*

I Teaching with the university

1	Preparation for teaching	• Clarity of aims, objectives and learning outcomes for each module
		• Preparation of content, learning materials, IT and visual aids
		• Estimation of student learning effort needed
2	Quality of actual teaching activity	• Evidence of effectiveness and excellence of lecturing, small-group work, practicals, fieldwork, project supervision, etc.
3	Value and range of teaching	• Amount of time spent on teaching
		• Experience of a wide range of teaching to a variety of, e.g. students, sizes of groups, content of intrinsic difficulty, service teaching, interdisciplinary teaching
4	Innovation in teaching	• Evidence of innovations in curriculum/programme design and/or teaching methodology, e.g. resource-based learning, learning through work, e-learning, problem-based learning, 'action learning', etc.
		• Collaboration in teaching – team teaching, etc.
		• Innovations of national/international repute in the teaching of the specific subject area
		• Short course developments; modular programme developments
5	Communication with students	• Evidence of effectiveness in student guidance and counselling, motivating students, the quality of marking and feedback on student's work, interpersonal relationships, availability and accessibility
6	Assessment practices	• Evidence of range of methods of assessment used, innovation in assessment techniques
		• Congruence of assessment and learning outcomes
7	Evaluation of own teaching	• Systematic and regular reflection on all the above practices
		• Regular use of peer/student evaluation
		• Continuing reflection on teaching in relationship to the overall teaching aims and objectives of the department, and the curriculum on offer as a whole

8 Management of teaching

- Programme leadership: chair of programme committees for curriculum development, quality assurance, student experience, etc.
- Responsibilities for learning support
- Staff/student liaison role
- Learning and teaching fellow

9 Teaching scholarship and research

- Evidence of scholarship
- Effect of scholarship on teaching
- Influence of research on teaching

10 Teaching and the world of work

- Benefits from employer contact
- Involvement of employers in curriculum design and teaching
- Placement of students

II External activity

11 Invitations to teach elsewhere

- National/international conferences, lectures, seminars
- Regular teaching visits to other university departments

12 Membership of professional groups and bodies

- Subject-based, teaching-based, interest-specific, e.g. assessment, recording achievement, curriculum development

13 Professional service to other universities and organisations

- As external examiner, consultant, quality auditor/quality assessor, subject reviewer/institutional auditor

14 Publications on teaching

- Critical reflection on teaching approaches, scholarly work and textbooks, compilations of teaching materials, publication of one's own pedagogic research and development, editorial work, refereeing for journals, etc.

15 Teaching grants contracts and fellowships

- Grants for teaching development work; contracts to provide programmes for other organisations, fellowships awarded

* The effectiveness of the teaching portfolio is also dependent of course on the effort and commitment that staff put in to it. You can help them in this by asking them to reflect on their professional practice using HERDSA (1997), 'Challenging Conceptions of Teaching: Some Prompts for Good Practice' or simply by posing the following questions:

- What are you particularly good at in teaching?
- What aspects of your teaching do you still need to work on?
- What interests or excites you in teaching?
- What have you discovered about your teaching?
- What is your philosophy of teaching?

Sources: adapted from University of Western Australia, 1998; Elton and Partington, 1993

- good performance and achievements (book launch, QAA outcomes, etc.) provide you with many opportunities in which to publicly congratulate staff on their success.

Most feedback, however, takes place one-to-one, in private, and it is these encounters you will likely find the most demanding. To get the best out of them you will find they are more constructive, for you, your department and the individual concerned, if you adhere to the following good practice guidelines.

- Be clear what you want to say in advance. Practise in advance if necessary.
- Start with the positive.
- Think of it as a two-way conversation in which you expect to talk for approximately 20 per cent of the time and listen for the remaining 80 per cent.
- Put yourself in the other person's shoes.
- Be open and honest and seek a genuine dialogue.
- Invite reflection and prepare to listen actively.
- Ask open-ended questions: What progress do you feel you've made since we last spoke? What things have gone well, less well? What has helped or hindered you in reaching your targets? What do you still need to do to achieve your goal?
- Acknowledge and recognise the individual's contribution and achievements.
- Always remember *goals*, and how these link with the individual, the department and the university's objectives.
- Be tolerant of emotional outbursts (anger, weeping, etc.) and be prepared to empathise.
- Be specific: always make your message clear and explicit, whether you are criticising or praising.
- Always try to combine critical feedback with support, organisational and personal: What help would you like me to offer you?
- Own the feedback: use 'I' not 'you' and no 'third parties'.
- Think behaviour, not person. Never criticise personality. For example, never say 'you are aggressive'. Quote examples instead. 'Some of your behaviours mislead others into believing you are – what can we do about it?' (i.e. always use behaviour as evidence of use or non-use of a competency).
- Think about the impact that *you* have on the situation and take responsibility for your own feelings. Think too what the feedback says about you.
- Discuss the causes of problems as well as the symptoms.
- Continuously check that your feedback has been accurately received – clarify, clarify, clarify . . .
- Be flexible – if an approach is not working then can you change tack? Don't impose solutions, develop options for consideration.
- Always be ready to listen as well as to speak.

Actively reflect afterwards on how accurately your feedback was received (see Box 5.8) (Boutall, 1997).

Box 5.8 How well do you give feedback?

Ideally you should always score 4 rather than 3. If less than 3 you must make a conscious effort to improve on the next occasion

The 1–2–3–4 feedback model

---

1 COMPLETE MISUNDERSTANDING

- NOT LISTENING
- COMMUNICATION UNCLEAR
- OTHER PARTY DOES NOT WANT TO LISTEN

---

2 INACCURATELY OR ONLY PARTIALLY REFLECTING BACK

- PARTIAL MISUNDERSTANDING
- FULLER EXPLANATION/GREATER CLARITY NEEDED
- DETAILS INCORRECT

---

3 ACCURATELY REFLECTING BACK

- LISTENING ATTENTIVELY
- EXPLAINING CLEARLY IN OWN WORDS
- USING OWN WORDS TO FEEDBACK

---

4 REFLECTING BACK MORE

- THE MEANING BEHIND THE FACTS
- CLARIFYING THE CONTEXT
- A SHARED INTERPRETATION
- ENGAGING WITH THE EMOTION
- UNDERSTANDING THE 'REAL POINT'
- ACHIEVING EMPATHY

Source: adapted from Boutall, 1997

Tackling poor performance

> Your organisation is only as strong as the weakest member in it.
>
> Sir John Harvey-Jones

You will quickly find that your success, or lack of it, in monitoring performance and giving feedback soon becomes apparent in the degree of trust that your colleagues are willing to place in you; that, and the way in which they respond to the professional challenges you set them. Not everyone will be alike of course. Ideally we would all want every colleague to be a high achiever who exceeded the standard of performance, and in reality you will probably find that there are indeed many in this position. It is equally likely too you will find a small number who are underperforming, i.e. who fall short of the standard of performance. What should you do?

Resolve to take action

The overwhelming temptation may be to do nothing at all. You could persuade yourself, for instance, that, given this matter involves only a small minority, and in the absence of any real pressure either from above or from other departmental colleagues, why should you not turn a blind eye? With everything else you have to do, others would surely understand why you would not want to devote a disproportionate amount of your time and energy on a handful of individuals – besides the benefits are unlikely to outweigh all the hassle that would be involved.

Nothing in fact could be further from the truth. You would be making a colossal error of judgement if you were to follow this path. For there is only one thing more corrosive of departmental morale than staff underperformance, and that is managers who tolerate it. It may well be unspoken, and it may be unwritten, but it is nearly always the case that everyone knows which staff are underperforming and, whenever the issue is addressed, everyone is usually only too keen to ask you afterwards, 'What took you so long to deal with it?'

Such behaviour and depth of feeling indicate just how important staff regard this issue to be. It goes to the heart of staff equity. And as such poses one of, if not the, most difficult tests you will face as a manager. Shirk it and you risk becoming a 'lame duck'. Embrace it and you have the opportunity to significantly improve staff performance and morale. Resolved to act, you will need both patience and understanding; that and equal measures of tact, imagination and perseverance.

Tackle the issue not the person

It is also essential you recognise:

* *Underperformance is not necessarily the individual's fault.* There could very likely be an *organisational* explanation for this apparent individual failing: lack of resources, poor management, unbalanced workload, etc. As such this matter should be tackled as an issue and not as a means of targeting individual staff for punishment. Indeed it is very unrewarding to think in terms of blame or fault in these situations, unless it really does turn out to be a genuine case of misconduct (which you would need to

handle under your university's disciplinary procedure; a process we will discuss later in Chapter 8). Put another way, you need to remember that individuals respond better to encouragement rather than punishment, so your focus should be a positive one aimed at improving performance, and not on apportioning blame or identifying 'passengers' for redundancy. You should therefore avoid labelling people as 'under-performers'.

- *Underperformance is not the same as unsatisfactory performance.* The latter means that an individual is performing at a level below that stipulated in their employment contract (and ought to be dealt with as above under your disciplinary procedure) whereas the former is concerned with individuals who are working below their level of capability. In instances of underperformance your university may also have a 'competency procedure' for staff. In either case it is important you consult with your human resources adviser and your line manager before initiating any formal procedure. Do not act alone.

- *Underperformance is not just about the individual staff member concerned. It is also about you, and your performance.* Indeed, painful as it may be, you need to remain open to the possibility that you – through your actions, assumptions you've made, the way you have organised workloads, delegated activities, communicated tasks, etc. – may be the chief factor responsible for the underperformance in the first place. Managing underperformance then involves a scrutiny of *yourself* and *your* actions as well as that of the staff member.

While underperformance may be one of the most difficult challenges you will face, it can also be one of the most rewarding experiences. It may stretch your beliefs and abilities in many contrasting ways and to a far greater degree than is usually the case: your respect for human values; your capacity to motivate and inspire; your creativity, and so on. However, few issues give you such an immediate sense of personal satisfaction as that which you experience in successfully resolving instances of underperformance.

Identify the nature and causes of staff underperformance

You can be alerted to instances of underperformance in very many ways: through letters of complaint or petitions from students and/or staff; through formal expressions of concern from course leaders or subject heads; a critical report from an external examiner or accredited external body; as a consequence of appraisal; staff absenteeism; staff self-admission; and so on.

Either way, you must first investigate the shortfall in performance: i.e. you must avoid jumping to conclusions too quickly. The common assumption is that poor performance happens either because the person can't do it (which makes it a training issue) or because they won't, in which case it becomes a 'rewards' issue. It may not, however, as we've noted, be nearly so straightforward. Incapability or unwillingness are only two of many potential causes of underperformance. You therefore need to focus on issues around:

- problem-solving;
- staff motivation;
- collaboration and consultation;
- fairness and justice.

More specifically, ask yourself is it because they:

- Don't know *why* they are supposed to be doing something.
- Don't know *what* to do.
- Don't know *what standard* they have to achieve a particular task. (If so, it is a communication issue – about strategic vision, specific objectives, standards of performance, etc. – which you need to put right.)
- Don't know *how* to do the task. (If so, it is a training and development issue and again your responsibility to take the initiative.)
- Simply *cannot* do the task. They don't have and cannot acquire the necessary skills. (If so, this is a recruitment and selection, or more likely a delegation, problem and usually the staff member is not responsible.)
- Are *stopped* from completing tasks by organisational constraints: resources, poor communications, poor management. (If so, it is again incumbent on you to take the initiative.)
- Simply *refuse* and *won't* do the task. (If so, this is a discipline issue – *but* only after the above questions have been asked.)

Agree a course of action – and review it

Keep an open mind, therefore you should:

- Act early – don't let the situation escalate until it becomes chronic. If it is one you have inherited do not ignore it, even if your predecessor did.
- Gather information to understand what the staff member is doing wrong (and also what s/he is getting right).
- Talk with them one-to-one. Give them a clear outline of the issue and specific feedback on their performance.
- Allow them an opportunity to respond.
- Listen to their reactions and try to get to the root cause of the problems.

Ask open questions; invite suggestions: What do you need to help you become more effective? What can I do to help you? Check tactfully whether any obstacles have hindered their performance; their colleagues or their domestic and personal circumstances.

If the staff member is responsible for the underperformance then together come up with ideas for tackling the situation. In doing so you must bear in mind that:

- people do not have unlimited potential, they cannot achieve things simply because they want to hard enough;
- people don't change that much.

You should therefore:

- not waste time trying to fix weaknesses, trying to put in what was left out (but)
- focus on, capitalise on strengths – try to draw out what there already is; this is hard enough by itself.

• Decide and agree on a 'training' course of action, starting with a key issue, e.g.: assistance in the preparation of lectures; peer review; team teaching; counselling; shadowing; change in workload; change in role; visits to other departments/institutions; pursuit of a course of study or relevant qualification.

• Consider nominating – and providing for – a mentor.

• Follow up to review progress and give further guidance on a regular basis; fortnightly or monthly depending on the seriousness of the issue.

• Gird yourself to run through several cycles of this process if there are a number of issues to address.

• Anticipate – and expect – a significant improvement in performance over a six-month period. In the event that satisfactory progress is not achieved, however – and it is unfortunately more than likely you will not be able to eliminate all cases of under-performance in this way – you will need to initiate your university's disciplinary procedure under guidance from your HR adviser as a means of securing performance improvement.

Motivating staff

> I feel that no rational person would work in the British higher education system, and that anyone who enters it under present conditions is engaged in a self-destructive act; it is an ill-paid, overworked line of work and has lost almost all the old pleasures.
>
> Alan Ryan, on resigning as Warden of New College,
> Oxford, May 2002

Staff underperformance, albeit restricted to a minority, will severely test your leadership capacity. It is not the only one you have to face, however. You will also be expected to meet the equally demanding challenge of ensuring that all staff members within your department are suitably and appropriately motivated. Another tall order, particularly given as we noted earlier the degree to which alienation, cynicism and demoralisation are seemingly rife in so many academic communities. Such is, in fact, the anger of staff about ever more intrusive accountability, their resentment of the increasing demands made upon them, their concern over the decline of collegiality, and their scepticism about the capacity of their institutional leaders, it is perhaps not as surprising as it may first appear, that university academics – undervalued, overlooked and unappreciated as they undoubtedly perceive themselves – should actually be top of the UK Job Misery Index. What should, and can you, do?

Faced with such unpropitious circumstances, as much externally as internally generated, you may feel that whatever you were to do the impact would be negligible. You would make little difference.

Not so. You need to reflect on the following key proposition:

•   Each individual's line manager is the most important factor in an employee's effectiveness.

You should not ever underestimate either your ability or your potential to make a difference. But how? By considering in the first instance what few HEIs seem to have done to date, i.e. seek to understand and cater to the wants and needs of their staff. This may sound straightforward enough, yet it is surprising how often employers, and not simply those in HE, fail in this regard. For example, Barrow and Davenport (2002), in their survey of the UK private sector, found that staff tended to value, in order of priority, recognition of their work, involvement in change, a job 'that gets the best out of me', role clarity, consultation, and 'management that motivates', however most organisations scored a satisfactory rating of less than 50 per cent in all six categories. Many private sector companies like their HEI counterparts, then, are failing either to understand the wants of their staff, or to meet them – or indeed both. Motivation is, in fact, a complex matter, particular to each individual. It is also one which you can affect dramatically either way, positively or negatively. As such, it is important you understand motivation theory, to use as a guide to your actions.

Theories of motivation

Motivation is about giving people good reason to make them want to do things well, to excel. Motivation theory is grounded in the context in which, and articulates the basis on which, all motivational effort must be directed. Three influential and well-known theories in particular are worthy of note.

Maslow's hierarchy of needs

According to Abraham Maslow, people's needs are satisfied progressively, beginning with their most basic physiological ones (e.g. the basics of food, warmth, shelter, rest) before rising up a hierarchy that embraces, in sequential order, safety needs (e.g. job security), social needs (e.g. sense of belonging), ego needs (e.g. recognition by others) and self-actualisation needs (e.g. the need for self-fulfilment) (see Figure 5.1).

What it says, wholly sensibly, is that people's motivations can only be satisfied if this hierarchy is respected – and conversely, you ignore it at your peril. Thus your efforts aimed at engaging colleagues, for example, in the departmental strategic plan are likely to be blighted if staff feel they have more pressing concerns about their work environment or for the security of their jobs. The hierarchy also reminds us that the work environment is also very much a social environment and indeed for some individuals it may represent the majority of the people contact in their lives.

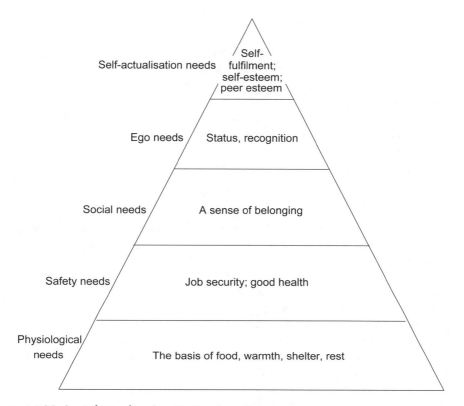

Figure 5.1 Maslow's hierarchy of motivational needs

Hertzberg's motivator / hygiene factors

Frederick Hertzberg's theory has more immediate practical relevance to the everyday work environment, and certainly offers a more detailed insight on how to develop positive motivation, and avoid demotivation. In it, Hertzberg identifies two categories of factors:

- hygiene factors: those things that switch people off if they cause negative feelings;
- motivators: those factors that can make people feel good.

The hygiene factors, or dissatisfiers, Hertzberg identifies are all external (environmental) factors that can affect the individual and include such things as: institutional policy and administrative processes; supervision; working conditions; salary; relationship with peers; personal life (and the impact of work on it); status; security.

The motivators, or satisfiers, in contrast, all stem from the intrinsic (internalised) qualities of human nature. They are all in varying degrees a force for positive motivation and include in ascending order of power: achievement; recognition; the work itself; responsibility; advancement; growth. The implication for managers then is a clear one. You should aim to:

- Nullify or at least minimise the effect of the hygiene factors, those aspects of work that give rise to gripes and dissatisfaction: everything from pay inequities, work-load differences, and bureaucratic systems to car parking facilities, smoking policy and access to the photocopier. Get these things right and you will avoid staff demotivation.
- Nurture and accentuate the key factors that create positive motivation within individuals, those aspects of work which give staff a deep sense of satisfaction: everything from professional development, promotion and responsibility to simple acknowledgement of a job 'well done'. Get these things right and you will ensure people will want to perform and to perform well.

Vroom's expectancy theory

Victor Vroom's expectancy theory, like that of Hertzberg, also offers us a practical application. In it, Vroom identifies principles linked to the achievement of goals chiefly the notion that:

- There is, or can be, a virtuous circle involved in this process; namely purposeful activity leads to goals and the liking for achieving them acts as a spur to people and the pattern repeats itself as new goals are set.
- The positive effect is multiplied in proportion to the degree which the goals are regarded as attainable. Thus the higher the probability of success the greater will be the strength of motivational feeling.

Again the implications for managers are clear. Set goals that are either too easy or hopelessly unrealistic and you will inspire no one. Give people a challenging target on the other hand and they may just surprise themselves, and you, in the process. As in other instances you need to be wary of a blanket approach. Individuals will need to be persuaded in different ways according to their beliefs and aspirations. Timing is also an issue, the most effective interventions are invariably at the outset when the task appears most daunting and the belief in accomplishing it less certain (Forsyth, 2000).

Motivation principles for managers

Motivation, as we've said, and as these theories exemplify, is a complex business: one which is affected by many disparate factors. Nonetheless we can discern a number of guiding principles to help us when we seek to motivate colleagues:

- *There is no magic formula* – no simple lever, least of all money, for maintaining or increasing motivation specifically in universities or indeed elsewhere.

- *Success, as ever, lies in the details* – in minimising the dissatisfiers and maximising the motivators. The motivational climate of your department is literally the sum total of all the pluses and minuses of the various individual factors, on both sides of the equation. As such it is essential you consider *all of them* on either side.

- *Continuity and consistency* – establishing a positive motivational climate takes time. It doesn't just happen overnight. It requires constant attention. Almost everything you do has motivational consequences. You should, therefore, always attempt to anticipate the effects, and equally importantly the side effects, of your actions. Thus the introduction of a new system aimed at cost saving, for example, will not secure the maximum positive effect if the process of complying with it is perceived as bureaucratic, and time consuming. Indeed, the lasting motivational effect may well be a negative one.

- *Differences in timescale* – motivation and performance levels do not rise and fall together. Rather performance always follows motivation. Thus if you keep your ear to the ground you may be able to prevent a drop in motivation adversely affecting levels of performance. Equally, you need to be patient and avoid overreacting if initiatives you take do not instantly yield the desired effect.

- *Always keep others in mind* – the things that motivate or concern your colleagues may not be ones you value yourself. Equally, what you believe is important may not be important to them. No matter. It is what *they* value that counts. You must be careful therefore not to dismiss matters and suggestions out of hand. Resist your internal censor. If not, you will at best be regarded as uncaring, and at worst may miss the opportunity to improve your motivational climate.

Your department's motivational climate

What about the motivational climate within your department? If you are to make a positive difference it is also important you understand the nature of your motivational climate; not least so that you will know the effect of the actions you decide to take. It may well be you feel that you know the atmosphere of your department well enough; indeed you may even feel you know it only too well! Even so, you should still be prepared to acknowledge that not everything may be as it appears; that signs and attitudes may not be what they seem; that departmental meetings, staff appraisals, informal gatherings and MBWA may have given you a sharp insight into the motivational climate, but maybe not a comprehensive picture or, indeed, an accurate one. Why not? This maybe due to any number of reasons: openness may not have been encouraged; the belief that no one ever seems to listen; the fear of reprisal; peer pressure; the lack of understanding; a lack of time; 'it is just simply not done around here'; etc. Whatever the reason, the point is, no matter how well you feel you know it, you should still be prepared to test your assumptions and allow yourself to be surprised.

Appalachian State University

The simplest way of finding out exactly how people feel is, of course, to ask them. You may not, however, as we've said, get either a frank or an honest answer in public settings, or even in private one-to-one conversations. A more reliable alternative, as many employers have come to recognise, is to survey staff opinion – a trend which is also growing among HEIs. Occupational stress surveys, for example, carried out institution-wide by external consultants, and often yielding unexpected outcomes, have become increasingly commonplace. Few universities, however, have matched the rigour, depth or honesty with which Appalachian State University, one of sixteen institutions that make up the University of North Carolina system, has attempted to assess their 'Faculty quality of life' (Durham *et al.*, 1998).

Working to a brief set by the provost's office, 'to design and implement a study of faculty to identify personal and institutional factors influencing their perception of the quality of life', the university's Hubbard Center for Faculty and Staff Support team developed a ninety-minute structured interview protocol derived from Senge's *The Fifth Discipline* (1990b). Following a pilot study of university administrators, the researchers (in male and female mixed pairs) interviewed a 10 per cent stratified random sample of forty-eight full-time, tenure track faculty members representing the demographic parameters of the population. The interviewers, with the interviewees' permission, hand-recorded or keyboarded the responses and then analysed the nature, frequency and context of them. In this way, they were able to identify several major themes: faculty perceptions, that is, which have given a clear direction to the university in its desire to maintain its tradition of strong faculty–student relationships and ensure faculty vitality and well-being. The team found that:

1   'Teaching and interactions with students have the greatest impact overall on faculty life.' (Teaching excellence is a primary mission of the university.)
2   'The department chairperson, departmental climate and relationships with colleagues can make academic life "heaven or hell".'
3   'Most faculty members feel they have difficulty balancing the demands of teaching, research and service as well as difficulty balancing personal and family lives with professional expectations.'
4   'Key incidents can have significant negative impact on overall perceptions of well-being.'
5   'A common faculty perception is that the institution is characterised by a reversal of the state and university motto, *esse quam videri*' ('here to be seen', i.e. staff do not think management 'walk the talk').

The Appalachian study is also remarkable in that it managed to fulfil the two essential preconditions for an effective opinion poll without involving an outside agency: namely, faculty perceived it to be not only a genuine initiative (as opposed to a gimmick), but also one which was organised in such a way they felt free to say what they really thought without fear of any comeback.

These conditions are difficult to replicate when it comes to your own department. The very fact of conducting a survey may be seen as an admission of failure or difficulty; even the sheer novelty may itself be sufficient to arouse suspicion. Nonetheless, even if your HEI does not want to take a leaf from Appalachian State University, you can still meet these preconditions in other ways. For example:

–   by linking your survey to, and making it part of, a key initiative: e.g. the formulation of your department's strategic plan; the department's annual review; a staff development action plan; as a response to an initiative from the university centre;
–   by allowing respondents the opportunity to remain anonymous if they wish;

Box 5.9 Faculty staff survey questionnaire in one UK 'new' (post-1992) university

Name (optional) _____

1   What three things do you *like* most about:
    (i)   your current job
    (ii) the university

2   What three things *concern* you most about:
    (i)   your current job
    (ii) the university

3   What do you consider to be the three main things you offer in contributing to the work of the university?

4   What do you regard as:
    (i)   your main achievement this year
    (ii) the university's main achievement this year

5   Are there any skills you have which are not fully utilised in your work?

6   What do you believe should be the new faculty's main goals and priorities?

7   What are the *values* you would most like to see/feel in the faculty on a day-to-day basis?

8   What three things could the faculty do to make a positive difference in your working life?

9   Any other comments you would like to make?

–   by explaining how the findings will be used and when you will also give feedback to staff.

In this way, you should be able to convince staff that you yourself do not have an ulterior motive (other than the well-being of the department) and that you are serious about eliciting a genuine and candid response (see Box 5.9 for an exemplar model of one such survey in a newly created faculty in a UK 'new' university).

There is, of course, one further prerequisite of such surveys, and that is to do with you rather than your colleagues. You've got to be prepared to listen, and to act, on what you might not like or wish to hear. Unless you are prepared to do so, you should not proceed with this idea. An alternative, or indeed an additional, approach, one which may not generate as incisive an outcome but no less a reflective one, is to conduct your own self-assessment of your:

(i)   Department – motivation is based on trust. To what extent do you and your colleagues have mutual trust in, and positive expectations of, one another? See Box 5.10.

(ii) HEI – what contribution does your institution make to the motivational climate in your department? What functional, economic and psychological benefits does your institution offer staff? In short, is your university a good employer? See Box 5.11.

Box 5.10 Assess the climate of your department

Trust is the set of expectations that one individual has in another individual, group or organisational unit. Mutual trust is the extent to which two or more individuals share positive expectations in one another. Think about members of your department while completing this questionnaire. The purpose of this self-assessment is to stimulate personal reflection and development.

Directions: The following statements assess various aspects of trust between you (as head) and faculty/staff in your department. Please use the following scale to indicate your level of agreement with each of the statements below:

Strongly disagree 1	Moderately disagree 2	Slightly disagree 3	Neutral 4	Slightly agree 5	Moderately agree 6	Strongly agree 7

Faculty and staff trust that I . . .

____ 1 am completely honest with them

____ 2 place our department's interests above my own

____ 3 will keep the promises I make

____ 4 am competent in performing my job

____ 5 express my true feelings about important issues

____ 6 care about their well-being

____ 7 can contribute to our department's success

____ 8 take actions that are consistent with my words

____ 9 share important information with them

____ 10 care about the future of our department

____ 11 can help solve important problems in our department

____ 12 have consistent expectations of them

____ 13 would make personal sacrifices for our department

____ 14 would acknowledge my own mistakes

____ 15 can help our department thrive in the future

____ 16 can be relied upon

I trust that faculty and staff . . .

____ 17 are completely honest with me

____ 18 place our department's interests above their own

____ 19 will keep the promises they make

____ 20 are competent in performing their jobs

____ 21 express their true feelings about important issues

____ 22 care about my well-being

____ 23 can contribute to our department's success

____ 24 take actions that are consistent with their words

____ 25 share important information with me

____ 26 care about the future of our department

____ 27 can help solve important problems in our department

____ 28 have consistent expectations of me

____ 29 would make personal sacrifices for our department

____ 30 would acknowledge their own mistakes

____ 31 can help our department thrive in the future

____ 32 can be relied upon

Definitions: *Trust* is the set of expectations that one individual has in another individual, group or organisational unit in terms of four dimensions (openness, caring, reliability and competence). *Mutual trust* is the extent to which two or more individuals have positive expectations in one another along the four dimensions.

Scoring: Record the sum of the scale values for the following questionnaire items. The potential range of subtotal scores is 4–28 and the potential range of total dimension scores is 8–56. Use your relative scores in each of the dimensions to assess the nature of mutual trust in your department. Subtotal scores less than 20 and total scores less than 40 indicate areas for possible improvement.

Openness

____ 1
____ 5
____ 9
____ 14
    ____ Subtotal

____ 17
____ 21
____ 25
____ 30
    ____ Subtotal
    ____ **Total**

Reliability

____ 3
____ 8
____ 12
____ 16
    ____ Subtotal

____ 19
____ 24
____ 28
____ 32
    ____ Subtotal
    ____ **Total**

Caring

____ 2
____ 6
____ 10
____ 13
    ____ Subtotal

____ 18
____ 22
____ 26
____ 29
    ____ Subtotal
    ____ **Total**

Competence

____ 4
____ 7
____ 11
____ 15
    ____ Subtotal

____ 20
____ 23
____ 27
____ 31
    ____ Subtotal
    ____ **Total**

Source: Shulman, 1998; adapted from Myers, 1991

Box 5.11 Is your university a good employer?

What messages does your institution give out to your staff? To prospective employees? To the outside world? What is the nature of the motivational situation in your university and how does it affect your department? Listed below are the dozen variables which constitute the 'employer brand' (the perception on which your reputation is based). Consider each in turn and rate them (1 being the most negative, 5 the most positive). Identify the shortfalls in the university and department which you need to address to realise your aspirations.

1   **Vision and leadership**
   - How clear is the existing vision?
   - Is it demonstrated by senior management?
   - Is the strategy to achieve the vision clear?
   - What is the style of leadership? Is it aligned with the vision?

2   **Policies and values**
   - What is the balance between reality and aspiration?
   - Are values implicit or explicit?
   - Are policies applied consistently?
   - Are values demonstrated in behaviour?
   - Are values linked to performance management?

3   **Fairness and cooperation**
   - Is equality and diversity taken seriously?
   - How do academic and 'non-academic' staff feel about one another?
   - What is the degree of cooperation between faculties/departments and central services?
   - What is the level of mutual respect?

4   **Corporate personality**
   - How would you describe your organisational culture? (see Chapter 2)
   - How does it manifest itself (language, artefacts)?
   - What is the balance between stability and risk-taking?
   - How far does the 'corporate culture' extend?

5   **External reputation**
   - To what extent are staff views coloured by their perceptions of external reputation.
   - Who are your key audiences? How do they feel about you?
   - Reputation for what? Cutting edge research; academic innovation; care for students; range of offerings; challenge to status quo, etc.

6   **Communication**
   - Do your people know what you are trying to do?
   - Are they engaged with you on this journey?
   - Do they feel they are listened to?
   - Are good practices and ideas shared across your university?
   - Do staff think their individual line managers are good communicators?

7   Recruitment and induction

- Do you attract the best people?
- What is the initial contact like for people who approach your institution?
- Does it match your external reputation?
- Does your recruitment process leave candidates (successful and unsuccessful ones) feeling good about themselves and you and your university?
- How does the 'first thirty days' affect new post-holders?

8   Performance management

- Is there clarity of standards and targets for all staff?
- What happens to those who are 'underperforming'?
- How do you bring out the best in people?
- Is performance management linked with your institutions plans and aspirations?
- Do all managers grasp the importance of performance management?

9   Development

- Is personal and professional development planning a feature for everyone?
- What do you do to encourage continuous improvement?
- Is promised development delivered?
- Is there development for the current job or career, or both?

10   Working environment

- What is the quality of your working environment?
- Physical – light, heat, decor, furniture
- Equipment including IT
- Amenities – restaurants, meeting places, etc.
- Do staff have 'social space'?

11   Reward

- Increments or performance-related pay?
- Benefits versus salary?
- Do you pay for scarcity/role of supply and demand?
- Pay for the job or pay for performance?
- How well do you see non-financial rewards?

12   Post-employment

- People die or leave – you hope most of them leave. What will they say when they've gone?
- How does your university look on their CV?
- What legendary figures have been members of your staff?
- Do you breed 'high-fliers'?
- How sensitive are you to the reasons people leave?

Source: adapted from Barrow and Davenport, 2002

Box 5.12 Prompts for improving the motivational climate in your department

Motivators	To maximise satisfaction
• **Achievement**	• Do all staff have SMART (and not DUMB) targets? • Do staff feel able 'to get the best out of their job'?
• **Recognition**	• Do you recognise staff achievements in departmental meetings – in writing – in the university's newsletter? • Do you celebrate staff achievements? • Do you reward staff achievements beyond the norm? • In what ways do you recognise lifetime achievement? • Is 'well done' and 'thank you' a regular part of your vocabulary?
• **Work itself**	• Do staff have the fullest opportunity to do what they do best? • Are all staff allocated to roles that are right for them? • Do you foster and encourage self-direction as well as accountability; do you have the balance? • Do you respect and value academic freedom (if not the freedom for academics to do what they like)? • Do staff have manageable workloads? • Do you involve staff in decisions affecting their role? • Do staff enjoy their work? • Do you engender a sense of fun? • Is leadership – from the top – seen as inspirational?
• **Responsibility**	• Do you give staff the opportunity to take on further responsibilities? • Do you encourage staff to 'take ownership' of their roles?
• **Advancement**	• Is your promotional ladder organised to recognise achievement in the most optimum way? Do you make full use of it? How do staff feel about it? • Do you give staff regular opportunities to add to their experience? • Do you encourage and support staff in developing their professional networks? • Do you show commitment to their career progression?
• **Growth**	• Do staff leave for positive reasons? • Do leavers go on to do bigger and better things? • Does your department breed 'high fliers'

Maintenance	To minimise dissatisfaction
• **Institutional policy and administration**	• What rules do you have and how do staff regard them? (intellectual property rights; workload allocations; consultancy arrangements; scholarly activity; conference expenses; smoking policy, etc.) • What systems are staff expected to use and how do they regard them? (quality assurance, student data, management information, finance, personnel, etc.)
• **Supervision**	• Is your management style appropriate for your department? • Do you consult properly? • Do you give staff the support they need? • Are you considered a good communicator? • Do you know how staff rate you?
• **Working conditions**	• Are working conditions seen as attractive? Do they meet staff expectations? • Is equipment regarded as suitable? • Are there additional facilities that are regarded as necessary? • Are staff involved in considering proposals for change?
• **Salary**	• Are salaries seen as fair internally? • Is there evidence of pay inequities? • How do salaries compare relative to those HEIs you regard as rivals? • Do you make the most of the salary flexibility available to you? • What benefits do staff have? Do you use them fully? Fairly?
• **Relationship with peers**	• Do staff willingly collaborate? • Do you have teams or tribes? • Do you foster and encourage peer group review?
• **Personal life conditions**	• Do staff have social space? How do they rate it? • Do staff work longer hours than they should? • Do you recognise the value of – and support – work-life balance? • Do staff confide in you?
• **Status**	• Do staff feel valued? • Does the way they are described in institutional publications support this? • What recognition is there of long service, special expertise and outstanding performance? • Do staff feel management supports their position within the university as a whole?
• **Security**	• Do all staff have a job role? • Do staff know what is expected of them? • Do staff know how they are performing? • Is corporate communication – internal and external – regarded as good? • Do you hoard information? • Is management seen as fair and robust? • Do you have an adult–adult employment relationship?

Think about how your dean or faculty/staff might complete this survey. Remember that it takes time to improve perceptions of trust in ongoing relationships. Work on the dimensions where your scores are the lowest to increase the overall climate of mutual trust. Develop an action plan to improve the climate of trust in your department and university.

These self-assessments, along with your anonymous staff survey and your own informal observations, should give you a clearer picture of the motivational situation in your department.

Having 'taken the temperature' you now need to *act* on it. It maybe that, if you have not already done so, you need to develop a modus operandi based on the leadership strategies highlighted earlier in this book. You will also find that the principles discussed in this chapter, on performance management, target-setting and feedback, can, when applied consistently, make a major positive difference. What else you can, and should, do will of course depend on your particular circumstances, though, given the nature of academic environments in general, it is likely you will find more freedom of manoeuvre with regard to the 'psychological contract' of staff, than their 'economic' one. Either way, you should leave no stone unturned. More specifically, you should consider at both macro- and micro-level the following:

(i)   All staff, and students for that matter, want and need four basic things: challenge, a sense of belonging, support and social space. Do you provide them? If not, what can you do about it?

(ii)   Research tells us, as we noted above, that staff tend to value, in order of priority: recognition of their work; involvement in change; a job 'that gets the best out of me'; role clarity; consultation; 'management that motivates'. Are your actions consistent with these priorities?

(iii)   Following Hertzberg, what can you do to minimise the dissatisfiers and maximise the motivators? Examine each one in turn – as outlined in Box 5.12 – and draw up an action plan for your department.

You will only realise your action plan, however, if you are able to maximise the potential of your staff. Staff motivation and staff development are both sides of the same coin. How though can you best encourage and facilitate staff development?

6 Developing staff

To discover and to teach are distinct functions: they are also distinct gifts and are not commonly found united in the same person.

Cardinal John Henry Newman, 1852

A mistake is only a mistake if it happens twice.

Merrill Lynch, Investment Bankers, Code of Practice

Staff development in HE has come a long way in a short time. From a cottage industry twenty years ago it is now an established, if not always accepted, feature of institutional life. Almost all UK universities have a staff development unit, or educational development unit, and in many instances both. Where once staff development was narrowly conceived in terms of teaching and learning improvement for individual academics, it is now more broadly identified, and rightly so, with professional development for all staff in line with predetermined institutional priorities. A recognised priority area itself, it is not uncommon for UK universities to devote 5 per cent of their staffing budget to staff development and training (Brew, 1995; Webb, 1996).

The learning organisation

The debate surrounding the growth and maturation of staff development within HE has, in turn, been influenced by the emergence and popularisation of a parallel phenomenon, the concept of the 'learning organisation'. Indeed, a book on staff development that doesn't make reference to this idea is now the exception rather than the norm. And for good reason, for the concept is transparently an attractive proposition: one that, as we noted in Chapter 3, could give organisations the leading competitive edge they yearn. More than that, the emphasis on learning, the values it espouses and the practical way forward it envisages, all resonate strongly with the way in which HE operates in particular. It should not surprise us then, even if it is rare, to have on this occasion a 'managerial concept' that is almost as well known and endorsed across HE as it is in the corporate world beyond. It is surely self-evident, advocates argue, that HEIs as 'institutions of learning', and latterly as champions of lifelong learning, should want, and seek, to be 'learning organisations' as well (Duke, 1992; Martin, 1999). What could be more logical, natural and desirable?

Unfortunately, the reality, however, could not be more different. The concept is well over a decade old and yet there is little evidence that *any* organisation has managed to transform itself into a 'learning organisation', either in HE or elsewhere. The view has formed that the goal may, in fact, be an unattainable one although others, notably John Burgoyne (2001), have admitted: 'our early thinking on the learning organisation had some naivety and was a bit happy-clappy. Because we came from self-development, there was a lot about love, trust and getting teams to share their needs and aspirations. While some of the values were quite appealing, there was a naivety about power relationships.' Still others maintain there was nothing new about the concept anyway (Garrett, 1995); that it was derived in large part from the pioneering work of Reg Revans (1984) (on action learning) and Chris Argyris and Donald Schon (1978) (on single-loop and double-loop learning) and that it was time for considering a new model, the *'learning, knowledge-managing, virtual organisation'*. Senge (1998) himself now counsels: 'Never say to staff, "we are going to become a learning organisation"' lest you leave yourself open to a hiding for nothing. Lastly, we should remind ourselves that, at one level, there can, in fact, be no such thing as a 'learning organisation' for the simple reason it is human communities who learn, not organisations.

That said, it would be wrong to conclude that, because of its failure in practice, the idea does not have merit. On the contrary, it still has value as an aspiration, as a modus operandi, and as a guide to what both you and your HEI should be doing, and, equally important, what you should not (see Box 6.1). In following it you will at least make progress towards this elusive goal (see Figure 6.1).

Box 6.1 Learning and non-learning organisations

Learning organisation

- Anticipates future problems
- Pays attention to external environment
- Continuously seeks improvement
- Problem-solving is based on conceptual analysis and understanding
- Problem-solving is organisation-wide and problem-centred
- Rewards for growth, initiative and creativity
- Job definitions encourage exploration, initiative and information-sharing

Non-learning organisation

- Reacts to current problems
- Pays attention only to internal operations
- Responds to accumulation of poor performance
- Problem solving is based on trial and error
- Problem-solving is compartmentalised and hierarchical
- Rewards for historical performance
- Jobs are narrowly circumscribed and risk-taking is discouraged

Source: adapted from National Commission on Education Briefing, 1995

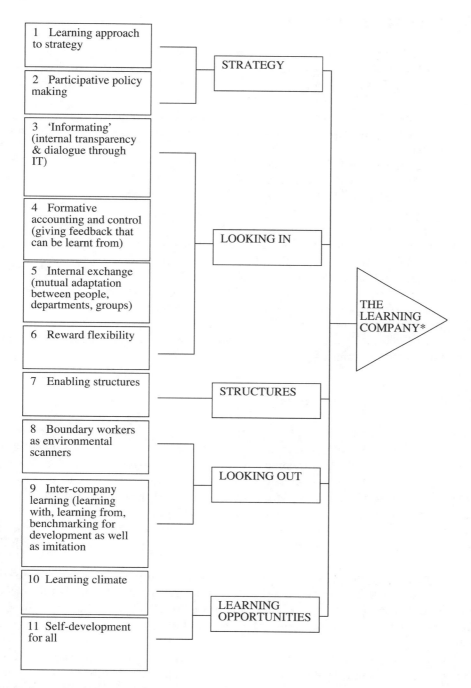

Figure 6.1 Distinguishing characteristics of the learning organisation

Source: adapted from Pedler, Burgoyne and Boydell, 1991

* The authors' preference for 'learning company' is an aesthetic choice. They believe it a more 'convivial' term than the 'learning organisation'.

Valuing staff development

HE has been very tardy about showing a *genuine* commitment to the idea of staff development. Too often the latter has unfairly and mistakenly been given a low priority and with it low status. This has been due in part to:

- perception: its (pejorative) association with low-level 'training';
- self-infliction: the repellent jargon ('staffdevelopmentese') used by some practitioners;
- a clash of cultures: the antipathy between the idea of staff development and the variety of cults prevalent within academic life (the 'gifted amateur', the 'intellectual', etc.).

It is also symptomatic of academic environments in general; in that the latter tend to be cultures of 'knowers' (the cult of the 'expert') rather than 'learners' and as Chris Argyris (1985) reminds us 'Why Smart People Have So Much Difficulty Learning' is because they think they know it all already.

Whatever the particular reasons, and no doubt they are difficult obstacles to overcome, it is important you do not succumb to them. You must seek not only to value staff development but *be seen to do so too* by making it one of your key priorities. To do that you first need to be clear what is meant by staff development and, equally, what your institution means by it.

What is staff development?

One additional reason why staff development has not been accorded the status and priority it merits in HE has been because of the way it has been conceived, often in a very narrow sense, as a tailored programme of activities aimed at remedying a specific skills deficit. While staff development can be about this type of provision it is by no means restricted to it. Indeed the phrase has sufficient elasticity that it can, and has been taken to, mean anything and everything. And herein lies the problem. To say you favour and value staff development can be seen to be just so much words. That said, we can, in fact, discern a degree of convergence on this issue in the literature.

At the *organisational* level, staff development is usually integrated with the institution's overall human resource strategy and 'is normally considered to include the institutional policies, programmes and procedures which facilitate and support staff so that they may fully serve their own and their institution's needs' (Webb, 1996).

At the *individual* level, staff development is concerned with the acquisition of something that is *new*: a new skill; a new way of seeing things; a new attitude; a new set of feelings; a new level of consciousness. It does not mean more of something that one has already: it is not simply an increase in knowledge or a higher degree of an existing skill. Rather development is a *different* state of being or functioning. Operationally, staff development is about learning in all its variety of forms including:

- education: those processes which result in formal awards up to and including postgraduate and professional qualifications;
- training: formal learning activities which may not lead to qualifications but may be undertaken at any time in a working career;
- development: informal learning experiences arising from the job; working with peers; liaising with partners and professional networks, etc. (Pedler *et al.*, 2001).

As one UK 'new' university has succinctly put it:

> Staff development is defined as a learning opportunity or activity which:
>
> - enhances the ability of individuals, teams and the institution to deliver the University's Mission and Strategic Plan;
> - enables staff to carry out their current and future roles effectively and to adapt to change;
> - assures the quality of teaching learning and research and the services which support them.

Put another way, staff development is about inducting staff into a 'community of practice' at both the institutional and disciplinary level; a process from which the individual and the institution should derive mutual benefit. Conceived in this way, staff development is, in practice, often guided by a number of working principles of which you need to be aware:

Expectations and responsibilities

It is usually anticipated that individual staff will take an active role in articulating their needs.

Heads of department carry the fundamental responsibility for ensuring that staff are enabled to perform their roles effectively and efficiently, and enjoy continuous learning opportunities through which their abilities and potential can be developed.

The principle of subsidiarity

As head of department, you are often granted a large degree of autonomy in fulfilling the responsibility you have been given: in the language you choose to use (or not); the way in which you determine development needs; the discretion you exercise in providing experiences; the way in which you manage resources to support development opportunities.

Emphasis on continuous professional development (CPD)

In keeping with the spirit of the 'learning organisation' concept, as well as recognising that in an age of lifelong learning 'what you learned last year is as important as what you achieved'. The near-universal tendency among HEIs, as elsewhere, has been to promote staff development as *a continuous and ongoing process*. You can anticipate you will be expected to establish behaviours and practices which actively encourage continuous professional development.

In what ways can, and should, you promote staff development? In the first instance:

- through understanding the strategic approach (or 'espoused theory') your own institution has towards staff development and using it as a *guide* for your actions;
- through understanding the nature of staff development in practice (or 'theory-in-use') in your institution and using it as a *means* of meeting the expectations your institution has placed on you;
- by exploring, considering and maximising the discretionary opportunities available to you.

Staff development in your university

Your own university's approach to staff development is, as we've noted, likely to be included in your institution's overall human resource strategy. What does this document tell you about the obligations you have to meet? What policy aims and objectives are laid down? What commitments are expressed? What guiding principles are enunciated? What statements of intent are made? Does it conceive of staff development as:

- Passive: a simple reporting mechanism on development activities?
- Active: anticipating performance improvement?
- Dynamic: establishing quantitative targets?
- Radical: establishing ratings and rewards alongside quantitative and operational performance criteria?

Does it commit your university to establishing a 'learning organisation'?

Either way, it is likely your university will anticipate adopting one of the following approaches (Harrison, 2002). Which one applies to your institution? What are the implications for you and your particular role?

A total or comprehensive approach

- This involves a systematic, full-scale analysis of all the organisation's training and development needs identified through discussion with all relevant stakeholders. It anticipates the establishment of an institution-wide staff development plan.
- It is favoured by institutions who regard their environment as relatively stable and those equipped with a robust specialist staff development function.
- *Risk*: development is confined solely to filling skills gaps in relation to current roles; it becomes disproportionately individual-led at the expense of institutional drivers.

A problem-centred approach

- This focuses on urgent problems facing the institution which require a training and development response. Development is selective and partial with the emphasis on flexibility rather than planning.

- It is favoured by institutions which regard their environment as highly unpredictable and those suffering severe resource constraint.
- *Risk*: development becomes preoccupied with responding to immediate needs and loses its long-term focus.

A business strategy approach

- This assumes that needs assessments and development plans must be produced and driven 'from the top' on the basis of the institution's key 'business drivers' (its own business strategy; operational priorities; the environmental changes it faces; etc.). It gives heads of department primary responsibility for staff development.
- It is favoured by institutions who regard their environment as highly competitive and those that are imbued with self-confidence.
- *Risk*: development fails to tap innovations 'bottom-up'; it becomes disproportionately business-led at the expense of individual professional fulfilment.

Such is the 'espoused theory'. To what extent, however, is this reflected in the way that staff development is actually delivered in practice. Is the practice consistent with the theory? Reflect on your own institution and consider if the 'theory-in-use' matches that of the 'espoused theory'. You can do this in a number of ways:

Perception and value

How is staff development regarded across your institution, and within your department? What value attaches to it?

Organisation

How is staff development formally organised in your institution? For example, via a faculty development committee, a small support unit, a large central unit, a central unit with departmental affiliates, a networked faculty development, an institutional 'ginger group', or do you have no formal provision?

Delivery

How is staff development 'delivered' in your institution, and within your department? Is it on-the-job or off-the-job? Ad hoc or systematic? Process- or event-driven? Remedial or developmental? Voluntaristic or comprehensive? Tolerated or evaluated? Implanted or embedded? A cost or an investment?

Role of staff and/or educational developer

Staff and educational developmental units can, in theory, fulfil a number of roles: as a provider of specialist services; a dispenser of advice; a counsellor; a collaborator; a broker; a controller, a 'change agent'; or indeed a variety of them. How does the unit operate in your institution? Is it consistent, in practice, with what your university is seeking to achieve in terms of staff development?

Model of practice

Staff development in many institutions is typically organised around one of three distinct approaches in practice (Brown and Somerlad, 1992):

- *fragmented*: one in which staff development is conducted as a singular ad hoc activity without reference to the needs or goals of the organisation;
- *formalised*: a 'systemic' approach based on an analysis of training needs;
- *focused*: one which regards training and development as continuous activities which are intrinsic to organisational well-being.

The tendency among organisations has been to evolve from a 'fragmented' approach to a 'focused' one via a more systematic 'formalised' phase. Such a trend is also consistent with the 'learning organisation' ideal (see Box 6.2). Which practical

---

Box 6.2 Emergent models of staff development

The fragmented approach

Training and development is:

- A cost not an investment
- Not linked to organisational goals
- Perceived as a luxury
- Based in a training department
- Primarily knowledge-based courses

The formalised approach

Training and development is:

- Systemic – part of career development
- Linked to human resource needs
- Linked to appraisal and individual needs
- Knowledge based courses plus a focus on skills
- Carried out by trainers and line managers

The focused approach

Training and development is:

- A continuous learning process
- Essential for organisational survival
- Linked to organisational strategy and individual goals
- On-the-job plus specialist courses
- Line manager's responsibility
- Tolerant

Source: adapted from Brown and Sommerlad, 1992

approach most closely resembles the staff development provision in your university? Again, is it consistent with your university's strategic staff development aim?

It may well be that in your institution the 'theory-in-use' is indeed consistent with the theory that is 'espoused'. You should not be too surprised, however, if it is not, for implementation naturally lags behind strategic formulation in practice. On the other hand, the mismatch should not be too great either. If it is, you should:

- seek clarification from your line manager;
- seek advice from your staff development officer: do not wait for them to come to you, they are nearly always only too willing to help;
- maintain good faith in the strategic approach articulated by your university;
- propose a practical way forward.

Remember that staff development is, as we noted earlier, about inducting staff into a 'community of practice' to the mutual benefit of them and their institution. As such, you cannot do worse, and more than likely you can do a great deal of good, than to use the design principles of the 'learning organisation' as your guide in determining staff development provision in your department (see Candy, 1998):

- Staff development should be:

    C   omprehensive
    A   nticipatory
    R   esearch-based
    E   xemplary
    E   mbedded
    R   eflective

- And have programme design criteria which are:

    L   inked and interconnected
    E   mpowering and transformative
    A   daptable and dynamic
    R   eflective and improvement-oriented
    N   on-hierarchical
    I   nteractive
    N   etwork- and group-based
    G   enerative and knowledge-creating.

Your university may have adopted these 'learning organisation' principles or indeed a similar model of development. Ultimately, however, it will be you who will have to implement it. How can you make the most of this opportunity, for your staff, your department and your institution?

Staff development in your department

Develop, agree and establish your own departmental staff development policy framework

You must first, as we've said, seek to understand the nature of staff development, the 'espoused theory' and the 'theory-in-use', within your institution. Beyond that, you must also seek to establish a similar clarity, as well as consistency, of purpose within your department. And the most effective way to do that is by developing and adopting a formal policy statement which makes this both explicit and transparent.

Departmental staff provision has too often been, and in many instances still is, a hotchpotch of academic tradition (concerning sabbaticals, conference support and the like) and ad hoc initiatives which are seldom coordinated or evaluated, and not always understood by those who might benefit from them; the process itself characterised by a lack of clarity over direction, the distribution of responsibility and the allocation of funding and resources. It is a condition which departments are increasingly spurning by formalising their staff development arrangements and it is a trend you would do well to emulate (Brew, 1995). Put another way, your first priority must be to develop your own *focused* approach at the local level.

It may be that you've inherited a staff development policy framework (in which case you should review it) or that you are starting from scratch. Either way, you should be aiming to develop and seek agreement on a framework appropriate to the needs of your department. It should be a comprehensive framework, too; one, that is, in which you address each of the following points.

Context

• Briefly outline the institutional and external environment within which your department operates.

• Explain how your staff development policy is linked to your departmental and institutional strategy.

• Outline the origins of your policy and how it was created; the process of consultation, etc.

Aims

• Elaborate the overall intentions of your policy, for example: to enhance the ability of staff to deliver the department's strategy; to carry out their current and future roles effectively; to adapt to change; to have job satisfaction; to achieve career progression; etc.

Objectives

• Specify the needs and priorities your policy will address, for example, in relation to: assessment practice; mode of teaching; learner support; student diversity; commercialisation; links to the community; research and innovation; and so on.

Guiding principles

• Identify the values and beliefs which underpin your policy, for example: commitment to individual empowerment; guarantee of equitable access; the establishment of a supportive, enabling framework; the opportunity for regular review.

Plan

• Specify the outcomes of your policy. Outline what you expect the department to achieve over the next 2 to 3 years. Set SMART targets: e.g. x per cent of staff formally qualified in teaching or members of professional teaching body; y per cent increase in the number of work-based learning opportunities for students; z per cent of the department's courses to be delivered by e-learning; a per cent increase in the number of students successfully completing their programme of study; b per cent of the department's income to be generated from 'third-stream' sources.

Delivery

• Identify the various ways in which the policy will be delivered, the emphasis being on the plural rather than the singular, that is all those mechanisms both on-the-job and off-the-job (see pp. 187–201).

Monitoring and evaluation

• Explain how you will measure the effectiveness of your staff development provision, the quality assurance process, for example: self-assessment; peer review; stakeholder evaluation; linkage to departmental decision-making.

Resources

• Specify the resources available to support the policy (for example, per capita allocation, discretionary allowance, departmental and central provision, the proportion of the staffing budget), and how the allocation will be managed (for example, staff development committee, line manager, institutional staff development manager, etc.).

• Indicate the level of support, or entitlements, which staff can expect to receive, including pro rata allowances for part-timers, for example: number of days study leave (typically thirty-five for full-time academic staff in UK 'new' universities); number of training days per year; conference expenses; materials allowance; professional membership subsidy; etc.

Identify and analyse staff development needs

The success, or otherwise, of your policy framework is dependent, in the first instance, on you having a sound grasp of the staff development needs in your department. Indeed an accurate and comprehensive needs analysis is a sine qua non of such frameworks. It is, however, not always easy to achieve, not least because individual staff themselves may not be sure what they need. Faulty methodology, poor application and insensitive communication can exacerbate this situation still further (Harrison, 2002). These are all pitfalls you must seek to avoid.

There are, in theory, a number of possible approaches you can take in determining individual development needs:

- Training needs survey: What training do you think you/they need?
- Competence study: What competency do you think you/they need?
- Task analysis: What tasks are required/do you do on this job?
- Performance analysis: How does this role impact on the performance of the department? What are, or should be, the critical accomplishments and how is each critical?

In practice, the tendency is to rely on an amalgam depending on the context in which you work. Thus training needs surveys, for example, tend to be used as a knee-jerk response to a series of complaints, as in 'how can we fix it?'

In the case of HE, where job roles are not always easy to define, however, the most fruitful way forward, as suggested earlier, is that based on standards of perform-ance and competency requirements. Having articulated job roles which specify these, you, and your colleagues, can use them as an objective measure in determining short-falls. Indeed, competency-based job roles provide you, and them, with a rich source of data by which you cannot only manage performance but also development too. As the assessment of needs is, or should be, a collective endeavour – on your part as well as theirs – it also follows that the more sources of information you can tap the greater likelihood there is of getting it right. In addition to *job roles* then, you should also consider the outcomes of the following.

Individual and team performance review

If you manage performance in your department in the way that's been suggested, you should find staff, both individually and collectively, becoming more confident in saying: 'Here's my personal (or team) strategic plan for the year? What do you think of it? What can you do for my personal (or team) development plan?' If they do not respond, then you need to prompt them explicitly: 'In view of the department's strategic plan and your own professional development to date, what competencies do you feel you need to acquire? And, what would be the best way, you think, of doing so?'

Course monitoring and review

Typically conducted formally on an annual basis, programme monitoring and review is now commonplace in virtually all university academic departments. This process invariably highlights issues or identifies problems and concerns. You need to distil the staff development implications.

Learning and teaching evaluations

The student evaluation of teaching, and that of course units, has likewise become increasingly formalised in many academic departments. What are the main areas for improvement?

Student feedback

Feedback from students is now canvassed with almost religious fervour and not solely with regard to learning and teaching. What do your questionnaire surveys, focus groups, student reps and staff–student committees tell you about the degree of student satisfaction? In what ways could staff development enhance the nature of the student experience?

External review

Universities have had, as we've noted, to become more accountable for the way they manage their affairs. To respond and to satisfy not just external examiners (of courses, as heretofore), but also those assessors, reviewers and auditors concerned with assuring quality in teaching (the teaching quality assessment, subject review and 'developmental engagement'), research (the RAE (research assessment exercise)) and overall well-being (the institutional audit). What are your department's strengths and weaknesses?

Equally, the QAA publishes extensive documentation on the purposes and processes of these quality assurance mechanisms. Measure your department against these benchmarks or better still have a 'critical friend' do so. What gaps do you need to make good?

Staff self-assessment surveys

Not a widespread practice, partly because the outcomes are not always reliable, and partly because staff very often mistrust such devices, regarding them as vehicles for admitting personal weaknesses. They can nevertheless be used to good effect provided you apply them tactfully, i.e. offer staff the opportunity for self-assessment but do not ask for the results of their self-assessment. Respect their desire to keep this information confidential to themselves. Instead ask staff for the outcomes of the process – to identify the staff development activities they wish to undertake (see Appendix 3).

Assess and determine how you will deliver staff development

Staff development is not just about 'content', it is about 'method' too. Once you have identified your department's development needs you need to consider the various ways in which you can address them, including those which your staff have indicated they would prefer. It is important you are flexible in this regard. Try not to let yourself, and others, be limited by any preconception you or they might have. Instead think of all the learning opportunities that can arise along the broadest of continuums: individual–collective development; professional–departmental development and the

Figure 6.2 'One size doesn't fit all': a comprehensive approach to planning staff development activity

interstices between them (individual–professional, individual–departmental, collective–professional, collective–departmental) (see Figure 6.2). What staff development you identify and how you deliver it will, of course, depend on your needs analysis and it may well be that your assessment leads you to focus heavily on one or two aspects of this schema. You should, however, arrange to ensure you do at least have some staff development activity planned for each of the different aspects of the model exemplified in Figure 6.2.

Establish a learning climate in your department

More than that, you should be proactive in seeking to establish a learning climate within your department. How? By using the following:

- being seen to be continuously learning yourself; by setting yourself challenging learning goals;

- continuously providing staff with learning opportunities both on- and off-the-job;
- providing new learning experiences from which colleagues can learn;
- not being afraid to encourage staff to challenge the traditional ways of doing things;
- tolerating mistakes by colleagues provided they try to learn from them;
- continuously helping staff to review, reach conclusions from their experiences and to decide what to plan next;
- building 'learning into the system' so that it is an integral not a marginal departmental activity.

You can do this last in a whole variety of ways; the conventional and not-so-conventional. Take the examples that follow. How many of these activities do you consciously promote? If not, why not? Consider the merits in each case of applying them (if you have not already done so) in your department.

Formal learning opportunities

- Dedicated periods of staff leave: sabbaticals, study leave.
- Off-campus workshops, seminars and conferences.
- Institutional and departmental workshops, seminars and conferences.

A common weakness of these events is that they often fail to attract colleagues beyond a dedicated minority: i.e. they suffer from the 'persistent absentee' and/or the 'not invented here' syndromes. Well-targeted events, however, based on an intimate knowledge of staff's individual learning needs, will help you to overcome this problem; to reach the parts of your department that other initiatives have failed to do before.

- Departmental 'away-days' or retreats.

Not an extended departmental meeting, or a protracted information-giving monologue, and not just a different location either. But rather a genuinely *different* interactive session held off-campus. One that has a clear purpose, on, say, a common problem, challenge or issue, is inclusive, nurtures team building and generates productive outcomes.

- National and institutional funded projects in developing learning and teaching.

Learning from one another

Audit of departmental expertise

How well do your colleagues know one another's expertise? – in learning and teaching innovation, external examining, quality assessment and review, research applications, refereeing publications, editing journals, handling committees, utilising new technologies, etc. Establish a simple departmental database using a common pro forma.

'Offers' and 'requests'

Establish a 'skills-swap' scheme which builds on the department's database of staff expertise. Staff members identify three areas in which they are willing to share their expertise with colleagues (in say, using WebCT or implementing equal opportunities) in return for help in addressing their own particular needs for help in, say, applying for European Union (EU) funding or writing up a book proposal. The advantages of such schemes are self-evident. Not only that they also, more importantly, bring staff needs out into the open in a non-threatening way. The scheme recognises, in other words, that when it comes to expertise we are often both experts and novices in equal measure.

Shadowing

This can be time consuming but is, nonetheless, a simple and very effective means of enabling staff to understand or learn to undertake the role of others – as programme leader, admissions tutor, assessment board chair, and the like. It is particularly useful when there is little written guidance yet there is relatively easy access to experienced practitioners.

Mentoring

Often cited yet not always understood or applied, mentoring is in fact the fastest growing method of professional development in all kinds of working environments today. Not simply in the conventional sense of helping new staff through their probationary period, but also in terms of career enhancement in general and, as we shall see later, in helping those disadvantaged in employment (such as women and ethnic minorities) overcome barriers to their progression in particular.

At its heart mentoring is a cooperative and nurturing relationship between a more experienced staff member and one that is less so. It is not a line management relationship. Or, put another way, when line managers attempt to act as mentors they invariably find the more formal aspects of their role (probationary review, workload allocation, performance appraisal, etc.) ultimately clashes with the cooperative ethos on which the mentoring agreement is based.

Peer observation and review of teaching

This was typically regarded with deep mistrust and suspicion until not so long ago, and still is in some quarters, peer observation and review has become the norm rather than the exception in most university departments. And for good reason too, for despite what the 'nay-sayers' may claim, by enabling staff to share their professional experience and expertise in confidence, peer observation is in fact one of the best ways in which staff can improve their teaching performance. To be fair, in those instances where peer review has not worked well, it can very often be because the scheme has been operated with a very different purpose in mind, for example as a basis for appraisal or promotion, or simply for making judgements about staff. To avoid this fate you need to ensure your scheme offers staff the guarantee of confidentiality. That way you are most likely to gain their confidence, if not always their consent. More than that, you will need to have clear ground rules for the process, as well as guidance on how participants should conduct each of the different aspects: the

pre-meeting, the observation itself and the post-observation feedback. Equally important, you should ensure staff are explicitly prompted to identify their professional
development needs, on the one hand, and disseminate their own examples of good
practice to the rest of their colleagues in the department, on the other.

Team reviews

Ensure your course teams and administrative teams get into the habit of reviewing
their work, not in a passive, reactive way on an annual basis, as is so often the norm,
but in a regular, systematic and ongoing fashion at every opportunity. Build reviews
into the calendar in the first instance, though ideally, they should become a normal
part of the daily routine.

Job rotation

Not always practicable, and potentially disruptive, but planned job rotation can be a
powerful means of not only developing new ideas, skills and expertise but also of
generating different perspectives, cross-fertilisation and very often a new and
improved way of doing things.

Departmental meetings

Learning and development may not be the primary business of meetings but is too
often a neglected aspect of such gatherings. Increase awareness and reflection by
including:

- Staff report-backs on workshops and conferences they have attended as a brief
  agenda item (literally five minutes). Reports should take the form of one side
  of A4 outlining in bullet point format the key learning points for the department.
- An appendix to the meeting minutes outlining in summary form the development activities of staff: papers published, grants secured, conferences attended,
  and so on.

Departmental focus groups

Much maligned, and not always fairly, focus groups are underrated and underused
in HE as a means of enhancing collective learning. Such groups, diverse in character,
can often be a useful source for helping your department to address particular
concerns (such as student retention, assessment workload, the integration of part-time
staff, and so on) or indeed to develop new initiatives (the production of a development handbook for staff, the creation of a 'good practice' guide on assessment, etc.).

Departmental newsletter

This works best, of course, if it is published on a regular basis. It is easier to maintain continuity, as well as interest, if you share the responsibility. Alternate the editors
and use it to celebrate learning achievements as well as inform staff of forthcoming
events.

Learning noticeboard

Provide a dedicated noticeboard. Get each of your teams to take it in turn to high-light and celebrate 'a learning theme of the month': this can be work- or non-work-related.

Lunchtime forums

Identify your main organisational group (or groups), course leaders, subject heads, research coordinators, or simply all departmental staff. Establish a regular meeting time, say the second Wednesday of each month, 12 to 2 pm – and stick to it.

You supply the food and refreshment and help (or better still ask one of your colleagues) to develop a programme of activities based on what the participants themselves have said they would like to do. Such forums typically choose to focus on an array of issues: ranging from the topical (the implications of 'top-up fees') to the local (a SWOT analysis of the department), the global (the new academic scholar), the theoretical (the multiple meanings of mass HE), and the practical (the institutional costing model for new courses). Either way, the participants in these informal gatherings nearly always derive, often to their surprise, far greater benefit in terms of knowledge, understanding and a sense of belonging, than they had originally expected.

Learning from others

Staff secondments and exchanges

This is a staple of staff development and typically takes place with other universities, and usually with an international partner institution. You should also consider second-ment opportunities for staff with partner employers. Indeed seconding staff into industry on a short-term basis (as opposed to bringing employers into academia) would arguably have a greater impact on your departmental culture than any other single factor.

Reciprocal workshops with other departments

This is too often an underestimated and underused practice. Departments all face common problems and issues, on the one hand, yet nearly always have varying levels of expertise, on the other. Reciprocal workshops and joint events with other depart-ments can be extremely valuable, then, in increasing learning through the sharing of ideas and expertise, in generating new and different perspectives on mutual concerns, and in addressing deficiencies (or 'skills gaps') particular to each. More than that, they are also likely, since individuals are more inclined to behave better in the company of others, to do so in less time, and with less rancour, than would be the case if these events were confined solely to the members of your department.

Partnering

This is a 'blind date' scheme aimed at increasing awareness and understanding of working practices and improving working relationships institution-wide. Strike up an agreement with central services (or, if already a central service, then with depart-ments), arrange reciprocal 'open days' and pair off staff who then have to explain what they do.

Visits to other institutions

Don't waste time 're-inventing the wheel' if it already exists elsewhere. In such instances, it is far more cost-effective to have staff visit other institutions than it is to bring in 'outsiders' to tell them how it is done. Not only that, such visits often deepen staff understanding as well as influence their attitude to change; a shift in developmental learning that would be unlikely to occur if they had attended an 'in-house' seminar instead.

Bringing in consultants

Often misused and occasionally maligned, consultants can, nevertheless, in the right circumstances, still give you considerable 'added value'. They come in all shapes and sizes and willingly perform any number of roles, most notably as 'doctor', 'detective', 'salesperson' or 'travel agent'. And herein lies the dilemma. For, on the one hand, you can use them in almost any circumstance, yet, on the other, you need to avoid using them in the wrong circumstances. The key cardinal principle to remember is that *consultants are there as 'outsiders' to help you do what you can't do alone*. As such, you should only use them as and when these instances arise – and only then.

To get the most out of them you also need to be honest, both with them and with staff, about the nature and purpose of their role, whether it be that of 'critical friend', impartial facilitator, advocate of new ideas, project manager or systems analyst, etc. That way, you should at least avoid the pitfalls that can so often stall a consultancy relationship before it is barely under way.

Benchmarking

The penchant for performance indicators, itself a consequence of the governmental drive for greater accountability, has become a commonplace activity both among and within many institutions. Try to ensure, however, you do not rely solely on indicators from like-minded departments, or QAA guidelines, as your only comparators. Consciously assess yourself, or invite others to assess you, against other third-party instruments: for example, the European Foundation Quality Model (EFQM) for business excellence, the Cabinet Office Charter-Mark, Investors in People, the Institute of Advice and Guidance. Succeed in this, and all else is likely to follow too.

Learning from you

Coaching

Training is specific, pre-planned and can take place on-the-job or off-the-job. It is about instructing, demonstrating, testing and applying in practice. Coaching is not like this at all – indeed it is just the opposite. Coaching is about helping others to help themselves through discussion, guidance, encouragement, observation and assessment. Or as the Industrial Society (1996) puts it, coaching is 'the art of facilitating the performance, learning and development of others'. Widely regarded as the elusive key to success in managing today's business organisation, it is, ironically, a practice more ideally suited, by its very nature, to academic environments than almost any other. As such, it is a golden opportunity you ought not spurn. Indeed you should regard coaching as one of the principal aspects of your role. Not everyone finds this easy,

Box 6.3 The ground rules for effective coaching

(i)   Planning: agree the topic or issue

Opportunities for coaching often arise from performance reviews and the regular one-to-one meetings you hold. They can also present themselves naturally at very short notice in day-to-day work (as, say, when changes occur). Either way, the activity must still be a planned one and mutually agreed to, by you and the individual.

(ii)   Identify the goals

The goals must be

- achievable;
- measurable through quality, quantity, cost and time.

It may be you are contemplating a proposal for external funding, a new academic programme, or changes to the system of support and guidance for students. Or, and perhaps more likely, you are seeking to persuade individuals to become more flexible in their views about the 'right' way to do a job, about how they manage their time, their order of priorities, the ways in which they channel their energies, etc. Either way, the objective is to agree the goal and the skill development to achieved, ideally volunteered by the individual. Avoid imposing the goal yourself.

(iii)   Promote discovery

Coaching is non-directive. You are there to encourage individuals to find their own solutions, not tell them how to solve their problems. There will of course be a tendency for prejudgements to exist on both sides and false information may well have been gathered from others. Your role is to help your coachee explore a situation, identify options and select a way forward: to discover, that is, the constraints, demands and full implications of the task they are undertaking. In doing so, you must ensure they pursue all lines of enquiry, draw out all the consequences for each and evaluate the likely outcomes of adopting particular courses of action.

(iv)   Set the parameters

Having set the goals and discussed the options, the next step is to set the parameters, i.e. establish clearly what has to be done and by when. You can both then monitor progress as well as take account of any risks which may exist.

(v)   Authorise and empower

It is essential that the individual does not charge ahead and find obstacles in every direction. Make sure they have right of access to information, attendance on courses and other colleagues as well as clerical support and expenses as appropriate. Inform other people who need to know what is happening.

(vi)   Recap and review

At the end of each session, make sure everything is clear. Ask the individual to recap the points discussed and agreed and note down the action points. Review these at the start of the next session.

Source: adapted from Industrial Society, 1996

however, and those that do are not always effective. Some believe they simply can't do it or think it not worth the effort, while others find it goes against the grain of their natural belief system, particularly those with a propensity towards a 'command-and-control' or parenting style of management. There is too no single right way to coach – different people and different situations require different approaches.

All that said, you will begin to overcome the doubts you may have, or alternatively improve your effectiveness, if you follow these two steps:

(i)   Follow the basic ground rules of coaching (see Box 6.3).
(ii) Have, or are prepared to acquire, the essential key competencies for effective coaching; i.e. the ability to be an active listener; ask open questions; establish trust and rapport; remain non-judgemental; and offer constructive feedback and evaluation (see Box 6.4).

If you succeed in mastering (i) and (ii) – in learning, that is, the art of coaching – you will be well-placed to avoid the pitfalls that so often blight coaching relationships (see Box 6.5). Put another way, you will have helped colleagues to uncover strengths and abilities they never knew they had and also learned something about yourself in the process.

Delegation

Delegation is one of those principles often widely admired in theory, yet rarely implemented to the same extent in practice. HE is no exception. If anything, indeed, delegation is less likely to occur in academic settings than in others. Why this is so is not difficult to discern. The strong beliefs in individual autonomy, intrinsic motivation and independence which characterise these settings, often lead to situations in which heads of department become reticent to assign particular tasks and duties, and even if they did the implication is that academic staff wouldn't want them (or have the time to do them) anyway. When combined with the other reasons often given for not promoting delegation – that it is too risky, it takes too much time and effort; that 'nobody can do the job as well or as quickly as I can' (along with the unexpressed anxiety that maybe they can), etc. – then it is not surprising perhaps that delegation should have met with such stiff resistance in practice. Even so, you must not allow yourself to fall into the same trap – otherwise your department will begin to exhibit the characteristics of those working environments in which delegation is conspicuous by its absence: namely underdevelopment, plateau performance, a climate of mistrust, silo thinking and a head constantly engaged in a losing struggle to stay on top of things.

Put another way, you need to set aside your fears and reservations whatever their origin:

*   if you have concerns about 'letting go' remember you can't possibly do everything yourself nor is it your job to; and besides, the rewards, in time saved and people developed, are potentially as great as the risk incurred;
*   if you feel insecure about staff making a better fist of it than you, remember you too will gain credit as well as them;

Box 6.4 Key skills for effective coaching

I Active listening

Good listening requires discipline and commitment to show people you value and respect their contribution. You can demonstrate this in a number of ways:

- Stop talking. You can't listen if you are talking
- Put the person at ease. Be attentive – look interested
- Allow air space – give the person room to talk
- Remove distractions– don't doodle or shuffle papers; maintain eye contact
- Show empathy – try to see their point of view from their position
- Be patient, do not interrupt and restrain emotions
- Avoid confrontation through criticism
- Ask questions and encourage the talker to respond
- Cut your mental chatter and concentrate

Be wary of the *barriers* to effective listening. Ensure your listening is not of the following kind:

- 'On-off' – cut out the distractions
- 'Red flag' – try not to get irritated
- 'Open ears – closed mind' – avoid jumping to conclusions too quickly
- 'Glassy-eyed' – fools no one. Save the daydreaming for later
- 'Too-deep-for-me' – concentrate harder, don't shut off
- 'Matter-over-mind' – be magnanimous. You can always make your point later
- 'Subject-centred not speaker-centred' – don't forget empathy
- 'Fact-driven' – keep with the flow, you can always check the facts later
- 'Pencil-driven' – ditto and make sure your maintain eye contact
- 'Hubbub' – switch off the noise and focus

II Asking questions

Questions guide and help the individual to establish understanding. Use different types as required:

- Open – the question that avoids a yes or no answer: encourages the individual to open up
- Fact seeking – ask for information by invitation, beware becoming interrogative
- Probing – asking for examples or direct specific instructions
- Reflective – use to respond to signals of feeling about what is being said. Identify strong feelings such as anger, frustration, worry, uncertainty and reflect these back
- Summarise – at intervals, summarise the discussion, the key learning points and action points. Focus information which shows you have been listening
- Suspend judgement – listen to information with an open mind. If you close your mind you will start asking closed questions and not gather useful information

III Feedback

Feedback is essential to the process of coaching so that progress can be evaluated. To be successful the key elements are:

- Give recognition for efforts made
- Ask what has happened – use probes
- Ask how things could have been done differently
- Ask what has been learned
- Ask what further actions are now necessary
- Suggest or explore other options

- Encourage the individual to implement agreed actions
- Be flexible to adjust your approach as needed – stay positive

IV Evaluation

- Evaluation should be based on an analysis of agreed measurements of progress
- You must therefore have clear objectives from the outset
- Ensure too that you monitor actual progress through regular contact with the coachee
- Ask for stakeholder evaluation as well as self-assessment
- Determine and agree conclusions and key learning and development outcomes

Source: adapted from Industrial Society, 1996

- if you simply don't trust staff, then remember that trust is a two-way street: you have to show trust yourself in order to earn the trust of others, i.e. it is down to you to take the first step to break the cycle of mistrust;
- if you think staff won't do it, you will never know unless you ask; don't under-estimate people's desire to take on a new responsibility: to feel valued and to have challenge in their work.

You need to recognise, in other words, the critical significance of delegation. It goes to the very heart of your capability as an academic leader for it is about enabling, developing, recognising and utilising the value of all those colleagues around you. Not only that, it is equally good for you, your department and your institution. It is, in short, like coaching, yet another essential art you must learn to master (see Box 6.6).

Learning for all

Inducting new staff
Deemed a high priority in theory, staff induction in practice is not always taken seriously in some university departments, and is occasionally overlooked altogether in others. This is a huge mistake on their part. In such instances newcomers are

---

Box 6.5 Coaching pitfalls you must avoid

- Unclear objectives
- Not agreeing goals
- Not assessing situation
- Losing objectivity
- Not agreeing next steps
- Hidden agenda(s)
- Solving their problems
- Being judgmental
- Trying to prove a point
- Imposing your view
- Not listening

Box 6.6 Principles of effective delegation

(i) What is delegation?

Delegation is the practice of giving one of your colleagues the authority to take decisions within defined areas of responsibility; in essence, to authorise someone to do a job on your behalf. It does not mean however that you abdicate responsibility for it. You still continue to be accountable, to 'carry the can' if things go wrong.

(Then again, risks can be minimised so long as you carry out the planning and timing in a proper fashion.)

(ii) The benefits of delegation

For you:	It will provide more time and energy to focus on what you're supposed to be doing, leading and managing (i.e. not doing yourself every single job for which you are responsible); it will also demonstrate to others you have confidence in yourself and your colleagues and that you are capable of being an effective leader.
For staff:	It can enhance their self-esteem, job satisfaction and professional development as well as their sense of being valued, of being in control.
For your department:	It brings a fresh perspective (and maybe a better one) to the task at hand, provides for cover in your absence and identifies a feasible future replacement.
For your institution:	It helps in developing future leaders (or 'succession planning'); increasing the levels of commitment and morale, and improving efficiency, effectiveness and productivity.

(iii) Planning for delegation

Before beginning, brainstorm your role:
- What do I do? Make a list of twenty or so different aspects of your job.
- Why do I do it? Should I keep it and why?
- Identify those tasks which you cannot delegate (such as matters of discipline, confidentiality, financial jurisdiction and the like) and approximately 6–7 you can (such as, for example, staff development coordination, pastoral support for students, new courses, liaison with external examiners, etc.)
- To whom could I give the job now?
- Have a one-to-one to assess their willingness. Don't assume that staff won't want to. Don't underestimate the impact of your willingness to assign authority to them. There is no surer way of demonstrating the trust and confidence you have in them.
- Who else should I be developing to do it and how?

(iv) Implementing delegation

- Clarify the objectives and identify the task and constraints with the individual.
- Brief them in a genuine, open and enthusiastic manner.
- Establish priorities, check resources and identify any training requirements.
- Agree target handover date and inform all relevant parties.
- Monitor and evaluate progress through regular one-to-ones in support.

(v) Pitfalls to avoid

- Underselling – don't trivialise the task or duty you're handing over otherwise it will be perceived as a boring chore.
- Overselling – don't over-hype it either, otherwise you may give the delegate a conflicting sense of priorities or worse still imbue them with self-doubt.
- Supervising too closely – resist the temptation to intrude on the delegatee the whole time.
- Supervising not nearly enough – don't let the delegatee flounder. Offer help and guidance to support them through their learning curve. Learn when to step in and when not.
- Usurping their authority – don't undercut or overrule the delegatee.

Source: adapted from Industrial Society, 1996

needlessly forced to expend more time and energy (and expense) in 'settling in', if indeed they ever do, than would ordinarily be the case. Equally, the department heads will have foresaken a golden opportunity to guide the newcomers' future contributions and behaviour at the very moment when they are most receptive to such influence. Put another way, induction is not simply an act of kindness, but is also a sound business practice and universally recognised as such within and beyond HE.

Universities which do not offer induction programmes to new staff are very much the exception than the norm. Such programmes usually focus, quite rightly, on introducing staff to the institution itself: its character and ethos (the history, mission, structure and organisation of the university, etc.) as well as the way it operates in practice, typically with regard to general matters such as health and safety, personnel, library and computing services, telecommunications and voice-mail, reprographics, and so on. The more adventurous programmes do not rely solely on information packs and presentations, but also seek to include tours (virtual as well as guided), treasure hunts, quizzes and receptions.

Either way, your role as head of department is to ensure your newcomers, whether experienced or probationary, are given the time and opportunity to attend them. More than that, you also need to make arrangements to cover all those epiphenomenal matters peculiar to your department (access to stationery, clarification on course development, conditions of service, etc.) which are not dealt with in your general institutional programme. You can do this in a number of ways:

- Through developing your own departmental guide for new staff; one, that is, which complements, not duplicates, your central induction programme. And do not forget, as so many do, to include a visit to your Students' Union as part of their itinerary.
- By appointing a mentor, or, if the circumstances warrant a less formal approach, a 'buddy', for each new member of staff, to help them through their first six months.
- By taking an active part yourself in their induction.

In this way, you will ensure that the induction process is, as it should be, *a planned and systematic one* and not one left to the vagaries of circumstance. The most critical aspect in the effective induction of new staff, however, is, as with so many other things, that of *attitude*. If you take it seriously, it is more likely that they will – and equally the reverse holds true. It is essential therefore that you start as you mean to carry on, otherwise you will be facing an uphill struggle from the outset. Remember too, induction is about initiating newcomers to your department's culture. If you are satisfied with 'the way we do things around here' then all well and good, if not you should use induction for what it is, an opportunity to begin again, to start afresh. Put another way, you can take advantage of the fact that new staff are not yet inculcated in the behavioural norms of your department as a way of changing how it operates. After all new staff, like students, have a tabula rasa when they first arrive. You need to do your utmost, then, to ensure that what they learn about your department is what you want them to learn.

Part-time staff

If universities were judged as employers solely on the basis of the experience of their part-time staff it is likely that few would emerge with their reputation intact, let alone enhanced. Routinely neglected, casual staff it seems, if reports are to be believed, occupy some nether world in which they are expected to meet the everyday demands of academic work (the development of schemes of work, the completion of module specifications, the marking of assessments and attendance at meetings) often without support, and occasionally without pay of any kind. Worse still, it appears that this shabby treatment is often justified on the basis that part-time staff have lower capabilities: a mistaken assumption which in itself is discriminatory, and which, in effect, has a disproportionate impact on those (women in particular) who do not always follow a conventional career path. Not surprisingly, teaching unions have accused universities of cultivating managers whose dominant mindset is one that views people as readily dispensable (Jaques, 1998; NATFHE 2001; UCEA (University and Colleges Employers' Association), 2000).

This is of course a path you should not follow. Put another way, you need to recognise that in itself there is nothing inherently wrong with casualisation. Indeed, so long as you do not come to rely on it too much (a staffing ratio of 80 per cent full-time to 20 per cent part-time is around the norm), casualisation, like induction, is another sound business practice. In this case it offers you flexibility in planning staff workload allocations and managing your departmental budget. It also will invariably bring in fresh ideas, new perspectives and expertise and very often a great deal of enthusiasm. Indeed, one of the enduring myths about relying on part-time teaching support is that it will have an adverse impact on quality. This is patent nonsense, as well as being dismissive of the energy, enthusiasm and talent which the great majority of part-timers bring to their work. When issues of quality do arise it is usually because part-timers have not been supported in the way they should have been, not because they lack capability. If you are to avoid falling into the same trap, you must make sure you respond to the needs of your part-time staff with the same consistency and resolution as you do those of your full-time staff. Not because you're legally obliged too (under European Union law part-time staff are entitled to the same employment rights as those of full-time staff; to do otherwise is to discriminate unlawfully), but because it is self-evidently the right thing to do: for them, for you and for your department. More specifically, you need to address the particular concerns that so often blights the part-time staff experience: the lack of access to accommodation, telephone, e-mail, printing, car parking, ID, and so on, and, most especially, their sense of isolation. You can do this in a number of ways by:

- organising a proper induction programme for part-time staff;
- establishing a policy for the development and support of part-timers; one that specifies explicitly the pro rata entitlements they can expect (initial training, desk space, access to library and computing facilities, invitations to 'away-days', etc.);
- ensuring all part-timers are included on your department and e-mail circulation lists so that they routinely receive the same information as full-time staff;
- including part-timers in your peer review of teaching schemes;
- fostering a part-time teaching network; bringing part-timers together socially and publishing a part-timers' directory listing contact details;
- appointing a mentor or 'buddy' for their period of employment;
- offering review and development opportunities in the same way you would full-time staff.

In this way, you should at least be able to ensure that your part-time staff will feel valued sufficiently to want to make the 'full' contribution they may have been prevented from, or felt unable to do so, hitherto. A situation which, in itself, will put your department one-up on very many others – and rightly so.

Celebrating diversity

> Everyone is different. Unique. Achieving diversity is about bringing together a rich mix of people, with differing perspectives and from different backgrounds, and creating an environment in which their differences are valued. A vibrant, open and creative culture. A culture in which ideas flourish. Where people thrive, grow and have fun. A culture where energy is unleashed. A winning culture for the 21st century.
>
> Unilever UK (Schneider, 2001)

> What do I think of quotas? Well, universities could do with a quota of people who understand that discrimination damages the quality of education. Maybe a small quota of people who recognise that publicly funded bodies have a responsibility to their locality. Perhaps another quota of people who can see that scholarship belongs to all kinds of body shapes and skin tones and that you cannot judge the quality of the thought by looking at the package.
>
> Gargi Bhattacharyya, UK university lecturer (Bhattacharyya, 2000)

The record of universities as employers of part-time staff has, as we've noted, not been a good one. The same can equally be said, unfortunately, with regard to their handling of equal opportunities. Indeed it was not until recently (2001–2) that all UK universities had managed to develop their own individual human resource strategies, and even then only at the insistence of the funding councils in some cases. To claim their share of the £330 million HEFCE (02/14, 2002) initiative on *Rewarding and Developing Staff in HE*, each HEI was required to not only submit a HR strategy but one which addressed six priority areas, including, in particular, equal opportunities (the others being recruitment and retention, staff development and training, equal pay and job evaluation, staffing needs review; and performance management). It was not until 2002–3, then, that all universities finally agreed to establish quantitative as well as qualitative targets in equal opportunities. Meantime the rest of the world had moved on – beyond 'the numbers' issue. Although historically deeply sceptical of 'equal opportunities' ('organisation man', you will recall, was meant not only to look alike but also to think alike: Whyte, 1956), the private sector nowadays has embraced not only minority representation but has also sought to create working cultures which celebrate individual diversity, as in the case of Unilever UK (Schneider, 2001). Not, admittedly, for the most part for altruistic reasons (that they believe it is socially or morally the right thing to do) but simply because diversity makes good business sense; it boosts 'the bottom line'. Either way, private sector performance in equal opportunities far outstrips that of HEIs, even among traditionally conservative businesses such as Ford Europe (also known as the 'multilocal multinational'), which is an irony in itself, given the principled stance that so many academics have taken for so long on this particular issue. It does us no favours then – and certainly none for our credibility in the world at large – if we do not seem capable of putting our own house in order.

We cannot, in our defence, certainly in the UK at least, claim that we have been ignorant of the matter either. The 1999 Employment and Ethnicity Report (Modood Report, 1999; see also Bett Report, 1999), for example, pointed out that only a third of universities had separate racial equality policies, while the Bett Report of the same year drew attention to gender inequalities in HE, and countless surveys have since confirmed what many already suspected, namely that, inter alia: all vice-chancellors and principals are white, and less than twenty of them are women; female professors account for less than 10 per cent of the professoriate; and the proportion of women in senior lecturer and researcher grades is little better than 1 in 5, while that of male and female British nationals from ethnic minorities is much lower still, 1 in 25; and so on (Finch, 2001). Nor can we claim to have had no support in the matter. The Commission on University Career Opportunity established by the Committee of Vice-Chancellors and Principals (CVCP) almost a decade ago, for instance, developed a full range of (detailed and still useful) guides to equal opportunities – on everything from setting out strategies and implementing them, to explaining harassment, to advice on avoiding age discrimination. Its successor, the Equality Challenge Unit (2002) set up in 2001, is likewise committed to working in partnership with HEIs to establish 'a higher education sector that promotes diversity and where equality of opportunity is a reality for all'.

We are likely to need such support more than ever too for the legislative pace in this area has quickened in recent years; most notably through the Race Relations (Amendment) Act (RRA), 2000 and the Special Education Needs Disability Act (SENDA), 2001 both of which extend earlier legislation (the Race Relations Act, 1976 and the Disability Discrimination Act, 1995) not only in making discriminatory behaviour on the part of HEIs illegal, but also in placing a new and enforceable positive duty on them in the way that they respond to the needs of these disadvantaged groups (CRE (Commission for Racial Equality), 2000; DRC (Disability Rights Commission),

2002). The 'equality challenge' then is a very tall order indeed for all universities and all university managers, and is one that you cannot, nor should you want to, shirk. What though can you do in your department to meet this challenge?

Recognise that equal opportunities is a key component of good management

Traditionally equal opportunities has not, as the record suggests, and despite protestations to the contrary, been a high priority in HE. Initially derided as a totem of political correctness, equal opportunities has tended to breed compliance with the legislative requirements on the one hand or generated heated debate on 'quotas versus targets' and 'affirmative action versus reverse discrimination' on the other. Either way, it is only recently, as a consequence of lobbying within and outside the sector (as well as, to be frank, a fair degree of internal shame), that equal opportunities has at last ceased to be a marginal activity. You likewise will need to, and can expect that your institution will require you to, 'mainstream' equal opportunities in your own department. This means you will in effect be held responsible, and rightly so, for the pursuit of equality goals. For many this will be a novelty, if not an issue. Others, however, may feel less comfortable with this notion. If so, you need to remember, and to recognise as others beyond HE have done, that equal opportunities is not only socially desirable and a moral right, as well as a legal requirement, it is also, at heart, a key component of good management.

Commit to making diversity one of your department's core values

Indeed, the real challenge ahead for HE, and one to which you should commit, is to follow the lead taken by those outside the sector (as well as that of some notable exceptions within, such as Tufts University, Massachusetts) who have gone that step further by moving 'beyond equal opportunities' to embrace 'diversity'. Unlike equal opportunities which is often perceived as little more than complying with the legal framework (or as treating everyone the same way), diversity, is about valuing people as individuals, respecting people's differences, and, above all, making the best use of these differences for the benefit of both the individual and the organisation (IPD, 1996; Schneider, 2001; Grass Roots Group, 2003). Thus, instead of the focus being only on particular groups – women, ethnic minorities, the disabled, and so on – *diversity is about all of us*.

As such, the 'equality challenge', then, is not so much a matter about helping 'them' to join 'us', but about critically looking at 'us' ourselves and rooting out all aspects of our culture which inappropriately exclude people and stop us from being inclusive – in the way we relate to current and prospective staff and students, institutional partners and, indeed, all other stakeholders. As organisations that are inherently intensely individualistic, universities are ideally placed to meet this challenge. Indeed the diversity aspiration is not only achievable, it goes to the very heart of the university's *raison d'être*. You therefore need have no qualms about, and should indeed take pride in, making diversity one of the core values of your department.

Understand how your university is attempting to manage diversity and identify the implications for you and your department

So much for the theory, what about the practice? How well do your university, your department and you measure up? As with so many other things there is no single right approach to managing diversity. All institutions will quite properly seek to do what seems best for them according to their particular circumstances and environment. That said, to manage diversity successfully we all, in the first instance, need to understand where we are now, what progress we've made, and what problems we still have to overcome. Without such understanding we cannot plan where we want to go in an informed manner. And, more particularly, as head of department you need to understand how your university is managing diversity both as a guide to your actions at the local level (to ensure consistency, address deficiencies, and so on), and also as an advocate for change across your institution. The diagnostic models outlined overleaf are designed to help you do just that. Use the one in Box 6.7 to assess your university's performance. Ask one of your colleagues to complete it too, and compare your findings.

However, a word of caution is in order. As indicated earlier, much of the public debate within the sector has centred on the setting of quantitative equality targets. And on that point you need to remember that, in the same way that 'access' for students without them achieving success is not really access at all (the 'open door' becomes in practice a revolving door), the same is just as true for equality targets: that is to say, a quantitative target *without a delivery strategy* of how your institution will achieve it is not really a target at all, merely an aspiration to take a leap in the dark. Moreover, while the target is important, it is still only a means to an end and not an end in itself. That said, no single element of the strategic implementation model is greater than any other. All eight in Box 6.7 are critical to effective implementation. How well then is your university managing diversity? In what areas is it doing well? In what areas, less well, and why? What are the main weaknesses? What are the implications for your department? What could you do to improve matters?

Assess your department's performance and draw up a diversity action plan

Turning closer to home, and as a prelude to developing your own action plan, you also need to determine how well you are managing diversity within your own department. You can, of course, do this on your own but since, as the model outlined in Box 6.8 illustrates, this involves gauging the perceptions of others both within and outside your department in addition to the monitoring of statistical information, you should consider setting up a small representative working group to help you reach a more objective as well as a more accurate assessment. It will also give reassurance to others and demonstrate your transparency in this matter. With the group, work your way systematically through each of the questions set out in Box 6.8 and log your conclusions.

Box 6.7 How well does your university measure up on diversity?

Consider the eight strategic implementation elements listed below; weigh up the positive and negative indicators in each case and rate how effective you think your university has been in that area.

Scale: 1 – Poor (all negative indicators); 2 – Marginal; 3 – Satisfactory; 4 – Good; 5 – Excellent (all positive indicators)

Strategic implementation element	Positive indicators	Negative indicators	Ratings
Organisational vision	• Vision of the university incorporates diversity • Clear diversity policy/statement • Policy outlines main areas of attention/objectives • Clear responsibilities indicated • Clear how it is to be used by different parts of the university • Linked to educational mission and values	• No vision • No policy • Vaguely worded • No objectives • No accountabilities • No statement of why necessary • Not linked to mission or values	___ ___ ___ ___ ___ ___
Senior management commitment	• Positive, visible support given by management team • Message communicated directly to staff • Managers practice what they preach • Preparedness to allocate resources • Clear understanding about what they want to achieve • Staff agree that management are committed	• Behaviour and words don't agree • Message rarely, if ever, discussed in public forums • No preparedness to allocate resources • Uncertainty about what they want to achieve • Staff would say management are not committed, that they are an obstacle	___ ___ ___

Auditing and assessment of needs	• Key HR processes are audited and re-audited for fairness
	• Staff are surveyed on their perceptions re diversity
	• Monitoring data is kept on:
	  – ethnic origin
	  – sex
	  – disability
	  – age
		• Processes are never audited
		• Staff are not encouraged to give their views
		• No data, or only poor data is available
		• Data is not kept up to date
		• Data is not reviewed regularly
		• Very little action takes place on the basis of the analysis
			___ ___ ___ ___

Box 6.7 *Continued*

Strategic imple-mentation element	Positive indicators	Negative indicators	Ratings
	• Data is regularly reviewed • Diversity successes/disasters are recorded and communicated • Action is taken on basis of analysis		___
Clarity of objectives	• Clear, quantifiable objectives are set • Timescale for achieving objectives are realistic • Objectives fit in with strategic objectives • A programme for action has been developed • Actions have been prioritised within the programme	• Unclear goals • Unclear or no timescales • Objectives and timescales are too ambitious, or are extremely conservative • Only targets/quotas and no objectives are set • Objectives do not fit in with strategic objectives	___ ___ ___ ___ ___
Clear accountability	• All staff are made aware of their responsibilities • Managers are made accountable for the way they select and manage their staff • Specific and diversity-achievable objectives are set for key staff • Staff are informed and trained in how they can meet their objectives	• Key staff are not given responsibilities • Managers have no accountability for diversity issues • Little or no training is provided • Personal objectives set are unrealistic and are ignored • Objectives are not understood	___ ___ ___ ___ ___
Effective communication	• Vision/policy is communicated to everybody • Policy is communicated to public • Variety of media is used in raising awareness of the issues • Information on progress is regularly fed back to staff	• Vision/policy is poorly communicated to staff • Policy is poorly communicated to public • There is limited use of different media • Messages are treated as one-off, not reinforced	___ ___ ___

| | • The views of staff are sought on how to proceed | • No follow-up on actions are planned | _____ |
| | • Awareness training is available for all | | |

Coordination of activity

- Champions for diversity have been established in different areas/departments
- Clear who has overall coordinating responsibility for diversity
- Role of the champions has been communicated
- Regular contact is maintained with other parts of the university to share experience
- Contact has been made with outside organisations in order to learn from them

- No one person or group has been given overall responsibility _____
- Lack of contact with other parts of the organisation; 'reinventing the wheel' _____
- No clear role for the champions has been established _____ _____
- Lack of direction for individuals or groups _____

Evaluation

- All actions taken are reviewed
- Evaluation is linked to strategic and diversity objectives
- Data is taken from a variety of sources
- Evaluation is an ongoing process
- Results are fed back to everyone

- Actions taken are not reviewed _____
- Evaluation is not linked to strategic and diversity objectives _____
- Data focuses on one or two areas – e.g. numbers employed _____ _____
- Information is not communicated _____

Scoring and interpretation

Add your rating scores together and divide by 8 to determine your overall institutional average. Universities rated as:

1 They are motivated by legal compliance. They focus on equality (treating everyone in the same way), rather then diversity (respecting people's differences). They are primarily reactive in implementing equal opportunities.

2 They recognise the value in going beyond simple compliance. They aim to support groups that have been historically disadvantaged, recognising the benefits to their internal and public image. Equity means being seen to 'do the right thing for disadvantaged groups'. Initiatives are ad hoc without any integrated plan.

3 They understand that certain diversity initiatives can improve recruitment and retention as well as efficiency. They evaluate diversity initiatives to identify programmes that will positively affect institutional life and view equality targets as a means to an end rather than the focus of the diversity strategy. They use an inclusive definition of diversity with the vision of creating an environment that is equitable for all.

4 They have internalised diversity as a core organisational value. Diversity is viewed as an essential element of continued growth and is integrated into all aspects of the institution and all staff consider themselves responsible for creating an environment that is fair and equitable for all.

5 They have achieved their internal vision of equity for all and now seek to foster diversity beyond their own boundaries – to their partners and in the local and regional community. Diversity needs no special internal consideration as its value, importance and necessity are firmly integrated into all aspects of institutional life.

Source: adapted from Kandola and Fullerton, 1998

Box 6.8 How well does your department measure up on diversity?

Staff statistics

1   Do you monitor staff profiles by: (a) age; (b) gender; (c) ethnicity; (d) disability?
2   Do you then benchmark these figures against: (a) other departments in your university; (b) equivalent departments in other regional, national or international universities.
3   Do you also monitor: (a) recruitment; (b) promotion; (c) appraisals; (d) salary; (e) leavers by these same groups?
4   Do you benchmark recruitment against the relevant external labour market? And do you review success ratios (the number of applications per appointee and number of applications for posts available) for different groups?
5   Do you review and compare promotion, salary and leavers across these different groups?

Internal perceptions

6   Have you ever run a focus group for: (a) staff who may feel excluded from the dominant culture; (b) staff drawn from the dominant culture?
7   Have you ever commissioned or conducted a specific diversity survey within your department? Did you analyse the results by each different group?
8   Have you ever included diversity-related questions in any of your departmental staff surveys?
9   Do you ever benchmark any of these staff diversity questions?
10 Do you know what the level of understanding and commitment is to diversity among your university's senior management group?
11 Do you know if your staff feel different about diversity from the way staff in other departments feel?

Student statistics

12 Do you monitor student entry by: (a) age; (b) gender; (c) ethnicity; and (d) disability; as well as by social class, educational qualifications and previous learning experience?
13 Do you then benchmark these figures against course intakes in: (a) other departments in your university; (b) equivalent departments in universities within your region and nationally?
14 Do your course teams also monitor student withdrawals by these same groups?
15 Do you benchmark recruitment against the relevant student market? And do you review the success ratios (numbers of applications per capita population; numbers of enrolments per number of applications) for different groups?
16 Do your exam boards monitor the number of: (a) first class honours graduates; (b) student failures by these different groups?
17 Do your exam boards review and compare performance across these different groups?

External perceptions

18 Do you genuinely cater to the needs of a diverse student body in your learning and teaching strategy and curriculum design? Is diversity covered in your surveys and measures of student satisfaction?
19 What proportion of your student market share is drawn from different groups? Is this in- or out-of-line relative to the nature and size of your portfolio market?
20 Do you analyse student feedback by: (a) age; (b) ethnicity; (c) disability; (d) disability; (e) religion?

21 In your market research do you identify the potential and diverse needs of different groups as a matter of course?

22 Have you ever run focus groups with: (a) female students; (b) ethnic minority students; (c) disabled students; (d) younger or older students?

23 Do you know how the local community and local educational providers regard your department?

24 Do you know how the senior management group, the board of governors and other departments regard your performance on diversity?

25 Does your appraisal of external partners include an assessment of their own equal opportunities policies and procedures? Do your external partners feel that their different ideas and ways of operating are welcomed?

26 What do your stakeholders think about your performance on diversity?

Source: adapted from Schneider, 2001

How well are you doing? Do you have all the necessary statistical information to hand? If not, what gaps do you have to make good? Is the analysis and evaluation of this information a routine activity within your department? Do you act on this information? How thorough is your understanding of the internal and external perceptions of your department? What does this picture tell you? What actions do you need to take to increase your understanding or to address the perceptions others have of your department?

In developing your action plan, you need to bear in mind (if you have not already done so) that it is precisely this sort of proactivity, in this instance the monitoring, review and revision of departmental practices, which in the cases of disability and race are now a legal obligation. Under SENDA, for example, it is illegal to treat staff or students, current and prospective, 'less favourably' if they have a disability, and HEIs are duty-bound to make 'reasonable adjustment' to ensure that they do not place anyone at a 'substantial disadvantage'. Similarly the RRA bestows a 'new enforceable positive duty' on HEIs to not only monitor their staff by ethnicity, but also to assess the impact on racial equality of proposed, as well as existing, policies and practices and to consult on them.

Make sure you practise what you preach

Diversity, however, is more than simply ensuring that appropriate mechanisms are in place. It is also about making sure that they do their job too – of capturing and analysing data and acting upon it. More than that, it is about effecting cultural change in the way your department behaves. As such it is incumbent on you to take the initiative, otherwise you run the risk that your action plan may fall short of the mark or, worse still, suffer the fate of so many other well-intentioned initiatives before it, and be dismissed as just another passing fad. Put the other way, you are more likely to establish diversity as a meaningful concept within your department if you are yourself seen to take it seriously, to give expression to your commitment, in short, to put into practice what you preach. You can do this in a number of ways:

Through your style of management

By not confusing the relationship between equality and effective management. Good management is not about giving a minority preferential treatment over others. On the contrary, it is about treating everyone fairly but not necessarily in the same way. In other words it is first and foremost about recognising, respecting and valuing people as individuals, each with their own unique characteristics, and responding to them on that basis 'to create a productive environment in which organisational goals are met efficiently and effectively by making the best use of everyone's talents and potential' (IPD, 1996).

In practical terms, this is yet another instance in which you must consider whether your style of management is the most effective one to achieve this outcome. Are you, for example, receptive to staff proposals for flexible working patterns? (A statutory requirement since April 2003 in the case of parents with children under six and those with disabled children under eighteen.) Would you be willing to extend the same right to those of your staff with responsibilities for caring the the elderly, even if it isn't a statutory requirement? More tellingly, do staff feel comfortable in approaching you about their personal welfare – about matters not immediately related to their work? If not, why not? Are you as committed to a work–life balance and 'family-friendly' arrangements as you should be (DfEE, 2000; CIPD, 2002)? Are you always open to fresh ideas on job enrichment? Check with others – to confirm this is so – even if you feel this is indeed the case.

By putting the case for diversity to others

To many 'equal opportunities' is a loaded term – one with a long history of unhelpful associations. 'Diversity' on the other hand appears to convey very little meaning at all. While this in itself is an advantage, the danger is that it will not become common currency unless you and your management colleagues take the initiative to make it so. Put another way, you cannot expect staff to be clear about what diversity is and why it matters if leaders and managers are themselves uncertain, or are not prepared, to make the effort to explain. Let us be clear then. Diversity, as has been explained – and in the everyday language that staff prefer – is about 'respect for the individual'. Diversity recognises, indeed celebrates the fact that each of us is different and unique, and that uniqueness is made up of a mix of visible characteristics (gender, ethnicity and some disabilities) and others that are not always immediately evident (sexual orientation, nationality, functional background, personality and so forth). To 'manage diversity' is to value these differences and seek to harness them to establish a vibrant working culture. *Why diversity matters*, then, is not solely for social and moral reasons but also business ones too: that is to say, diversity is important because it is about:

- using people's talents to the full;
- ensuring that selection decisions and policies are based on objective criteria and not on unlawful discrimination, prejudice or unfair assumptions;
- making your university more attractive to prospective applicants: becoming an 'employer of choice' for staff and a 'university of choice' for students;

- improving retention, making recruitment easier;
- generating greater staff commitment, loyalty and productivity;
- getting closer to students, clients, partners and other stakeholders;
- operating internationally with success;
- sustaining a healthy society;
- avoiding the costs of discrimination.

By 'walking the talk', not just 'talking the talk'

Getting others to understand the significance and value of diversity is an important first step. Staff will not be fully convinced, however, and understandably so, until they see by your actions that you are sincere in your commitment to it. You must, therefore, 'walk the talk' as well as 'talk the talk' if you want diversity to mean more to staff than merely so many fine words. Your style of management, as we've noted, is important in this respect. You need to go further, however, if you want to make diversity a living reality. You should:

- Establish your own departmental steering group to coordinate and review: your monitoring and data collection activity; the deliberations of your exam boards, programme teams and focus groups; the outcomes of your market research surveys; and the implementation of your action plan.
- Commit a proportion of your annual budget to support and progress equal opportunities within your department.
- Integrate diversity into your performance review discussions.
- Run awareness-raising and skills-building workshops for all your staff.
- Hold regular 'surgeries' – at least three times a year – with 'minority' staff.
- Celebrate your department as a *living* community as well as a *learning* community: recognise the major festivals of the principal religions; organise a Christmas party for your staff's children; establish a 'keep in touch' scheme to support women on maternity leave; host 'open days' for the local community (not just prospective applicants); invite one of the major disabled societies or the local race equality council to nominate a representative to sit on your equal opportunities steering group; etc.
- Volunteer your department as a pilot for your institutional job evaluation scheme (typically, higher education role analysis (HERA)) addressing inequalities in pay.
- Sign up to join one of your central bodies with institution-wide responsibilities for equal opportunities. Under the RRA, for example, your university will have, or should be establishing, equality teams in: student admissions, support and employment; student assessment, teaching and achievement; student learning support and development; staff employment, welfare and discipline; etc. These will be headed by lead officers and supported by data controllers overseen by your racial equality or equal opportunities action group. Similar mechanisms may also be in place with regard to policy formulation and implementation on 'joining up disability', 'work–life balance', 'measuring diversity', and 'promoting dignity at work' (by tackling harassment), etc.

Box 6.9 The basic legal principles of equalities legislation

Principle

Employers are free to decide on the skills, knowledge and qualities that they want from employees

Theory

- Employment decisions should be based on merit but all aspects of the recruitment and selection process must be free from bias and unlawful discrimination
- The law demands you give fair and equal respect to all applicants
- The law does not demand that you give preference to individuals because they are from an under-represented section of society

Practical implications

- Positive discrimination: i.e. the policy or practice of positively favouring an individual from an under-represented group – as in, for example, seeking to increase the number of female or ethnic minority job candidates – is an illegal one in the UK under the Race Relations and Sex Discrimination Acts.
- Quotas: i.e. the practice of suggesting that minimum levels or numbers of people from certain groups should be employed – as in, for example, a university should have at least 50 per cent female employees – is illegal in UK.
- Targets: i.e. where a workforce is skewed toward or away from certain groups it is perfectly legal to set targets that indicate how the numbers might be changed, for example, a university in an area where 10 per cent of the population is black but whose workforce is only 2 per cent may set a target – in those areas where recruitment is primarily local – to try and make the percentage of black people employed more representative by encouraging more to apply. To avoid discrimination against white people however, decisions to appoint must still be based solely on merit.

Targets are:

- Guidelines to illustrate imbalances within the workforce.
- About helping people ensure they do not accidentally discriminate when they are employing.
- About trying to encourage different people to consider particular jobs when they are seeking employment.

Organizations are more likely to stay within the law if they have their own clear policies, procedures and practices that support diversity and equality	Internal guidelines on good practice will ensure organizations adhere to the law	The risk is that the organization does not follow its own guidelines in practice. If it has a written policy and does not follow it then its actions are automatically unfair. The rule: 'failure to follow procedure is automatically unfair', applies. For example, a male employee who harasses a female colleague may warrant instant dismissal but if you do not invoke the written disciplinary procedure and follow its requirements you may find a counter claim for unfair dismissal from the male employee.
Employers are legally responsible for the actions of their employees except where the employer has taken clear steps to ensure discrimination does not take place	'Clear steps' meaning that the employer has provided guidelines on how to treat people equally, together with the necessary training	If the guidelines and the training are ignored the employee could be held personally liable for their actions. In many instances both the employer and employee may be held liable for discrimination.
All employees are treated equally	This includes direct discrimination which occurs when an individual is treated less favourably than someone else in similar circumstances because of their gender, marital status, ethnicity, nationality, disability or sexual orientation	Instances of direct discrimination are typically obvious and easy to identify.
A provision, criterion or practice which may have a disproportionate effect on men or women is indirect sex discrimination	Derives from rules which prima facie may appear to apply equally to everyone, however closer examination suggests they are likely to discriminate	Not as transparent as direct discrimination but nevertheless discriminatory in its effects. For example, working patterns and hours which adversely affect staff with childcare responsibilities; dress codes and health and safety requirements which do not respect religious custom; etc.

Source: The Grass Roots Group, 2003

Box 6.10 How do you measure up on diversity?

1   Age: What proportion of the UK is now aged over 40?

   a)   1 in 10
   b)   1 in 5
   c)   1 in 3

2   Gender: What percentage of the UK workforce do women represent?

   a)   Under 25 per cent
   b)   35 per cent
   c)   Over 40 per cent

3   Ethnicity: What percentage of new start-up businesses are opened by Asian businessmen and women each year?

   a)   2 per cent
   b)   9 per cent
   c)   15 per cent

4   Sexual orientation: What percentage of gay, lesbian and bisexual men and women conceal their sexuality because of fear of intimidation?

   a)   None
   b)   22 per cent
   c)   64 per cent

5   Disability: How many disabled people are there in the UK?

   a)   Fewer than 1 million
   b)   Up to 5 million
   c)   Over 8 million

6   Discrimination is estimated to account for what percentage of the pay gap between men and women?

   a)   Less than 10 per cent
   b)   25 to 50 per cent
   c)   Around 75 per cent

7   What percentage of British doctors were born overseas?

   a)   25 per cent
   b)   7 per cent
   c)   15 per cent

8   What percentage of disabled people in the UK use wheelchairs?

   a)   Less than 5 per cent
   b)   More than 10 per cent
   c)   Almost 50 per cent

9 What is the number of students over the age of 25?

  a) 43 per cent
  b) 25 per cent
  c) 19 per cent

10 What proportion of gay men experienced at least one violent attack between 1995 and 2000?

  a) 1 in 3
  b) 1 in 5
  c) 1 in 20

11 When evaluated, a marking system for exam papers is shown to produce results for male students that are lower than comparable papers from female students. This might be evidence of:

  a) Discrimination
  b) Bad behaviour
  c) Not discrimination

12 A student who is a wheelchair user is offered a university place on condition that she finds her own accommodation. No other student has this condition placed upon them. This is:

  a) Lawful
  b) Inconvenient
  c) Unlawful

13 A lecturer refuses to stop writing on the white board in order to turnaround and speak directly to students to enable a person who lip reads to access the lecture. This is:

  a) Unlawful
  b) Rude
  c) Lawful

14 Monitoring reveals that black students are less likely to secure work placements for a vocational course. This is likely to be:

  a) Discrimination
  b) Coincidence
  c) Not discrimination

15 More African-Caribbean than Chinese students are disciplined for persistently playing very loud music in halls of residence after 2.00 am. This is likely to be:

  a) Discrimination
  b) Coincidence
  c) Not discrimination

How did you do? *Answers*: 1 – c; 2 – c; 3 – b; 4 – c; 5 – c; 6 – b; 7 – a; 8 – a; 9 – a; 10 – a; 11 – a; 12 – c; 13 – a; 14 – a; 15 – b

Scores: 15 – Excellent; 1–4 – Very good; 12 – Good; 10 – Fair

Source: The Grass Roots Group, 2003

- Lobby your HR department or your central equal opportunities body to draw up your own institutional staff 'charter for diversity' based on 'respect for people' if your university has not already done so. If support is not forthcoming then hire a consultant and draw up your own departmental one.
- Make a formal commitment to, and ask others to follow suit in signing up for, the leadership challenge initiated and organised by the Commission for Racial Equality.

Through understanding the legal principles and how to apply them

As you will be judged by your actions, and given that the pace and degree of legislative change in equal opportunities is probably greater than in any other area of your managerial responsibilities, it is imperative that you keep abreast of such changes, however daunting this may seem. Not only so that you know what you will or are supposed to be doing, and what you will be legally bound to comply with, but also because you will be in an *informed* position to counter the lack of awareness and misunderstanding which, surprisingly, still prevails on these matters despite all the attendant publicity. Such ignorance can often lead staff to draw the wrong conclusion (as in 'I don't want to have to shortlist someone from an ethnic minority as a makeweight'), which in turn can make them feel vulnerable and threatened and ultimately resistant to the notion of diversity, even though the premise on which their opposition is based is an erroneous one. It is a trap you must make sure you do not fall into yourself. You can best avoid doing so through developing an understanding of the key basic principles of equalities legislation, as outlined in Box 6.9, and how they are applied in practice.

For example, you should know:

- In the case of recruitment and selection, the law demands you treat all applicants with fair and equal respect whatever their background. You cannot, however, seek to increase the number of female or ethnic minority staff by only shortlisting female or ethnic minority job candidates. This is positive discrimination and is illegal in Britain under the Race Relations and Sex Discrimination Acts. It is perfectly legal, however, to take 'positive action' to elicit applications from such disadvantaged groups or to meet the needs of such staff currently in post who, because they are disproportionately fewer in number, may feel isolated and ultimately prohibited from achieving their full potential. The successful Athena Project, for example, which offered mentoring support to women in science, engineering and technology in UK HEIs is just one such instance of this type of initiative (*Athena Guide*, 2003).

- You cannot impose quotas such as 'The X department must have two members of ethnic minority academic staff by 2005' for your department. Such quotas are unlawful and must be avoided. On the other hand, it is perfectly legitimate for you to set a target such as 'The department of X wishes to initiate representation by staff from visible ethnic minorities in its senior staff (principal lecturer upward) within two years and to increase this representation by the year 2006'. Such targets are different from quotas in that they are aspirational in character, and signal your intention to address an imbalance you have recognised in your staffing profile, relative perhaps to local or national population norms. They do not imply, however, that you intend to discriminate against white people. That said, you should ensure that your aspirational target is reflective of the relevant recruitment pool, i.e. it is realistic and achievable, otherwise it could lead to demotivation and discouragement in the event of not being met.

• How thorough is your understanding then? Use the quiz in Box 6.10 to make a preliminary assessment. Whether you did well or not (and hopefully you did manage to answer twelve or more questions correctly), the important point is that you are, as with the other aspects of diversity, proactive in this regard. That is, do not wait for, or rely on, others such as your HR department, to provide you details of the latest initiatives. Seek them out yourself. The Equality Challenge Unit, for instance, has published guidelines on action planning and monitoring covering all aspects of diversity. Immerse yourself in them, know them, and apply them. Put another way, knowing the pitfalls is half the battle, knowing what to do, the other. When combined with the other initiatives outlined above you will be well on your way to internalising diversity as a core value. Indeed, you will know you have reached that point when your department and your university accept that in embracing diversity, they stand a much better chance of succeeding than those departments and institutions that don't.

Recruiting and selecting staff

> I was gifted at an early age – the minute I saw a person I could see the flaw in that person. It was like a curse.
>
> V.S. Naipaul

> How can I possibly know what other members of the faculty promotions committee were thinking and on what basis they arrived at the different statements they made in the committee meeting.
>
> Cambridge professor giving feedback to a failed professorial candidate, May 2000

Diversity and staff development both take effect from a common starting point: the recruitment and selection of new staff, and also their induction. The latter we have covered, but not as yet the former. The appointment of new staff is a process with which many will not only be familiar but also feel comfortable about. And prima facie it has a chronological symmetry, from job analysis and job design through to advertisement, interview and selection, which makes it appear a relatively straightforward process.

Yet therein lies its main weakness. It is precisely because we approach this activity with such certainty – after all, who doesn't like to think they are the best judge of character and ability – that the probability of making mistakes also becomes that much greater: the temptation to 'cut corners' in determining the nature of the appointment or in specifying the job criteria; the over reliance on a single selection method; the propensity to appoint those in your own self-image, and so on. Indeed, it is hard to identify another process quite so prone to flaws in practice as that of appointing staff. There is a very real danger, if you are not careful, that you may end up however unwittingly appointing someone who is not only unsuitable (which happens more often than many care to admit) but also falling foul of the discrimination laws in the process. As most of us now operate in a climate of ever-increasing resource constraint you will, moreover, have squandered a golden opportunity to improve your staffing resource, which you can ill afford to lose.

The purpose of this final section is to show how you can avoid these pitfalls, or, more positively, what you can do to give yourself the best opportunity of both promoting diversity, and of making the 'right' appointment for you and your department: to demonstrate that, indeed, you do have the attributes of a good employer.

To appoint or not? Making the business case

The first rule in making the right appointment is *to think through precisely what you're looking for*. Seems obvious, and it is, yet it is still surprising how many fail to do this adequately in practice. Why it is not always given the full attention it deserves is usually because the recruiters have fallen into the classic trap of making one, if not two, false assumptions. The first is that since vacancies arise as and when people leave or retire, the case for filling them is self-evident. And the second is that, if the last person who did the job was really good, then they must have a clone to replace them. To avoid a similar fate it is important you keep an 'open mind' as to both the need for an appointment, as well as its nature. You should ask yourself the following questions about all vacancies, whether arising from expansion or from staff who have left:

- Is there really a staffing gap in our provision? In the case of growth, is it more imagined than real? What is the hard evidence, as opposed to speculation? If a staff leaver, what specialist (not generic) expertise has the department lost? What is the nature of the staff workload we have to make good – its size, breadth, distinguishing features?
- If there is a gap, what is the most *appropriate* way of filling it? By reorganising the workloads of remaining staff members? By hiring a part-timer(s)? By making overtime payments? By subcontracting the work? Or, by recruiting a full-blown replacement?
- What other staffing shortages do you have in your department? Are they similar in size or nature as this new one? How do these relate to your department's strategic objectives and your long-term staffing requirements: the different skills mix, the age profile of your staff, and so on? What area should take priority? Why?
- If you require a new appointment, how will that person's role be similar to and different from the previous incumbent?

Don't rush these questions: the more you reflect, the more value you are likely to get from trying to view the vacancy in a different and broader light. You may ultimately decide on one of the above options and not appoint at all, or alternatively you may use the vacancy (or 'saving') to fund a new appointment in another aspect of your department's work altogether. Then again, after due consideration, you may decide you do indeed need a full-blown replacement. Either way, you will more than likely have to present an appointment 'business case' (or rationale) to your HR department, university or faculty staffing group for their approval before you can proceed.

From their perspective this exercise is very much a business one – and rightly so. It is a matter of budgetary numbers. How many students do you have? How many staff members? What is your staff–student ratio? What is the average staff workload? What proportion is your part-time staffing complement? How much and how many are your sources of research and enterprise income? What are your department's mid-term priorities? What and where is the market demand?

As such you need to understand their orientation and respond to them on that basis: do not feel obliged, as so many do, to write a lengthy narrative extolling the virtues of your department. Such non-quantified commentaries clog up the work of staffing committees with regular monotony, are never appreciated by its members, and leave them second-guessing the author's intention. Instead save your time and theirs by outlining your rationale in a short concise statement (no more than one side of A4) that includes the pertinent facts and numbers.

Preparing the job description and person specification

Your business case approved, you then need to draw up a job description and a person specification. These HR tools are, of course, a well-known staple of the recruitment process and, as in the first step of determining the nature of the appointment, are just as easily overlooked precisely for that reason. While this may not be so much an instance of familiarity breeding contempt, there is often a tendency in practice to treat them far less seriously than they ought to be. This is a fatal mistake. Indeed the difficulties that often arise during the final stages of selection can invariably be traced back to misunderstandings and flaws in the original design of these two documents. In the worst instances some selection panels even manage to confuse the two.

To avoid this outcome you will need to make sure you not only differentiate the two, but that you consider each of them with due regard to accuracy and detail as well as diversity. Your HR department will be able to advise on these matters and it is very likely that your institution may well have developed its own 'in-house' style. Either way, there are common ground rules you can, and should, follow:

The job description

A job description or job purpose or role definition is a summary report of information relating to a particular job. They can, as we noted earlier, come in a variety of forms, ranging from the competence-based ones illustrated in Appendix 1 to more conventional ones which list a range of duties. Either way, whichever you prefer, you should ensure that your job role:

– is written in a style that is clear, concise and gender neutral;
– keeps words to a minimum, avoids duplication, yet gives prospective candidates sufficient information to decide whether to proceed with with an application;

- identifies the 'principal accountabilities' (or duties) attached to the post;
- explains where the post is located in the organisational structure.

In other words it should specify, in a way that is precise and accurate as well as non-discriminatory, all the critical determinants of the post (as exemplified in the specimen outline shown in Box 6.11): that is the job title, location, line management relationship, job purpose, main tasks and employment terms and conditions (Torrington and Hall, 1995).

The person specification

The person specification, by contrast, outlines the characteristics that an individual would need to possess in order to fulfil the requirements of a job. Typically expressed in terms of the qualifications, experience, skills and abilities required of applicants, the person specification is based on, and derived from, the job description. It is not drawn up, nor should it ever be despite the temptation in practice to do so, either parallel with or in isolation from the job description. To do that would risk jeopardising the entire appointment process for it is the person specification which forms the basis for the next stages.

In devising your person specification you should (as shown in the case of the specimen outlined in Box 6.12) take account of the following:

- Avoid overestimating the characteristics of the person required to do the job, otherwise you risk restricting your potential pool of applicants or alternatively appointing someone who is overqualified. Thus in the case of educational requirements, for example, you should stipulate the minimum necessary for satisfactory performance.

- Do not assume that qualifications guarantee skills such as organisational ability, oral and written communication and teamworking (this assumption is often a critical failing in HE).

- Consider the importance of potential. Skills can always be learned but deep-seated personality traits may never alter. Thus the potential to be able to learn a task may be an acceptable substitute for a person who has already obtained those skills, particularly if the latter is not as suitable as the former for appointment. Remember too, some skills may have been developed from work experience which under-represented groups may have been unable to obtain.

- Take care to avoid unlawful indirect or direct discrimination such as: length of experience (which indirectly discriminates against women who have had career breaks to raise a family); specific qualifications (which may exclude people who have gained the required knowledge or skills in other ways, or who may have equivalent qualifications from an another country); size or physical strength of candidates (instead, specify the capability needed and request evidence during the selection process) (CUCO, 1997).

Box 6.11 Job role for a learning and teaching fellow

Job title   Faculty learning and teaching fellow

Job purpose

- To provide leadership in learning and teaching innovation across the faculty.
- To contribute to the realisation of the university's learning and teaching strategy.
- To act as a role model for continuous professional development in learning and teaching.

Reports to   Faculty director of learning support and development.

Campus base   City campus.

Key responsibilities

- Take the lead in at least one of the faculty's prioritised areas of development, namely: assessment of learning; e-learning and e-tutoring; problem-based learning; progress files; student-centred learning; work-based learning.
- Provide individual expertise in relation to an aspect of learning and teaching.
- Work collaboratively with subject groups, programme teams and individual tutors to enhance the student learning experience, e.g. subject reviews, programme validation.
- Proactively disseminate best practice in learning and teaching innovation across the faculty.
- Contribute to the development and implementation of strategies to embed new approaches to learning and teaching across the faculty.
- Work with other members of the team of fellows to enhance and develop learning and teaching across the faculty.
- Participate actively in regional, national and international forums on learning and teaching innovation.
- Act as a role model for continuous professional development.

Terms and conditions

Job title	Title retained beyond term of office.
Length of office	Three years (subject to annual review).
Appointment	0.5 FTE (full-time equivalent).
Responsibility allowance	£2,500 per year (throughout duration of office).
Number of appointments	Three.
Date of appointment	Start of academic year.
Eligibility	All staff engaged in teaching and/or the support of learning.

Box 6.12 Person specification for a learning and teaching fellow

Criteria	Priority (1, 2)	Method of assessment
1 Qualifications		
a) Education to first degree level	1	Application form
b) Recognised teacher training qualification	2	Application form
c) Achieving or seeking accreditation from the HE Academy	1	Letter of application
2 Skills/knowledge		
a) Knowledge of contemporary approaches to learning and teaching in HE	1	Presentation, interview
b) Ability to communicate ideas clearly, in writing and orally	1	Presentation, teaching portfolio
c) Ability to empathise with staff from a wide variety of academic backgrounds	1	Interview
d) Ability to use a variety of means to support staff development in learning and teaching	1	Letter of application, interview
3 Experience		
a) Successful track record in teaching and/or support for learning	1	Letter of application
b) Awareness of changes in HE curriculum	1	Presentation, interview
c) Experience in one of the specified priority areas with demonstrable achievement	1	Application form, interview
4 Personal qualities		
a) Innovative	1	Letter of application
b) Resilient, self-confident and credible	1	Presentation, interview
c) Energy, enthusiasm and good humour	1	Presentation, Interview

1 Priority 1 indicates essential criteria - extremely unlikely that a candidate would be successful if unable to satisfy any one of these.
2 Priority 2 indicates desirable criteria - candidates failing to satisfy a number of these are unlikely to be successful.

• Distinguish between those characteristics which are essential and those which are desirable, thereby avoiding being unnecessarily restrictive.

• Write (as in the case of the job description) in a style that is not only gender neutral but also clear, concise and accurate. For example, you should avoid using terms such as 'a good/sound educational background', what do you mean by 'good' or 'sound'? 'Relevant experience in a related field' is another, what do you consider 'relevant' or 'related'? Likewise 'previous experience required' – it is possible to have had ten years' bad experience. Stipulate the type, level and quality of experience you require.

- Reflect on, and determine, how best you will 'evidence' these characteristics; through the application form, personal portfolio, interview, presentation, psychometric test, cv, etc.

Advertising, shortlisting and selection

Advertising

When advertising you ought to have two main aims: to reach as many potential applicants as possible, and to enhance the image of your department and institution in the process. It is important you do not lose sight of either one. In the case of the former, you should advertise in the appropriate newspapers (the national education press, etc.), journals (professional, specialist) and electronic networks in such a way as to secure an optimum balance between coverage and cost and also one that is most likely to produce a reasonable field of candidates to do the job. In doing so, you should also consider both the local and ethnic community press, as well as take 'positive action' to encourage job applications by explicitly stating you would welcome them from women or men or minority groups in those instances where few or no members of that sex or group have been employed in your organisation in the previous year.

Every recruitment exercise is also a marketing opportunity. You therefore need to give careful consideration to the impression your advertisement conveys. UK universities have traditionally been slower than their counterparts in the US to acknowledge this reality. While American universities have in many instances articulated distinctive 'positioning statements', some UK institutions by contrast have still not moved beyond proclaiming to the outside world that they are a 'no smoking employer', or that they are not yet equipped to handle on-line applications. The absurdity inherent in such notions, the idea that of all the things they could tell strangers about themselves they should choose these in particular, beggars belief. It is likely to disappear, however, as the new competitive environment presaged by the White Paper will force institutions to take their 'brand image' and target markets far more seriously than ever before. The danger then, of course, is that universities may veer to the other extreme – to that of hype and 'spin'.

Either way, from your perspective you need to ensure that your advertisement is not only accurate, logical and non-discriminatory in language, but that it also conveys the 'right message': the one that intuitively reflects your core purpose and values, your key strengths and aspirations, etc. If it does not, you risk putting off those who may be ideally suited, and attracting others who are more likely not. The same also holds true of the 'further information' pack you send prospective applicants. Don't opt for the lazy way out, as others sometimes do, and rely on 'a glossy' and the standard institutional application form. It is just not good enough. In both cases:

- think of the lasting impression you are giving to those who do not proceed with an application, as well as those who do; and
- give your advertisement and further information the 'personal touch' and customise them in the same way you expect prospective candidates to do with their applications.

Your HR and marketing departments have the specialist expertise to help get your message across. Make sure you use them.

Shortlisting

If your advertisement, job description and person specification are equally consistent, as well as accurate, then the shortlisting of applicants should, in theory, be relatively straightforward. You can also make the task easier by asking prospective applicants to explicitly address the individual criteria laid down in the person specification in a 'letter of application' or 'supporting statement'. That said, practical difficulties arise in some instances simply from the sheer volume of applications (particularly in subjects where market supply outstrips demand) as well as from the potential for discrimination. Either way, you can best overcome such difficulties by sticking to the following shortlisting conventions:

- Operate on the principle of inclusion rather than exclusion so that the process is positive, looking for strengths rather than shortcomings.
- Use only the original agreed criteria on the person specification. Do not allow the introduction of any new criteria or the use of any criteria that may lead to discrimination (i.e. age, gender, race, marital status, religion, disability or sexual orientation).
- Consider only the facts and do not make any assumptions, thereby avoiding the risk of stereotyping while also ensuring that internal and external applications are treated alike.
- Prepare your shortlist with at least one other person, if not the whole selection panel.
- Use only desirable criteria when a large number of applicants appear to meet the essential criteria. In such instances, you and your selectors should each compile a personal list of, say, ten candidates. Reveal them to one another and seek agreement. There should be a high degree of consensus if you have each followed the process properly. If not, seek to reduce the areas of disagreement by classifying candidates as 'strong', 'possible' or 'maverick'. Continue the discussion until you all agree a final shortlist or, as some tend to favour nowadays, an initial 'long-list'. In either case take care to guard against including compromise candidates: those who are not strong but also are offensive to no one.
- Record, for feedback purposes, the reasons, in each case, for shortlisting, or not shortlisting, individual applicants.

Selection

Interviewing, of course, is the most common method of selection. Yet it is not always the most appropriate or the most accurate of devices. Indeed, its critics claim that not only are interview panels invariably flawed, but that at worst unstructured interviews are little better than using astrology to assess candidates. What is clear, as most now recognise, is that used on their own interviews are not a reliable predictor of future performance. As such, most organisations now use a variety of selection methods in appointing staff, not so much as an alternative to interviews, but rather as a complement to them. HE is no exception. It is as commonplace now, for example, to ask prospective tutors to give a presentation, or submit a teaching portfolio, as it is to ask managers to take psychometric tests or attend an assessment centre (Torrington and Hall, 1995).

You, too, need to give this matter due consideration when making your own appointment. To what extent would it help your decision-making to ask candidates to deliver a mini-lecture, lead a research seminar, give a presentation, offer a SWOT analysis on your department or the future of HE, take a personality test, etc. Equally, you need to remember that *selection is a two-way process* and that you should give candidates both the opportunity to visit your department and to meet informally with staff members. As for the interview itself there are a number of simple, yet important, steps you can, and should, take to address the flaws in the process and make it a more reliable one.

- *Arrange recruitment and selection training for all panel members*. It is common practice nowadays to ensure that all interviewers are trained in awareness of equal opportunities. You only have to reflect on your own personal experience as an interviewee, however, to realise that this is not nearly enough. Too often a cosy assumption is made – and here academia is conspicuously more guilty than others – that any reasonably educated individual can interview effectively at the drop of a hat. More than that, interviewers are often unaware of the very things that bring the process into disrepute, such as their own predisposition to bias. Research, for example, tells us that interviewers very often decide to accept or reject a candidate within the first three or four minutes ('the first impression' syndrome), and then spend the remainder of the interview seeking to confirm that their initial impression was right. Evidence also suggests that we all tend to approach interviews with a mental model of a 'typical'

Box 6.13 Interview rating errors to avoid

Rating error	Consequence
Halo	Impressive performance in one area leads to a good rating in all areas
Horn	Poor performance in one area taints rating in all areas
First impression	Forming opinion (good or bad) early; first impression influences all later perceptions
Recency	Opinion based on recent observation influences rating for the whole period
Leniency	Consistently rating higher than deserved
Severity	Consistently rating lower than deserved
Central tendency	Avoiding extremes; rating everybody in the centre categories
Clone	Giving better ratings to individuals who are perceived to be similar to oneself
Spillover	Continued downgrading for poor performance in past rating areas

interviewee and are therefore susceptible to the 'contrast tendency': i.e. we overreact either positively or negatively when a highly qualified or very weak candidate is preceded by an average one. Indeed as interviewers we are prone to committing, as Box 6.13 illustrates, a whole host of errors in the process (ACAS (Advisory, Conciliation and Arbitration Service), 1988; Hanscombe, 1998). A professional development programme will not of course eliminate all these errors but, in helping to raise the level of awareness and consciousness about such flaws among members, it should at least enable them to avert the most obvious pitfalls in making their final selection.

- *Make sure everyone knows, in advance, what to expect.* In the case of:
  - Candidates; where, when and to whom do they report; the activities and tasks they are expected to undertake; the time and place of interview.
  - Panel members; who they are; where and when they should gather (typically thirty minutes before the first interview).

There are no hard and fast rules on the size and composition of interview panels. Nevertheless you should always aim to interview with at least one other person (of the opposite sex) and ideally with a small representative group of three or four (anything bigger becomes progressively more unwieldy) which should also include your HR staff relations adviser. Although the panel has a collective responsibility, it is also a good idea to have one member specifically designated to act as the group's monitor with regard to equal opportunities. Check too that your HR representative circulates interviewers with a candidate information pack – containing the interview schedule, job description, person specification, advertisement and individual applications – at least three days prior to the interview.

  - Support staff and facilities.

Confirm that candidates have been asked if they need any prior assistance in attending the interview; that arrangements have been made for hotels, transport, car parking and refreshments and that reception staff know who is expected, when and for what purpose.

- *Develop and agree a structured interview plan – and stick to it.* There are, despite what some of your colleagues might argue to the contrary, a number of compelling reasons why interviews should be structured, which you ignore at your peril:

- it makes sure you cover all the relevant areas (as well as avoid the irrelevant ones);
- it is what the candidate will expect: a structure within which to operate;
- it looks professional: structure lends the process a sense of coherence and direction;
- it makes the most effective use of the time available;
- it can act as a memory aid for panel members when making and comparing notes on candidates;
- it makes it easier to compare candidates;
- it is the most reliable guarantor of eliminating discriminatory practice.

Rehearse these arguments with any of your panel members who may beg to differ. Then seek to agree a structure based on:

- the specific criteria which will be used for assessing the candidates, i.e. those articulated in the person specification;
- the areas of questioning to be put to *all* candidates by each member of the panel related to these criteria;
- the order in which each panel member will ask their particular set of questions; you need to ensure the process is a systematic one and not one in which panel members 'jump about' in posing questions of the candidates simultaneously; make the sequence a logical one so that conversation flows naturally;
- a common length of time, typically no more than forty-five minutes followed by 5–10 minutes in which members can write up their notes immediately after each candidate has been interviewed;
- the number of candidates to be interviewed: you ought not to exceed four in any one session and allow for comfort breaks in between.

- *Set aside your preconceptions and seek to ensure each interviewee has the opportunity to give of their best.* Once agreed, it ought not to be too difficult, hopefully, to get your colleagues to stick to this plan. You still though have the problem of how to get what you want from each of the candidates. There are, of course, as is well known, a number of interview strategies you can deploy: the 'sweet and sour' strategy; the 'stress' strategy; the 'problem-solving' strategy; and so on. The one typically used in both HE and elsewhere, and rightly so, is the so-called 'frank and friendly' approach for the very practical reason that the less interviewees feel threatened and the more they are relaxed, the more likely it is they will be forthcoming in the information they offer (Torrington and Hall, 1995). You have a critical role to play, then, in ensuring that both the tone and the style of the interview follows this approach. You can do this in a variety of ways:

- Arrange the seating as informally as possible by having a low table or nothing between the interviewers and candidates. Barriers such as large tables and use of telephones during an interview can be threatening and can get in the way of effective communication.
- Attempt to put the candidate at their ease. Adopt a friendly, easy manner. Be attentive. Project a sense of peacefulness and quiet. Smile and make eye contact without being overbearing or relentless. Introduce the panel and yourself. Explain the interview format.
- Seek to establish a rapport. Try to find something non-controversial that genuinely interests you about each of the candidates: 'I noticed with interest that you mentioned . . . on your application form. Can you fill me in on some of the details?' Show empathy: 'I would have found the situation you're describing very frustrating/demanding. How did you feel about it? So what did you do as a result? How did you deal with that?
- Take care with the range and type of questions you and your colleagues use; choose the right type of question for the particular circumstances (see Box 6.14).

Box 6.14 Questioning techniques to employ

Type of question	Nature of question	Purpose
Open	What, when, why, how 'Tell me about'	• To get the candidates to open up • Establish rapport • Explore opinions, attitudes and feelings
Probing or 'follow through'	Concentrates on specific points: – 'What exactly . . .' – 'Describe to me step-by-step' – 'Can you give me an example to help me understand'	• To get under surface of initial answer • Clarify uncertainties • Test validity of a more general response
Closed	Prompts short or yes/no response	• To confirm basic facts • To avoid strain at the start of a discussion or to bring discussion back on the rails [Use sparingly, and always follow up with an 'open' question. Do not misuse either. For example, do not ask 'Was your last job challenging?' Instead rephrase as: 'What did you find challenging about your last job?']

Avoid Leading, multiple and hypothetical questions

- Rule out questions that imply the candidate is going to be treated differently in the interview or the job because of their race, gender, disability or sexual orientation. For example, do not allow questions such as: How will you cope as the only woman/disabled person/black person in the department? Do you think people will take you seriously as a female manager?
- Prepare your questions for the candidates. Your questioning technique is extremely important but so, equally, is the subject matter you choose to talk about. Research tells us, for example, that *past behaviour in a given situation is very often the best predictor of future performance* (Torrington and Hall, 1995). As such, it makes far more sense for you to spend time probing candidates on this aspect of their previous experience than it does in canvassing their opinion on the various matters at hand. Again you should do this by asking 'behavioural questions' related to the specific competencies in the person specification: as in, for example, 'Can you think of a time when . . . ?'.

  - you had to organise others in the completion of a major project;
  - you changed your style of teaching or delivery of the course in response to student feedback;
  - you had to make a decision about two conflicting priorities;

- – a member of your course team was not 'pulling their weight';
- – you identified a potential problem which you successfully averted;
- – you had to make a difficult decision concerning the allocation of resources;
- – 'Walk me through the situation';
- – 'Tell me your part in it';
- – 'What happened as a result of what you did/said?';
- – 'What was the outcome?'.

- Remember to leave time for the candidates to ask their questions.

- *Watch out for rating bias in yourself and your panel members when making your final selection.* You should not judge candidates (nor allow your panel members to) until all the interviews have been completed and all available information (including that of feedback from presentations, tests, etc.) has been gathered together. Your panel should then review each candidate's performance in turn, not initially against one another but rather against the demands of the job:

- Systematically use a common rating system (strong, average, weak; 1–10; etc.) based on the selection criteria. Easier said than done. Enlist your colleagues' support in ensuring you all avoid the classic interview rating errors (see Box 6.13).
- Do not make any assumptions. Be especially wary of members expressing unease about candidates if their feelings cannot be substantiated by reference to the agreed selection criteria.
- Keep all the information in context; do not focus only on one or two issues.
- Make assessments based on the answers given and the behaviour demonstrated.

- *Compare candidates.* Once completed you are now in a position to compare candidates and reach a final decision. If there is disagreement you should seek to resolve it by reference to the selection criteria. In making your decision you should also consider a second-choice candidate, in case your preferred candidate declines the offer.

- *References.* Finally, you should check the candidate's references do not contain any negative or unexpected information. (As references can be subjective and open to abuse and error, consulting them prior to interview can often prejudice panel members for or against candidates.) If doubt is expressed then check the matter with the referee and if necessary recall the candidate for a second interview. If not, then offer the appointment to the candidate. Once accepted, remember that staff development begins with the interview. Make arrangements for their induction and offer them the opportunity to identify their professional development needs.

7 | Managing change

There is nothing constant except change.

Heraclitis, *c.*500 BC

There is nothing more difficult to take in hand, more perilous to conduct, or more uncertain in its success, than to take the lead in the introduction of a new order of things.

Machiavelli, 1513

Habit is habit and not to be flung out of the window by any man but coaxed down-stairs a step at a time.

Mark Twain

'University damned as incompetent.' 'University in £8 million crisis faces break up.' 'Blairite Vice Chancellor brought low by high ambitions quits as University fails inspection.' 'A Radical Mission that ended in Failure.' Such were the screaming broadsheet headlines in November 1998 which hailed the 'naming and shaming' of Thames Valley University (TVU) as the UK's first 'failing' university; an unprecedented event which many believed had 'profound implications' – in the questions it raised 'into the way HE is run' and 'academic quality and standards assured' – not only for the institution itself, 'but for the entire HE sector' (Alderman, 1999).

The size, scale and nature of the failure sets TVU apart from other HEIs, but it is not, of course, the only institution to have experienced difficulty in managing change. Indeed, instances where change has faltered in universities are as commonplace, if not more so, than those where change has been successful. The University of Cambridge's 'botched attempt' to introduce a new computerised accounting system (Capsa), for example, is yet another illustration of this tendency. Not only that but, as with TVU, it also stands as a salutary warning to other institutions of the inherent dangers in managing change and of the dire consequences it can wreak when things go awry. In this instance, an independent inquiry found that Cambridge's implementation of the new Capsa system in 2000–1 had proved to be an 'unmitigated disaster' characterised by moments of 'high farce', 'hard to credit naivete' and 'fallacious' financial reports. So much so, indeed, that it not only 'wasted £10 million of public money' but it had also, in the way that the new system hampered and delayed access to research grants, invoices, salaries and expenses, 'almost brought the University to its knees' in the process (Baty, 2001; Owen, 2001).

Knowing these risks, you could be forgiven for wanting to avoid change altogether. As a head of department, however, you do not have the luxury of this option, for change – the commitment to it and the management of it – is a sine qua non of the role. Every generation likes to believe that it lives in an age of change, and our own is no exception. Indeed one of the most *unchanging* articles of human faith, as Heraclitis reminds us, is the conviction of every generation that the world is changing faster than ever. And while this may be an erroneous belief on the part of our own generation, as we noted in Chapter 1 on globalisation, it does hold true in the case of higher education. For again, as we saw in Chapter 2, universities have experienced changes in their role and function over the past quarter century that are unprecedented in their history. Such changes, we noted, were more externally imposed than internally generated. Either way, the implications for you are the same. Others, above and below, will be looking to you to articulate, to implement and to change the model, sometimes in circumstances in which change is planned, and also in those when it is not. More than that, you will be expected, and should want, to secure the genuine *commitment* of staff to change, as opposed to their mere *compliance* with change. How though should you approach this most difficult of tasks?

The purpose of this chapter is to help you succeed in managing this process: namely in securing staff commitment to, as well as managing the implementation of, change. The chapter does so in the spirit that we learn as much if not more from things going wrong, as we do from when they go right. It contrasts the experience of TVU's attempts to implement change, with those of university innovators in the US and Australia. In doing so, it explains the nature of change, the approaches to change and how to manage change, as well as identifying the distinguishing characteristics of the university innovators.

TVU: an insider's perspective

'No one in the rest of higher education,' said the new deputy vice-chancellor, 'has undergone the degree of change you've been expected to undertake here.' 'He doesn't know the bleedin' half-of-it,' muttered the head of student services, sitting beside me.

'TVU is unlike the score or so of other universities I have been involved with,' the hard-faced consultant troubleshooter explained to the academic board 'in that its difficulties do not appear to be confined solely to issues of finance or of quality but to a unique combination of both. The university is now losing a quarter million pounds a month . . .' – thereby confirming what everyone already knew. For the main teaching building which once used to groan under the weight of student numbers now stood eerily quiet.

'The thing is,' the lecturer in European Studies, staring redundancy in the face, pointed out, body shaking and voice racked with emotion, 'what you've got to understand is that none of this is our fault.'

And yet it had once been all so different. TVU, an amalgamation of four very different institutions – Ealing College of Higher Education, Thames Valley College, Queen Charlotte's College of Health Care, and the London College of Music – was formed in 1992 and sought to build on the traditions of its antecedents. At a time when many university mission statements were largely indistinguishable, invariably seeking to be 'all things to all people' or simply plain anaemic, TVU had no ambiguity about its sense of purpose. It was committed to 'supporting mass participation in HE as a contribution to equality and social justice' and aimed 'to become a student-driven institution, committed primarily to teaching and learning and playing a major part in the educational, cultural and economic life of the region'. 'We were constantly struck,' the QAA Special Review team later reported, 'by the way in which this [laudable mission] permeated many of our meetings with staff at all levels from the vice-chancellor to the most junior support staff.' This sense of mission produced a student body of 'remarkable variety'; one in which nearly two-thirds of the university's 28,000 students in 1996–7 were part-timers, 59 per cent over 25, 48 per cent from ethnic minorities, and one-third from abroad (QAA, 1998). As the local paper put it, TVU was not 'a university of dry academics, teaching well-off middle class youths' but rather 'a place of learning for single parents, people with jobs, and ethnic minorities, teaching them things they wanted to learn and would find useful' (Tear, 1998).

The university, however, did not confine itself solely to promoting access per se. Building on established strengths in hospitality, nursing, business studies and languages (indeed linguistics achieved the same rating (5) as that of Cambridge in the 1996 RAE), the university sought to carve a distinctive niche in catering for the needs of the creative and cultural industries in West London and the Thames Valley. Not an unrealistic ambition in view of the university's location or for an institution that could count Pete Townshend from The Who, Ronnie Wood from the Rolling Stones and the late Freddie Mercury from Queen among its alumni. That the ambition was later realised was also due in no small part to a number of honorary professors, including, among others, David Frost, Jeremy Isaacs, Michael Grade, Howard Goodall and Jenny Abramsky, who all very much wanted to help, and indeed made a generous contribution towards TVU's development.

TVU, furthermore, also sought to pioneer what were then relatively new ways of learning – electronic-, media- and resource-based – as a substitute for, rather than an addition to, traditional teaching and learning strategies: to move away from what is a very narrow teaching and learning environment (in which students attend lectures at a set time and place, complete assessments that are often 'bolt-on' courses and learn passively under the tutor's control) to one that would be much broader and holistic in scope. It offered an environment in which students could tap a wide range of learning resources (their student peers, the most underused resource in HE, the library, computing and multiple media facilities, etc.), and organise their learning around assessments which would be central to their courses, and in which, above all, they would be active participants in the process under the tutor's guardianship. Central to this new environment were the learning resource centres (LRCs), which both integrated and housed multiple learning technologies and were established on the two main campuses in Ealing and Slough. The latter, named after the university's first chancellor, Paul Hamlyn, was an award-winning design conceived by the architect, Richard Rogers. Not dissimilar to the Eurostar terminal at London's Waterloo station, the new LRC, in marked contrast to the faded campus buildings (*c.*1960s) that surrounded it, was, and is, indeed, a stunning learning showcase. So much so in fact that when Tony Blair and David Blunkett came to open it the former enthused: 'What is so remarkable about what I have seen here today is that this could form the benchmark for what could be done right throughout the country. Why I wonder can't every university be like TVU'. 'Things then' were 'only supposed to get better' – but they didn't; they fell apart in spectacular fashion. What went wrong then and why?

Many universities have had to wrestle with the common dilemma of how to do 'more' (teach more students) with 'less' (resources) and still maintain quality in an environment which has become increasingly competitive and in which the pressure for change is unremitting. TVU was no different though – since it had no significant financial resources or any realisable assets (other than building stock) and was operating within 40 per cent of the space norms recommended by HEFCE – its problems were relatively more acute than most. Either way, it is difficult to fault the case the vice-chancellor made for change or the vision of the 'new learning environment' he articulated. On the contrary, if one accepts (and one ought to) the argument that 'radical external changes call for radical internal changes' then it not only offered a far more appealing prospect than 'death by a thousand [funding] cuts' but also a genuinely attractive alternative environment for learning: one indeed that met the challenge facing all of us – of turning 'mass time' into 'quality time' for students. This was no reckless or foolhardy venture, then, but rather an imaginative aspiration ahead of its time – that has indeed stood the test of time.

And yet herein lay the source of the university's problems. For like almost every other change initiative that fails to achieve its original promise, the rationale very often still makes sense on paper. This is because such analyses invariably pay too much attention to what is 'above the waterline' (where any inconsistencies are transparent) and too little to what is going on 'below the waterline' (where inconsistencies are often hidden) (Scott-Morgan, 1999). This was the case at TVU; or, as the QAA put it:

> For its success [change] needed very careful and comprehensive planning, effective leadership, prior infrastructural development, good communications, fail-safe contingency plans, fully tested information systems, a realistic timetable and goodwill on the part of all staff. We believe that these were all pre-requisites, not merely desirable options, the absence or failure of any one of which would be likely to jeopardise seriously a successful outcome.

Put another way, making sense on paper is one thing, putting it into practice quite another altogether. The university failed, in essence, not because its aspirations were unsound, but because it attempted to do too much too quickly, in an internal environment that was ill-prepared for change, and came unstuck. This experience warrants closer inspection not least because, in comparing it with the successful innovators I visited as a Churchill Fellow, it is possible to identify the particular reasons for TVU's failure, but also, more importantly, for the lessons we can learn from it.

There were in fact a number of reasons why TVU failed in its attempt to manage large-scale change:

The very nature of the change itself – and its consequences

The implementation of the 'new learning environment' anticipated a change in the traditional role of the tutor from that of 'director of learning' (or information deliverer) to that of 'facilitator of learning' (or curriculum designer). And yet, as fundamental a change as this represented, and in some instances it would require tutors to alter their deep-seated habits of a lifetime, it did not attract anything like the opprobrium that was directed towards the related changes that were made to the curriculum. Changes, that is, whose impact in practice had the opposite effect to what staff and students might reasonably have expected: that is, they weakened rather than strengthened the university's curriculum.

For example, the university offered prospective undergraduates an à la carte selection of 269 different pathway (or course) combinations. But in restricting modules to a single pathway, it simultaneously confined students, much to their chagrin, to a set menu of study. Thus the Jean Monnet Professor of Politics, who regularly attracted more than fifty students to her module on the politics of the European Union when it was offered university-wide, found it rendered unviable when its intake was restricted solely to the small cohort of students majoring in politics. Languages too, once a mainstay of the institution, was a rendered a marginal activity – an outcome as unnecessary as it was damaging.

The inadequacy of the consultation process

Consultation, and the participation and commitment that goes with it, is an essential prerequisite for any change process that seeks to be an effective one, and at TVU an extensive and lengthy consultation did indeed take place over a period of nine months. Such was the 'general lack of trust' among staff, however, that this process was never perceived to be anything other than as the QAA put it 'a hollow exercise'. Or as one senior academic put it: 'If you ask a question you are deemed to be either mad or bad and when you don't you are accused of not being engaged.'

This modus operandi contrasts sharply with the model of best practice, noted in Chapter 3, used by George Mason University, Virginia, in determining their visionary guide, 'Engaging the Future'. Their plan was produced by a faculty group task force working to a brief set by the Provost's Office and was the outcome of a process that embraced alumni, the local Round Table organisations and legislators. So successful was this initiative in championing 'university citizenship' that the Commonwealth of Virginia adopted it as mandatory practice for all its universities.

The failure to anticipate the full extent of the changes

The phenomenon of unintended negative consequences, where the secondary effects of change nullify those of the primary, is not an unusual one. On the contrary it has been such a common occurrence as to prompt the formulation of a law in its name,

Tutt's (1985) law of unintended consequences which states that: 'Social systems frequently respond to change in the opposite way to that intended by those who initiated the change.' This is not a variation of Murphy's famous law that 'anything that can go wrong will go wrong', but rather an acknowledgement of the inherent risks involved if we rely on an oversimplistic cause and effect relationship when designing change. It is a law we too often ignore to our cost.

In the case of the 2003 White Paper, for example, its focus necessarily, and quite properly, is the *domestic* UK audience many of whom support the aspirations (if not the means) it sets out with regard to world-class research, teaching excellence, wider access, and so on. In articulating how this will be achieved, however – through the creation of seventy (departmental) centres of teaching excellence, the introduction of a six-star research rating, etc. – the impact of such changes from an *international* perspective do not appear to have been considered. For the perception likely to be drawn, unintended though it may be, is that UK universities have only seventy departments where teaching is excellent, and that research outside of Oxford and Cambridge, say, in a subject such as Physics, is of minor consequence.

TVU fell foul of the same tendency when it sought to establish an internal market in which 'colleges' ('comprising a small management group') commissioned courses and 'schools' (or 'repositories of staff') ran them; the intention being to incentivise schools and staff to develop, in line with the university's (legitimate and pressing) aspirations, profitable new income sources. In practice this artificial internal division – one in which the colleges sought to exercise a supervisory role over schools, who in turn regarded them as supernumerary – had the effect of reducing the status of tutors as the QAA put it to that of a 'hired hand'.

This conception of the tutor's role is strikingly at odds with practice elsewhere. Australia's University of Ballarat, for example, has sought to broaden, not narrow, the traditional concept of scholarship by putting the late Ernest Boyer's theoretical model into practice, an initiative it believes will more accurately reflect the tutor's range of work. Similarly the University of Western Australia and Queensland University of Technology both encourage competition as a means of promoting change but do so in a way – through departmental awards for excellence in teaching and learning – that fosters, not fractures, academic teamwork.

Opting for the 'big-bang' approach and piling one fundamental change on top of another

Again good practice tells us that when planning change which is both significant in scope and fundamental in character (i.e. the very sort TVU was contemplating), it is prudent to undertake a trial implementation (usually centred on a 'piloting programme') in the first instance. Then if all goes well, and with lessons learned, implement the change in a measured (usually phased) way. The 'new learning environment' went ahead without any such 'trial-and-error' planning, and was implemented simultaneously across all three levels of all undergraduate programmes in one fell swoop in September 1997. This was in spite of the fact, as the QAA put it, that it was 'a very ambitious attempt to restructure the academic organisation and culture of the university at its most basic level' and even though 'some staff had warned' of the recklessness of such a 'big-bang' approach.

Nor was that all. This change was introduced on the back of another innovation of equally far-reaching significance that had been set in motion the previous year: the 'root and branch' restructuring and centralisation of all the university's academic-related administration (or ARA). This initiative was designed to replace, as explained to the senior management group, 'the current individuated craft-style system of administration with a post-industrial one to cater for mass student numbers'. Its ramifications in practice, however, were extraordinary: misplaced assignments, missing exam marks, unregistered students and unknown class sizes. Indeed the chaos that was to envelop the university – and set in train the sequence of events that led to the newspaper allegations of 'dumbing-down', the QAA Special Review, the resignation of the vice-chancellor and the 'naming' and 'shaming' of TVU – all stem from this common source. Put another way, the first phase of the ARA introduced in September 1996 – an administrative reorganisation that involved the transfer of local and specialist staff from schools into a central registry, just as school re-sit exam boards were due to sit that year – was a spectacular own goal from which the university spent much of the next two years trying to recover. A human error that was compounded still further by an inadequate examination IT software system, that could not cope with either the volume or complexity of the university's patterns of assessment, which meant that the errors, inaccuracies and omissions outstanding from the re-sit boards of September 1996 rolled over into, and were indeed added to by, those exam boards of the following year. The consequences of this were dire and the university's reputation suffered as a result, and deservedly so. TVU became 'the university that's hip, that's cool, and loses its degree results' and one mother's well-publicised 'run-around nightmare' trying to obtain her son's course results served to underline the point (Wynne-Jones, 1997; Reid, 1997). And yet this situation was by no means irretrievable and the university, as the vice-chancellor rightly later pointed out, made significant progress in unravelling this assessment imbroglio.

Less publicised, yet infinitely more intractable, were the contemporaneous difficulties encountered in student timetabling and classroom allocation. The introduction of a new student support system meant that each student was supposed to be allocated a 'director of studies' and a named pathway. In practice, however, this condition proved impossible to fulfil using the new timetabling software system, for it was programmed in such a way as to print an individual student timetable based on a director of studies or a pathway, but not both: that is, a student could not be allocated a director of studies unless they were registered on a pathway but they couldn't register on a pathway unless they also had a director of studies. This was a devilish 'Catch 22' that had hellish consequences and brought the university to the brink of paralysis. Literally thousands upon thousands of individual student timetables were published centrally of which more than two-thirds, because of the technical shortcomings, were erroneous. From a student perspective it was akin to going to the bank knowing you have money in your account but not being able to access the cashpoint machine for want of a PIN code. Or having a valid ticket for the football match but not being allowed through the turnstile. Not surprisingly student bewilderment and puzzlement soon gave way to frustration and irritation and ultimately anger and full-blown rage. A terminal breakdown was avoided only by foresaking technology in favour of establishing local emergency 'paper systems' or, as the QAA expressed it, through the 'Herculean and ad hoc efforts of dedicated individuals'.

Again university innovators such as George Mason demonstrate that there are alternative ways of realising similar aspirations, without necessarily entailing fundamental restructuring. The award-winning New Century College, for instance, was set up to offer students 'the finest small college education within the context of a large state university'. It is one in which students, underpinned, ironically, by an individuated craft-style system, learn actively and collaboratively to design their own 'intellectual map'. In other words, it is one that could not only have diminished the 'long tail' of students which the QAA identified at TVU, but which would also have motivated administrators, not demoralised them.

The failure to recognise that change imposed from above cannot, and does not, work

The idea that change will only occur, and can only occur, if it is 'driven from the top' is, as Senge (1995) reminds us, a deeply entrenched popular belief. It is almost uniformly an unquestioned assumption that persists in spite of abundant evidence to the contrary – that top management in universities, as well as in business, have largely been impotent in transforming their organisations. It is a very wrong-headed notion too: one that is, ironically, in an 'age of empowerment' and 'flatter organisations', not only deeply disempowering (in that it implies the way to empowerment can only be achieved by recourse to hierarchical authority), but also, even more importantly, that overlooks the crucial fact that *values are only values if they are chosen voluntarily* and as such cannot be imposed from the top. Thus initiatives that are solely top-down are at best likely to evoke *compliance* with change rather than a genuine *commitment to it*. And in some instances actually move an organisation backward, rather than forward.

This is essentially what happened at TVU. Taken together, the anticipated changes to the university's organisation, system, processes and culture were of such magnitude that they needed, as the QAA noted, 'goodwill on the part of all staff' if they were to stand any chance of success. This prerequisite was conspicuous by its absence at TVU. Indeed the very period during which many of the above changes were being introduced (November 1996 to May 1997) was itself overshadowed by industrial action on the part of the lecturer's union, NATFHE. This action, such as the withholding of student assessment marks, was consciously aimed at undermining the implementation of these changes. This nadir in the relationship between management and staff was, of course, not inevitable, but it was also no surprise either, and stemmed from a number of different sources.

First, there was the notion of the 'student-driven' university; a novel, and indeed revolutionary, concept in what (if not rightly) has traditionally been a 'supply-led business'. It became an issue from the outset precisely for that reason. For while many staff, like their counterparts in other 'new' universities, were by inclination, and in practice, 'student-centred' in their teaching and learning and always keen to support students, at TVU they felt threatened by the idea of being 'student-driven', and with good reason. The initial estate rebuilding programme, centred on an extensive refurbishment of the Students' Union, served to confirm their suspicion. But it was the way the concept was used in a coercive sense rather than, as it should have been, as a guiding aspiration, that convinced many staff their interests and concerns were being overridden – that they were not just of secondary but of minor importance.

Second there was, as the QAA observed, the 'very poor' industrial relations within the university; the legacy of a long-standing dispute over the contractual terms under which academic staff were employed. In essence, the Ealing NATFHE branch took the view that management should honour the local employment agreement that pre-dated the new national professional contract, while the directorate maintained that the former had been superseded by the latter, and besides staff were not being required to do anything other than was asked of their counterparts at other 'new' universities. This initial disagreement grew over five years into an increasingly bitter and acrimonious dispute that became ideological and personal as well as industrial in character. The dispute was protracted: in the directorate view, because some branch officials, i.e. those known to be active within the Socialist Worker's Party, were bent on doing so for their own ends, over and above the interests of their members (that the latter were in essence 'sheep' led by 'wolves'); and in the union's view, because management persistently refused to recognise their grievances over staff workloads. Neither side covered itself in glory – and it had knock-on self-defeating consequences, not least the exclusion of academic staff from the recruitment and admissions process over the critical summer period, which in turn undermined staff commitment still further.

Lastly there was the leadership, and in particular the vice-chancellor's approach to the management of change. We noted in Chapter 2 that although leadership and management are not mutually exclusive, a critical difference between the two emerges in the way that leaders and managers are perceived by their staff. A management relationship, for example, can be perfectly satisfactory, and often very productive, when both sides approach it in a cool, calm and purposeful manner. A leadership relationship, on the other hand, will not succeed in this way: it must involve emotion, passion and a stirring of the blood. The vice-chancellor, Mike Fitzgerald, certainly did that. Not least through the well-documented unorthodoxy of his 'image' – the spiky peroxide hair, the dangling earring, the zany ties, the Armani suits, the Cuban cigarillos, the office jukebox, the chauffeur-minder, etc. To his followers he was universally known as 'Mike', and to his detractors as 'the celestial ear-ring', 'the anti-Christ' or simply 'that man'; only the eccentric ever referred to him as 'Dr Fitzgerald' or 'Vice-chancellor'. These epithets, of course, grew out of more than a simple assessment of image – there were other far more substantive aspects. No one, for example, doubted his passionate commitment to the values he espoused, his visionary capabilities, or indeed his intellectual agility. Where scepticism did arise and grew, however, was in the way this vision was to be realised.

Taking his cue from management writer Gareth Morgan, the vice-chancellor, in his very first paper on the university's academic organisation, for example, explained that the management philosophy would be more 'hands-off' than 'hands-on' within an institution that would be 'more human and value-based' and centred around 'networks' rather than 'hierarchies' (Fitzgerald, 1992). The reality, however, in the eyes of many staff, never lived up to this expectation. Indeed it seemed to be the very opposite of what had been intended: 'to build up rather than devolve down', 'to empower staff and students', 'to maximise flexibility and simplicity', 'to create a learning organisation', etc. This perception was compounded further by the overtly hierarchical 'top-down' approach that the vice-chancellor took in managing change. As a visionary, and as a putative transformational leader, the vice-chancellor's approach, based on Richard Beckhard's (1992) 'model for the executive management of transformational change', may have seemed to be both a logical and a natural one. It was ultimately, however, an ill-judged one, because by their very nature such approaches render staff invisible – as if they are not 'to act' but to be 'acted upon' (Trowler, 1998). For all these reasons then it is no surprise that staff were 'seriously disaffected' and felt 'a sense of estrangement' from the institution, as the QAA put it. Nor is it any wonder TVU was unable to either implement the planned changes, or generate a genuine commitment on the part of staff to the proposed changes.

The myth of 'dumbing-down'

That said, a myth developed from this failure of leadership and management, linking it to an alleged 'dumbing-down' of academic standards which in turn led to the unwarranted demonisation of the university both in the media and across the HE sector. It is a canard that ought to be set right:

The central charge of the *Sunday Times* (26 October 1997) that the university 'deliberately lowered standards in order to pass students' was, the QAA concluded, 'without foundation'. What had happened, and what had led to the initial allegation, is that the initiatives described above – chiefly the ARA and the inadequate IT exam software system combined with the localised NATFHE industrial action – produced a chaotic situation in the summer of 1997; one in which students identified as needing to re-sit had not been given proper notice of this requirement. Rather than delay the re-sits as should have happened, the pro-vice-chancellor in the vice-chancellor's absence instructed the re-sit assessment boards to pass students who had achieved 30 to 39 per cent. The well-intentioned impulse behind this instruction was that students should not have to suffer through no fault of their own. The unintended and unforeseen consequence, of course, would be to allow students to pass who might otherwise have failed. As such this instruction, as the QAA pointed out, was 'almost immediately countermanded by the vice-chancellor and not implemented'; and its perpetrator, the pro-vice-chancellor, paid the price for her error of judgement and resigned.

The failure of any assessment management system is, of course, not only deplorable but also indefensible if it means that students obtain better awards than those to which they are entitled. Even so, as one independent quality assessor has noted, we 'need to put this into perspective'. For although the QAA found TVU's assessment regime 'inherently unstable', the number of students who actually did receive a degree class higher than they should have done (later rescinded) did not exceed the number of fingers on one hand.

Nor is the QAA itself without blemish in this regard. For despite the damning indictment of the Special Review, the report is itself, as the independent assessor pointed out, 'short on hard evidence'. Not only that, but even more remarkable, was the fact that the reviewers chose not to derive any of their judgements from the QAA's own teaching inspection reports: namely the four QAA subject reviews – Sociology, Linguistics, Modern Languages and American Studies – which TVU underwent between 1995 and 1997; ones in which the university not only scored around the average (19.25) for TQAs in 'new' universities during this period, but were, in fact, *above* the average specifically for 'quality assurance and enhancement' (3.25 compared to the 3.19 average). Put another way, the Special Review and the (four) TQAs can't both be right – which begs the question: who quality assures the QAA and how?

The partiality of the review was underscored further by the three paragraphs devoted to TVU's international partnerships, which the QAA found to be 'less than fully rigorous'. Though again the independent assessor claimed to 'have read far worse overseas audit reports and continuation audit reports all relating to "old" universities that paint pictures at least as depressing as that painted in the review of TVU' without, however, attracting 'the clamouring for blood' as happened with TVU.

The focus on personalities and institutions (the former vice-chancellor versus the former head of the QAA; the QAA versus UUK (Universities UK)) and on sector-wide issues (the quest for a quality assurance mechanism acceptable to all stakeholders; the failure of governance; the desire to avoid 'another TVU', etc.) has meant that those who suffered most from the demonisation have been overlooked, not least:

- those large areas of TVU (professional, postgraduate, FE and health sciences) which were relatively unaffected by all the changes, yet whose reputations were impugned as a consequence;
- the hundreds of students who had their initial learning experience of higher education so unnecessarily blighted;
- the scores of staff who lost their livelihoods.

These were the true victims and the real tragedy of TVU. An outcome not fatal in consequence, but one that was as unnecessary as it was wasteful, and a salutary lesson to all who seek to implement large-scale change in HE.

The university innovators

TVU is a very good example of what *not* to do in implementing change. One that stands in sharp contrast to the university innovators, such as George Mason, Virginia, University of Ballarat, University of Western Australia, Queensland University of Technology and the University of Phoenix, identified earlier. This begs the question: what is it that distinguishes successful university innovators from less successful institutions? The innovators themselves are, in fact, very different types of HEIs: each with contrasting cultures, structures, traditions and orientations. It is nevertheless possible to discern a number of significant distinguishing characteristics which these successful innovators share in common (see Box 7.1).

These similarities, indeed, are not restricted solely to these distinguishing traits but also extend further to include the actual processes, or change levers, which the innovators used in implementing change. These are specific 'soft' and 'hard' processes which they all consciously harness to telling effect (see Box 7.2). From the collective experience of these innovators, as well as that drawn from TVU, we can identify a number of key principles that can help you in your own efforts to successfully implement change (see Box 7.3).

The innovators show that it is possible for institutions of learning to become more like 'learning organisations'. That smart people don't just know, they can learn too. It is, in short, an example we would all do well to follow. How though can, and should, you put it into practice?

Box 7.1 The distinguishing characteristics of university innovators

(i) 'Liberated' leadership

Innovators have a well-developed consciousness concerning the importance and significance of leadership both in the manner in which it is practised and the way it is developed.

Their approach to leadership is invariably non-hierarchical and often genuinely transformational (Kouzes and Posner, 1995): i.e. it rests on the exercise of consensual rather than top-down power. Put another way, university presidents and provosts did not dictate change or a vision, but sought rather to nurture others through the transparency of their own individual actions and the use of informal as well as formal networks and forums.

More than that, they view leadership as a distributive phenomenon and have sought to cultivate leadership qualities at all levels (course leader, head of department, dean of faculty, senior general staff) and across different groups (minorities and women in particular). Their intention is to 'liberate' leadership 'by enabling those closest to the job to take their own decisions'.

Significantly, the various 'cults' which Middlehurst (1993) identified as acting as a brake on leadership development in UK universities (the 'gifted amateur', the 'intellectual', etc.) are conspicuous by their absence among innovators.

(ii) Champions of 'university citizenship'

Innovators are proactive in attempting to give 'meaning' to membership of their respective communities. Conversely, they are also 'listening organisations' with a common aspiration to reach out to all their eligible members on an equitable basis.

(iii) 'Learners' as well as 'knowers'

Innovators are self-conscious about their limitations. And though they conspicuously avoid faddism and jargon, they are to all intents and purposes 'learning organisations' even if none of them explicitly claims to be one.

(iv) Client-focused

Innovators have an acute sense of self-identity, which does not recognise 'stakeholders' as such, but highlights rather the transactional nature of the relationship between the institution (as an entity in its own right) and a diverse range of clients.

(v) Masters of technology

Innovators recognise that IT is a means to an end and not an end in itself; that the key variable in teaching and learning is not computing provision per se, but rather the quality of the interaction between student and teacher. As such, they integrate IT as appropriate to their needs. Technology is the servant to the innovators, not the master.

Box 7.2 Change levers used by university innovators

'Soft' processes

(i) Tapping collegiality as an aspiration

Collegiality, as Ramsden (1998) reminds us, is one of those models which is fine in theory but rarely found in practice. Inward-looking, unwieldy, self-interested and occasionally destructive, Ramsden argues that collegiality has had a rather better press than it deserves. On the other hand, in an age of mass higher education and 'new managerialism', collegiality – and, with it, the virtues of unselfish collaboration and shared decision-making – have acquired meanings of iconic proportions. And it is these sentiments which the innovators have successfully harnessed in fresh and pioneering ways.

(ii) Working with – and not against – the organisational culture

Of the three broad approaches that tend to be used in managing change – power/coercive; normative/re-educative; and rational/empirical – the innovators employed a mix of the last two, but rarely the first (Quinn, 1995). Put another way, they accepted that culture is a 'process' and not an 'entity' that can be moulded; that universities don't have cultures per se but rather that they *are* cultures.

(iii) Focus on groups rather than individuals

While accepting that universities are intensely individualistic organisations, the innovators recognise that substantive change can only be secured in a collective fashion. Hence they shifted the focus of their interest, and their resources, away from the 'lone teacher/scholar' to that of the group: the course team, subject group, research unit, department and faculty.

'Hard' processes

(iv) Questioning of sacred cows

The innovators were also proactive in encouraging the questioning of established customs and practices. Whether it was the status of academic tenure, the efficacy of the directorate, the notion of the 'academic year', or the outsourcing of halls of residence, no aspect of university work was beyond scrutiny.

(v) Reframing the academic staff 'contract'

As the task of innovation has become more complex, universities have been driven to harness specialist expertise (sometimes in-house but often outside the institution) for aspects of academic work (the design and development of learning resources, delivering instruction, mentoring students, etc.) that conventionally were always undertaken by academic staff.

This being the case, the innovators all attempted to modify their contractual relationship with academic staff in such a way as to reflect more accurately the precise nature of the work actually done by tutors. In some instances, by ignoring tenure as at Phoenix, in others by establishing 'research professorships' and 'teaching-only' appointments as at QUT (Queensland University of Technology), or by hiring 'senior contract' professors in partnership with private enterprise as at GMU .

(vi) Performance management

The innovators have likewise also initiated and established processes of performance management (or more accurately 'performance and development management') in much the same way as outlined in Chapter 5.

Indeed their processes mirror contemporary best practice in this area as outlined by Armstrong and Baron (1998): namely, the innovators' approach is developmental rather than judgemental, flexible rather than monolithic, based on 360 degree feedback rather than top-down appraisal, and owned by departments and subject groups rather than the personnel or HR function. In short, they have all sought to link individual staff development with institutional goals in an innovative way

Box 7.3 Lessons we can learn from university innovators in managing change

(i)   No magic pill

There is no exact method or prescribed formula in managing change; no pill which will guarantee success.

(ii)   The 'art of conversation': a core process

Significant change depends on dialogue and commitment as much as imagination and perseverance. That what is conventionally regarded as the 'soft stuff' of the process (i.e. how we talk to one another, when we do it, the way in which we do it, and, most critically, how we value it) is ironically the 'hard stuff' in managing change successfully.

(iii)   Top-down change cannot – and does not – work

Top-down change we noted earlier can only evoke at best compliance with change rather than a genuine commitment to it.

The experience of the innovators, on the other hand, suggests that the role of people at the top of organisations is to create the climate in which initiatives can flourish. Not so much a case of 'top-down' or 'bottom-up' as 'anywhere up'.

(iv)   Leadership qualities can, and should, be tapped at all levels

A corollary of effective leadership from the top is the recognition by the innovators that leadership is an attribute not confined to a particular position in a hierarchy. On the contrary, they harnessed the skills of leadership at all levels within their institution. In essence, they understood something which others have been slow to recognise: namely, that our traditional conception of leadership, 'the captain-of-the-ship' image, stands in need of revision.

Managing change in your department

> We trained hard, but it seemed that every time we were beginning to form up into teams, we would be reorganised. I was to learn later in life that we tend to meet any new situation by reorganising, and a wonderful method it can be for creating the illusion of progress while producing confusion, inefficiency and demoralisation.
>
> Petronius Arbiter, *c.* AD 66

Make your department a 'pocket of good practice'

Effective leadership, as we noted in Chapter 3, is about nurturing others in a quiet subtle way. It is about developing informal networks to get people 'on board' and establishing a climate in which initiatives can flourish. It is definitely not about dictating change nor about 'a vision'. These guidelines apply just as much to all leaders as they do to those at the top. In fact when it comes to change, this is even more the case, for it is the departments which are the key organisational units in taking change forward. As such you need to recognise your responsibility, accept it and make the most of it.

You should not underestimate your scope for local discretion in matters of change. We have noted how change that is solely 'top-down' will not lead to a change in values – nor, for that matter, as Petronius Arbiter reminds us, does the penchant for internal restructuring so prevalent in many HEIs. In fact, you will find that individuals will carry on much as they did before once the initial reorganisation is over. We have also seen at TVU how, when faced with chaos, individuals will quite naturally self-organise. It follows then that you should never, nor indeed allow any of your colleagues to, consider change as a matter beyond their influence; an activity in which, as 'passive victims' or jaded cynics, they have no real part to play. On the contrary you, and they, have the opportunity to take charge of your own destiny in this regard, *no matter the particular circumstances in the rest of your institution*. Whether you are surrounded by upheaval or inertia you can, and should, aim to make a real difference by being an agent of 'good practice' within your department, in effect by seeking to establish your department as 'a pocket of good practice' within your university (Butcher and Atkinson, 1999).

Your leadership style is very important in this respect, as too is the need for common sense. Relying on these alone however will not suffice. Common sense approaches for instance, such as those based on rational linear understandings of change, often prevent us from recognising the true and full complexity of change. For example:

- the notion that top-down change, as we've seen, does not always work as anticipated: the law of unintended consequences;
- that change begets change, i.e. the process of change is a dynamic one and changes themselves change as they are implemented and adopted;
- that any 'implementation gap' (the difference between planned change and reality) may be due to nothing other than the working out of either one or another of the two above;

Box 7.4 The ten fundamentals of successful change management

1   Change invariably stems from changes in the environment both internal and external.

2   Change must presage a new model for the future.

3   Change will not succeed unless there is dissatisfaction with the old and genuine belief in the new – people must have a reason.

4   Major change is always painful and requires different ways of behaving, thinking and perceiving. People must be involved – resistance is normal.

5   Change is 'lumpy' – people, systems and processes change at different rates in different ways.

6   As line manager you must drive it and support it too – as 'designer', 'teacher' and 'steward' (Senge, 1990a).

7   'Play the ball where it lies'. Work with the good practice you've got. Avoid deficit models of current practice. Avoid importing models form elsewhere (those 'not invented here').

8   Change is an ongoing process, not an event.

9   Change is unique to each organisation. Celebrate your individual landmarks of success.

10 Change is contingent on effective communication, listening to feedback and acting on it – on you 'walking the talk' not just 'talking the talk'.

- that a change approach which works in one setting may not do so in another, i.e. approaches need to be customised according to the purpose, audience and context of change;
- that the well-known axiom, 'If it ain't broke, don't fix it' is often a wrong-headed one since it only applies in the unlikely event of a stable environment.

We have also seen, as with TVU, the folly of not following a textbook approach to the management of change.

It is an error you can seek to avoid by familiarising yourself with the theory as well as the practice of change (Trowler, 1998; Fullan with Stiegelbauer, 1991; 1993; 1999). This chapter is based on the theory and models of change, but this is no substitute for first-hand understanding of the different perspectives on change (structural, political, symbolic and human resource) (Armstrong, 2000; Trowler *et al.*, 2003), or analytical approaches to change (systemic conflict versus strategic choice) (Cameron and Quinn, 1998; Pettigrew *et al.*, 1992), or indeed the various ways of managing change (technical, political, cultural) (Tichy, 1983). 'There is' too, as Kurt Lewin (1951) reminds us, 'nothing so practical as a good theory'. The more your practice is informed by change theory and evidence, therefore, the less likely you are to fall foul of these common sense approaches, and the more prepared you will be for change in all its nuances. That said, there are too certain fundamentals, ten aspects, if you will, of successful change management – tenets which you should adhere to (see Box 7.4).

Understand and recognise the different approaches to managing change – their strengths and limitations

You should also be aware that there are, in fact, three broad approaches you can take in managing change: power/coercive; normative/re-educative and rational/empirical (Quinn, 1995), each of which has their particular strengths and limitations (see Box 7.5). In practice most people tend to rely on a blended approach, drawing on two if not all three of these different strategies.

In developing your own approach you will, of course, need to consider: the nature of anticipated change (fundamental or incremental); the likely degree of resistance; the culture of your department; and the motivation of your staff. That said, in developing change, you also need to remember too that the nature of HE environments are such that:

* power/coercive strategies rarely, if ever, work nor should you have to rely on them – they can backfire, as we saw at TVU;
* incremental changes are more likely to be successful in the longer term than a 'big-bang' approach;
* the autonomy of individual scholars notwithstanding, you should have due regard for the nature and strength of the existing *group* cultures (the course teams, subject groups and research centres) in which individuals operate.

Reflect on your own experience of change and use that when helping others to understand the nature of the change process

Think about your own psychological contract – the key things you valued about a job you had in the past or indeed your current role. All those aspects that were not part of your formal contract: your sense of autonomy and self-responsibility; the respect and esteem of your peers; your reputation; the comfort of your surroundings; and so on.

Next, think how you felt when a change impinged on or permanently removed any of these things. What was that experience like? Confusing, messy, hurtful, a necessary evil, no bad thing . . .?

Now consider how a change you have to implement will affect those things your colleagues might value: not whether *you* would be concerned if you were doing that job but whether *they* are likely to be concerned.

Empathy is an essential skill if you are to successfully implement change; that, and an understanding of the contours of the change process. Even on reflection, change rarely seems to have the appearance of symmetry, yet we can discern at least three different stages – each with their own needs and demands which you must master, the pre-adoption, adoption and implementation phases. Or what Kurt Lewin has dubbed the process of 'unfreezing, changing, refreezing'. The work of psychologist William Bridges (1991) on loss and grieving is particularly useful here, both in explaining the nature of these various stages, as well as in identifying practical strategies we can apply that will help individuals overcome them (see Box 7.6). Two aspects of this process merit further explanation.

Box 7.5 Approaches to managing change

Approach	Assumption	Strength	Weakness
Rational/empirical (or 'systems-thinking')	• People are rational • Once a proposal is clearly explained individuals see it is in their best interest and subscribe	• Based on the logical and rational analysis of the evidence • Individuals respond more positively to change when the process and details are explained	• Individuals don't always embrace change even if it is in their best interests (e.g. smoking, in spite of health warnings) • Encourages an instrumental attitude • Emphasises bureaucracy and control over emotional commitment
Normative/ re-educative (or individualistic)	• Individuals are affected emotionally and personally by their work experiences • Recognises the importance of organisational culture as a force for or against change	• Most effective in overcoming individual resistances to change • A 'bottom-up' approach that focuses on 'winning hearts and minds'	• It is slow • Not everyone will 'buy-in' to the change • Underestimates the power of alternative cultures (e.g. subject groups)
Power/coercive (or authoritarian)	• The individual desiring the change has more power than the individual who is expected to comply with it	• Upholds the legitimacy of the hierarchy • Can yield short-term benefits	• Essentially manipulative • Creates resentment and is ineffective in the long term

Source: adapted from Quinn, 1995

Box 7.6 Practical strategies for managing change

The three-stage process of change	*What you should do*
(i) Attending to endings	
• Involves letting go of existing practices • Marked by feelings of loss and resentment and maybe even emotional outbreaks, illogical claims and threatening behaviour	• Accept and expect emotional behaviour • Acknowledge the quality of what is lost; treat the past with respect • Share information; relate change to larger environment, internal and the external ('the bigger picture')
(ii) Managing the transition zone	
• Involves seeking out and giving support during the transition time; i.e. the period of waiting before the new situation has emerged • Marked by frustration, tension and polarisation among staff	• See the change as an opportunity • Get staff involved working on changes • Identify scenarios; develop a shared purpose and vision, a plan and a part to play for all staff
(iii) Launching a new beginning	

• Involves making beginnings as positive as possible
• Marked by individual acceptance and understanding of change
	• Ensure that each individual staff member knows the answer to:
	  – What is the new shared vision; what will it look like?
	  – What is the new purpose – what is it for?
	  – What is the plan – how will we get there?
	  – What part will each individual play?

Source: adapted from Bridges, 1991

Identifying and presenting your case for change

You may initiate change, or have change imposed upon you, either internally or externally. Either way, you still have to convince others (and maybe even yourself) of the need for change. Kurt Lewin developed a model – that of *force field (or equilibrium) analysis* – which helps us do just that. Lewin postulates that in any given situation there are forces within organisations that are ('driving') 'pressures' for change, and forces that are 'resistances' to change. Thus when the forces for change are stronger than the resistant forces, change will occur; likewise when the forces against change are stronger than the pressures for change, change will not occur.

Consider then your own particular circumstances and instance of change:

- List all the driving forces, for example: the negative economic imperative (to do 'more' with 'less'); the positive pedagogic imperative (the consensus between employers and educationalists on graduate transferable skills); new learning technologies; student diversity; legislative compliance; etc.

- List all the resisting forces, for example: resource limitations; perceived threat to autonomy; the perception of imposition; the loss of status and esteem; the preference for tradition; the lack of faith in those proposing the change; the belief that something has been overlooked; new skill requirements; risk aversion; the 'not-invented-here' syndrome; etc.
- Examine each force and assess its strengths. Consider the possible consequence of each force and assign each one a numerical value.
- Identify those forces over which you have some influence or control – and those you do not.
- Analyse the list to determine the efficacy of the proposed change and, assuming the balance is in favour, how you can implement it.

In theory, you have several natural courses of action: e.g. to increase the strength of the drivers or to add new drivers. In practice, however, conventional wisdom tells us it is far more effective to focus on diminishing the effect of resisting forces (reducing their strength, removing them or best, of all, turning them into drivers) than it is to emphasise the strength of the drivers.

Put another way, people want a *positive* reason to change (e.g. 'It will bring benefits both to myself and to our students') not a negative one (e.g. 'My job will be on the line if I don't go along with it') – other than in the immediate short term the latter is never, despite what many seem to believe, a key motivator for change. Identifying the areas over which you have some influence will also tell you where to focus your efforts when implementing the changes.

That said, you must first prepare a 'situational analysis' – a story or picture of 'where we are now' – which explains to your colleagues the circumstances which have prompted the need for change. Again, in doing so, conventional wisdom tells us it is helpful if you identify two dimensions of the 'prompt' for change (Trowler *et al.*, 2003):

- *Chronic* features, i.e. those long-term concerns you may have about particular aspects of professional practice, for example: the over reliance on a singular mode of assessment; an ethos that is 'knowledge-centred', not 'learner-centred'; a pedagogy that is too traditional; techno-phobia; etc.
- *Conjunctural* features, i.e. new circumstances such as a government or institutional policy change; a new source of funding; the appointment of new staff; etc.

And use the latter to create an immediate impetus for change; that is, to stimulate action on the former.

Put another way, you should use your analysis as an opportunity not only to depict the present scenario, but also to identify and challenge your department's blind spots. To get leverage that is in taking change forward.

Reducing the resistance to change

Rationality will get you so far, but the real challenge in managing change lies in supporting and guiding people through this painful process. You need not only to have empathy, as we've said, but also to have sincerity and genuine respect, if you are to succeed. You should also focus, as we've indicated, on reducing resistance (as opposed to increasing the strength of the driving forces) to change. How?

First, recognise the notion 'No-one likes change' for what it is – yet another popular myth. Humans have always been the most adaptable of species and many not only embrace change, but enjoy it too. Seek out those around you who support the proposed changes and get them to articulate and share with others new (and better) scenarios which the changes could bring.

And next, take your cue from Senge (1994; Senge *et al.*, 1999) and seek to build a shared vision of the change with staff – to surface and test the 'mental models' held by staff.

We discussed earlier how to build a shared vision in strategic planning and the same principles apply here; the second 'discipline', however, requires further explanation.

'Mental models' are the premise on which we base our understanding of the world around us – the assumptions (and prejudices) which underpin our knowing and doing. Unearthing and recognising one's own mental models, as well as those of your colleagues, is vital if you are to reduce resistance and work towards a shared goal. This is no easy thing, however, for as noted by Argyris and Schon (on whose work Senge's concept is based), people, and professionals in particular, quite naturally tend to construct 'defensive routines' which help them disguise their vulnerability in the workplace (Argyris, 1985, 1990; Argyris and Schon, 1978, 1996). So strong is this motivation, indeed, that despite what we may think our basic human tendency is to act according to four basic values:

- to remain in control;
- to maximise winning and minimise losing;
- to suppress negative feelings;
- to be as 'rational' as possible – that is, to define objectives and to evaluate behaviours in terms of whether or not the objectives are achieved.

The consequence of this mutual concern to save face, not surprisingly, is that we spurn listening, stifle debate and block learning. And, more often than not, without ever even realising we're doing so. This task of defusing 'defensive routines' is, in fact, even more demanding in the case of HE. For these activities – the questioning of assumptions, the weighing of evidence and the analysis of reasoning – are, by their very nature, at the heart of academic work. And while academics themselves are invariably quick to dissect the research of their colleagues, they are far less inclined to turn the spotlight on to their own reasoning and ways of analysis. Even so it is a task you cannot baulk. You must get your colleagues to consider their own assumptions – to walk up and down their own 'mental ladder of inference', if you will; that is, to examine their own actions and beliefs about their environment as they see it. You can do this in a number of ways:

- Lead by example: hold off on your own assumptions and be open about your own defensiveness; e.g. 'I am feeling uneasy about this because . . .'; 'I don't quite understand it. Can you help me see this better?'; 'It is threatening to me too . . .'.

- Get staff involved in working on the changes through one-to-ones, small groups and departmental workshops.
- Identify and showcase examples of good practice in your department already in place.
- Bring in an outside consultant to run a creative thinking workshop to identify and develop alternative scenarios. Develop pictorial as well as written scenarios.
- Use 'management by walking about': regularly cited, often underestimated, and too rarely practised.
- Recognise and be sensitive to the fact that staff respond to and deal with change in different ways at different rates:

  - those who thrive on it, the 'swimmers' who enjoy it; i.e. those you should encourage and leave to get along with it;
  - those who have problems with it, the 'strugglers' who have difficulties staying afloat; i.e. those for whom you should arrange appropriate training and support;
  - those who retreat from it, the 'copers' who withdraw from other professional activities; i.e. those who are the most taxing and also often overlooked who are best dealt with through a searching one-to-one.
  - those who shun it, the 'nay-sayers' and the 'mossbacks' who work around it or seek to change it, often in creative ways; i.e. those for whom you should gird yourself for the long haul: try to negotiate and be tolerant unless the change is mandatory.

A final point: consensus is always desirable, though rarely found in practice. Fortunately it is not essential either. It is though, as you know, a value close to the heart of many academic communities. Following the guidelines above will bring you closer still to the realisation of this elusive aspiration.

8 Managing up and managing the 'down side'

In war, resolution; in defeat, defiance; in victory, magnanimity; in peace, goodwill.

Winston Churchill

We all crave satisfaction in our work. Yet for many it is a desire that remains unfulfilled. Job satisfaction scores in America, Britain and Europe have, in fact, dropped successively in each of the past three decades – today less than half (47 per cent) profess to be 'extremely satisfied at work' (Oswald, 2003). In HE, as we noted in the introduction, this trend is even more marked; an outcome that has been attributed to, among other things, the adverse impact of university management. We have, however, seen how you can use your role in the way you lead by example, formulate strategy, manage performance, develop staff, celebrate diversity, handle change, and so on – to make a *real* and *positive* difference to the working lives of those around you. This, though, begs the question of your own sense of satisfaction. For the same sources of dissatisfaction that affect staff apply equally to you. In both cases it is not so much the long hours of work, the relatively low pay or job insecurity. It is, tellingly, the very nature of the work itself the relationship you have with your line manager, and the capacity you have to work in a self-directed way, which are the real indicators and shapers of professional well-being.

What, though, can you do to overcome or alleviate the adverse effects that these sources of dissatisfaction can bring? How can you manage these less attractive and more difficult, though no less important, aspects of your role? This chapter seeks to demonstrate how you can sustain your sense of self-worth, as well as your belief in the intrinsic value of what you do and what you contribute. In doing so, it explains how you can – and should – work with your line manager, maximise your political resources, make effective presentations, manage your budget, handle complaints, discipline and grievances; and also how to manage redundancies.

I   MANAGING UP

Working with your line manager

The relationship between you as manager and those who you manage is, quite properly, at the heart of any text in management. It is, though, not the only management relationship you must master. You do, in fact, need to be effective in managing five different ways: 'managing yourself', 'managing across the organisation', 'managing outwards' (beyond your organisation),'managing upwards', and also 'managing downwards' (Forrest, 1997). Of these, 'managing up' is often the most neglected – to the detriment of both parties. This is a very grave error. For, in the same way that you are the most important factor in your own staff's effectiveness, so too is your line manager in regard to you. Simply because you may have had no choice in deciding who your line manager is, you should not behave as if the relationship is somehow predetermined.

On the contrary, you must be *proactive* in this regard. You should make a deliberate and conscious effort to reach both a mutual understanding with your line manager (there are no 'bosses' in a 'learning organisation', simply co-learners) as well as an effective working relationship. And you should attempt this no matter how inauspicious or difficult your own particular circumstances may seem. For it is not just in your interest that you have a good working relationship, but also in your line manager's and, more critically, your university's interest too. How should you do this?

- *Understand the 'organisational world' from their perspective. What does your line manager want?*

Put yourself in their shoes and attempt to understand both the theory and the reality of their job. (You can of course also do this literally by 'shadowing' them in their work over a short period.)

Consider, in the first instance, the nature of their job on paper – where it lies in the institutional structure and the particular job role. It is always revealing to read your line manager's job description, for it invariably describes their role in relatively straightforward terms. Make a point of doing so if you haven't already. If you are denied access then seek an explanation.

Try to gauge the day-to-day reality of their work: the external and internal pressures; the competing interests; the political overtones; the demands on time; the institutional objectives to meet; the traumas; the satisfactions; etc. Remember, too, that organisations always look different at different levels and, as a rule, perceptions of stability, order and predictability typically diminish the further up the institutional hierarchy you climb.

Consider the 'added value' they bring to their role. Think about your manager's contribution to the university: what are the particular individual, and maybe even unique, skills, experience and abilities that your manager brings to the role? How do they choose to carry the role out? What is their management style? What aspects of the job do they seem to enjoy most, or spend more time on? What aspects of the role are easier for them to carry out than you might have expected? In answering these questions you will distill the personal 'added value' which your manager contributes, i.e. those qualities which your institution would lose if he or she were to be run over by a bus tomorrow; ones indeed which might not ever be replaced (even if the duties of the post remain unchanged), for their successor might have a totally different profile.

Either way, it is on this 'added value' area that you should focus. For it is here you have the best opportunity of reaching a mutual understanding. You will also gain a better insight of their likely reactions to proposals and recommendations. That said, remember too that you are not required to like or admire your manager (though it helps), nor do you need be similar in personality. Indeed, you may be completely different in personality, yet still make an ideal partnership.

Try to look at yourself from their point of view. What do they want from you? They will, of course, have quite specific demands depending on the particular nature of your role. As a general rule, though, your manager will want you to help them.

-   Keep them informed on an ongoing basis. Avoid springing last minute surprises on them. Line managers really resent this, so, no matter how great your immediate difficulty, talk it through with them before it reaches crisis point. *Don't* conceal it. By doing this, you will at least both have time to deal with the difficulty, and you may even manage to keep a level temperature between the two of you.
-   Put forward solutions, not problems. Their world is full of people telling them why something can't be done. Don't add yourself to this list. Take the initiative. Instead of presenting them with a problem to handle, show them how the problem can be resolved. This way you may also avoid having solutions imposed upon you.
-   View issues from their perspective. Not only does this show your understanding but it will also lead to better decision-making too.
-   Be able to cover for them in their absence, which may in turn lead to your own promotion.

If you have a good manager they should also be seeking to raise your profile by providing you with opportunities – through delegating responsibilities, sponsoring management development activities, etc. – to broaden your experience and understanding so that you can be even more effective in your role.

•   *Considering your own expectations of your line manager: What do I want?*

Reflecting on your own expectations can help you in two ways:

-   it allows you to examine whether or not your expectations are, in fact, reasonable, and not wholly unrealistic, ones;
-   it provides a basis on which you can negotiate the 'ground rules' by which you and your manager agree to work together.

Again individual expectations will vary. Even so you should be able to expect your manager to commit themselves to helping you by willingly agreeing to:

- keep you informed on an ongoing basis;
- have a sound understanding of your role;
- be supportive while respecting your autonomy;
- act as an adviser on how to sort out specific problems;
- openly support your decisions (unless they're truly misguided);
- be prepared to listen to new ideas;
- give you regular feedback on the good things and the 'not so good';
- give you opportunities for professional development;
- recognise your achievements;
- maintain honesty, exercise patience and practise consistency.

The last one may be an ideal, and difficult to sustain in practice, but there is no reason why it cannot be a shared aspiration.

- *Negotiating and establishing a working agreement with your manager.*

Having an appreciation of your manager, of their personal contribution as well as their role, and having clarified your own expectations, you now have sound basis on which to reach a mutual understanding that will benefit you both. One, that is, which ideally plays to each of your strengths. You should, in the first instance at least, aim to agree and divide your duties and responsibilities on this 'horses for courses' basis. This initial allocation can, of course, be revised as you develop in your role. Whatever the specifics of your particular circumstances you should also aim to ensure that you and your manager agree the following:

- a set of 'ground rules' for working together; and that you review them, consciously, on a periodic basis *and* at least once a year;
- to have regular one-to-one meetings (typically one hour, every other week) on the same basis, and conducted on similar lines, as those which you have with colleagues in your own department.

The benefits of establishing a good working relationship with your manager are exponential: mutual support leads to mutual trust and respect, which in turn leads to greater autonomy and increased responsibility; the very things we identified at the outset which nurture professional well-being.

- *If however you are unfortunate enough to have a bad manager . . .*

You should:

- Recognise that, in the short term, even that can have advantages in that you can learn from them – what *not* to do. Observe what they fail to do, or do in the wrong way, and vow never to make the same mistakes yourself in the future.

- Try to create a group network of your peers inside and/or outside your institution, if you don't already have one. Such groups are extremely helpful as a source of both support and ideas.
- Know that, in the long term, bad managers always come undone as a result of their actions – one way or another.

• *And if you are unfortunate enough to have a truly noxious manager ...*

You should:

- recruit a mentor to help you work out ways of coping with and managing the situation; mentors, of course, are not limited to this 'defensive' role but they can be an invaluable safety valve for your frustrations;
- seek advice and support from your HR department through your staff relations adviser, or directly from your head of personnel.

If neither of these work then you should consider the following, but only as a last resort:

- Going over your manager's head and appealing direct to their line manager;
- taking out a grievance against your manager: if it is not commonplace you can depend that such action will stall, at least temporarily, the most insensitive and obdurate of bullies;
- invoke the Public Interest Disclosure Act 1998 (or 'Whistleblowers' Act') and appeal direct to your board of governors if the concerns you have about your manager are ones of malpractice which threaten (not just your own interests but also those of) the institution (HEFCE 01/20, 2001).

If you decide that it is not appropriate to take any of the last three steps, then resolve to:

- Stand your ground, dig in and keep the faith; (or)
- work out an exit strategy (or indeed do both).

Building and maintaining a power base

> I seen my opportunities and I took 'em.
> G.W. Plunkitt, Tammany Hall ward boss,
> New York City, 1905

One effective way of managing up – whether or not your relationship is good or bad – is to help yourself make the most of your political resources. We are all familiar with the phrase: 'power corrupts and absolute power corrupts absolutely'. Power, however, is an inescapable feature of organisational life and one you will have to come to terms with if you are to be a truly effective manager. This does not mean, though, that you have to be manipulative or coercive, or seek personal advantage at the

Figure 8.1 The main sources of organisational power

Source: based on Morgan, 1997

expense of others. People of course can and do use power in this way – and that is the point. Power in itself is not inherently evil; like energy it is neither good nor bad. Its moral or immoral use stems from the actions of individuals in pursuit of their own agendas (Morgan, 1997). What you should be aiming to do, and will indeed be expected to do by your colleagues, is to maximise your power to advance the interests of the department. You should also be seeking to promote those of your institution as well as your own. How?

Make an inventory of your political resources

There are more than a dozen important sources of power within organisations, ranging from the formal (such as control over resources and information, etc.) to the informal (such as interpersonal networks), and from the concrete (control over technology) to the abstract (the management of meaning and symbolism). In broad terms these can be categorised under four main types of power base: authority, expertise, resource control and interpersonal skill (see Figure 8.1). Or, put the other way, from an individual perspective power comes from:

Box 8.1 Make an inventory of your political resources

The following questions are designed to help you think about the political resources you have. They are divided between the four types of power base: authority, expertise, resource control and interpersonal skill. The questions help to identify whether you have the particular type of power in each section, but there is space for you to add additional indicators of your own. The more positive indicators you have, the greater your power.

1   Do you have formal authority?

(a)   Do you have the formal right (say, in your job description) to make decisions, other than trivial ones?

(b)   Do other people need your approval before they take action?

(c)   Do you supervise someone else's work?

(d)   Do your decisions significantly affect important long-term aspects of your institution's work?

(e)   Does your manager typically support your decisions and not overrule them?

(f)   Do you encounter any resistance to your right to make decisions, supervise others or give approval from colleagues, peers or more senior managers?

(g)   _____

(h)   _____

(i)   _____

'Yes' answers to any of (a)–(e) indicate your possession of authority.
'Yes' to (d) indicates a high level of power based on authority.
'Yes' to (f) suggests a reduction of your political resources which you may need to do something about.

2   Do you have the expertise?

(a)   Does it take a year or longer to learn to do your job adequately?

(b)   Do you need a qualification to do your job?

(c)   What is the highest qualification in your field – do you have it?

(d)   Are you the only person in your institution who can do your job?

(e)   If you were to leave your institution would they have difficulty in replacing you?

(f)   Does your knowledge and skill relate to a major aspect of the institution's work?

(g)   Do people frequently consult you and follow your advice?

(h)   Do more senior managers clearly show that they value your contribution?

(i)   _____

(j)   _____

(k)   _____

'Yes' to any of (a)–(h) indicates your possession of expert power, but 'no' to (g) and (h) suggests a lack of perception of your expertise by others, and you may need to do something about this if this political resource is to be fully used.

3   Do you control resources?

(a)   Can you give or withhold access to the following resources of your oganisation:

(i)   money

(ii)   information (non-trivial)

(iii)   promotion

(iv)   training and development

(v)   senior managers and other powerful people

(vi)   computers and other operational or administrative facilities

(vii) 'perks'

(viii) _____

(ix)   _____

(x)   _____

(b)   Are others aware that you can give or withhold access to these things, perhaps because you have on occasion refused them?

(c)   Do others have alternative access to these resources?

'Yes' to any of the items in (a) indicates that you have power based on resource control.
'No' to (b) suggests that you may need to do something about this in order to fully use this political resource, but 'yes' to (c) in reference to any resource indicates a low level of power in relation to that resource, to which you may not wish to draw attention.

4   Do you have interpersonal power?

(a)   Are you on good terms with a number of people in the institution across different departments and hierarchical levels?

(b)   Do you know who the powerful people are, and are you on good terms with them?

(c)   Do people confide in you?

(d)   Do you usually speak at meetings?

(e)   Are you an 'active listener' – you make sure you have understood the other person's point of view?

(f)   Do you make sure that other people take your views seriously when it matters to you?

(g)   Do you avoid being either passive or aggressive in formal or informal discussion with others in the institution?

(h)   Can you hold the attention of a group or larger audience?

'Yes' to any of these questions indicates your power based on interpersonal skills.
'No' to any of (d)–(h) suggests that training and development would help you develop your political potential.

Looking back over your answers to these questions you will probably have found that you have in some degree each of the types of power base. If you give yourself a rating for each of the four types on the chart below, you will have a profile of your political resources.

Profile of political resources					
High	5				
	4				
Medium	3				
	2				
Low	1				
		Authority	Expertise	Resource control	Interpersonal skill

- your formal position: your role;
- your personal authority: the personal characteristics you have (articulacy, empathy, humour, intelligence, dynamism, physical appearance, etc.) that others find attractive or influential or persuasive;
- your expertise: both real and imagined (by others);
- your access to information;
- your ability to recognise and seize an opportunity: to be 'in the right place at the right time'.

Box 8.1 is designed to help you to explore and recognise your political potential. Complete the questionnaire and determine your political profile.

Conducting a power/dependency analysis of your position

As well as making an assessment of your political resources you also need to go further and examine your position in relation to that of others; in particular those with whom you have the most interaction. Think of your own immediate power network – those individuals in positions upon whom you depend – and begin mapping them out as suggested in Figure 8.2. You will probably find that, on the surface, your network of dependencies is in fact a fairly simple one. This is quite normal and you may find that you need to make a real effort to answer the questions set. If you do, it is more likely that you will be able to identify the true complexity of the network of power and influence in which you operate. Enlist the support, if you can, of a

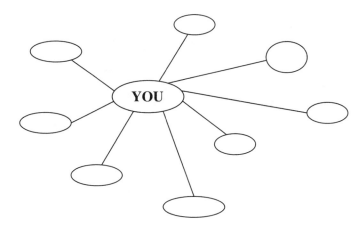

Figure 8.2 Analysing your network of power

This diagram represents the network of contacts you have in carrying out your role. Use it to identify the people with whom you have the more important interactions, regardless of their position in the hierarchy. Then consider the following questions:

(a) What kinds of power do they have in relation to you?
(b) What kinds of power do you have in relation to them?
(c) What interests are they pursuing (both pragmatic and psychological)?
(d) What interests are you pursuing?

Consider in particular what evidence there is for (c) and alternative interpretations of it.

trusted colleague or peer – as indeed you should in the case of the previous questionnaire too. It will not only make the task easier but should also ensure the outcome is more accurate than if you were to rely solely on your own self-assessment.

Drawing up an action plan to realise your political potential

How did you get on? Is the analysis of your 'power net' consistent with the inventory of your political resources? What are the differences? Can you account for them? What does your political profile tell you? What areas do you need to work on? What are you going to do about it?

- Consider those individuals at the top of your institution – do they have any characteristic(s) in common?
- Consider too where your institution is headed and what characteristics might be needed in the future.
- Commit to 'making your own luck' and draw up an action plan that will realise your full political potential.

Making effective presentations

> What puzzles me is how anyone can write sentences such as 'The act of approval integrates considerations of not only academic integrity but resource efficiency and fitness for purpose as measured against university strategic direction and culture paradigm' without their face crashing onto their keyboard with boredom. For management speak is not only depersonalised, it is clanking, repetitive, ungrammatical and full of non sequiturs.
>
> Gary Day, UK university lecturer, 11 October 2002

One simple and common way of trying to exercise influence is through the presentation of ideas or analyses to your manager or peers orally or, more typically, in writing. As this is the *raison d'être* of HE you could be forgiven for thinking that we are equally as incisive in the way we communicate within our institutions as we are in our research or our teaching. The sad truth is that you could not be more wrong. For much of what passes for internal communication often has the hallmarks of a poor student essay: ill prepared, ill thought out, long-winded and sloppily executed. Or, just as depressing, it bears the imprint of the bureaucratic 'dead-hand'. Or, worse still, it is littered with the pseudo-jargon (pretentious words that are neither definite nor fixed in meaning: 'synergy', 'holistic', 'end product', 'problematise', 'actioned', 'joined up thinking', and so on) that has come to dominate subject disciplines and academic life in much the same way as it has business, the professions and government.

This is not a path you should follow if your aim is to be understood (indeed many use jargon precisely to avoid just such transparency) and, contrary to what many academics believe, it is also very unlikely to persuade your manager into supporting your idea or proposal. Put another way, and as many institutions have increasingly begun to recognise, including even the funding councils, there is no substitute for plain English, plus brevity and precision.

More specifically, you should observe the following when preparing your proposal – or executive summary, if it is a report:

- It should be no more than one to two sides of A4. Lengthy tomes are as off-putting to your manager as they are to you, and they are likely to receive more of them than you are. You risk your proposal being given short shrift if you are not considerate in this regard.
- It should be written in a clear simple style and structured in a bullet point or short paragraph format, i.e. it should be 'easy on the eye'.
- It should be written from the perspective of the reader and not from your own. If your first words are 'This paper . . .' your proposal will not stand out from the pack, and your audience will be entitled to conclude that you, like the lazy reviewer who begins 'This book . . .', has not expended much thought on enlisting their attention. Think, instead, of an arresting opening that takes them from where they stand, in point of knowledge, to the proposal you are setting out before them.
- It should be organised around a basic framework in which you:
  - state the problem, the issue or idea;
  - identify the causes and effects; the pros and cons; etc.;
  - list the possible solutions, alternatives, options;
  - make a recommendation – i.e. you make it easier for them by cutting down what they have to do – to either agree or disagree; conversely you also make it more difficult for them to procrastinate too.

- It should be consistent with the virtues of a good research paper: one that is based on a love of order, accuracy, logic, honesty, self-awareness and imagination (Barzun and Graff, 1992).

Similar principles apply when it comes to oral presentations:

- Ascertain how long you are expected to speak and who and how many are expected to attend. The first question will help you determine the amount and kind of material to present; the second, the appropriate vocabulary, tone and degree of complexity. Knowing the characteristics of your audience you can pitch your remarks at the right level.
- Write your script 'for the ear' and not 'the eye' as any good lecturer does. Do not write long sentences or begin with qualifiers. Do not go from one main point to another without a break. Use more signposts than are necessary for print, etc. In the past lecturers used 'overheads' to *complement* what they had to say; nowadays presenters are too often led by the all-pervasive Powerpoint technology into confining what they say to what is literally on the screen. Do not fall into the same trap. Concentrate on your message, not the technology.
- Focus on getting across your key points (issues, ideas, conclusions) – six at most – and *only* them. Remember the longer and quicker you speak the less likely you are to be heard.
- Believe in what you are saying, and believe it matters how you say it. Your audience is not there to attend a reading. Practise your delivery so that it adds value

to the printed word; and maintain a good pace too; about 125 words a minute (Barzun and Graff, 1992; Siddons, 1998; Grant, 1997).
- Recognise that, as with the written word, the key to an effective presentation is thorough preparation. As Churchill himself put it, after one long rambling oration: 'I am sorry to have made such a long speech but I did not have time to write a shorter one.'

Managing your budget

One of the very first demands your manager will make is that you deliver your budget: that you, in effect, not only break even on your budget, by keeping your expenditure within limits and achieving your income targets, but also (ideally) generate a surplus. This responsibility can be an unnerving one for even the most experienced head of department, let alone the newly appointed head for whom it is very often a novelty. It is also an activity that, traditionally at least, and efficiency gains notwithstanding, we have not managed that well either. Whether for their own reasons, or because of the particular budget setting arrangements within their institutions, heads of department have too often been *reactive* rather than proactive in managing their budgets. This again is not an example you should copy. For the competitive and straitened circumstances in which your department operates (let alone your institution) make it imperative you take the initiative in this regard. How?

- Recognise and understand the basic principles of what budgets are and why we have them (see Box 8.2).

- Recognise and understand the principles underpinning your own budget.

The *nature* of your budget, for example, are you head of:

- a 'profit centre'? – a centre that has revenue as well as costs attributed to it;
- an 'investment centre'? – a centre in which not only profit but the investment required to generate the profit is measured (or more likely);
- a 'cost centre'? – a centre in which only costs are measured.

The *sources* of your budget, for example:

- the proportion of your income that is funding council grant, tuition fee income, research grants and contracts, commercial activity, endowments and investments, etc.;
- the proportion of your expenditure that is: (a) staffing costs (academic, administrative, technical, part-time, overtime, etc.); (b) general costs (consumables, staff development, equipment, travel and subsistence, telephone, postage, etc.).

The *basis* of your budget – the way in which it was (or could be) formulated, for example:

Box 8.2 Budgets and their purposes

What is a budget?

A budget is 'a plan quantified in monetary terms, prepared and approved prior to a defined period of time, usually showing expected income to be generated and/or expenditure to be incurred during that period and the capital to be employed to attain a given objective' (Chartered Institute of Management Accountants).

Why do we have budgets?

- To define the objectives of the organisation and thus provide a framework for the individual departments to operate within.
- Provide a system whereby the resources of the organisation are used most efficiently.
- To indicate the efficiency and effectiveness with which the activities of the organisation have been coordinated.
- To identify and quantify areas that have exceeded or fallen short of the targets.
- Allow management to rectify adverse variances and capitalise on favourable variances.
- Provide a basis for revising the current budget and preparing a future budget (forecasting).
- Provide some centralised control over diverse activities and responsibilities.
- Provide a stabilising influence in seasonal or cyclical activities (profiling).
- Provide a means of focusing on the important issues and highlighting areas where individuals can make a contribution.

- The incremental budget: this is the traditional 'base + adjustment' approach where the budget is based on what has happened in the past with any forecast changes built into the plan.
- The rolling or continuous budget: this reduces the level of uncertainty by allowing money to flow from one year to the next.
- The three level/probabilistic budget: this analyses the degree of future uncertainty and projects three possible outcomes (the most likely, the best and the worst) thereby setting the parameters within which the actual budget out-turn is expected to fall.
- The zero-based budget: this budget is built up 'from scratch' by estimating the resources needed to deliver (and assure the quality of) the level of forecasted activity.
- The activity-based budget: in this budget overheads (i.e. all costs that are not direct) are allocated in line with the cost drivers (student numbers, staffing and building) that actually (and not speculatively) influence the way overheads operate within the institution: that is to say, overheads are not apportioned indiscriminately, as in the case of the traditional 'top-slice' approach, but in line with the way in which resources are actually consumed, as determined by the institution's particular 'resource allocation model'.

The *institutional framework* within which your budget is set. What are the key objectives of your institution's financial strategy and the implications for your budget and your department? For example, they could be: to establish a central strategic priorities investment fund; to fund specific capital projects; to build up a financial reserve; to obtain 50 per cent of income from non-funding council sources; etc. (HEFCE 02/34, 2002).

Knowing your budget in this way is the first step towards establishing control over it. It will mean you will never be fazed or paralysed by any set of 'dead' figures that is put before you. It will give you the confidence to, for example:

- challenge both the accuracy and the assumptions on which your budget is based; and
- monitor your university's policy on matters of institution-wide interest (e.g. on internal recharging, overhead allocation) and ensure it is being fairly and consistently applied across all budget centres in keeping with the government's requirement that all HEIs establish a 'transparent approach to costing' (JCPSG (Joint Costing and Pricing Steering Group), 2000).

You should also take comfort in the knowledge that: whatever your budget, people are your biggest asset and, so long as you've adhered to the principles of performance management set out earlier, you will be close to maximising the potential of what is typically your department's most expensive resource.

(If you have not, however, you are likely to have a shortfall which cannot be made good through savings from the general (or non-pay) costs of your budget. Nor should you attempt to do so either. The demotivational consequences of cuts to, say, your travel and conference budget, for example, far outweigh any savings it may generate. You should instead go back and review your initial staff workload allocations and part-time teaching budget.)

Even so, you need to go further and recognise that the three most important things in budgetary management are *planning, planning* and *planning*!

For your budget is, or should be, in essence no more than your strategic plan translated into another language. The pity is that not all institutions or heads of department (to their mutual detriment) appear to recognise this. Indeed, it too often happens that heads of department, by choice or force of circumstance, get caught up, as we've noted, in a reactive cycle; one in which they are given an operating budget – see how much they can spend – passively monitor it – then hope for the best at the end of the financial year (see Figure 8.3).

To avoid this trap, or to break out of this cycle, you need to:

- Go back to the first principles of your department's strategic plan. What are your department's objectives; the targets; the critical milestones? Are they quantifiable? For example: to decrease reliance on Treasury funding by 10 per cent; to reduce part-time staffing costs by 10 per cent; to increase the proportion of income from CPD short courses by 25 per cent, etc. Do you anticipate the cessation of existing activities or the development of new ones? Is your course portfolio planning sensitive to 'product life-cycles'?
- Conceive of your plan and budget as *dynamic*, not static. Take a leaf from the military strategic planners who determine their objectives, and then work backwards.

Proactive: How to do it?

Budget Model

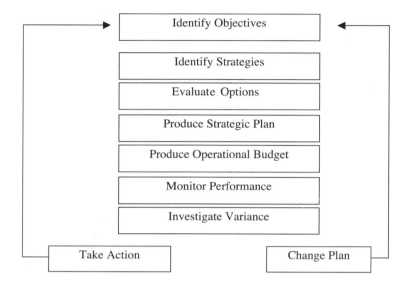

Reactive: How not to do it?

UNIVERSITY BUDGET MODEL

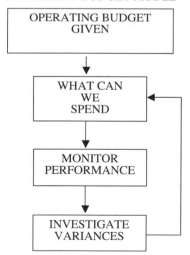

Figure 8.3 Managing your budget

What do you need to do to achieve your objectives? What do you need to do today in the next three hours – never mind the next three years – to make it a reality? Review both your plan and your budget in the light of your actions. If they are dynamic you ought never to move beyond Year I of your plan (see Figure 8.5).

- Recognise that the approach on which your budget is based may not be conducive to forward planning: e.g. the traditional 'base + adjustment' budgets may be fairly simple to manage and make it relatively easy to draw comparisons (with previous year's results and current forecasts), but they do not highlight any inefficiencies in the existing order of things, nor do they reflect any risks or opportunities either. As such you should enlist the support and expertise of your management accountant to apply the budgeting techniques noted above (the activity-based, the zero-based and the three-level) to your own budget, as a means of bringing these to the fore – and act on them.
- Work with your management accountant in actively managing your budget, for example:

    – divide your general cost items by twelve, plot the expenditure and monitor it;
    – identify expenditure items that are 'lumpy'; e.g. one-off capital projects, the part-time staffing budget;
    – profile your budget by plotting when and how you will spend it;
    – prepare a budget forecast over three months, six months and nine months; try to match expenditure with planning; your accuracy with this, as with everything else, will improve with practise.

None of this is rocket science but when you have put all the elements together, you can ensure that your future is not left to chance – that it is one you can manage and control.

Preparing a business plan

As government has successively levied greater fiscal accountability on HEIs, so too, in turn, have institutions themselves done the same within their own domains. And it is increasingly the case that if you wish to develop a new course or research proposal, or apply for a public grant, you will only be permitted to do so on the basis that you have a sound business plan. How best can you meet this requirement?

View it as a requirement that is there to help you – and not hinder you. For business planning is simply:

- the structured management of business ideas from concept to delivery through agreed stages (see Figure 8.4);
- a tool to help you capitalise on strengths, pioneer opportunities, redefine weaknesses and minimise threats.

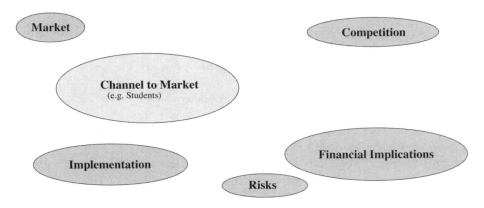

Figure 8.4 The key elements of business planning

It also:

- provides a means of targeting and measuring commercial activity;
- provides an accurate indication of costs and implications;
- avoids wasted effort and duplication;
- operates as an 'early warning' system should things go wrong.

Or, put another way, it turns conventional academic planning on its head by ensuring that any development activities are market-driven, not supply-driven (Luffman *et al.*, 1996).

- *Present your proposal on the basis of a systematic examination of the various stages of the business planning process outlined in Figure 8.5.*

Overview & SWOT Analysis

►Environmental Review

- The Market
- Competitors
- Channel to Market (e.g. Students)

►Implementation

- Who
- How
- By When

►Financial Implications

- Cost
- Income

►Risk Assessment

Figure 8.5 Preparing a business plan

A SWOT analysis of your proposal

- Strengths – What does your department have that others don't? What are your unique selling points (USPs)?
- Weaknesses – What are the risks? What could you lose? How much will it cost?
- Opportunities – What is the target market? Why will they buy it? What is the market size? What market share are you expecting? How is this divided up over time; what is the build-up?
- Threats – Who are the known competitors with similar offerings? How strong are they? How long have they been in the market? What is the size of their market share – their turnover? What do you know about their offer (e.g. pricing information)?

The logistics of implementation

- How will you sell to this market? Who will carry out this activity? What are their targets?
- What marketing support is needed (brochures, advertising, attendance at exhibitions)? Who needs to be involved to make the project work, directly and indirectly (e.g. support services)?
- What timelines are you working to and why?
- What are the key delivery stages in the process?
- Are there any special requirements (e.g. weekend provision only)?

A breakdown of costs and income

- What are your investment costs – your forecast of up-front development costs?
- What are the costs of your recruitment and marketing activity?
- What are the costs associated to delivery?

In all three cases make sure you allow for full cost recovery and include all direct costs (e.g. salary, consumables), indirect costs (e.g. library, premises) and overhead costs (i.e. those costs incurred whether the activity runs or not, e.g. fuel, rates, lighting, maintenance).

- How has your pricing been based? What is your market intelligence? Are you seeking to:

  - grab the market – penetration pricing;
  - make a fast return – skimming the price;
  - offer a quality product – premium pricing;
  - looking for economies of scale – economy pricing;
  - exploit different perceptions – differential pricing.

- What are your income forecasts (pricing × student numbers)? How much activity does it represent? Is it genuinely realistic?

An assessment of risk

Outline the risks which may cause changes to the plan, for example: delays in course development; difficulty in targeting the market; rival activity; quality issues.

- Financial sensitivity: What are the implications of changes in costs and income over time? What would be the financial impact of an increase in the cost of development or a shortfall in student recruitment?
- Cost-benefits: What impact (high, medium, low) would the development have on the overall activity the department? What is the likelihood (high, medium, low) of this development not succeeding? What are the risks for the department in *not* pursuing this development, i.e. the cost of foregoing the opportunity (HEFCE 01/24, 2001)?

II MANAGING THE 'DOWN SIDE'

Handling complaints, discipline and grievances

> At the heart of our political system is a culture which cares more about the right process than the best outcome.
>
> James Strachan, Chair, UK Audit Commission, May 2003

Tricky, demanding and unpleasant are all accurate ways of describing this 'shadow side' of your role. It can equally, however, be an illuminating, instructive and enhancing experience too. In the popular imagination, handling complaints, discipline and grievances is about apportioning blame, seeking retribution, meting out punishment or scoring points. A belief unwittingly given substance by the (necessary) formal and elaborate way in which almost all HEIs have introduced procedures (adversarial in character) to deal with them. This is not the place to consider the efficacy of your institution's procedures; suffice to say that this is not their intended purpose, and nor should it be yours. On the contrary, your focus in all three instances should be on *seeking to bring about improvement*:

- in the provision of service (complaints);
- in the performance levels or conduct of staff (discipline);
- in the nature of working relationships (grievance).

Put another way, you should be seeking to turn each of these 'negatives' into a 'positive'. How? Simply, but critically, in the way you approach them and the manner in which you handle them.

- *Recognise the complaint, grievance or discipline issue as an opportunity to enhance quality.* This may seem perverse as a guiding principle in these instances, but, given quality is one of those curious features which is visible only in its absence, they do, in fact, present you with the best opportunity you're likely to have to make a real difference in this regard. For they offer you the rare chance 'to take the lid off' your

Box 8.3 Quality in higher education

1	The 'exceptional' view	–	synonymous with excellence, e.g. student services
2	The 'perfection' view	–	consistent with flawless outcomes, e.g. the world-class university
3	The 'fitness for purpose' view	–	fulfilling a customer need, e.g. the QAA
4	The 'value for money' view	–	a return on investment, e.g. the funding council
5	The 'transformation' view	–	a change from one state to another, e.g. learning and teaching

Source: based on Harvey, 1995

surface reality; to probe the 'backstage' and 'under-stage' of your department (Becher, 1996) – to unearth it, learn from it, to influence it and to improve it.

Such instances also constitute a reminder, as well as a test, of your commitment to quality. Quality of course is not conceived in any singular way in HE. Some institutions purport to offer 'value for money', others 'fitness for purpose' and still others 'service excellence' (see Box 8.3). Either way, complaints, grievances and disciplinary matters are, by their very nature, likely to breach such commitments. It is incumbent on you to meet this challenge.

• *Be prepared to engage in critical self-reflection on your own role in these matters.* Complaints, grievances and matters of discipline are rarely cut and dried. They often raise other issues to do with working practices, or the involvement of other parties, or may, indeed, be symptomatic of a more fundamental problem. They are as likely to be about you too, if not directly then indirectly, about what you may or may not have done. You must, therefore, be prepared to put your own self-justification to one side and critically reflect on your own role as a contributory factor in these matters (Moores, 1994).

• *Take responsibility for the issue; accept the buck and do not pass it.* In all these cases the procedures governing them invariably, and quite properly, lay down very specific guidelines on how they should be handled: the various stages, the conduct of the hearing, the right of appeal, and so on. As such they can be very protracted for they each usually have a 'built-in escalator' whereby, if the issue remains unresolved, it can be referred ever upward. To the extent, indeed, that at the final stage there is usually provision for some form of independent or external arbitration, through the board of governors, a visitor or an ombudsman. It is also the case that the portent of such matters often grows exponentially, as if 'it takes on a life of its own', and what may have started as a simple misunderstanding between a student and a lecturer has developed into a full-blown disciplinary concern. It is down to you to ensure this does *not* happen. You should always endeavour to reconcile such differences – to nip them in the bud – before they get out of hand. Or, if they *are* out of hand, take responsibility for dealing with them under the particular procedure. Do not hide behind the procedure nor make a fetish of it either. The 'letter of the law' is important and you should follow it, but keep your eye on your overall objective – the 'best outcome'.

- *Remember you have 'a duty of care' to staff as well as to students and other stakeholders.* And while it is the case that the majority of complaints are likely to raise legitimate concerns there will be some, a vexatious minority, that do not. Again, it will be up to you to weed these out in timely fashion.

How then should you handle these matters?

Complaints

Identify the nature of the complaint

This may seem, and may well be, straightforward. But it is not always so. Indeed it can often take time, patience and skilled questioning to 'get to the bottom' of a complainant's concern. As a first step ask them, if they have not already done so, to submit their complaint in writing on one side of A4.

Appraise the significance of the complaint

(a) Does it arise, for example, from a misunderstanding on their part, a difference of expectation or a failing on the part of your department for which there is collective culpability?
(b) Or is it about the (alleged) conduct or incompetence of a member of your staff and therefore (potentially) serious.

Determine how to proceed

- If (a), telephone them and explain your position or send them a letter of apology. Resolve to investigate your department's collective failing and aim to avoid a repeat.
- If (b), formally write to them inviting them to a meeting to discuss their complaint. Offer them the opportunity to bring a friend, or Students' Union (or legal) adviser with them if they wish.
- If you receive a student petition, agree to meet with two student representatives. Do not be cajoled into meeting the whole group. It may jeopardise any subsequent investigation and, if unwarranted, totally undermine your colleague and leave you looking unprofessional too.

- If the complaint was an anonymous one, do not ignore it. Have an informal word with the staff member. It may be you have a mischevious complainant in your midst. On the other hand it may be symptomatic of a problem brewing. Seek to both reassure and help your colleague resolve any difficulty.
- At the meeting seek to clarify and thoroughly understand the nub of the complaint. Summarise it to the complainant and get them to confirm it.
- Write to the member of staff outlining the complaint and invite them to a meeting to discuss the matter. Offer them the same rights as the complainant. Indicate too that the nature of the meeting is an informal one.
- Unless it is an issue of gross misconduct, e.g. theft, assault, aggravated harassment, etc., you should *never* invoke the disciplinary procedure before a staff member has been given the opportunity to answer any charges that have been made against them (ACAS, 2000).
- In the interim complete any further investigation that may be necessary, including the interview of any third parties.

Determine how to act

Having interviewed both parties and considered the case you must determine what to do next. You can choose to:

- uphold the complaint;
- reject the complaint as unfounded, unproven or vexatious;
- take no action;
- take informal action, e.g. counselling and development;
- invoke the competence procedure if it is a matter of poor performance;
- invoke the disciplinary procedure if it is a matter of conduct.

Whatever you decide, you should summarise your findings in a short report and inform both parties of the outcome accordingly.

Discipline

Handling cases of discipline is, or should, not be so different in practice from the way you deal with complaints. For the same principles and processes – keeping an open mind, gathering the facts, the interview, the written record, etc. – apply in both instances. The main difference, of course, lies in the formality of the procedure and its potential consequences, up to and including dismissal. For these reasons, then, you need to be absolutely certain it is the correct path to follow. Or, put another way, be sure you are only invoking it:

- as a 'last resort' and not as your 'first port of call';
- because you have given informal oral warnings or reprimands in the past that have had no effect and you've now exhausted the limits of your authority;
- because the nature of the case merits it:

- *misconduct*, e.g. abusive or threatening behaviour including: bullying; sexual, social or racial harassment; regular unauthorised absence; constant unsatisfactory timekeeping; wilful refusal to carry out a reasonable request; negligence which causes unacceptable loss, damage or injury; the deliberate breach of health and safety regulations; etc.;
- *gross misconduct*, e.g. theft, fraud, arson, physical assault, aggravated harassment; total incapacity due to the influence of alcohol or illegal drugs (having already exhausted the existing procedures in place for health-related abuse); etc.;
- *incompetence*, having already exhausted the competence procedure for tackling poor performance.

If any of the above do not apply then you should not proceed. Indeed it is unlikely your HR department will allow you to because you will not have satisfied 'the test of reasonableness' by your actions; i.e. one of the three critical factors (the others being the grounds for dismissal and the veracity of the procedure itself) which employment tribunals take into account in their adjudication of appeals (ACAS, 2000).

If this test is also satisfied then you should proceed but do so with the support of your manager and HR adviser. In the preliminary investigation make sure you always have someone else in attendance with you when meeting the other party. And in the knowledge that, when it comes to the formal hearing, you – and you alone – will be acting as 'chief prosecutor', while the director of HR takes on the role of chair.

Your aim is, and must remain, one of seeking improvement in conduct or performance, and not one of retribution.

Grievances

Grievances are no different either, in the sense that, like discipline, every effort should be made to resolve them in an informal way. They typically arise out of long-standing differences, but might also be sparked by a single incident – but they should be the exception not the rule. (If they are the norm in your department, then there is something seriously amiss with your management style, or the motivation and performance of your staff; issues which you should address with urgency.)

Either way, the grievance procedure allows individuals to exercise their right to raise matters of concern or to have problems addressed – issues which you may have underestimated or been unaware of – and by the same token it offers you the opportunity to put things right. As such you should act promptly and fairly, as indeed you are required to, and with due regard to natural justice.

If a grievance is taken out against you

- Take it seriously without being defensive.
- Do not take offence.
- Focus on the complaint not the individual.
- Consider the complaint through their lens not yours. Is it symptomatic of another issue?

- Prepare to defend – or apologise for – your actions.
- And most importantly: explore ways you can move forward in resolving these differences to each other's benefit.

Managing redundancies

> Even people who are unhappy about the outcome of a process will have less dissatisfaction and fewer dysfunctions than they might otherwise have if they understand the process through open communications and see that it was fair . . .
>
> De Nisi, 2000

If you are lucky you may avoid having to manage redundancies. If not, you should prepare yourself for what is one of the most challenging, and unpleasant, duties you will ever have as a manager. As with discipline, redundancy is, or should be, the very last resort. The process is also subject to external statutory requirements, if not to an agreed internal procedure. And again, like discipline, has similar misconceptions attached to it. Redundancy is not about dismissal: it is the job, not the individual, that is redundant. It is also, in practice, voluntary, far more often than it is compulsory. And while it can be a brutal process it doesn't have to be that way. And that's the point. For, no matter how inauspicious the circumstances, all staff that leave should be able to do so with their dignity and respect intact. And it is your responsibility, once a redundancy programme has been agreed, to help ensure this is the case (Rothwell, 2000). Put another way, redundancy is nearly always a painful process for everyone involved, for leavers, stayers and you alike. Even so, you should realise, and accept, that you can still make a real and positive difference, despite how unpropitious your situation may seem; that you can, in fact, by seeking to minimise the stress on those who leave and upholding the morale of those who remain, render the process far less traumatic than it would otherwise be. How?

- *Do all that you can to avoid a redundancy situation in the first place,* principally through your institution's human resource strategy.

A 'redundancy' arises when the employer ceases 'to carry on the business for the purpose of which the employee was employed' or 'in the place where the employee was employed' or where 'the requirements of the business for employees to carry out work of a particular kind has ceased or diminished' (ACAS, 2002). Your HR strategy, if it is an effective one, will have taken just such scenarios into account. And, more particularly, will have been based on a planned forecast of existing and future staffing needs institution-wide. This way, if a redundancy situation arises then at least job losses should be minimised. Careful HR planning will also help to improve job security among staff as well as avoid knee-jerk reactions to immediate problems at the expense of longer-term staffing needs.

Additionally, specific practical initiatives may minimise or avoid a redundancy situation, e.g.: natural wastage; restricting the recruitment of permanent staff; reducing (or curtailing) the use of temporary staff; filling vacancies from among existing staff; reducing (or curtailing) overtime; retiring all staff at the normal retirement age and (if permissible) seeking applicants for early retirement; retraining and deploying staff elsewhere in the institution.

• *Use full, proper and early consultation on the redundancy proposals.* In the UK employers are legally obliged to have a consultation period of at least thirty days if the intention is to make twenty to ninety-nine employees redundant and at least ninety days in cases where more than one hundred employees are affected. Your institution may also have a formal policy or a formal agreement with trade union or employee representatives setting out the procedure to be followed. Either way, the golden rule is that consultation should take place as early as practicable in order to provide an opportunity for all parties to share the problem and explore the options. You also need to:

– Remember to consult beyond those immediately at risk and with individual staff not just their representatives. Failure to do so could result in an employment tribunal granting a 'protective award' to any, and every, individual who complained you did not fulfil this requirement (ACAS, 2002).
– Remember that 'notice of consultation' is not 'notice of redundancy' and it is possible that more acceptable alternative ways of tackling the problem or of minimising hardship may emerge during this period.

• *Have a compelling business case for the proposed redundancies.* The process is one thing and should be relatively unproblematic. Where the contention invariably lies is in the substance of your proposals: the reasons for the redundancies; the number and categories of staff involved; the selection procedure; and the method for calculating redundancy payments (over and above the statutory entitlement).

First and foremost is your rationale. Your business case must be a compelling one and, more importantly, must be equally convincing to others too: staff, their representatives, managers and governors alike. If not, you will encounter serious opposition – and rightly so. Put another way, a legitimate business reason, for example a sustained shortfall in student numbers and recruitment, is not by itself sufficient. You must *demonstrate* it as well. That is, you must offer a thorough and systematic analysis of all the factors that have given rise to the particular circumstance (based, for example, on market research, sector norms, etc.) as well as an explanation why you believe the area (e.g. course, subject, service) is no longer viable, and, having considered institutional needs and requirements, likely to remain so. That a redundancy programme would in essence be in the best overall interests (or 'greater good') of the institution. Your business case is akin to drawing up a business plan, the difference being in the outcome usually associated with it: retrenchment rather than growth.

In determining the number of jobs lost you will ironically find it easier to start from the opposite premise. How many staff do you need – and will you need – to 'roll-through' and 'roll-out' the provision of your course, subject or service while still maintaining quality. This figure subtracted from your overall staffing complement will give you the number of jobs surplus to requirements. Implicit in this 'zero-based' approach – in building up your budget 'from scratch' on the basis of the number of staff needed to provide for the number of registered students – is that there is a consensus on the level of provision needed to maintain quality: the requisite staff–student ratio, the level of service, and so on. As there will be no such consensus your safest option is to draw up your contingency plans based on published sector norms. Either way, you should anticipate having to produce and reproduce successive resource plans – outlining the best case, worst case and most likely case scenarios, etc. – many times over as the consultation develops and the process gets under way. The other unacknowledged aspect of this approach is that it often shows in stark relief just how small a contribution, in business terms, research makes to institutional viability. Contrary to the popular belief that research is often the critical factor in keeping institutions afloat, it is in fact a luxury that only a few HEIs can afford.

- *Agree and establish selection criteria that are objective and transparent, and applied consistently.* The method of selection is typically just as contentious as the number and category of staff involved, and for good reason. For the less objectively and less precisely criteria are defined, the greater is the risk that staff are liable to discrimination or unfair selection for redundancy. The desirability of avoiding such an outcome, and indeed the legal imperative to do so, is rarely disputed. Where the real difficulty often lies, however, is not so much in the commitment to establishing objective and transparent criteria but in agreeing the very nature of the criteria in the first place, and typically it is even more difficult to prioritise and weight the individual criteria once they are agreed.

The number, nature and weighting of the specific criteria that are finally agreed will of course depend on your local circumstances. Even so, they should not only be objective but also, if they are to be perceived as legitimate, consistent with the strategic direction of your institution and department. And again, as in the case of the recruitment of staff, you need to take particular care to ensure that they are not directly or indirectly discriminatory on the grounds of sex, race or disability (see Box 8.4). Finally, should your 'notice of redundancy' not yield a sufficient number of volunteers (and you should make every effort to ensure that it does, given the far more demoralising effect of compulsory severance), you need to ensure that the criteria are *applied* with as much care as when they were drawn up. As a fail-safe best practice, it may be worth setting up an internal appeals process. This not only has the advantage of bringing a speedy resolution to legitimate individual grievances but also reduces the likelihood of any future complaint to an employment tribunal.

- *Offer staff help and assistance in finding alternative employment.* Again employers have a statutory obligation to allow staff who are under notice of redundancy 'a reasonable amount of paid time off' to look for another job or to arrange training. Good employers of course can, and do, offer a whole lot more; typically, access to an outplacement service which usually provides workshops on financial planning, job searching and self-marketing as well as one-to-one specialist sessions on careers guidance (ACAS, 2002).

- *(And more importantly) understand the effects of the change on staff and support them throughout this process.* Textbook theories will tell you that staff go through four different stages before coming to terms with redundancy: negation, self-justification,

Box 8.4 Specimen selection criteria for redundancy of academic staff

Criteria	Scoring (0–5 points)

Qualifications
- Higher degree; teaching; professional body

Teaching and learning
- Competence in delivery of subject
  - as evidenced by external examiners' comments, teaching materials, etc.
- Contribution to scholarship
  - evidence of scholarship integrated in practice of teaching and learning
  - application of IT in the curriculum
  - willingness to gain experience of commercial application of the subject
  - specific module/programme development
  - evidence of innovation in the curriculum

Breadth and depth of experience
- Spread of subject specialisms
- Spread of levels taught
- Programme leadership and management
- External examining
- Competence in personal tutoring

Research
- Refereed publications eligible for the RAE
- Number of research students

Workload
Number of teaching contact hours
Amount of funded research work

exploration and, ultimately, resolution. And it is indeed the case that some staff, a minority, will pass imperceptibly through these stages and move on (De Nisi, 2000). What it doesn't prepare you for, however, is the way in which many staff go backwards and forwards through these stages, as they work through their feelings, before finally coming to resolution. And still others, another sizeable minority, can go through all these different stages on the same day – every single day of the week. You can best help staff through this by the following:

- Resist the natural tendency to withdraw; and deal *visibly* with the reality of the situation by talking to staff and being with staff. This is not the time for hiding. Communication, communication and communication are the watchwords.

- Counsel them. You do not have to be a professional counsellor nor are you expected to be. Counselling, in a management sense, is a way of responding and relating to someone so that they feel clearer about what is concerning them and are then better able to help themselves and make their own decisions. It means in practice you should:

  - be non-directive, non-judgemental;
  - have empathy;
  - respect confidentiality;
  - help to release tension;
  - help to release creative energy;
  - recognise the individual wants it (counselling) and ensure ownership of the problem stays with them.

Put another way, there are, in this context, three stages to the counselling process:

- getting the story: listening, interpreting and responding;
- understanding the situation: exploring, focusing and giving feedback;
- moving on: developing strategies, gaining acceptance.

All this of course is a lot easier said than done. Nor should you underestimate the task, for it is an emotional roller coaster of epic proportions for them – and also for you. And in that sense it is important that you recognise, as should your manager and HR department, that you too will need support and possibly counselling during this process.

It may also transpire that you too are to be made redundant. If so:

- Remember and recognise that the same cycle of stages – negation, self-justification, exploration and resolution that staff go through applies equally to you too.
- Probe the legitimacy of the business rationale. Suggest alternative courses of action. Be realistic, not fanciful. And stick to business reasons not appeals based on emotion.
- Play the accountants at their own game. Think of all the extraneous factors they may have missed. Take them beyond the zero-based approach. Present them with the 'doomsday scenario'. Make them rethink.

After you have accepted the business case for the decision, then:

- Resolve to be as professional and as responsible as you always have been until you leave.
- Don't waste time beating yourself up or seeking to blame others.
- Don't be coy either about trying to secure the best severance package you can. Ask your employer to pay for outplacement counselling and for any legal costs. Try to negotiate salary in lieu of notice and to keep any non-pay allowances you may have been given in your role, e.g. your mobile phone number, laptop computer, etc.

- Recognise too, that even redundancy can have 'a silver lining'. For although it may be traumatic, it forces you, in the same way as with staff, to hold a mirror up to yourself; to look inwards, to reflect and re-evaluate your priorities; to realise indeed the genuine qualities and marketable skills you have; and to understand that it is not the end of the world – that it is a job, not life; that you always have choices and there are always opportunities.

9 | Managing yourself

Let he who would change the world first change himself.

Socrates

I know that the only way to live my life is to try to do what is right, to take the long view, to give of my best in all that the day brings and to put my trust in God.

Queen Elizabeth II, 25 December 2002

To succeed as a leader and manager you must master as, we have seen, a whole variety of different skills and competencies. There is one remaining skill, however, we have yet to consider; one that completes the full complement, and that is of course, how you manage yourself. This again is a skill which, like many others, is too often taken for granted. Because it seems self-evident, many managers tend to overlook it or consciously disregard it in practice, that is they either underuse the ability, or sacrifice it in the face of (apparently) more pressing concerns. This again is a grave error, for it can harm them both ways. On the one hand, they may inflict ill health on themselves and, on the other, they may damage their credibility in the eyes of their staff. The point is, you cannot expect to make a good job of managing other people and situations unless, and until, you can effectively manage yourself.

This ability – to self-manage, to keep on learning – is in fact one of the distinctive hallmarks that characterise strong leadership (Eglin, 2003). It is, however, not very straightforward to master and the evidence suggests that many managers have considerable difficulty in doing so (Quinn, 1995). The incessant demands, the competing priorities, the information overload and the degree of expectation in the environment in which we operate today, all make it harder than ever, and the inward journey of self-exploration and realisation can also be an uncomfortable and possibly a painful one too. Even so you owe it to yourself, as well as to others and to your institution, not to shirk or neglect this responsibility. On the contrary you should indeed be diligent and purposeful in fulfilling it. How though can, and should, you organise yourself – be yourself, look after yourself, and develop yourself. This last chapter seeks to explain just that.

Organising yourself

> Are the least effective managers the ones who look like they are doing the most?
>
> Bruch and Ghoshal, 2002

Many managers in academia, as elsewhere, are often frenetically busy. Their diaries 'wall-to-wall' with meetings, they dash hither and thither, constantly checking their e-mail, making countless phone calls, despatching memos and extinguishing fire after fire. It certainly looks impressive – and also *seems* impressive. Unfortunately the sad truth, often acknowledged, if unspoken, is that most of this activity for much of the time achieves very little. Indeed Bruch and Ghoshal (2002) found in their decade-long study of 'busy managers' that fully 90 per cent of them squandered their time in all sorts of ineffective activities: that is, they may have thought 'they were attending to pressing matters' (grappling with strategic issues, focusing on cost savings, devising creative approaches to new markets, etc.) but 'they were really just spinning their wheels' in an unproductive way. Only a 10 per cent minority, the 'purposeful action-takers', spent their time in a committed, purposeful and reflective manner. The difference between the two groups being that the latter managed to combine two particular traits – *energy* and *focus* – in a far more effective way than the other three categories which made up the 90 per cent majority (see Figure 9.1):

- 40 per cent 'distracted managers': highly motivated and full of energy, they switch from one activity to the next at a rapid rate. They are not driven, however, by any strategic imperative and as such are unable to lead others.

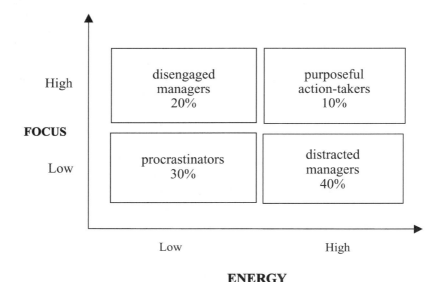

Figure 9.1 The 'busy manager syndrome': managerial behaviours

Source: adapted from Bruch and Ghoshal, 2002

- 30 per cent 'procrastinators': these managers can't even get started. Experience has taught them that whatever they do they won't make any difference to anything. They are unable to motivate others.
- 20 per cent 'disengaged': focused but not driven or excited by what they do. They lack the energy to deal with problems or drive things through.

How can you avoid being a victim of this 'busy manager' syndrome? What can you do to ensure you are a 'purposeful action-taker'?

- Do not confuse being active with being productive. Do not be so absorbed with routine tasks and fire-fighting that you have little time or energy for issues that require reflection, systematic planning or creative thinking.
- Do not blame your institutional environment. Do not spend your time on making the inevitable happen. Focus your energy and your will-power on what you're paid to do – make happen what otherwise won't happen.
- Do not be constrained by extraneous factors, such as your manager, your peers, your job role. Do not be swayed by those around you even if they look busy and sound busy. Instead decide *first* what it is you must achieve and then manage your way through those around you.

Put positively:

- Stave off the instinctive feeling that you must look busy no matter how powerful that feeling may seem. Make an appointment with yourself for thinking and develop your own personal strategic plan. Identify three to four priorities – *the things that would really make a difference to your department* (for example: developing an e-learning infrastructure for your courses; establishing a work-based learning programme with local employers; hosting a learning and teaching conference; leading a partnership bid for regional or European funding; etc.) Let these be a guide to your actions and your planning over the term, semester and year ahead.
- Set up a seven-day time log and record how you currently use your time. This does not have to be the time consuming chore it may appear and, provided you are honest with yourself, it can also prove self-revelatory. Simply note down how you spent the hours in a day over a one-week period: teaching, meeting, supervising, telephoning, e-mailing, socialising, reflecting, etc. Compare how you used this time in proportion to the priorities you set yourself. How does it 'fit'? Is there consistency in your actions? What areas are you neglecting? What aspects can you change to improve matters?
- Consider the 'top twenty-one time-wasters' outlined in Box 9.1. Go through the list and identify those time-wasters you experience. To what extent are they really a necessary or inevitable aspect of your role? Why do you tolerate them? What can you do about them?

Enrol on a time management course. We all feel we've been there already. Simply put, time management involves addressing three basic elements: clarifying goals, forward planning and making effective use *of* time *at* the time (Maitland, 1995).

Box 9.1 The top twenty-one time-wasters

1　Frequent interruptions – telephone or other

2　Indecisiveness

3　Meetings that are too long or not really necessary

4　Switching priorities midstream

5　Lack of objectives, priorities or daily plan

6　Personal disorganisation

7　A cluttered office

8　Inability to delegate effectively

9　Shuffling paperwork around

10　Restrictions on equipment or materials

11　Chasing people

12　Trying to do too much – unable to say 'No'

13　'Butterflying' from one task to another leaving them all unfinished

14　Poor quality information or communication

15　Excessive socialising

16　Office procedures not properly set up

17　Unclear division of responsibility or authority

18　Always checking up on others

19　Plunging into a task without planning

20　Poor self-discipline

21　Exhaustion – as a consequence of the above!

Source: Industrial Society survey cited in Warren and Toll, 1997

Nevertheless we should not be too grand to think we know everything there is to know. There is often something new to learn, that little extra that could make a difference (Adair, 1988).

Pay particular attention to those primary activities that could make all the difference to the way you operate and how effective you may be:

• *Delegation*: never do a task that someone else can do. Do not let guilt, fear or pride keep you from delegating (see Chapter 6).

• *Meetings*: challenge the value of all meetings that do not have a clear, useful purpose. A good chair will review the effectiveness of their meetings on a periodic basis (see Chapter 4). Prompt them lest they forget. Alternatively, propose that you use your internal institutional auditors to conduct an independent review to improve the effectiveness of meetings. Always ask the chair to cancel meetings if there is no substantial business.

- *Brainstorming*: these are best done on your own in your own way, or in an activity forum designed for that express purpose. Ignore the hype and avoid conventional brainstorming group sessions. They never work (Allan *et al.*, 1999). Often dominated by one or two strong personalities (while the others struggle to think in the babble going on around them): at best such 'freewheeling, blue-sky' sessions typically recycle old ideas and, at worst, constitute so much 'social loafing' (high-profile activity of the most menial, and wasteful, kind) (Furnham, 2002).

- *Handling paperwork*: process it as soon as you can. If you've let it build up then set some time aside for a stress-busting blitz. Mark and label four empty filing trays: 'Deal with', 'Distribute', 'Read', 'File' – and arm yourself with sufficient plastic bin bags for the most important category – the 'Discard' pile. *Handle each piece of paper once only*. Don't read it. Skim it and determine what to do with it. Don't use your desk as a filing space, use project folders or 'bring forward' files for work in progress. And don't transfer piles of paper on your desk to piles of paper in other parts of the office.

- *Handling electronic data and e-mails*: the principles are no different to those of handling paperwork. You need a simple and logical grouping of material arranged in folders, sub-folders and file names. Likewise with correspondence: the message may be instant but your reply need not be. Judge each e-mail on its own merits, not that of 'net-etiquette'. Discipline yourself to checking your e-mail once or, at most, twice a day.

- *Prioritising tasks*: distinguish between what is *important* and what is urgent. Prioritising activities ensures you are not just involved in routine maintenance tasks; that you are proactive, not simply reactive. If you have several items of urgency and importance, do the hardest one first. Do the most important items during that portion of the day when you perform best and the most trivial when your energy levels are lowest.

- *Working with an assistant*: establish regular one-to-one 'business meetings' every other week. Review your diary with them on a weekly basis. Have them filter your post and phone calls. Don't dump on them. Delegate interesting and responsible work, not simply the mundane. Keep them informed.

Being yourself

> Be not another's, if thou canst be thyself.
> Paracelsus (Swiss physician)

The importance of understanding your own values and behaviours – of knowing yourself, valuing yourself and being yourself – is self-evident. If you don't understand and accept yourself it is nearly impossible to understand and accept others. Many managers often find this genuinely difficult, however, while others shy away from it altogether. Either way, their impact on those around them is, as we noted in Chapter 4, often one of the last things they ever learn about themselves.

Much of this apathy, difficulty or resistance is often related to the amount of experience and proficiency that managers have in their role and, in particular, to the way in which they respond to feedback. One of the main problems about receiving feedback of course, and why we instinctively shy away from it, is that we may not like what we get. Negative information is never particularly pleasant and we often resort to all kinds of strategies to deflect it including: denial ('It's not true'); flight ('I've got another meeting to go to'); rationalisation ('I can explain that . . .'); shifting the blame ('That was because somebody else. . .') or attacking the source ('He's an idiot anyway') (Pedler *et al.*, 2001).

To be effective as a manager however you must strive to overcome this natural inclination. For the key to overcoming defensiveness in others – to help them learn, to build up trust with them, to better understand them – is, as Socrates reminds us, by *confronting the defensiveness within ourselves first*. Put simply, if you are a role model of sensitivity, openness and learning then you will more than likely cultivate the spread of these same qualities in those around you. It is also the case that if you don't really understand yourself then you will not develop and grow in your role as you should, nor realise your latent potential (Quinn, 1995).

How then can you be less defensive? How can you understand yourself better, value yourself, be yourself?

- *Recognise the true scope and flexibility for change in your relationships with those around you.* We all have different aspects which we choose to 'open' or 'hide' from view as well as 'blind spots' which others see and we do not. Likewise we all have aspects that lie 'unknown' both to ourselves and to those around us (as in the 'Johari window' depicted in Figure 9.2). In Figure 9.2, the quadrant sizes are not fixed: in relationships they will of course change with the passage of time. You can, however, exercise more direct influence through your willingness, on the one hand, to explore your current lack of self-awareness in areas 2 and 4, and on the other reveal more of yourself to

Your values, motives and behaviours . . .

	Known to Self	Not Known to Self
Known to others	1 OPEN	2 BLIND
Not known to others	3 HIDDEN	4 UNKNOWN

Figure 9.2 The Johari window

Note: named after the originators Joe Lufts and Harry Ingham those around you. Or, put another way, you can direct your energy, skills and resources into increasing quadrant 1 at the expense of 2, 3 and 4.

- *Remember that in any given situation we never see things as they are, only as we are; and that we always have a choice* – to change the situation, to change ourselves, leave the situation, or decide to live with the situation.

- *Use personal self-reflection*; a 'backwards review'. Start a personal journal: a review of critical incidents describing what happened, who was involved and what they did. What did you *want* to say or do? What did you *actually* say and do? On reflection, how do you feel about it now? What have you learned? What are you going to do about it?

- *Remembering that our 'concept of self' is neither fixed nor permanent*: that it may have been conditioned by powerful external influences (parents, family, school, neighbourhood) in the past but need not be so in the future. Our self-concept is made up of three critical parts: our self-ideal (the person we would most like to be); our self-image (or inner mirror of how we see ourselves and think about ourselves); and our self-esteem (how we feel about ourselves). All three are malleable and can be built up, not to create a super-inflated ego (though of course that can and does happen) but rather in nurturing a wholesome self-respect or positive self-image. Put another way, low self-esteem does not have to be a lifetime condition, nor the realisation of our self-ideal an elusive goal (Turner, 2002).

- *Recognise how conditioned beliefs can prevent you from managing yourself.* These typically manifest themselves in a number of ways, for example:

  - major debilitating devices, for example: negative thinking; irrational fear and worry; procrastination; complacency; our past mistakes and failures; the conditioned negative attitudes (the 'No syndrome') inherited from childhood ('I'm just no good with maps');
  - unrealistic expectations with which to beat yourself up, for example: 'I must be perfect in everything I do'; 'I must have the love and approval of others at all times'; 'I have a right to rely on others to give me what I want';
  - self-fulfilling prophecies, for example: 'My background, childhood and past must continue to determine my feelings and behaviour' (also known as 'Died at 20, buried at 70');
  - irrational assumptions, for example: 'Unhappiness is externally controlled'.

Whatever their source, their effect is much the same: to deny us true self-management. Can you identify any of your own conditioned beliefs that may be holding you back from managing yourself?

- *Seek to overcome your conditioned beliefs, thinking and behaviour by cultivating your higher self (your inner friend), not your lower self (your inner enemy).* Much easier said than done of course. At its most sophisticated this involves contemplation, visualisation and activating your superconscious, often, as in the case of sports players, with the help of a coach. You too may wish to consider this option. It is not as fanciful as it may seem. Indeed a half day at a recognised assessment centre is, as many have discovered, a small investment when set against the rewards it may bring. Alternatively you can access the wealth of self-development literature on this subject which offers advice on everything from drawing up action plans for thirty-day mental diets to practical tips on using the 'Affirmation method' ('Yes, I can do this . . .') (Turner, 2002; Pedler *et al.*, 2001).

- *Develop your own personal mission statement*. Not, that is, a missionary tract, but rather an expression of what you want to be, your purpose in life, your values. An anchor in other words you can use as a source of guidance in your professional life. Again this can be a very demanding task. It involves going back to first principles – your basic beliefs about people, work, family, religion, politics, life and death – and teasing out and questioning your 'taken-for-granted' assumptions. The process will force you to articulate and define your personal 'sense of mission'. And the statement will add meaning to what you do, explain what you do and also be a source of comfort in both good times and bad.

- *Elicit feedback through formal self-assessment instruments*. For example, the Myers-Briggs (personality) type indicator (1977) will provide you with insight on the deeply-held ways in which you prefer to work – extrovert or introvert, senser or intuitive, thinker or feeler, judger or perceiver – as well as offer a character profile for your particular category: ENTJ, ISTP, INFP, ESFJ, etc. The Thomas-Kilmann conflict mode instrument (1974) will enable you to assess the particular style you have learned (and can modify) in handling workplace conflict – competing, accommodating, avoiding, collaborating, compromising.

- *Test your own perceptions against those of others through 360 degree feedback*. For example, the visionary leader behaviour questionnaire (Sashkin, 1995) is a well-established formal instrument which will give you 'contextual feedback' on your leadership behaviour, your leadership characteristics and your effect on your institution as a leader.

- *Respond to feedback in a constructive way*. Do not dodge it in the ways outlined above. If you feel the criticism is justified then listen, ask for details, seek to clarify and understand, ask for examples and try to establish a way forward. If you feel the criticism is unjustified, do not ignore it or dismiss it. You still need to build and maintain a useful relationship with that person and they must have some reason for making it. Try and establish the source. Is it past history, a case of bad timing, or a legitimate difference of view? If you receive positive feedback then don't put yourself down by trivialising it ('You're only saying that to be kind'); don't be seduced by your own brilliance either otherwise you will remain blind to other aspects of yourself; learn to accept it with good grace ('Yes, I was pleased with the way that went.').

Looking after yourself

If you don't control pressure, then pressure will control you.
Terry Venables, football coach

Well, there's work-life balance and then there's work . . .'
Female vice-chancellor, UK 'new' university

Rarely a day goes by without one report or another reminding us that stress is the most prevalent health problem of our ever faster moving world, that we do not do nearly enough to balance work with life and that children are showing increasing signs of the stress-related illnesses that affect their parents. All very true of course – and not surprising. We live in a world in which our personal and private space is more cramped than ever, where the journey to work can be as stressful as work itself, where the noise levels are three times greater than they were in 1970 (a decibel hell that no doubt has Thomas Carlyle spinning in his grave); and where new technology ensures we cannot only communicate but are also accessible on a 24/7 basis. Not only that. We often work in environments which encourage, if not celebrate, Stakhanovism as a virtue; those working very long hours, regularly going without sleep and rarely taking up their full leave entitlement. All of which begs the question: how well do you manage to look after yourself? Or, put another way, what can you do to manage the (apparent) contradiction between sustaining high performance in your role on the one hand, while maintaining a healthy work-life balance on the other?

- *Appreciate the nature of stress; that it is particular to each individual and can be good as well as bad.* In essence, stress is the response we make to the (perceived) relationship between the demands made upon us and our ability to cope. As such it varies from individual to individual. A competitive Type A person, for example, might find certain circumstances stressful whereas a more sanguine Type B person might not. Generalisations are therefore difficult, though it is apparent that we do *benefit* from 'stress' so long as we perceive it to be healthy. Problems arise when we experience 'overstress' (see Figure 9.3). We also need to remember that many people do love their jobs and don't regard work as a chore.

   If, on the other hand, you do have feelings of resentment, maybe because you are in a role which you don't enjoy but you have commitments that mean you can't quit, then remember that, as we noted above, you still have options: to change the situation; to change yourself; or to put up with it. The best way forward very often is to start by reassessing your priorities and changing your attitude and approach to your work (Warren and Toll, 1997).

- *Learn to recognise the symptoms of stress and how they may apply to you.* Stress can affect us in many ways and to varying degrees – from sore eyes (minor), to migraine (major), to ulcers (last chance) and, in the worst circumstances, to 'burn-out' or even death (see Box 9.2). Consider, then, how you feel when under pressure or when experiencing a stressful event; notice where in your body you feel the effects. Do these correlate with any of the symptoms listed in Box 9.2? Begin to identify precisely what situations make you feel like this; and talk it over with your doctor if appropriate.

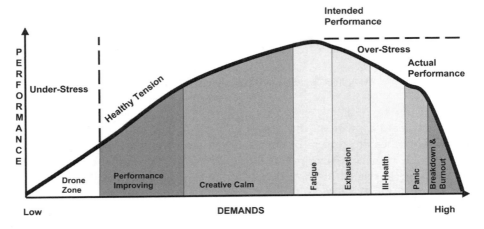

Figure 9.3 The stress curve

Source: adapted from Kelly (1998); Warren and Toll (1997)

Box 9.2 What does stress do to us?

Stage 1 – Minor
- Frequent infections/colds
- Sore eyes
- Overreaction to situations
- Speeding up, talking too fast, walking too fast
- Overeating and drinking
- Sweating
- Making more errors than usual
- Absent-minded/forgetful

Stage 2 – Major
- Emotional outbursts
- Extreme irritability
- Dyspepsia and gastric symptoms
- Heartburn
- Constipation
- Tension headaches
- Aching muscles
- Migraine

- Insomnia
- Loss of energy
- Comfort tricks: smoking/drugs/drinking
- Anxiety/depression
- Clumsiness

Stage 3 – Last chance
- Cotton wool head
- Ulcers
- Palpitations
- Chest pains
- Cardiac symptoms/incidents
- Extreme depression/anxiety
- Exhaustion

Stage 4 – Too late
- Burn-out *
- Physical or mental breakdown
- Death

* Burn-out can be defined as 'a state of physical, emotional and mental exhaustion marked by chronic fatigue, feelings of helplessness and hopelessness, and the development of a negative self-concept and negative attitudes towards work, life and other people'.

Source: based on Miller *et al.*, 1994

Box 9.3 How vulnerable are you to stress?

Mark against each of these statements:

F – Frequently
O – Occasionally
N – Never

_____ I am able to organise my time effectively

_____ I meet people with whom I can talk

_____ I have one or more friends to confide in about personal matters

_____ I am able to speak openly about my feelings when angry or worried

_____ I give and receive affection

_____ I keep a check on tensions in my body and have ways of reducing them

_____ I make sure I do something that relaxes me after a stressful time

_____ I take a quiet time for myself during the day

_____ I do something for fun at least once a week

_____ I walk, rather than drive or ride, whenever possible

_____ I use the stairs rather than a lift when practicable

_____ I take reasonably energetic exercise at least twice a week

_____ I have regular conversations with the person/people I live with about domestic issues

_____ I have an absorbing interest or hobby apart from work

_____ I am clear about my sense of values and what is important in my life

_____ I am the appropriate weight for my age, height and build

_____ I eat at least one hot balanced meal a day

_____ I limit my drinks of tea, coffee, chocolate and cola to three or less a day

_____ I keep within the recommended limits for alcohol of 21 units (men) or 14 units (women), spread over a week

_____ I give myself treats

Now check how many Fs, Os and Ns you have. 17 or more Fs and Os indicate you are probably pretty stress fit. 5 N's or more suggest you have an increasing vulnerability to stress and need to take action to turn them into Os or Fs.

Source: adapted from Warren and Toll, 1997

Family	Work	Leisure
Partner	Personal Development	Financial
Home	Health	Friends

Figure 9.4 Balancing your 'nine lives'

You should also reflect on the fact that while 'burn-out' and recovery from it is not unusual (some even manage to survive a second bout), it is not a condition that you will recover from professionally (and likely as not physically) should you experience it a third time (Kakabadse, 2001).

• *Assess and monitor your stress fitness level and your work-life balance.* Complete the questionnaire in Box 9.3 to assess how vulnerable you are to stress and how it manifests itself in your life, What do you need to do to improve your level of stress fitness?

In the case of Figure 9.4 take each one of your 'nine lives' in turn and grade them on a scale of 1–10 on the basis of (a) quality (1 – poor, 10 – good) and (b) time spent (1 – a little, 10 – a lot). What does your profile tell you? Where are you doing well, less well? What are your areas of neglect? What is the relationship between the time spent and the quality outcome? What can you do to strike a more even balance?

Repeat these two activities on a three monthly basis to monitor your progress.

• *Think of stress fitness in a positive not negative way; of improving your well-being (from within) not that of overcoming 'a problem' (from without).* Sustained high performance is not simply about managing stress. It is about physical and emotional strength as well as brainpower; it is about aligning mind, body and spirit together in such a way as to achieve peak condition. The 'high-performance pyramid' illustrated in Figure 9.5 is a mirror image of Maslow's hierarchy of needs. Consider the condition of your needs. Identify the ones you must nurture (Loehr and Schwartz, 2001).

Draw up your own personal stress fitness action plan. Just as the media regularly remind us about the prevalence of stress, so, too, are we inundated with advice on how to tackle it – from quick fixes on 'how to be happy', 'how to detox', to lifestyle planning and exercise regimes, to object lessons in full-blown therapy. The difficulty is not that there is a choice, but that there is so much it can seem disabling, even contradictory. That said, these various schema tend to be built around a number of key organising principles (the need for exercise, relaxation, and so on). These are some practical 'tips' you may want to consider in drawing up your action plan.

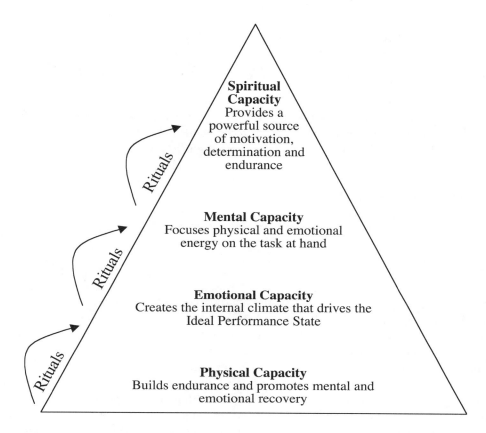

Figure 9.5 The high-performance pyramid
Source: adapted from Loehr and Schwartz, 2001

- Always accept 100 per cent responsibility for how you feel. You may not be responsible for all that goes on around you but you can always control your reaction to it.
- Learn to develop positive thinking techniques.
- Do regular physical exercise: cycling, swimming, running or gym work. Two thirty-minute cardiovascular workouts a week will keep you ticking over. Three will increase your fitness levels. Charles Dickens chose to walk twenty miles a day as a means of staving off manic depression.
- Learn to use muscle relaxation techniques.
- Develop a more balanced diet. Avoid processed foods and drink 1.5 litres of water a day.
- Practise the 3Rs: rest, reflection and renewal. Take regular 'time outs' as well as time off. Stakhanovism is a vice. Those who achieve a good balance between work and leisure have more energy and more commitment to their job.
- Build in treats as a reward for hard work or to sustain you in hard times.
- Find someone you can really talk to, your 'speaking partner'.

- Join a peer support group.
- Learn to listen to the person who knows you best . . . you!
- Do unto others as you would have them do unto you.
- Increase your spirituality through study, meditation, fasting or prayer.
- Go regularly to places that renew you.
- Avoid moaners.
- Put yourself in situations where people are having fun. Management is a serious business but you don't have to be po-faced about it all the time.
- Do all those healthy things you know you ought to do.

Developing yourself

> The life which is unexamined is not worth living.
> Socrates

HE management is not only held in low esteem within the sector, but outside it too. 'Bogus professionalism' is the pejorative term most commonly used by Whitehall departments – in private, if not in public – to describe the way in which universities are led and managed. A criticism that is not without foundation and has more credence in the area of self-development than perhaps in any other aspect of the HE manager's role; an outcome, ironically, for which we only have ourselves to blame. Put another way, the strong commitment to, and practice of, continuous professional development (CPD) that is characteristic of so many professional groups has until recently been conspicuous by its relative absence within HE. The point is: CPD should not be, nor should you consider it, a matter of optionality. It is no less than a lifetime obligation and responsibility. You cannot expect staff to do it if you do not practise it yourself. Nor can you expect to create, as we discussed in Chapter 6, an authentic learning climate within your department without practising it. More than that, however, CPD is primarily about *you* – about 'doing your best', aspiring to 'be the best', not being complacent, working on improvement, being curious, etc. It is, in essence, the key to your professional growth and fulfilment. And, as such, it is an activity you can embrace positively, rather than negatively as a forced expectation. Indeed an opportunity for you to relish, not spurn. How then can you make the most of it? What can and should you do to develop yourself?

- *Conduct a self-assessment of your learning needs.* You should by now, if you completed the self-assessment tools earlier in this book, have built up a reasonably clear picture of your own profile as a manager. If not, then consider again Boxes 3.7, 3.8, 4.2, 4.19 and 8.1 in particular, along with any feedback you received. Remember to bear in mind, too, that you should determine your skill needs in terms of three broad areas:

- personal skills, e.g.: creativity, problem-solving, decision-making;
- skills with other people, e.g.: communication, negotiation, teamwork;
- skills with things, e.g.: new learning technology, IT equipment.

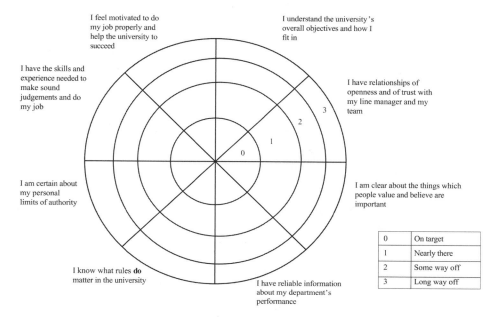

I feel motivated to do my job properly and help the university to succeed

I understand the university's overall objectives and how I fit in

I have the skills and experience needed to make sound judgements and do my job

I have relationships of openness and of trust with my line manager and my team

I am certain about my personal limits of authority

I am clear about the things which people value and believe are important

I know what rules **do** matter in the university

I have reliable information about my department's performance

0	On target
1	Nearly there
2	Some way off
3	Long way off

Figure 9.6 How well do you fit your role?

With this in mind reflect on your role and draw up your needs analysis based on a consideration of:

– Your levels of personal and professional satisfaction: write down the three major sources of satisfaction, and the three of dissatisfaction, in terms of dealing with people and managing activities in each of the following: your job, your career and your life.
– Your perception of your degree of 'fit' with your role: complete the dartboard questionnaire illustrated in Figure 9.6.
– Your perception of your needs against a common template: the competing values framework developed by Quinn (1995) integrates four contrasting models of management – human relations, open systems, internal processes and rational goals – and identifies the eight specific (and prima facie conflicting) roles (× 3 competences = 24) that every manager must ultimately master if they are to be wholly effective in their post: innovator, broker, producer, director, monitor, coordinator, facilitator and mentor (see Figure 9.7). Take each of the eight roles in turn and consider: what do I know about myself in this role? How could I play this role more effectively? Which of the twenty-four competences do I really need to work on?

• *Identify your developmental stage as a manager.* Management is no different to any other activity in that it is a learning process: there is no reason why we cannot master it, if we have appropriate knowledge and experience, as well as skill and ability. On the other hand, it is not that easy either. Where are you on the road to mastery?

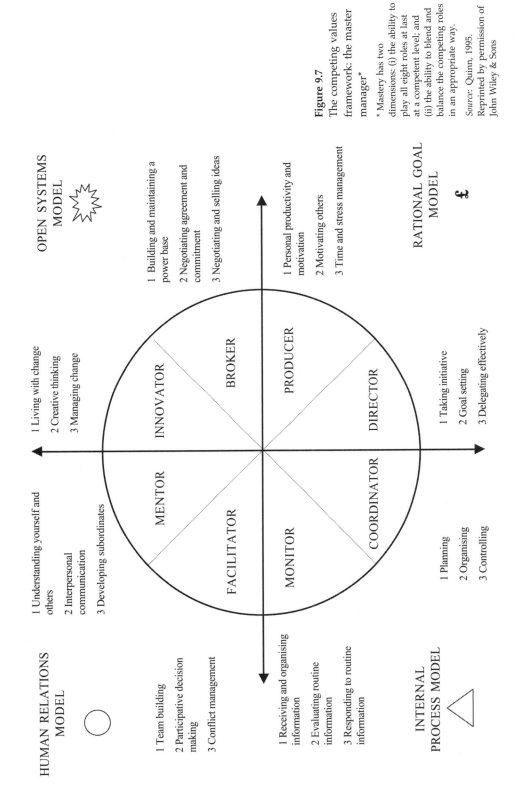

HUMAN RELATIONS
MODEL

1 Understanding yourself and others

2 Interpersonal communication

3 Developing subordinates

1 Team building

2 Participative decision making

3 Conflict management

OPEN SYSTEMS
MODEL

1 Living with change

2 Creative thinking

3 Managing change

1 Building and maintaining a power base

2 Negotiating agreement and commitment

3 Negotiating and selling ideas

1 Personal productivity and motivation

2 Motivating others

3 Time and stress management

RATIONAL GOAL
MODEL

£

1 Receiving and organising information

2 Evaluating routine information

3 Responding to routine information

INTERNAL
PROCESS MODEL

1 Planning

2 Organising

3 Controlling

1 Taking initiative

2 Goal setting

3 Delegating effectively

INNOVATOR

BROKER

PRODUCER

MENTOR

DIRECTOR

FACILITATOR

MONITOR

COORDINATOR

Figure 9.7
The competing values framework: the master manager*

* Mastery has two dimensions: (i) the ability to play all eight roles at last at a competent level; and (ii) the ability to blend and balance the competing roles in an appropriate way.

Source: Quinn, 1995.
Reprinted by permission of John Wiley & Sons

- the novice stage: following rules and procedures;
- the advanced beginner stage: you will have worked out the unwritten rules as well (the norms, conventions and accepted practices in your role);
- the competent stage: thinking independently for yourself;
- the proficient stage: you will have learned to unconsciously 'read' evolving situations;
- the expert stage; doing what comes naturally, as if having a 'sixth sense'.

Use the models developed by Pedler *et al.* (2001) and Quinn (1995) to determine your stage of development. What do you think of it? How do you feel about it? What can you do to start to move into the next one?

• *Diagnose your natural learning style and seek to strengthen your ability in other learning styles.* We all learn in a combination of (four) different ways, as activists, reflectors, theorists and pragmatists. This, in turn, has implications for the kinds of activities and situations that suit, or do not suit, our development as learners. Use the learning style questionnaire developed by Honey and Mumford (1995) to determine your prefererred learning style. Consider how you can take advantage of learning opportunities that dovetail with your style. Equally reflect on how you can build up your learning strength, by developing those learning styles for which you do not currently have a strong preference.

• *Remember to consider the full range of potential learning opportunities open to you* – planned as well as unplanned, 'within the job' as well as 'away from the job' (see Chapter 6). Some unwittingly restrict the scope of their opportunities, and hence their prospects for development, by making artificial distinctions between these four areas. Make sure you do not fall into the same trap. Try to think of learning as a seamless activity running through all aspects of your life (Forrest, 1995).

• *Develop your own personal strategic action plan.* In Chapter 3 we discussed how you could establish a strategic plan for your department. You can, and should in fact, use and apply the same principles with regard to your professional development: that is, ask yourself the following questions. What is your vision, your personal dream? What are your aims, capabilities (resources) and opportunities? Are they aligned with one another? Where are you now? What will help you get to where you are going? What do you have to do today?

• *Keep a learning log.* Underrated, and underused, personal journals of this nature are, as many of the professional bodies now recognise, a powerful means of sustaining professional development. At their simplest such logs provide a record of your answers to three basic questions: What did you do? What did you learn from it? How might you use this now and in the future? Completing the answers not only helps you to review your experiences and to monitor your progress, but you will also find it disciplines you to search out and take learning opportunities – as well as being a source of comfort and ideas you can draw on in difficult situations.

• And finally – *Make a pact with yourself.* Commit to becoming a master manager.

Principal lecturer
job role

Role map analysis of a principal lecturer in UK (post-1992) 'new' university

Role definition	Job purpose: why do I exist?
Principal lecturer	• To take a major responsibility for quality and innovation in teaching and learning within a faculty and for ensuring the continuing academic and professional development of faculty colleagues
	• To take a leading role in learning and teaching innovation
	• To act as a role model and mentor for colleagues
	• To make a major contribution to academic quality in the faculty by providing continuing academic leadership on a subject and ensuring the ongoing development of students, colleagues and the curriculum in that area
	• To contribute to enriching the learning experience of students within the faculty
	• To lead on the development of specified, high-quality modules/programmes which understand and meet students' needs
	• To ensure that these modules/programmes meet the university's commitment to equality through development of the curriculum and by diversifying the range of students
	• To support colleagues in the delivery of modules/programmes by actively seeking to incorporate student evaluation as part of their continuing improvement

Core responsibility to head of department for –	How success is measured (the standard of performance)	Skills, styles and qualities needed (the requisite competencies – the 'how')

Students

Key competences (the 'what')

- Contribute to enriching the learning experience of students in the faculty
- Encourage and enable colleagues and students to develop modules/programmes which identify and meet students' needs
- Contribute to the personal tutorial and pastoral care systems of support for students
- Encourage and enable students to participate in the work of the faculty

- Students' evaluation of their learning experience is positive and their objectives are achieved
- Students' views and opinions are actively sought in the development of new modules/programmes and tutorial/support systems
- Faculty committees, task groups, etc. have active student membership or representation

- Ability to encourage and motivate students and to create a culture in which they feel empowered to express views
- Ability to resolve issues of concern for students and to achieve conflict resolution

Teaching and learning

Key competences (the 'what')

- Act as a role model for educational innovation through one's own approach to teaching and learning and utilisation of a wide range of techniques and methods, including resource-based learning
- Identify internal and external good practice and innovation in teaching and learning strategies; share and promote this within the faculty
- Act as a facilitator, mentor and support for colleagues in their professional development as teachers
- Utilise and experiment with a variety of self, peer and student assessment and evaluation methods, including resource-based learning
- Communicate effectively one's own subject

- Recognition through the quality management process, including student evaluation
- Regular communication takes place, including workshops/ seminars
- Ongoing professional development activities and one-to-one support are offered to colleagues
- Recognition through the quality management process
- Curriculum content reflects current thinking and developments in the subject area
- Curriculum delivery reflects current developments in teaching and learning strategies

- Interest in teaching and learning; willingness and ability to use and experiment with a variety of teaching and learning approaches and methods
- Ability to disseminate information and knowledge in an enthusiastic and non-patronising way to stimulate curiosity
- Ability to motivate, coach and support; knowledge of individual learning styles and development needs
- Knowledge of assessment and evaluation theory and methods; ability to respond constructively to evaluation
- Communication, presentation and interpersonal skills
- Ability to be proactive and to manage projects

Core responsibility to head of department for –	How success is measured (the standard of performance)	Skills, styles and qualities needed (the requisite competencies – the 'how')

knowledge, update colleagues and students, and make a major contribution to curriculum development across the faculty and the university
- Lead and promote special initiatives in teaching and learning in the faculty and ensure resulting good practice is embedded in the curriculum

Staff

Key competences (the 'what')

- Provide support, advice and guidance to one or more specified subject groups/programme teams in the delivery of high-quality modules/programmes - Have a responsibility within the faculty for delivering the university's commitment to equality in all aspects of the recruitment and development of teaching staff	- Members of subject groups/programme teams feel valued and supported and have full access to information and guidance - The teaching staff profile and participation in staff development activities reflect the university's commitment to equality	- Ability to offer advice and guidance in constructive and supportive ways - Demonstrate a clear commitment to equality and the ability to act as role model in carrying out equal opportunities good practice

Programmes and quality management

Key competences (the 'what')

- Provide proactive, continuing, academic leadership in a subject area and make a major contribution to raising the standards of academic quality in the faculty - Encourage and enable students and colleagues to participate in a range of monitoring and evaluation activities to assess the effectiveness and appropriateness of module/ programme delivery	- Recognition through the quality management process - Effective and open processes of evaluation are in operation, participated in and acted upon - The appropriateness of modules/programmes for existing and potential students' needs is regularly evaluated - The extent to which equality issues are explored in the curriculum is regularly evaluated	- Demonstrate a strong commitment to one's own ongoing academic development and updating - Understanding of quality issues, processes and management - Knowledge of needs of existing students and under-represented student groups and a strong commitment to increasing access - Persuading and motivating skills; ability to ensure open

Core responsibility to head of department for –	How success is measured (the standard of performance)	Skills, styles and qualities needed (the requisite competencies – the 'how')
• Lead and promote the development of modules/ programmes which encourage wider participation and which meet students' needs • Actively promote and meet the university's commitment to equality as integral to the content and curriculum development of modules/ programmes		debate on equality issues and to take action on negative feedback

Communication

Key competences (the 'what')

• Make a major contribution to effective communication for students and colleagues in the faculty • Contribute to and participate in lateral communication across the university	• Information, views and ideas are communicated proactively, openly and consistently • Regular meetings and communication takes place with colleagues in other faculties and in university-wide services	• Ability to use effectively a range of communication styles and methods and to encourage people in their ideas and views • Ability to communicate and share ideas in an open, supportive and non-confrontational atmosphere

Strategy and policy formulation

Key competence (the 'what')

• Contribute to the development of strategies to realise the university's mission and the faculty's aims and objectives	• Teaching and learning strategies are developed which inform and are influenced by the faculty's plans and which help to realise the university's mission	• Knowledge of the aims and objectives of the faculty and the university and how these relate to teaching and learning strategies; ability to contribute to policy formulation and strategic planning

Additional responsibilities
• A principal lecturer would be expected to take on one or more of the following accountabilities during his/her teaching career in the university

Core responsibility to head of department for –	How success is measured (the standard of performance)	Skills, styles and qualities needed (the requisite competencies – the 'how')

Subject quality group coordination

Key competences ('the what')

- Coordinate the activities of a subject group within the faculty and be responsible to the head of department for its work
- Ensure the effectiveness of the quality management process in module delivery and subject group operation and be responsible to the head of department for the assurance of quality management
- Coordinate resources for a subject group

- Achievement of agreed objectives and targets for the subject group
- Recognition through the quality management process of the effectiveness of the subject group operation
- Continuous improvement in the efficient and effective use of resources

- Persuading, motivating and negotiating skills
- Strong commitment to quality and excellence; ability to respond to perceptions of quality and to implement and monitor change
- Ability to match resources to needs; ability to predict and identify shortfall and duplication

Programme leadership and direction

Key competences ('the what')

- Lead and direct one or more major programme teams within the faculty and be responsible to the programmes manager for their work
- Ensure recruitment and admissions procedures and practices in specified programmes are in accordance with academic board and faculty policy
- Ensure the effectiveness of the quality management process in specified programme delivery and programme team(s) operation and be responsible to the programme manager for the assurance of quality management
- Coordinate resources for one or more specified programme teams, including the resource

- Achievement of agreed objectives and targets for the programme team
- The programme(s) profile broadens and diversifies; equality issues and monitoring are an integral part of all procedures and practices
- Recognition through the quality management process of the effectiveness of programme team(s) operation
- Continuous improvement in the efficient and effective use of resources

- Persuading, motivating and negotiating skills
- Ability to develop a common understanding among admissions staff of the meaning and importance of quality and social justice
- Strong commitment to quality and excellence; ability to respond to perceptions of quality and to implement and monitor change
- Ability to match resources to needs; ability to predict and identify shortfall and duplication

Core responsibility to head of department for –	How success is measured (the standard of performance)	Skills, styles and qualities needed (the requisite competencies – the 'how')
for the provision of personal tutorial and pastoral care systems for students		

Research and scholarly activity

Key competences (the 'what')

All teaching staff are required to engage in a programme of self-management scholarly activity for which they will be accountable on an annual basis to their head of department

However, it is recognised that a principal lecturer might wish to make a particular contribution to research and scholarly activity in a faculty in the following ways:

Core responsibility to head of department for –	How success is measured (the standard of performance)	Skills, styles and qualities needed (the requisite competencies – the 'how')
• Lead and coordinate a research group, including securing research funding • Help to create a research environment in the faculty by encouraging and supporting colleagues to engage in research activities • Make a major contribution to the research profile of the faculty through personal research activities and publications • Coordinate staff development activities in research methodology and skills • Develop and promote resource-based learning	• Achievement of agreed objectives and targets for the research group including increase in research funding • The number of staff engaged in research activities increases • Increase in research papers and publications; research profile of faculty rises and is recognised externally • Increase in workshops, seminars, guidelines, etc. • Use of resource-based learning materials and techniques increases across the faculty	• Persuading, motivating and negotiating skills • Ability to identify, generate and repeat a variety of sources of funding; ability to optimise research opportunities • Ability to act as coach, mentor and facilitator; ability to motivate and encourage • Ability to self-motivate and to meet deadlines; commitment to achieving recognition for the faculty as well as for personal academic achievement • Ability to disseminate information and knowledge in a non-patronising and empowering way • Strong commitment to and belief in benefits of resource-based learning

Core responsibility to head of department for –	How success is measured (the standard of performance)	Skills, styles and qualities needed (the requisite competencies – the 'how')

External relations

Key competences (the 'what')

• Contribute to the establishment, development and monitoring of strategic alliances and partnerships with other education and training providers • Contribute to the development of the external reputation and profile of the faculty • Contribute to the increase of sources of income for the faculty, including special funded projects	• Wider and increased participation in programmes at or with the university • Increase in applications by students and staff wishing to join the faculty • Increase in faculty representation on external forums and bodies • Sources of income increase and diversify	• Demonstrate a commitment to widening access and to meeting the needs of the university's partners • Ability to promote the faculty marketing, liaison and networking skills • Ability to identify, generate and repeat a variety of sources of income; ability to optimise opportunities

Annual evaluation of department contributions

Annual evaluation of department contributions to institution building at Arizona State University

Relevance		Status		Grade	
PR,	of primary relevance	EX,	exemplary	A	Excellent
SR,	of secondary relevance	AVG,	typical; average	B	Good
NR,	not relevant	MIN,	absent or minimal	C	Fair
				D	Unsatisfactory
				E	Failing

		Relevance	Status	Grade
I	**Creating a quality learning environment**			
A	Special classes being offered			
	1 Writing intensive			
	2 Time flexible (jumbo, stretch)			
	3 Honours			
	4 New student seminars			
	5 Enhancements (lab; reading; recitation; discussion sections; field trips)			
	6 Broadened perspective (integrative; capstone; inter-, cross-, and multi-disciplinary; senior seminar)			
	7 Enrolment limited			
	8 Faculty taught			
	9 Undergraduate research experience			
	10 Innovative instruction (collaborative learning; critical inquiry; learning cycle; technological enhancement)			
B	Special facilities/support			
	1 Mediated learning labs/classrooms			
	2 Tutors/advisers (hours extended)			

			Relevance	Status	Grade
	3	Modern equipment/adequate stations			
	4	Colloquia, symposia series			
	5	Audio/visual support			
	6	Class scheduled in appropriate facilities			
C		Special efforts at enrichment/recognition			
	1	Honours societies, majors clubs			
	2	Organised study groups			
	3	Student awards			
	4	Development of 'involvement profiles' (job résumé)			
	5	Junior fellows program			
	6	Conference paper presentation support			
D		Attracting student talent			
	1	Scholarship support			
	2	Recruitment activities			
	3	Campus visits			
	4	Student preparation for awards competition			
	5	Co-enrolment of majors in the honours programme			
E		Department climate (attentiveness/sensitivity to students)			
	1	Faculty/student diversity			
	2	Protected classes mentoring/networks			
	3	Undergraduate printed guidebook			
	4	Senior reception			
	5	Programme of study workshops			
	6	Student interviews			
	7	Brown bag lunch discussion groups			
	8	Social events for all			
F		Efforts at continuous improvement			
	1	TA (Teaching Assistant) training/evaluation/mentoring			
	2	Graduate training attentive to future requirements of the professoriate			
	3	Faculty development			
	4	Unit development (retreats)			
II		**Building/sustaining nationally prominent programmes**			
A		Encourage and support faculty research/creative activity			
	1	External funding			
	2	Publication			
	3	Invited presentation			
	4	Editing/reviewing			
	5	Clusters of strength			
	6	Collaborate with faculty in other disciplines			
	7	Career development grants			
	8	Support of interdisciplinary activities			
	9	Collaboration with industrial partners/national labs			

		Relevance	Status	Grade
	10 Access to special facilities (e.g. NASA's space telescope), collections, archives, etc			
B	Provide leadership for the discipline			
	1 Hold office in the national professional organisation			
	2 Serve as programme director, section head in federal agencies			
	3 Serve on panels, boards, accreditation bodies			
	4 Host/organise conferences and workshops			
	5 House national/international journals			
C	Build graduate student quality			
	1 Graduate student recruitment visits			
	2 Entry qualifications of enrolled students			
	3 Ph.D. and Master's enrolments			
	4 Graduate school admission of undergraduate majors			
	5 Appropriateness of teaching assistant workload			
	6 Competitive of stipends			

III Serving the broader institution

		Relevance	Status	Grade
A	Full and effective use of resources			
	1 Space and facilities appropriately utilised			
	2 Faculty time and effort directed and distributed appropriately			
	3 Staff utilisation optimised to work to be accomplished			
	4 Resourcefulness in handling instructional replacement (due to the unavailability of faculty because of leaves, unfilled positions, understaffing, etc.)			
B	Responsiveness to institutional needs			
	1 Offer courses responsive to demand			
	2 Income generating activity			
	3 Providing coursework to support general studies			
	4 Summer bridge offerings			
	5 Use of faculty in undergraduate, lower division courses			
	6 Supporting interdisciplinary instruction			
	7 Providing quality advising			
	8 Support university-wide student recruitment/career days			
C	Unit culture			
	1 Depth of concern for, loyalty to the university			
	2 Service on committees at all levels			
	3 Good communication between chair and faculty			
	4 Appropriate levels of consultation/shared governance			
	5 Effective internal problem-solving mechanisms			
D	Active outreach			
	1 Service on state boards/councils			
	2 Sponsorship of external events			

		Relevance	Status	Grade
3	Workshops for school teachers			
4	Campus events for high school students (science fair)			
5	Hosting community college personnel, high school counsellors			
6	Participation in faculty ambassador's programme			
7	Operation of clinics, labs, museums, galleries			
8	Programmes for the disadvantaged			
9	Participation in state and local organisation			
10	Hosting campus tours			
11	Participation in alumni events			
12	School demonstrations			
13	Radio, television programming			
14	Telefund groups			
15	Friends groups			
16	Newsletters			

Staff self-assessment survey

Staff retain Sections 1 and 2 and return Section 3 to you

SECTION ONE – ASSESSMENT

Current work performance

(i)   *Professional knowledge of present job*

    A   _____   Inadequate
          _____   Tendency to A
          _____   Tendency to B
    B   _____   Thorough knowledge of job

(ii)   *Quantity of work (speed and consistency) in producing required results*

    A   _____   Fair
          _____   Tendency to A
          _____   Tendency to B
    B   _____   Usually high output

(iii)   *Quality of work (extent to which results meet requirement)*

    A   _____   Passable
          _____   Tendency to A
          _____   Tendency to B
    B   _____   High quality

(iv)   *Attitude towards job*

    A   _____   Passable
          _____   Tendency to A
          _____   Tendency to B
    B   _____   High quality

(v)   *Judgement and analytical ability (extent to which decisions or actions based on a sound appraisal of the situation and reached by logical reasoning)*

    A   _____   Conclusions sometimes inaccurate
          _____   Tendency to A
          _____   Tendency to B
    B   _____   Sound judgement

Personal characteristics in relation to the job

(i) Personality and acceptability

    A   _____   Impact and effect on others not always favourable
         _____   Tendency to A
         _____   Tendency to B
    B   _____   Make a very good impression

(ii) Ability to communicate

    (a) Verbal (at meetings, discussions, interviews)

    A   _____   Verbal communication not always effective
         _____   Tendency to A
         _____   Tendency to B
    B   _____   High standard of presentation

    (b) Written (reports, memoranda, letters)

    A   _____   Limited, basic writing skills
         _____   Tendency to A
         _____   Tendency to B
    B   _____   Writes very well

(iii) Mental, alertness and initiative (initiative, grasp of new ideas, with problem-solving, etc.)

    A   _____   Tend to follow precedent
         _____   Tendency to A
         _____   Tendency to B
    B   _____   Constructive and creative thinker

SECTION TWO: DIAGNOSIS

Assessment of learning needs/objectives for continuous development

*Learning needs
(tick as appropriate)*

Rate your ability in:

	High	Low	
Assessing other people's capabilities	_____		☐
Decision-making	_____		☐
Delegating	_____		☐
Giving instructions	_____		☐
Problem-solving	_____		☐
Judgement	_____		☐
Leadership/initiative	_____		☐
Listening	_____		☐
Planning	_____		☐
Public speaking	_____		☐
Running meetings	_____		☐
Self-discipline	_____		☐
Selling ideas	_____		☐
Thinking/creativity	_____		☐
Understanding other people	_____		☐
Use of time	_____		☐

SECTION THREE: ACTION

Department staff development programme

You can, of course, address your particular learning needs in a number of (informal) ways and in a variety of settings (both at work and outside the workplace).

In order that the department may help you fulfil your learning needs, I would be grateful if, in this particular instance, you would complete the questions below and return this sheet (and this sheet only, not pages 1–2) to your head of department.

1   Please identify (up to) three staff development activities that you would like the department to organise and be willing to participate in: (e.g. chairing meetings, dealing with people; team building, minute-taking; IT training; self-appraisal; handling discrimination, delivering (better) lectures; writing a Ph.D., getting published, maximising research, etc.):

(i)   _____

(ii)   _____

(iii)   _____

2   In what ways, would you prefer these activities were provided: via (please rank in order of preference: 1, 2, 3. . .)

——	Resource pack	——	Task group (focus)
——	Practical demonstrations	——	Informal, ad hoc
——	Seminars (teach-each-other events)	——	Any of the above
——	Formal lectures	——	Other (please specify)
——	Workshops		

3   When would you prefer these activities were organised (please tick as appropriate):

——	Beginning of academic year	——	Half day
——	Inter-semester	——	Full day
——	End of academic year	——	One hour sessions
——	Year round	——	Early morning
——	Other (please specify)	——	Lunchtime
——	Late afternoon	——	Weekend
——	Evening	——	Other (please specify)

Signed (optional) _____   Date _____

Source: CIPD assessment cited in Harrison, 2002

References

ACAS (Advisory, Conciliation and Arbitration Service) (1988), *Employee Appraisal*, London.

ACAS (2000), *Code of Practice on Disciplinary and Grievance Procedures*, London.

ACAS (2002) *Redundancy Handling*, London.

Adair, J. (1983) *Effective Leadership*, Pan Books, London.

Adair, J. (1988) *Effective Time Management*, Pan Books, London.

Alanbrooke, Lord (2001) *War Diaries, 1939–1945: Field Marshall Lord Alanbrooke*, Weidenfield and Nicholson, London.

Albury, D. (1997) *The Future and Management of Higher Education*, Office of Public Management, London.

Alderman, G. (1999) 'Innocence Amid TVU Slaughter', *THES* (*Times Higher Education Supplement*), 23 July.

Alexander, M. (2001) 'Strategy and Strategic Process: From Theory to Reality', *Top Management Programme 61*, Cabinet Office, London, unpublished paper.

Alimo-Metcalfe, B. and Alban-Metcalfe, J. (2002) 'The Great and the Good', *People Management*, 10 January.

Allaire, Y. and Firsirotu, M.E. (1984) 'Theories of Organisational Culture', *Organisation Studies* 5 (3): 19–26.

Allan, D., Kingdon, M., Murrin, K. and Rudkin, D. (1999) *How to Start a Creative Revolution at Work*, Capstone, London.

de Alva, J.K. (2002) 'The For-Profit University', UUK Conference, The Future of Higher Education: Profits, Partnership and the Public Good, 14 June.

Argyris, C. (1985) *Strategy, Change and Defensive Routines*, Pitman, Boston, MA.

Argyris, C. (1990) *Overcoming Organisational Defenses*, Prentice-Hall, Englewood Cliffs, NJ.

Argyris, C. and Schon, D. (1978) *Organisational Learning: A Theory-in-Action Perspective*, Addison-Wesley, Reading, MA.

Argyris, C. and Schon, D. (1996) *Organisational Learning II: Theory, Method and Practice*, Addison-Wesley, Reading, MA.

Armstrong, M. (2000) *Strategic Human Resource Management: A Guide to Action*, 2nd edn, Kogan Page, London.

Armstrong, M. (2001) 'Changing the Culture: Rewarding and Developing Staff in Higher Education', Improving Performance Management in Higher Education Conference, 22 October, Capita, London.

Armstrong, M. and Baron, A. (1998) *Performance Management: The New Realities*, The Institute of Personnel and Development, London.

Athena Guide to Good Practice, 1999–2002, The Athena Project 22, Equality Challenge Unit, London.

Babbidge, H.D. and Rosenzweig, R. (1962) *The Federal Interest in Higher Education*, McGraw-Hill, New York.

Baer, M., Hellman, D.A., Porter, R. and Watson, M. (1998) 'Creating a New Home for Faculty: Implementing Departmental Planning', Northeastern University, Boston, MA.

Bargh, C., Bocock, J., Scott, P. and Smith, D. (2000) *University Leadership: The Role of the Chief Executive*, Society for Research into Higher Education (SRHE) and Open University Press (OUP), Buckingham.

Barnett, R. (1990) *The Idea of Higher Education*, SRHE and OUP, Buckingham.

Barnett, R. (2000) 'The University is Dead, Long Live the University', *THES*, 11 February.

Barrow, S. and Davenport, J. (2002) 'The Employer Brand', People in Business, London, unpublished paper.

Barzun, J. and Graff, H.F. (1992) *The Modern Researcher*, 5th edn, Harcourt Brace Jovanovich, London.

Bass, B.M. (1985) *Leadership and Performance Beyond Expectations*, Free Press, New York.

Baty, P. (2001) 'Cambridge Debacle May Lead to Inquiry'. *THES*, 9 November.

Becher, T. (1996) *Academic Tribes and Territories: Intellectual Enquiry and the Cultures of Disciplines*, SRHE and OUP, Buckingham.

Beckhard, R. (1992) 'A Model for the Executive Management of Transformational Change' in G. Salaman (ed.), *Human Resource Strategies*, Sage, London.

Belbin, M. (1990) *Management Teams: Why they Succeed or Fail*, Butterworth-Heinemann, London.

Bell, D. (1966) *The Reforming of General Education: The Columbia College Experience in the National Setting*, Columbia University Press, New York.

Bennis, W. and Nanus, B. (1985) *Leaders: The Strategies for Taking Charge*, Harper and Row, 1985.

Bett, M. (1999) *Independent Review of Higher Education Pay and Conditions* (Bett Report), Universities and Colleges Employers Association (UCEA), London.

Bhattarcharyya, G. (2000) 'Feelgood is No Good', *THES*, 31 March.

Blake, R.R. and McCanse, A.A. (1991) *Leadership Dilemmas: Grid Solutions*, Butterworth-Heinemann, Oxford.

Blanchard, K. and Johnson, S. (2000) *One Minute Manager*, HarperCollins, London.

Boutall, T. (1997) *The Good Manager's Guide*, Butterworth-Heinemann, London.

Boxall, P. and Purcell, J. (2002) *Strategy and Human Resource Management*, Palgrave Macmillan, Basingstoke.

Boyer, E.L. (1990) *Scholarship Reconsidered: Priorities of the Professoriate*, Carnegie Foundation for the Advancement of Teaching, Princeton University Press, NJ.

Brew, A. (ed.) (1995) *Directions in Staff Development*, SRHE and OUP, Buckingham.

Bridges, W. (1991) *Managing Transitions: Making the Most of Change*, Addison-Wesley, Reading, MA.

Brodie, I. (2001) 'Great Leaders were Grumpy' *The Times*, 1 September.

Brown, H. and Somerlad, E. (1992) 'Staff Development in Higher Education – Towards the Learning Organisation?', *Higher Education Quarterly* 46: 174–190.

Brown, J.S. and Duguid, P. (1996) 'Space for the Chattering Classes', *THES*, 10 May.

Bruch, H. and Ghoshal, S. (2002) 'Beware the Busy Manager'. *Harvard Business Review*, February: 5–11.

Buckingham, M. and Coffman, C. (2001) *First, Break All the Rules: What the World's Greatest Managers Do Differently*, Simon and Schuster, London.

Burgoyne, J. (2001) 'Tester of Faith', *People Management*, 22 February: 32–4.

Burns, J.M. (1978) *Leadership*, Harper and Row, New York.

Butcher, D. and Atkinson, S. (1999) 'Upwardly Mobilized', *People Management*, 14 January: 28–33.

Cameron, K.S. and Quinn, R.E. (1998) *Diagnosing and Changing Organisational Culture*, Addison-Wesley, Reading, MA.

Candy, P.C. (1998) 'Disciplinary Discourses, Departmental Differences and Distributed Development', University of Ballarat, Victoria, unpublished paper.

Churchill, W. (1996) *Memoirs of the Second World War*, Houghton Mifflin, Boston, MA.

CIPD (Chartered Institute for Personnel and Development) (2002) *The Guide to Work Life Balance*, London.

Clark, B.R. (1983) *The Higher Education System: Academic Organisation in Cross-national Perspective*, University of California Press, Berkeley, CA.

Clark, B.R. (1998) *Creating Entrepreneurial Universities: Organisational Pathways of Transformation*, IAU Press, Pergamon, Oxford.

Coaldrake, P. and Stedman, L. (1998) *On the Brink: Australia's Universities Confronting their Future*, University of Queensland Press, St Lucia, Queensland.

Cohen, D. (1998) 'Universities to the Power of 21'. *Guardian*, 27 July.

Cohen, M. (2000) 'Poisonous Exercises: A Dartboard and a Map Could Do Better than the RAE', *THES*, 22/29 December.

Cohen, M.D. and March, J.G. (1986) *Leadership and Ambiguity: The American College President*, 2nd edn, Harvard Business School Press, Boston, MA.

Covey, S.R. (1989) *The Seven Habits of Highly Effective People*, Simon and Schuster, New York.

CRE (Commission for Racial Equality) (2000) *Strengthening the Race Relations Act*, CRE, London.

CUCO (Commission on University Career Opportunity) (1997), *Guidelines on Recruitment, Selection and Promotion for Universities and Colleges in Higher Education*, CVCP, London.

Cunningham, V. (2000) 'Fine Mess We're In', *THES*, 13 October.

CVCP (Committee of Vice-Chancellors and Principals) (2000) *The Business of Borderless Education: UK Perspectives*, CVCP, London.

Daniel, J.S. (1996) *Mega-Universities and Knowledge Media: Technology Strategies for Higher Education*, Kogan Page, London.

Daniel, J.S. (1998) 'Open as to Places: An Academic Community on which the Sun Never Sets', SRHE Annual Conference, University of Lancaster.

Dann, J. (2001) *Test Your Emotional Intelligence*, Institute of Management, London.

Deal, T.E. and Kennedy, A.A. (1982) *Corporate Cultures: The Rites and Rituals of Corporate Life*, Addison-Wesley, Reading, MA.

Dearing Report: National Committee of Inquiry into Higher Education (1997) *Higher Education in the Learning Society: Summary Report*, HMSO, London.

De Nisi, A.S. (2000) *Human Resource Management*, Houghton Mifflin College, Wilmington, MA.

DfEE (Department for Education and Employment) (2000) *Changing Patterns in a Changing World: Work–Life Balance*, London.

DRC (Disability Rights Commission) (2002) *The Disability Discrimination Act: A Senior Manager's Guide*, London.

Drucker, P. (1974) *Management: Tasks, Responsibilities, Practices*, Heinemann, London.

Drucker, P. (1993) *Post-Capitalist Society*, Harper, New York.

Duke, C. (1992) *The Learning University: Towards a New Paradigm?* SRHE and OUP, Buckingham.

Durham, H., Claxton, C. and Butts, J. (1998) 'Building a Learning Organisation: Assessing Faculty Quality of Life', Appalachian State University, Boon, NC.

Earwaker, J. (1991) 'Boo to the Barbarians', *THES*, 29 March.

Egan, G. (1995) 'A Clear Path to Peak Performance', *People Management*, 18 May: 34–7.

Eglin, R. (2003) 'Give the Young Turks a Helping Hand to the Top', *Sunday Times*, 30 March.

Elton, L. and Partington, P. (1993) *Teaching Standards and Excellence in Higher Education: Developing a Culture for Quality*, 2nd edn, CVCP, London.

Equality Challenge Unit (2002) *First Annual Report*, London.

Erban, P. (2001) 'Competency Frameworks in Performance Management', Improving Performance Management in Higher Education Conference, 22 October, Capita, London.

Fiedler, F.E. (1978) 'The Contingency Model and the Dynamics of the Leadership Process' in L. Berkowitz (ed.), *Advances in Experimental Social Psychology*, vol. 11, Academic Press, New York, pp. 59–112.

Finch, J. (2001) 'Why I Believe the Drive for Equal Opportunities Needs New Impetus', *THES*, 16 February.

Fitzgerald, M. (1992) 'TVU: Academic Organisation', 17 June, unpublished paper.

Flexner, A. (1930) *Universities: American, English, German*, Oxford University Press, Oxford.

Forrest, A. (1995) *Fifty Ways to Personal Development*, The Industrial Society, London.

Forrest, A. (1997) *5 Way Management: Maximise Your All Round Impact*, The Industrial Society, London.

Forsyth, P. (2000) *How to Motivate People*, Kogan Page, London.

Fraser, A. and Neville, S. (1993) *Team Building*, The Industrial Society, London.

Frean, A. (2001) 'Boardroom is Playground for Mummy's Boys', *The Times*, 8 September.

Frost, P.J., Moore, L.F., Louis, M.R., Lundberg, C.C. and Martin, J. (1991) *Reframing Organisational Culture*, Sage, London.

Fullan, M. (1993) *Change Forces*, Falmer, London.

Fullan, M. (1999) *Change Forces: The Sequel*, Falmer, London.

Fullan, M. with Stiegelbauer, S. (1991) *The New Meaning of Educational Change*, Cassell, London.

Furnham, A. (2002) 'Getting the Most from a Meeting', *Sunday Times*, 29 September.

Garratt, B. (1995) 'The Learning Organisation: An Old Idea That Has Come of Age', *People Management*, 21 September: 25–8.

van Ginkel, H. (1995) 'University 2050: The Organisation of Creativity and Innovation', *Higher Education Policy*, 8 (4): 14–18.

Goddard, J. (1999) 'Signs Point to the Learning Corporation', *THES*, 30 July.

Goleman, D. (1996) *Emotional Intelligence: Why it can matter more than IQ*, Bloomsbury, London.

Grant, A. (1997) *Presentation Perfect: How to Excel at Business Presentations, Meetings and Public Speaking*, The Industrial Society, London.

Grass Roots Group (2003) *Respect for People: Charter for Diversity*, Tring, Herts.

Halsey, A.H. (1992) *Decline of the Donnish Dominion*, Clarendon Press, Oxford.

Handy, C. ((1993) *Understanding Organisations*, Penguin, London.

Hanscombe, S. (1998) 'Make the Right Impression', *The Times*, 21 June.

Harrison, R. (2002) *Learning and Development*, 3rd edn, Chartered Institute of Personnel and Development, London.

Harvey, L. (1995) Editorial, *Quality in Higher Education*, 1:5–12.

HEFCE (Higher Education Funding Council for England) (2000) *Strategic Planning in Higher Education*, 24, Bristol.

HEFCE (2000) *Better Accountability for Higher Education*, 36, Bristol.

HEFCE (2001) *Funding Higher Education in England*, 14, Bristol.

HEFCE (2001) *Guide for Members of Governing Bodies of Universities and Colleges in England, Wales and Northern Ireland*, 20, Bristol.

HEFCE (2001) *Good Practice to Risk Assessment*, 24, Bristol.

HEFCE (2001) *Rewarding and Developing Staff in Higher Education*, 16, Bristol.

HEFCE (2002) *Rewarding and Developing Staff in Higher Education: Good Practice in Setting Human Resource Strategies*, 14, Bristol.

HEFCE (2002) *Financial Strategy in Higher Education Institutions: A Business Approach*, 34, Bristol.

HEFCE (2003) *Joint Consultation on the Review of Research Assessment*, 22, Bristol.

HERDSA (Higher Education Research and Development Society of Australasia) (1997) *Challenging Conceptions of Teaching: Some Prompts for Good Practice*, Milperra, NSW, Australia.

Hersey, P. and Blanchard, K.H. (1992) *Management of Organisational Behaviour*, 6th edn, Prentice-Hall, Englewood Cliffs, NJ.

Honey, P. and Mumford, A. (1995) *Using Your Learning Styles*, 3rd edn, Ardingley House, Maidenhead.

House, R.J. (1988) 'Power and Personality in Complex Organizations' in B.M. Staw (ed.), *Research in Organizational Behaviour*, vol. 10, JAI Press, Greenford, CT, pp. 305–57.

Hunt, J. (1992) *Leadership: A New Synthesis*, Sage, London.

Industrial Society (now renamed The Work Foundation) (1996) 'Effective Middle Management; Essential Skills', London.

IPD (Institute of Personnel and Development) (1996) *Managing Diversity: An IPD Position Paper: A Vision for the Development of Equal Opportunities*, IPD, London.

Jacoby, R. (1997) 'Intellectuals: Inside and Outside the Academy' in A. Smith and F. Webster (eds), *The Postmodern University? Contested Visions of Higher Education in Society*, SRHE and OUP, Buckingham.

Jaques, D. (1998) *Supporting Part Time Teachers in Higher Education*, Universities and Colleges Staff Development Agency, Briefing Paper 56, University of Sheffield, Sheffield.

Jarratt Report (1985) *Report of the Steering Committee for Efficiency Studies in Universities*, Committee of Vice-Chancellors and Principals (CVCP), London.

Jaspers, K. (1946) *The Idea of the University*, Macmillan, London (originally published 1923).

JCPSG (Joint Costing and Pricing Steering Group) (2000) *Transparent Approach to Costing* [in universities], vols I and II, Office of Science and Technology, London.

Kakabadse, A. (2001) 'Leadership and Context', *Top Management Programme 61*, Cabinet Office, London, unpublished paper. See also Pickard, 2001.

Kakabadse, A. and Kakabadse, N. (1998) *Essence of Leadership*, International Thompson Business Press, London.

Kandola, R. and Fullerton, J. (1998) *Diversity in Action: Managing the Mosaic*, 2nd edn, Chartered Institute of Personnel and Development, London.

Katzenbach, J.R. (1997) 'The Myth of Top Management Teams', *Harvard Business Review*, Nov.–Dec.: 83–91.

Kay, J. (2000a) 'Dream World', *Guardian*, 28 November.

Kay, J. (2000b) 'So We Agree Not To Agree?', *THES*, 24 November.

Kelly, D. (1998) 'The Pressure's On!', Stress Management Video, BBC, London.

Kemmis, S. and Maconachie, D. (1998) *Strategic Repositioning: A Case Study of Rapid Change at the University of Ballarat*, Department of Employment, Education, Training and Youth Affairs, Canberra.

Kerr, C. (1963) *The Uses of the University*, 3rd edn, Harvard University Press, Cambridge, MA.

Kerr, C. (2001) *The Gold and the Blue: Academic Triumphs*, University of California Press, Berkeley, CA.

Kotter, J.P. (1990) *A Force for Change: How Leadership Differs from Management*, Free Press, New York.

Kouzes, J.M. and Posner, B.Z. (1995) *The Leadership Challenge*, Jossey-Bass, San Francisco, CA.

Krahenbuhl, G., Linder, D. and Collins, J. (1998) 'Faculty Work Reconsidered: An Integrative Model', Arizona State University, Tempe, Arizona, unpublished paper.

Krinsky, I. and Weber, S. (1997) 'New Manager Assimilation', *American Association of Higher Education Bulletin*, 49 (9): 11–13.

Laurillard, D. (2001) *Rethinking University Teaching: A Conversational Framework for the Effective Use of Learning Technologies*, 2nd edn, Routledge Falmer, London.

Lewin, K. (1951) *Field Theory in Social Science*, Harper and Row, New York.

Likert, R. (1967) *New Patterns of Management*, McGraw-Hill, New York.

Loehr, J. and Schwartz, T. (2001) 'The Making of a Corporate Athlete', *Harvard Business Review*, January: 120–8.

Lucas, A.F. (1995) *Strengthening Departmental Leadership*, Jossey-Bass, San Francisco, CA.

Luffman, G., Lea, E., Kenny, B. and Sanderson, S. (1996) *Strategic Management: An Analytical Introduction*, 3rd edn, Blackwell, Oxford.

McGregor, D. (1960) *The Human Side of Enterprise*, McGraw-Hill, New York.

Macintyre, B. (2001) 'Bush Gets America Down to Business', *The Times*, 17 February.

McNay, I. (1995) 'From the Collegial Academy to Corporate Enterprise: The Changing Culture of Universities' in T. Schuller (ed.), *The Changing University?* SRHE and OUP, Buckingham.

McNay, I. (1996) 'Work's Committees' in R. Cuthbert (ed.), *Working in Higher Education*, SRHE and OUP, Buckingham.

McNay, I. and Dopson, S. (1996) 'Organisational Culture' in D. Warner and D. Palfreyman (eds), *Higher Education Management: The Key Elements*, SRHE and OUP, Buckingham.

Maddix, R.B. (1998) *Team Building*, 2nd edn, Kogan Page, London.

Maitland, I. (1995) *Managing Your Time*, Institute of Personnel and Development, London.

Martin, E. (1999) *Changing Academic Work: Developing the Learning University*, SRHE and OUP, Buckingham.

Melody, W. (1997) 'Universities and Public Policy' in A. Smith and F. Webster (eds), *The Postmodern University? Contested Visions of Higher Education in Society*, SRHE and OUP Buckingham.

Middlehurst, R. (1993) *Leading Academics*, SRHE and OUP, Buckingham.

Miles, R.E. and Snow, C.S. (2003) *Organisational Strategy, Structure and Process*, Stanford University Press, CA.

Miller, L.H., Smith, A.D. and Rothstein, L. (1994) *The Stress Solution*, Pocketbooks, New York.

Mintzberg, H. (1973) *The Nature of Managerial Work*, Harper and Row, New York.

Mintzberg, H. (ed.) (2002) *The Strategy Process, Concepts, Contexts, Cases*, 4th edn, Pearson Higher Education, Herts.

Modood Report (1999) *Ethnicity and Employment in HE*, Policy Studies Institute, London.

Moores, R. (1994) *Managing For High Performance: A Practical Guide*, The Industrial Society, London.

Morgan, G. (1997) *Images of Organisation*, 2nd edn, Sage, London.

Murlis, H. and Hartle, F. (1996) in 'Does it Pay to Work in Universites?' in R. Cuthbert (ed.), *Working in Higher Education*, SRHE and OUP, Buckingham.

Myers, M.S. (1991) *Every Employee a Manager*, 3rd edn, Prentice-Hall, Engelwood Cliffs, NJ.

Myers, P. and Myers, K.D. (1977) *Myers-Briggs Type Indicator*, Oxford Psychologists Press, Oxford.

NATFHE (National Association of Teachers in Further and Higher Education) (2001) *Justice for Agency Lecturers*, June, London.

NATFHE (2002) Survey, *The Lecturer*, June.

National Commission on Education (1995) *Learning in the New Millennium*, Briefing 5, Paul Hamlyn Foundation, London.

National Conference of University Professors (1996) *The Case for Universities*, Policy Document No. 6, London.

Newman, J.H. Cardinal (1976) *The Idea of a University*, Oxford University Press, Oxford (originally published 1853).

Oswald, A. (2003) 'Life Can Be a Beach, If You Let It', *Sunday Times*, 2 February.

Owen, G. (2001) 'Cambridge Amateur Culture Led to Chaos', *The Times*, 3 November.

Pedler, M., Burgoyne, J. and Boydell, T. (1991) *The Learning Company: A Strategy for Sustainable Development*, McGraw-Hill, London.

Pedler, M., Burgoyne, J. and Boydell, T. (2001) *A Manager's Guide to Self Development*, 4th edn, McGraw-Hill, London.

Pelikan, J. (1992) *The Idea of the University: A Re-examination*, Yale University Press, London.

Peters, T. (1987) *Thriving on Chaos: Handbook for a Management Revolution*, Pan Books, London.

Pettigrew, A., Ferlie, E. and McKee, L. (1992) *Shaping Strategic Change: Making Change in Large Organisations; The Case of the National Health Service*, Sage, London.

Pickard, J. (2001) 'Ruling Classes: What Does It Take To Be a Leader', *People Management*, 9 August: 21–5.

Porter, M.E. (1998) *The Competitive Advantage: Creating and Sustaining Superior Performance*, Simon and Schuster, London.

Pratt, J. (2000) 'How Will Our Soul Be Saved', *THES*, 29 September.

QAA (Quality Assurance Agency for Higher Education) (1998) *Special Review of Thames Valley University*, 9 November, Gloucester.

Quinn, R.E. (1995) *Becoming a Master Manager: A Competency Framework*, 2nd edn, John Wiley and Sons, London.

Ramsden, P. (1998) *Learning to Lead in Higher Education*, Routledge, London.

Reed, M. and Hughes, M. (eds) (1991) *Rethinking Organisations: New Directions in Organisation Theory and Analysis*, Sage, London.

Reid, E. (1997) 'Run-around Nightmare', *Guardian*, 14 October.

Revans, R.W. (1984) *The Origins and Growth of Action Learning*, Chartwell Bratt, Bromley.

Robins, K. and Webster, F. (eds) (2002) *The Virtual University? Knowledge, Markets and Management*, Oxford University Press, Oxford.

Rose, M. (2000) 'Target Practice', *People Management*, 23 November: 44–5.

Rothwell, J. (2000) 'How to Break the News of Redundancies', *People Management*, 23 November: 46–8.

Russell, C. and Parsons, E. (1996) 'Putting Theory to the Test at the OU', *People Management*, 11 January: 30–4.

Sanders, C. and Goddard, A. (2001) 'Cambridge is Worth 170 Guildhalls', *THES*, 13 July.

Sashkin, M. (1995) *The Visionary Leader*, HRD Press, Amherst, MA.

Sashkin, M. and Rosenbach, W.E. (1993) 'A New Leadership Paradigm' in W.E. Rosenbach and R.L. Taylor (eds), *Contemporary Issues in Leadership*, Westview Press, Boulder, CO.

Schein, E. (1997) *Organisational Culture and Leadership*, 2nd edn, Jossey-Bass/Wiley, London.

Schneider, R. (2001) 'Managing Diversity', *People Management*, 3 May: 27–31.

Schuller, T. (ed.) (1995) *The Changing University?* SRHE and OUP, Buckingham.

Scott, P. (1995) *The Meanings of Mass Higher Education*, SRHE and OUP, Buckingham.

Scott, P. (ed.) (1998) *The Globalisation of Higher Education*, SRHE and OUP, Buckingham.

Scott, P. and Watson, D. (1994) 'Managing the Curriculum: Roles and Responsibilities' in J. Bocock and D. Watson (eds), *Managing the University Curriculum: Making Common Cause*, SRHE and OUP, Buckingham.

Scott-Morgan, P. (1999) 'Hidden Depths', *People Management*, 8 April: 38–46.

Senge, P. (1990a) 'The Leader's New Work: Building Learning Organisations', *Sloan Management Review*, 32 (1): 7–23.

Senge, P. (1990b) *The Fifth Discipline: The Art and Practice of the Learning Organisation*, Random House, London.

Senge, P. (1994) *The Fifth Discipline Fieldbook: Strategies and Tools for Building a Learning Organisation*, Nicholas Brealey, London.

Senge, P. (1995) *Leading Learning Organisations: The Bold, the Powerful and the Invisible*, MIT Press, Cambridge, MA.

Senge, P. (1998) 'Faculty Work in Learning Organizations', Sixth American Association of Higher Education Conference on Faculty Roles and Rewards, Orlando, FL.

Senge, P., Kleiner, A., Roberts, C., Ross, R., Roth, G. and Smith, B. (1999) *The Dance of Change: The Challenge of Sustaining Momentum in Learning Organizations*, Nicholas Brealey, London.

Shulman, G. (1998) 'Leading a Quality Department: A Learning Organisation Perspective', Miami University, Oxford, OH, unpublished paper.

Siddons, S. (1998) *Presentation Skills*, Institute of Personnel Development, London.

Sizer, L. (1982) 'Assessing Institutional Performance and Progress' in L. Wagner (ed.), *Agenda for Institutional Change in Higher Education*, SRHE, Guildford.

Smith, A. and Webster, F. (eds) (1997), *The Postmodern University? Contested Visions of Higher Education in Society*, SRHE and OUP, Buckingham.

Smith, P.B. and Peterson, M.F. (1988) *Leadership, Organizations and Culture*, Sage, London.

Snoddy, R. (2002) 'The BBC's Popular Vulgarian', *The Times*, 15 February.

Soames, M. (ed.) (1998) *Speaking for Themselves: The Personal Letters of Winston and Clementine Churchill*, Doubleday, London.

Syrett, M. and Hogg, C. (eds) (1992), *Frontiers of Leadership*, Blackwell, Oxford.

Taylor Report (2001) *New Directions in Higher Education Funding*, Universities' UK, London.

Teaford, J.C. (1984) *The Unheralded Triumph: City Government in America, 1870–1900*, Johns Hopkins University Press, Baltimore, MD.

Tear, Y. (1998) 'Mike Fitzgerald: The Man with the Plan', *Ealing Gazette*, 20 November.

Thomas, K.W. and Kilmann, R.H. (1974) *Thomas-Kilmann Conflict Mode Instrument*, Consulting Psychologists Press, Palo Alto, CA.

Tichy, N.M. (1983) *Managing Strategic Change*, John Wiley and Sons, New York.

THES (*Times Higher Education Supplement*) (2000) 11 February, 25 February, 31 March, 14 April; (2003) 7 February.

Toffler, A. (1991) *Power Shift: Knowledge, Wealth and Violence at the Edge of the 21st Century*, Bantam Press, London.

Torrington, D. and Hall, L. (1995) *Personnel Management*, 3rd edn, Prentice-Hall, Engelwood Cliffs, NJ.

Trow, M. (1973) *Problems in the Transition from Elite to Mass Higher Education*, Carnegie Commission on HE, Berkeley, CA.

Trowler, P.R. (1998) *Academics Responding to Change: New Higher Education Frameworks and Academic Cultures*, SRHE and OUP, Buckingham.

Trowler, P., Saunders, M. and Knight, P. (2003) *Change Thinking, Change Practices: A Guide to Change for Heads of Departments, Programme Leaders and other Change Agents in Higher Education*, Learning and Teaching Support Network, Generic Centre, York.

Turner, C. (2002) *Born to Succeed: Releasing Your Business Potential*, Texere, London.

Turner, D. (1998) *Liberating Leadership: A Manager's Guide to the New Leadership*, The Industrial Society, London.

Tutt, N. (1985) 'The Unintended Consequences of Integration', *Educational and Child Psychology*, 2: 20–38.

UCEA (Universities and Colleges Employers Association) (2000) *Guide to Good Practice on Fixed Term and Casual Employment in Higher Education*, UCEA, London.

University of Western Australia (1998) 'A Guide to the Teaching Portfolio', Centre for Staff Development.

Urry, J. (1999) 'Locating HE in the Global Landscape', *SRHE News*, Society for Research into Higher Education 39, London.

Vroom, V. and Yetton, P.W. (1973) *Leadership and Decision-Making*, University of Pittsburgh Press, Pittsburgh, PA.

Warner, D. and Palfreyman, D. (eds) (1996) *Higher Education Management: The Key Elements*, SRHE and OUP, Buckingham.

Warner, D. and Palfreyman, D. (eds) (2001) *The State of UK Higher Education: Managing Change and Diversity*, SRHE and OUP, Buckingham.

Warren, E. and Toll, C. (1997) *The Stress Work Book: How Individuals, Teams and Organisations Can Balance Pressure and Performance*, Nicholas Brealey, London.

Webb, G. (1996) *Understanding Staff Development*, SRHE and OUP, Buckingham.

Weick, K. (1976) 'Educational Organisations as Loosely-coupled Systems', *Administrative Science Quarterly*, 21 (1): 1–19.

White Paper (2003) *The Future of Higher Education*, DfES, London.

Whyte, W.H. (1956) *The Organisation Man*, Simon and Schuster, New York.

Wood, J., Brinig, M. and Clark, R. (1997) 'Engaging the Future: Report of the President's Faculty Task Force on the Future of the University', George Mason University, VA.

Woodcock, M. (1989) *Activities for Team-Building*, Gower, London.

Wynne-Jones, R. (1997) 'The University that's Hip, Cool and Loses Its Degree Results', *Independent on Sunday*, 30 November.

Index